JANE AUSTEN, EARLY AND LATE

Jane Austen, Early and Late

FREYA JOHNSTON

PRINCETON UNIVERSITY PRESS

PRINCETON & OXFORD

Published by Princeton University Press
41 William Street, Princeton, New Jersey 08540
6 Oxford Street, Woodstock, Oxfordshire OX20 1TR

press.princeton.edu

All Rights Reserved

Library of Congress Control Number 2021940446
ISBN 978-0-691-19800-2
ISBN (e-book) 978-0-691-22981-2

British Library Cataloging-in-Publication Data is available

Editorial: Ben Tate and Josh Drake
Production Editorial: Jill Harris
Jacket Design: Layla Mac Rory
Production: Danielle Amatucci
Publicity: Alyssa Sanford and Amy Stewart
Copyeditor: Jennifer Harris

Jacket art: Bernardo Bellotto (1721–1780), *The Ruins of the Old Kreuzkirche, Dresden,* 1765. Oil on canvas. Inv. 638. Photo: bpk Bildagentur / Gemäldegalerie Alte Meister, Staatliche Kunstsammlungen Dresden / Elke Estel / Hans-Peter Klut / Art Resource, NY.

This book has been composed in Arno

Printed on acid-free paper. ∞

Printed in the United States of America

10 9 8 7 6 5 4 3 2 1

For SPP

CONTENTS

ILLUSTRATIONS

ACKNOWLEDGEMENTS

I AM GRATEFUL to the prompt, courteous, and helpful staff of the various institutions in which Austen's manuscripts and ancillary materials are held: the Bodleian Libraries, Oxford; the British Library; the Jane Austen House Museum at Chawton; the Library of St John's College, Oxford; Hampshire Record Office; Winchester College Fellows' Library; the National Library of Scotland; and the New York Public Library. Katharine Beaumont kindly allowed me to consult and photograph her copy of Oliver Goldsmith's *History of England*, containing the annotations of Jane Austen and various other members of her family. I am very grateful for Dr Beaumont's permission to make use of some of those images in this book, where they will appear in print for the first time. Deirdre le Faye was immensely helpful and quick in responding to queries, making suggestions, and supplying materials. My thanks to Peter Sabor for his advice on how to find books owned and written in by Jane Austen. I learned a great deal from those who read and responded to draft versions of my argument: Seamus Perry, Dan Sperrin, Kathryn Sutherland, and the anonymous readers of my proposal. Many thanks are also due to my excellent copyeditor, Jennifer Harris, and to all the team at Princeton University Press for their expert help, advice, and enthusiasm: Bob Bettendorf, Josh Drake, Jill Harris, Dimitri Karetnikov, and Ben Tate.

Parts of two chapters have appeared in slightly different form elsewhere: 'Jane Austen's Past Lives', *Cambridge Quarterly*, 39 (2010), 103–21, and 'Jane Austen's Universals', *Essays in Criticism*, 68 (2018), 211–33.

This book started to take shape while I was preparing a new edition of Austen's *Teenage Writings* with Kathryn Sutherland; I am thankful to her for encouraging me in that work as well as in this one, and for all she has done to enable my own and other people's research into Jane Austen. Hers is the most recent and most detailed presentation and textual-critical account of Austen's fiction manuscripts, a five-volume print edition that builds on an earlier digital resource (https://janeausten.ac.uk). These extraordinarily rich texts and commentaries offer countless hints of the novelist's working methods and creative debts throughout her writing life. My book is, in turn, indebted and responsive throughout to Sutherland's work.

ABBREVIATIONS

Bibliography	David Gilson, *A Bibliography of Jane Austen*, rev. edition (Winchester: St Paul's Bibliographies; Delaware: Oak Knoll, 1997)
Collected Poems	*Collected Poems and Verse of the Austen Family*, ed. David Selwyn (Manchester: Carcanet, 1996)
Emma	*The Cambridge Edition of the Works of Jane Austen: Emma*, ed. Richard Cronin and Dorothy Macmillan (Cambridge: Cambridge University Press, 2005)
Family Record	Deirdre le Faye, *Jane Austen: A Family Record*, 2nd edition (Cambridge: Cambridge University Press, 2004)
Goldsmith, *History*	Oliver Goldsmith, *The History of England, from the Earliest Times to the Death of George II*, 4 vols. (London: T. Davies; Becket and De Hondt; and T. Cadell, 1771)
JAFM	*Jane Austen's Fiction Manuscripts*, 5 vols., ed. Kathryn Sutherland (Oxford: Oxford University Press, 2018)
JALM	Brian Southam, *Jane Austen's Literary Manuscripts: A Study of the Novelist's Development through the Surviving Papers*, Continuum Studies in Jane Austen, new edition (London and New York: Athlone Press, 2001)
Juvenilia	*The Cambridge Edition of the Works of Jane Austen: Juvenilia*, ed. Peter Sabor (Cambridge: Cambridge University Press, 2006)
Letters	*Jane Austen's Letters*, ed. Deirdre le Faye, 4th edition (Oxford: Oxford University Press, 2014)

Memoir	J. E. Austen-Leigh, *A Memoir of Jane Austen and Other Family Recollections*, ed. Kathryn Sutherland (Oxford: Oxford University Press, 2002)
MP	*The Cambridge Edition of the Works of Jane Austen: Mansfield Park*, ed. John Wiltshire (Cambridge: Cambridge University Press, 2005)
NA	*The Cambridge Edition of the Works of Jane Austen: Northanger Abbey*, ed. Barbara M. Benedict and Deirdre le Faye (Cambridge: Cambridge University Press, 2006)
OED	*Oxford English Dictionary*, 2nd edition, ed. John Simpson and Edmund Weiner (Oxford: Clarendon Press, 1989)
P&P	*The Cambridge Edition of the Works of Jane Austen: Pride and Prejudice*, ed. Pat Rogers (Cambridge: Cambridge University Press, 2006)
Pers	*The Cambridge Edition of the Works of Jane Austen: Persuasion*, ed. Janet Todd and Antje Blank (Cambridge: Cambridge University Press, 2006)
S&S	*The Cambridge Edition of the Works of Jane Austen: Sense and Sensibility*, ed. Edward Copeland (Cambridge: Cambridge University Press, 2006)
Tomalin, *Jane Austen*	Claire Tomalin, *Jane Austen: A Life*, rev. edition (London: Penguin, 2012)
TW	Jane Austen, *Teenage Writings*, ed. Kathryn Sutherland and Freya Johnston (Oxford: Oxford University Press, 2017)

———

Jane Austen's underlinings in manuscript are reproduced in some print editions (*Juvenilia, Teenage Writings*) in the form of italics; in others (*Letters, Jane Austen's Fiction Manuscripts*), they are shown as underlined. When quoting, I have followed the practice of the edition in question. In the appendix, when transcribing marginalia from hitherto unseen photographic images of Goldsmith's *History of England*, I have reproduced underlined words in underlined form so as to remain as close to the original image as possible.

JANE AUSTEN, EARLY AND LATE

Introduction

HER SIX COMPLETED novels may have been published within the narrow
span of six years and two months, but Jane Austen lived long enough and wrote
a sufficient quantity of work in the course of three decades to have identifiably
early, middle, and late phases in her authorial career. Or, to borrow the categories employed by her first biographers, she began with 'juvenile tales' and
'childish effusions', moved on to 'betweenities', and ended with 'novels' proper.
To consider the body of her work in this way is to progress in a straight line
from immaturity to maturity, from 'how she ought *not* to write' into 'the right
direction' (*Memoir*, pp. 42–3, 186).

The trouble with this view of things is that it does not square with the
compositional record. Austen preserved, returned to, and revised her earliest
unpublished works long after she became a published author. The book-
length fictions with which she made her name cannot be securely demarcated from the shorter juvenilia in terms of when they were composed, or
according to their subject matter, or on the basis of their author's concern
and affection for them.[1] Nor, it seems, would even her nephew James Edward Austen-Leigh—a man who voiced strong objections to the public appearance of Austen's first known writings—necessarily have argued that
there was a firm division between the teenage and adult works. Not, at least,
in terms of style. 'Perhaps the most characteristic feature in these early productions', he wrote, 'is that, however puerile the matter, they are always composed in pure simple English, quite free from the over-ornamented style
which might be expected from so young a writer' (*Memoir*, p. 40).

---

1. See Kathryn Sutherland, *Jane Austen's Textual Lives: From Aeschylus to Bollywood* (Oxford:
Oxford University Press, 2005), p. 204.

Like many literary careers, Austen's begins and ends in manuscript compositions left unpublished until long after she died. These writings, which emphatically display what her great-niece, Mary Augusta Austen-Leigh, summed up as 'strong family instincts and quick power of observation', emerged piecemeal into print, initially in the context of biographical accounts by her relatives.[2] After her death, family members retained control of her manuscripts for decades, permitting only the gradual and partial release of texts deemed a risk to the status of the increasingly renowned six novels. Austen's first known literary works are fair copies or transcriptions dating in the earliest case from around 1787, when she was eleven or twelve, and concluding in mid-1793, when she was seventeen. It is not known how long a gap there may have been between the creation and subsequent transcription of these works (accompanied, perhaps, by some fresh composition); it might have been a matter only of weeks or months. Now referred to collectively as 'juvenilia', or 'teenage writings', these twenty-seven pieces were originally entered into three stationer's notebooks styled 'Volume the First' (Bodleian Library, MS. Don. e. 7), 'Volume the Second' (British Library, Add. MS. 59874), and 'Volume the Third' (British Library, Add. MS. 65381). The contents of the three books are not arranged chronologically, although Austen seems to have begun to transcribe with that intention. The earliest entries (c. 1787–90) are to be found in 'Volume the First'. But so are the last, from 1793. All three volumes contain later revisions and corrections, not all of them in Austen's hand. Some changes seem to have been implemented during the first transcription, but others are clearly made later.[3] This material is already, at the point of being written down, the result of some kind of authorial re-reading, and of second thoughts if even of the most cursory kind. It is therefore not quite evidence of a primary creative process working itself out on the page, but of an author returning to something in order to record it and in the process also correcting, supplementing, or otherwise altering it. When she re-read and wrote out her work, Austen's revisions were fitful and opportunistic, perhaps the effect of sharing the texts

2. Mary Augusta Austen-Leigh, *Personal Aspects of Jane Austen* (London: John Murray, 1920), p. 13.

3. See for example *JAFM*, vol. 1, pp. 132–3, where the word 'must' in the first story of 'Volume the First' is corrected to 'first'; this correction 'appears from ink and hand to have been made on an occasion distinct from the general copying of this piece'.

with others, or of having them read aloud to her as she wrote them down.[4] The teenage works then circulated across generations within a close group of relatives and friends who kept and sometimes changed those works as they saw fit.

Austen's tiny one-act 'The Mystery an unfinished Comedy'—perhaps composed as an afterpiece for her family's 'private Theatrical exhibition' in 1788 (*TW*, p. 275)—was the first of the teenage writings to appear in print, in the second edition (1871) of Austen-Leigh's *Memoir of Jane Austen*. In this context, it was offered 'as a specimen of the kind of transitory amusement which Jane was continually supplying to the family party' (p. 40).[5] In the first edition of the *Memoir* (published on Austen's ninety-fourth birthday, 16 December 1869, but dated 1870), the author had printed none of his aunt's juvenilia, explaining that 'it would be as unfair to expose this preliminary process to the world, as it would be to display all that goes on behind the curtain of the theatre before it is drawn up'.[6] (The theatrical analogy remains a commonplace in the period, as it had been in the eighteenth century; fending off a would-be biographer, William Wordsworth offered 'One last word in matter of authorship; it is far better not to admit people so much behind the scenes as it has been lately fashionable to do'.[7]) In the second edition of the *Memoir*, retaining exactly the same language of resistance to exposure, Austen-Leigh also chose to include— as his specimen display of all that goes on behind the curtain before it is drawn up—an early, very short drama.

'The Mystery' is the only one of Jane Austen's teenage works to be dedicated to her father, the Rev. George Austen, who had seemingly unworriedly sanctioned the same early satirical experiments about which Austen's late nineteenth-century relations expressed such anxiety. Having his name at the head of this work might have given it some additional, and reassuring, authority in the eyes of his descendants. Billed as 'unfinished', 'The Mystery' is an intergenerational drama of comically thwarted disclosure; thwarted, at least as far as the audience is concerned. Older and younger generations mingle in

---

4. See for example *JAFM*, vol. 1, pp. 130–31, where the correction of 'Thro'' to 'Threw' suggests that 'at this point JA may have been copying from dictation'.

5. On the Austen theatricals, see *Family Record*, p. 63.

6. J. E. Austen-Leigh, *A Memoir of Jane Austen* (London: Richard Bentley, 1869 [dated 1870]), p. 62; *Memoir*, p. 43.

7. Wordsworth to Barron Field (16 Jan. 1840), *The Letters of William and Dorothy Wordsworth*, ed. E. De Selincourt, rev. Alan G. Hill, 4 vols. (Oxford: Clarendon Press, 1978–88), vol. 4: *The Later Years, 1821–1853*: part 1: *1821–28* (1978), p. 440.

the cast list. 'Old Humbug' and 'Young Humbug' recall Old and Young Hamlet; they also reflect the young author's assumed identity as 'your most Hum.^le Servant', where humility is transparently a pose. The names 'Corydon' and 'Daphne', conventional for rustic lovers, come from ancient pastoral and its English imitators, literature that—like the somewhat jaded, clapped-out atmosphere of dramatic comedy conjured by the name 'Spangle'—would have been well-known to Austen's parents (there is another Corydon in 'Frederic & Elfrida', *TW*, p. 8 and p. 275 n.).[8] The more everyday, home-grown names of 'Colonel Elliott' and 'Fanny Elliott' anticipate characters in Austen's later fiction ('Fanny' in *Sense and Sensibility* and *Mansfield Park*; 'Elliot' in *Persuasion*).[9]

'The Mystery' permits nothing to reach fruition in terms of our understanding of character or action. In the first scene, Corydon—as befits a swain—enters a garden, only to say he is interrupted and swiftly to leave again. Old and Young Humbug are then discovered, 'talking'. The father tells the son he wishes him to follow his advice, and the son agrees; we never learn what the advice is about. In the second scene, women are sewing and a 'narration' has 'nearly concluded' because Mrs Humbug has 'nothing more to say on the subject'. We might guess that while the men in the garden have been discussing careers, the separate group of women indoors has been discussing love. Or perhaps the 'advice' given by Old to Young Humbug relates to the same narration that is being concluded among the women inside the house. But nothing is explicitly said to this effect. The conclusion of scene 2 is that Fanny, thanks to Daphne's whispered communication, now knows 'every thing about it'—whatever 'it' may be. So she too determines 'I'll go away'. Mrs Humbug and Daphne then also declare 'And so will I', and the audience is none the wiser. The mirror episode at the end of scene 3 sees the Colonel whisper *his* secret to a sleeping Sir Edward. The need to share is thereby satisfied, with no risk incurred of damaging publicity (*TW*, pp. 49–51).[10]

---

8. 'Corydon' in defined in the *OED* as 'A generic proper name in pastoral poetry for a rustic'. Thomas Love Peacock's *Melincourt* refers to 'the character of *Corydon sospiroso*' ('sighing Corydon'), and to 'lords, baronets, and squires, all Corydons, sighing'. *Melincourt*, 3 vols. (London: T. Hookham, Jun., and Co.; Baldwin, Cradock, and Joy, 1817), vol. 1, p. 16; vol. 2, p. 2.

9. Two other surnames in the teenage writings resurface in the later fiction: Annesley and Musgrove ('A Collection of Letters', pp. 138, 145). A Mrs Annesley, companion to Miss Darcy, appears in *P&P*; the Musgrove family in *Pers*.

10. On Austen's style as a combination of 'wish and refusal', whereby a 'secret is kept and told', see D. A. Miller, *Jane Austen, or the Secret of Style* (Princeton, NJ: Princeton University Press, 2003), p. 59.

The author's definitive 'Finis' wraps up 'The Mystery', a work that is both complete and abruptly broken off. This text has rightly been said to anticipate Austen's later fiction in that it 'provides a model in miniature of the kinds of narrative and dramatic reticence on which her mature novels depend'.[11] Games with suppressed or evacuated content and vanishing protagonists continue from 'The Mystery' and 'Jack & Alice' (whose 'Hero' never enters his own story, other than in a brief narratorial report of his death, *TW*, p. 20) into the longer and later compositions. The 'intelligent, gentlemanlike' apothecary Mr Perry— quoted, summarized, or invoked at least seventy times in *Emma*—never appears in his own person (vol. 1, ch. 2, p. 18). The joke of his pervasive yet invisible authority flares suddenly into view when he is reported (by Miss Nash, to Harriet, who then repeats the story to Emma) to have remonstrated with Mr Elton on 'how shabby it was in him, their best player, to absent himself' (vol. 1, ch. 8, p. 72). Here, the character with whom Mr Woodhouse encourages us to associate the 'best' qualities, the man whose words are constantly, admiringly, circulated around Highbury—and someone we are never permitted to approach except through other people's accounts of him—is indirectly presented as telling off another character, 'their best player', for having left the stage because of 'a *lady*'. Some readers might recall at this point that Austen's authorial identity, at least in her first published work of fiction, *Sense and Sensibility*, was that of 'A LADY' (it was advertised on 31 October 1811 as 'a New Novel [. . .] By Lady—'). In her lifetime, she never appeared on her own title pages as 'Jane Austen'.[12] It is she, as a 'lady' and author, who causes the absence of Mr Perry, not the 'lady' ostensibly in question, Harriet Smith—or even Emma Woodhouse, the real object of Mr Elton's attentions, whose tussles for control of the narrative make her a storyteller with whom Austen's narrator is competing throughout the novel.

'The Mystery' bespeaks, intentionally or not, the Austen family's habitual exclusivity and inwardness, its self-sufficiency and opacity to outsiders. The function of 'The Mystery' in its late nineteenth-century biographical setting is akin to that of Jane Austen's handwriting—which, far from being mentioned

---

11. Bharat Tandon, *Jane Austen and the Morality of Conversation* (London: Anthem, 2003), p. 62.

12. The title page of *Sense and Sensibility: A Novel*, 3 vols. (London: T. Egerton, for the author, 1811), states that the novel is 'BY A LADY'; 'assertively and modestly', as Tony Tanner remarked, 'the name [is] withheld, the sex proclaimed'. 'Jane Austen: "By a Lady"', *New York Times* (6 May 1979), p. 266. The advertisement appeared in the *Morning Chronicle*, no. 13254 (31 Oct. 1811), p. 1, col. 4, and thereafter with slight variations in the wording. See also *A Family Record*, p. 188.

in that same setting as a way of apprehending the character of the author, was described by her niece Caroline Austen in a marvellously self-enclosed piece of redundant effusion as something that 'remains to bear testimony to its own excellence' (*Memoir*, p. 171).[13] The Austen family tendency to close ranks and take cover within its own private little world was remarkable. One relative, Philadelphia Walter, described the clan as 'all in high spirits & disposed to be pleased with each other'.[14] This 'hard humorous family' was, as E. M. Forster put it in a 1932 review of Austen's letters, 'the unit within which her heart had liberty of choice; friends, neighbours, plays and fame were all objects to be picked up in the course of a flight outside and brought back to the nest for examination'.[15] Austen-Leigh himself was mildly prickly on the subject: 'There was so much that was agreeable and attractive in this family party that its members may be excused if they were inclined to live somewhat too exclusively within it' (*Memoir*, p. 19).[16] Within that closed circle was another, yet smaller one, that of the two sisters who were

> everything to each other. They seemed to lead a life to themselves within the general family life which was shared only by each other. I will not say their true, but their *full*, feelings and opinions were known only to themselves. They alone fully understood what each had suffered and felt and thought. Yet they had such a gift of reticence that the secrets of their respective friends were never betrayed to each other. (*Memoir*, p. 198)

13. Austen family papers held by the Hampshire Record Office include a letter analysing Jane Austen's handwriting (8 Feb. 1893); it begins: 'I receive the impression of precision.— exactitude—Underlying the surface of this character seem to be many deep qualities which at first sight would not be recognized. Much tender regard for the feelings of others strikes me— This writer would not act impulsively or under pressure—Devotion to what appears to be duty is strong. Reserve forms a considerable ingredient in this character keeping many qualities in the shade' ('Character, given by Mrs Wingfield when holding a letter written by Jane Austen', [n. p.]. 23M93/64/4/1/2, Hampshire Record Office).

14. See *Austen Papers 1704–1856*, ed. R. A. Austen-Leigh (London: Spottiswoode, Ballantyne & Co., 1942), p. 131.

15. E. M. Forster, 'Miss Austen and Jane Austen', *Times Literary Supplement* (10 Nov. 1932), pp. 821–2.

16. One of the closest parallels to Jane Austen's circle on this score is offered by the Burneys' 'familial culture' of collaborative play, creation, and performance (musical and theatrical), as discussed in Lorna J. Clark, 'Teaching "The Young Idea How to Shoot": The Juvenilia of the Burney Family', *Journal of Juvenilia Studies*, 1 (2018), 20–36 (p. 21).

Heralding the author's later experiments in novelistic reticence, 'The Mystery' also encapsulates the Victorian biographer's view of Austen's career and the dearth of event that appears to characterize her life. The play stages a reluctant act of disclosure in the simultaneous (and successful) hope of preserving its secrets. G. K. Chesterton remarked that 'A very real psychological interest, almost amounting to a psychological mystery, attaches to any early work of Jane Austen'. He did not propose a solution, suggesting instead that Austen was a genius who was 'born, not made', a claim which only deepens the very real interest as well as the near-mystery.[17] With its conclusion in which nothing is concluded at the 'End of the Ist Act', young Austen's 'The Mystery' might nevertheless, as its author suggests, be considered a perfectly finished thing, since it is left 'as *complete* a *Mystery* as any of its kind' (*TW*, p. 49). The mystery is complete, even if the work in which it appears is not finished, because it remains unrevealed to us; indeed, it is impossible to solve. The most finished of literary works is the one in which the answer is never discovered or shared. There may be an additional comic element in play, involving an Irish use of 'completely', such as is invoked in relation to solving a mystery in Thomas Love Peacock's 'The Dilettanti' (1812–3):

> Comfit. M^r O'Prompt! will you do me the favor to clear up this mystery?
> O'Prompt. Oh bless your old soul! you must not apply to me: for, by the faith of St Patrick, I'm bothered completely.[18]

The pun on or joke about 'complete' in Austen's early spoof persists into her later works of fiction, where several characters' (often suspicious) habit of referring to something as 'quite complete' or 'very complete' or 'most complete' is already undoing the work of finitude that it describes.[19] Such wording gestures

---

17. Jane Austen, *Love and Freindship and Other Early Works Now First Printed from the Original MS.* (London: Chatto & Windus, 1922), 'Preface', p. xiii.

18. 'The Dilettanti' (1812–3), in *The Works of Thomas Love Peacock*, eds. H.F.B. Brett-Smith and C. E. Jones, 10 vols. (London: Constable & Co.; New York: Gabriel Wells, 1924–34), vol. 7: *Poems and Plays* (1931), p. 356. Compare *Headlong Hall* (1816), in which Sir Patrick O'Prism declares 'by my soul, I'm bothered completely'. [Thomas Love Peacock], *Headlong Hall* (London: T. Hookham, Jun., and Co., 1816), p. 73.

19. For 'quite complete', see for example *Emma*, vol. 1, ch. 14, p. 129; for 'very complete', see for example *MP*, vol. 2, ch. 8, p. 295, *Emma*, vol. 3, ch. 2, p. 355; for 'most complete', see for example *NA*, vol. 1, ch. 9, p. 61, *S&S*, vol. 1, ch. 11, p. 252, *MP*, vol. 1, ch. 6, p. 62. *Emma* has more examples than any other Austen novel of 'complete' and its cognates.

to the larger moral point that 'complete truth' is a truly uncommon property of 'any human disclosure' (*Emma*, vol. 3, ch. 13, p. 470); these communications will almost always retain an element of uncertainty or inconclusiveness.

'The Mystery', of all Jane Austen's early texts, best reflects or rather anticipates, in comically miniaturized and accelerated form, the family biographer's insistence on a 'personal obscurity' in his subject that is 'so complete' as virtually to strangle the memorial impulse (*Memoir*, p. 90). The playlet takes the 'gift of reticence' to its logical conclusion in betraying virtually nothing of what its characters are talking about. Its position within the biographical narrative of 1871 may officially serve as evidence of 'the first stirrings of talent' within the young Austen; perhaps even more importantly, it is made to introduce the mature novelist's reported opinion that 'such an early habit of composition' should not be encouraged (*Memoir*, p. 42). Releasing one tantalizing fragment of the teenage author's compositions, Austen-Leigh could not allow himself to do so without making it part of a general campaign against such writing's existence. That campaign that is all the more curious in view of his own early compositions and collaborations with his aunt in her unpublished works: he supplied continuations to 'Evelyn', and 'Kitty, or the Bower', the two unfinished tales in 'Volume the Third'.[20] It was his own career as an aspiring teenage novelist that prompted Austen's famous description of her writing as 'the little bit (two Inches wide) of Ivory on which I work with so fine a brush, as produces little effect after much labour' (*Letters*, 16–17 Dec. 1816, p. 337).

In November 1814 Austen wrote to her niece Anna about the latter's novel, 'Indeed, I <u>do</u> think you get on very fast. I wish other people of my acquaintance could compose as rapidly'; one month later, to Anna's younger half-sister Caroline, she repeated the sentiment even more emphatically: 'I wish I could finish Stories as fast as you can' (*Letters*, pp. 296–7, 301).[21] The desirability or not of completion as it relates to completeness—the need to have done, even if elements of the work are left undone or uncertain—is rehearsed in many of Austen's early as well as late pieces of fiction. The opening tale in 'Volume the First', 'Frederic & Elfrida', is dedicated to Martha Lloyd in gratitude for 'finishing my muslin Cloak'. The story that follows shows an interest in muslins ('the different excellencies of Indian & English', *TW*, p. 5) and an even stronger desire to reach the finish line. The first chapter is already

20. See Kathryn Sutherland, 'From Kitty to Catharine, James Edward Austen's Hand in *Volume the Third*', *Review of English Studies*, 66 (2015), 124–43.

21. Compare 'you write so fast' (to Anna Austen, 9–18 Sept. 1814, *Letters*, p. 288).

wrapping things up: 'so ended this little adventure, much to the satisfaction of all parties' (*TW*, p. 3). As an adult, Austen remained averse to protracting the final stages of her stories, on one occasion imputing to the reader her own impatience to have done:

> The anxiety, which in this state of their attachment must be the portion of Henry and Catherine, and of all who loved either, as to its final event, can hardly extend, I fear, to the bosom of my readers, who will see in the tell-tale compression of the pages before them, that we are all hastening together to perfect felicity. [...] I leave it to be settled by whomsoever it may concern, whether the tendency of this work be altogether to recommend parental tyranny, or reward filial disobedience. (*NA*, vol. 2, ch. 16, pp. 259, 261)[22]

In Austen's first compositions, characters are thrust forward as finished without any effort to lend them plausibility; stories break off without the distribution of just rewards and punishments, or in some cases any events deserving the name. Tragedies are 'not worth reading', perhaps because they imply a sort of justice or completion for which the young author has no appetite ('The History of England', *TW*, p. 124). Two other early works in 'Volume the First' are, like 'The Mystery', styled 'unfinished' in their titles while sporting 'Finis' as their last word ('Sir William Mountague an unfinished performance'; 'Memoirs of Mr Clifford an unfinished tale—', *TW*, pp. 34–6). Many years later, Austen wrote 'Finis' and the date (18 July 1816) at the end of *Persuasion*, before deciding to re-write the last chapters (*JAFM*, vol. 4, p. 282), suggesting perhaps a continued sense of the provisional as far as endings were concerned.[23] In her published novels, the resistance to finality that shapes her early tales becomes a moral problem or question as well as a joke about the limits of novelistic 'pictures of perfection' (*Letters*, 23 March 1817, p. 350). There is sometimes, too, a perceptible impatience with the generic requirements of marriage fiction which seems in turn to generate a refusal quite to conclude, or an ending that is wilfully inadequate. For the teenage Austen, partiality of

22. Compare the last paragraph of 'Lady Susan': 'I leave him therefore to all the Pity that anybody can give him' (*JAFM*, vol. 3, pp. 639–41), and a deleted passage in a draft closing chapter of *Persuasion*: 'Bad Morality again. [...] I [...] shall leave it to the mercy of Mothers & Chaperones & Middleaged Ladies in general (*JAFM*, vol. 4, p. 269).

23. 'The three Sisters' ('Volume the First') and 'Lesley-Castle' ('Volume the Second') are described in their titles as 'unfinished' but do not have 'Finis' written at the end (*TW*, pp. 52, 62, 96, 119).

feeling and narration such as that which governs her 'partial, prejudiced, & ignorant Historian' (*TW*, p. 120)—'partiality' in the twin senses of incompleteness and personal bias—is a matter of eluding detection, a game of impersonation without responsibility or consequences.

———

There was nothing sudden or spectacular about Jane Austen's rise to widespread acclaim. It has taken an especially long time for her earliest writings to gain critical attention and discussion, let alone interest and praise. Richard Simpson, reviewing Austen-Leigh's *Memoir* in 1870, was exceptional in construing her teenage works as direct evidence of her development from a 'critic' into an 'artist':

> She has left many manuscripts, which her family refuses to publish, on the ground of their not being worth it. None of them were intended for publication; they were exercises, not studies. What she wrote was worked up by incessant labour into its perfect form.[24]

Simpson's brusque appraisal ('refuses to publish', 'not being worth it') is a fair representation of how Austen's family treated and regarded her teenage works. The first appearance in print of these largely burlesque 'exercises' was hesitant and grudging—permitted only after much throat-clearing and in the context of a growing public appetite for information about her authorial and biographical origins—and did not begin until more than three decades after her death. No complete text of the juvenilia was published until the twentieth century. Those who might have been expected to champion their arrival in print could seem as regretful as her own family that these minor works had ever seen the light of day. R. W. Chapman, introducing Austen's 'Volume the First' to her public with an apologetic grimace in 1933, ended his preface on a cautionary note:

> *It will always be disputed whether such effusions as these ought to be published; and it may be that we have enough already of Jane Austen's early scraps.* [...] *But perhaps the question is hardly worth discussion. For if such manuscripts find their way into great libraries, their publication can hardly be prevented.*

24. Richard Simpson, unsigned review, *North British Review* (April 1870), repr. in *Jane Austen: The Critical Heritage*, 2 vols., ed. B. C. Southam (London: Routledge & Kegan Paul; New York: Barnes & Noble, 1968–87), vol. 1: *1811–1870* (1968), pp. 241–65 (pp. 243, 253).

That Chapman would have preferred to adopt a more drastic course of action than to publish is suggested by a chilly final sentence, extraordinary from a man who devoted so much of his life and work to preserving Austen's words: '*The only sure way to prevent it is the way of destruction, which no one dare take*.'[25] Brian Southam—also responsible for ground-breaking work on the juvenilia—continued to refer to Austen's teenage compositions in the reluctant, disparaging vein established by the author's family, suggesting that we need not regret the (putative) loss of more of her early works.[26] Chesterton, introducing 'Love and Friendship' (1790) and a selection of other writings by young Austen, wrote of one transitional fiction, unpublished in her lifetime: 'I hope I may be allowed to say that I for one would have willingly left "Lady Susan" in the waste-paper basket'.[27] As late in the day as 1989, the great grand-daughter of James Edward Austen-Leigh and co-founder of the Jane Austen Society of North America was confidently imagining that Austen felt 'ashamed' of her early writings, described here as 'tedious': 'The juvenilia, I believe, could well have been left [. . .] in a drawer, for study by scholars, who I venture to suspect are pretty much the only people who ever really peruse them'.[28] In comments such as these, Austen's early writings—'trifling enough', according to David Cecil—acquire a status akin to that of the tawdry treasures that Harriet Smith consigns to the flames when her romance with Mr Elton is finally proved to be a sham (*Emma*, vol. 3, ch. 4, pp. 366–9).[29] Unfortunately, as far as Chapman and Southam were concerned, the same could not be done with the '*early scraps*'.

Such attitudes to Austen's first known works resemble that of Leslie Stephen to the Brownings' letters (Austen's letters have routinely incurred similarly dismissive responses): 'It does not follow that because I want fact not fiction I therefore want all the facts, big and small; the poet's washing-bills, as well as his early drafts of great works'.[30] The point Stephen is making does

---

25. R. W. Chapman, 'Preface' to Jane Austen, *Volume the First* (Oxford: Clarendon Press, 1933), p. ix.

26. *JALM*, pp. 18–19.

27. *Love and Freindship and Other Early Works*, 'Preface', p. x.

28. Joan Austen-Leigh, 'The Juvenilia: A Family "Veiw"', in *Jane Austen's Beginnings: The Juvenilia and Lady Susan*, ed. J. David Grey, intro. Margaret Drabble (Ann Arbor, MI, and London: UMI Research Press, 1989), pp. 173–9 (pp. 177, 178).

29. David Cecil, *A Portrait of Jane Austen* (London: Constable, 1978), p. 59.

30. Leslie Stephen, 'The Browning Letters', in *Studies of a Biographer* [1898–1902], 4 vols. (Cambridge: Cambridge University Press, 2012), vol. 3, pp. 1–35 (p. 30).

not quite fit the case of Austen's teenage compositions; they are neither 'washing bills' (although these can be crucial, as in *Northanger Abbey*, vol. 2, ch. 7, p. 176; ch. 16, p. 260) nor quite, *pace* Q. D. Leavis, 'early drafts of great works' (although many of them both anticipate and overlap with the later novels).[31] But the instinctive critical sense that it would be better for certain juvenile, unfinished, or otherwise seemingly trifling materials *not* to have survived—that the persistence of some kinds of literary evidence is to be lamented rather than celebrated—has long governed one strain of reaction to these works. It is reflected in how little has been written about them. Would she had blotted a thousand such tales, rather than taken such pains to secure them.

Austen's early works are, like the houses of the Musgrove family in her last completed novel (indeed, like the Musgroves themselves), preserved 'in a state of alteration' (the author's, and her family's), 'perhaps of improvement' (*Pers*, vol. 1, ch. 5, p. 43). Recent critics of these writings have adopted Dr Johnson's stance when he professed that 'All knowledge is of itself of some value. There is nothing so minute or inconsiderable, that I would not rather know it than not'.[32] But they have not always known what kinds of knowledge or evidence the juvenilia might constitute, or what they could suggest as points of critical enquiry and comparison. James Sutherland hailed 'Love and Friendship' as 'a remarkable performance [. . .] for a girl of fifteen', but what he found remarkable about it was primarily the 'subtlety' that, even in this rather 'crude' work, keeps 'breaking in, and we become aware of that cool intelligence that was to preside over all her mature writing'.[33] A. Walton Litz was and is representative of many in his wish to accord the early tales a subordinate, preparatory role, 'chiefly important in relation to [Austen's] major novels', while stressing that 'it would be a mistake to place too much emphasis on the relationships between these fictions and the later novels'. Doing 'too much' of anything is by definition 'a mistake'; in any event, it is not clear how this sense of critical priorities fosters Litz's conclusion that the teenage writings 'are remarkably self-sufficient': parodies and burlesques are necessarily reliant on something

31. See Q. D. Leavis, 'A Critical Theory of Jane Austen's Writings', *Scrutiny*, 10 (1941–2), 61–87, 114–42, 272–94; and 12 (1944–5), 104–19. Her theory is discussed in chapter 1.

32. *Boswell's Life of Johnson: together with Boswell's journal of a tour to the Hebrides and Johnson's diary of a journey into North Wales*, ed. G. B. Hill, rev. and enlarged L. F. Powell, 6 vols., 2nd edition (Oxford: 1934–64), vol. 2, p. 357.

33. James Sutherland, *English Satire* (Cambridge: Cambridge University Press, 1962), p. 119.

that exists before and outside themselves. Wanting to insist that these tales are mostly 'self-explanatory' seems to be part of Litz's apprehension that attending to the sources and origins of the teenage writings might provoke the same loss of perspective and the same indecorum that are dramatized by young Austen in those very burlesque tales; hence the critic's attempt 'to avoid wherever possible the byways of literary detection', to resist being misled.[34] Rather than look back to investigate where these riotous early works came from, Litz is determined to look forward, to concentrate on where they were going. He may be unusually keen to acknowledge these texts as a starting point, but he sounds keener still to get away.

Fashions exist in editing and criticism, as in anything else. One generation of editors and critics will incline more favourably to late than to early work—however those categories and divisions are construed—the next, by way of reaction to its predecessor, will find reasons to prefer first thoughts to second. In the choices he made about how to present Austen's incomplete working drafts of 'The Watsons' (c. 1805), *Persuasion* (1817), 'Sanditon' (1817), and 'Lady Susan' (date unknown), R. W. Chapman was himself inconsistent. He offered clean transcriptions of the first three texts, retaining contractions and oddities of spelling but removing corrections or deletions and recording them in textual notes. However, in the case of the fairly short novel-in-letters 'Lady Susan'—a beautifully written fair copy of uncertain date which has almost no corrections or deletions—he altered the appearance of his transcription in order to make it less polished than the actual manuscript. In so doing, he could not but change the character of the work. Where Austen had scrupulously demarcated one speech from another, beginning each on a new indented line and thereby presenting her text in dramatic as well as epistolary form, Chapman ran the speeches together, ignoring the paragraph and line breaks and the visual separation of one speaker from another.[35] The editor's intervening hand here combines with that of the unwitting author to achieve a collaboration of uncertain purport.

---

34. A. Walton Litz, *Jane Austen: A Study of Her Artistic Development* (New York: Oxford University Press, 1965), pp. 18, 24.

35. For commentary on this intervention, see Sutherland, *Jane Austen's Textual Lives*, pp. 207–10; *JAFM*, vol. 1, p. 20. For direct comparison of Austen's manuscript with Chapman's edition, see *Jane Austen's Lady Susan: A Facsimile of the Manuscript in the Pierpont Morgan Library and the 1925 Printed Edition*, intro. A. Walton Litz (New York and London: Garland Publishing, 1989).

Chapman's aim was presumably to lessen the strikingly theatrical appearance of these dialogues within letters—a quality that early epistolary Austen shared with her beloved Samuel Richardson—and instead to make the tale look more like the draft of a later conventional third-person novel. Her nephew reported that Austen's

> knowledge of Richardson's works was such as no one is likely again to acquire [...] Every circumstance narrated in Sir Charles Grandison, all that was ever said or done in the cedar parlour, was familiar to her; and the wedding days of Lady L. and Lady G. were as well remembered as if they had been living friends. (*Memoir*, p. 71)

She may have collaborated with her niece in transforming *The History of Sir Charles Grandison* (1753–4) into a comic play, *Sir Charles Grandison or The happy Man*.[36] Whether she did so or not, the young Austen seems to have responded to epistolary fiction as a form of theatre, with the potential for dramatic adaptation and performance.[37] When it came to transcribing successive letters in 'Lady Susan', it would therefore make sense for her to have given unusual care and attention to the division of one speaker and speech from another. In Chapman's version of the text, with this aspect of its presentation altered, Austen's unpublished manuscript has been made to appear less directly imitative of an eighteenth-century predecessor and more directly preparatory for her later published fiction. Rather than look back to the 1750s, this version of 'Lady Susan' looks forward to the 1810s (estimates of the novella's date of composition range from 1793 to 1812, giving it an uniquely mobile position in Austen's career; see *JAFM*, vol. 3, pp. 297–8).[38] The text is subtly reconfigured by Chapman so as to suggest imminent renunciation of the epistolary mode, and thus to fall in with 'teleological assumptions about the development of narrative forms' as

---

36. See Mark Kinkead-Weekes, *Samuel Richardson: Dramatic Novelist* (London: Methuen, 1973); Penny Gay, *Jane Austen and the Theatre* (Cambridge: Cambridge University, 2002); Paula Byrne, *Jane Austen and the Theatre* (London: Hambledon and London, 2002).

37. Brian Southam claimed the playlet was composed by Austen—the 53-page manuscript appears to be in her hand—but this is unlikely. Family tradition ascribes it to a very young Anna Austen (later Lefroy); see *JALM*, pp. 136–40; Sutherland, *Jane Austen's Textual Lives*, pp. 246–7.

38. On establishing the date of the text, see also Janine Barchas, *Matters of Fact in Jane Austen: History, Location, and Celebrity* (Baltimore, MD: Johns Hopkins University Press, 2012), pp. 45–6.

most influentially rehearsed in Ian Watt's *The Rise of the Novel: Studies in Defoe, Richardson and Fielding* (1957).[39]

The fact that 'Lady Susan' was not completed, other than by a relatively brief non-epistolary conclusion, seems to endorse Chapman's reading of its place within Austen's career and in the historical development of the novel. Fictional letters had to be abandoned in order for the author and her genre to progress. From now on, Austen would strive to finish and to publish, and those finished publications would not be epistolary. But there is at least one other way of reading 'Lady Susan'. If it is a failure—and it is far from clear why it should be considered as such—it might be for reasons that have nothing to do with the letter-form. Perhaps, in its very conclusion in multiple marriages, a younger Austen would have considered 'Lady Susan' a let-down. The heroine, a beautiful villain, ends up yoked to an empty-headed (albeit rich) man. She gains respectability, and the price is freedom. Lady Susan's triumph cannot but feel pyrrhic, at least by comparison with the fate of a comparably resourceful, albeit far less developed, heroine, Eliza in 'Volume the First':

> No sooner was she reinstated in her accustomed power at Harcourt Hall, than she raised an Army, with which she entirely demolished the Dutchess's Newgate, snug as it was, and by that act, gained the Blessings of thousands, & the Applause of her own Heart. ('Henry & Eliza', *TW*, p. 32)

If we accept Southam's suggestion that 'Lady Susan' was composed in two phases, across a period of perhaps ten years or more, significant alterations could have been made to the draft during fair copying, and the 'Conclusion' may well have been a late addition.[40] Between starting and finishing 'Lady Susan', how might Austen and her attitude to conclusions have changed? The possible ten-year divide between the author who wrote most of the tale and the author who brought it to a close might even be alluded to in the two women—a decade apart in age—who appear in the very last sentence of 'Lady Susan': 'For myself, I confess that I can pity only Miss Manwaring, who coming to Town & putting herself to an expence in Cloathes, which impoverished

---

39. David Owen, 'The Failed Text That Wasn't: Jane Austen's *Lady Susan*', in *The Failed Text: Literature and Failure*, ed. José Luis Martínez-Duenãs Espejo and Rocío G. Sumerilla (Newcastle upon Tyne: Cambridge Scholars Publishing, 2013), pp. 81–96 (p. 88: citing Elizabeth Heckendorn Cook). On the choice of epistolary form as 'regressive', see ibid., pp. 86–7.

40. See *JALM*, pp. 45–52; B. C. Southam, *Jane Austen: A Students' Guide to the Later Manuscript Works* (London: Concord Books, 2007), pp. 26–7.

her for two years, on purpose to secure him, was defrauded of her due by a Woman ten years older than herself. / FINIS' (*JAFM*, vol. 3, p. 641). Could this 'Conclusion' be written in the voice of an older Austen, ironically confessing to pity 'For myself', the younger author she once was—someone who is now being defrauded of her right to this work by a mature Austen who has sailed in and married off her characters, thereby putting an end to and a dampener on things? If so, the irony would be compounded by the fact that the marriage for which Miss Manwaring had been planning (and spending) is itself left unaccomplished; it is the price of authorial completion.

———

Partly because of their perceived status—until very recently—as mere trifles, partly because of the 'damage [...] done to these early works by the determined tendency to consider them only or chiefly in light of the great works to come', very few readers encounter Austen's first writings before they have read her mature fiction (and relatively few thereafter).[41] Thanks to the efforts of two pioneering critics and editors, Christine Alexander and Juliet McMaster, that is in the process of changing. The Juvenilia Press, established by McMaster and developed by Alexander, has published editions of the early works of (among many others) Jane Austen, Maria Edgeworth, Hannah More, and Sophia Burney. Alongside the International Society for Literary Juvenilia (launched in 2017) and the *Journal of Juvenilia Studies* (begun in 2018), whose work the Society supports, the Juvenilia Press has fostered knowledge of and enthusiasm for childhood and teenage writing across the globe. Its originators have always put teenage Austen at the fore of their activities and productions. In 2005, McMaster and Alexander edited a collection of essays, *The Child Writer from Austen to Woolf*, in which Margaret Anne Doody suggests that, if we read 'early works' looking solely for evidence of 'the mature author', we will be missing out.[42] Alexander's edition of Austen's *Love and Freindship and Other Youthful Writings* appeared in 2014; in 2016, McMaster published a collected edition of her own essays, *Jane Austen, Young Author*, in which she discerned an 'ethic of energy' and 'ethic of sympathy' that persist from the juvenilia into

41. Jane Austen, *Catharine and Other Writings*, ed. Margaret Anne Doody and Douglas Murray (Oxford: Oxford University Press, 1993), 'Introduction', p. xxx. See also pp. 86–7.

42. Margaret Anne Doody, 'Jane Austen, That Disconcerting "Child"', in *The Child Writer from Austen to Woolf*, ed. Christine Alexander and Juliet McMaster (Cambridge: Cambridge University Press, 2005), pp. 101–21 (p. 101).

the later novels. This book, like McMaster's, finds 'the continuity as notable as the discontinuity' between the teenage and the adult writer.[43]

Jane Austen, Early and Late examines her first known works and their reception, initially within and then, gradually, outside her own familial circle. It focuses on the dubious chronology of her compositions, her likely sources and influences, on her comic and stylistic repertoire, and on the relationship of her earliest known manuscript works to the later, celebrated novels. In so doing, it considers the ways in which authorial careers tend to be presented, by critics and biographers, in terms of the subject's development from childhood to maturity, and asks whether such a pattern best captures the achievements of this novelist; indeed, whether it makes sense to refer to an 'early' or a 'late' Jane Austen at all.

Another interdisciplinary field within which this study of the early and the late writer might have been cast is that of age studies (or ageing studies, as it is sometimes known). Recent work in this area has stressed Austen's keen sense of the varieties of growth and experience, the losses and gains that come with maturity, and the associations of ageism with sexism in her lifetime.[44] As a precocious child and premature old maid, Austen perhaps merits the description bestowed on Jude Fawley's son, Little Father Time, in *Jude the Obscure* (1895): 'Age masquerading as Juvenility'.[45] For Edward Said, writing on late style, the boy embodies a 'sense of accelerated decline' alongside 'compensating gestures of recapitulation and inclusiveness'. This uncanny combination well describes the character of Jane Austen's unpublished work, 'a montage of beginnings and endings, an unlikely jamming together of youth and age': Kathryn Sutherland has remarked that her manuscripts 'appear to represent early and later drafts compacted into one' (*JAFM*, vol. 1, p. 44).[46]

───────

43. Juliet McMaster, *Jane Austen, Young Author* (Farnham: Ashgate, 2016), pp. 8–9.

44. See for example Devoney Looser, *Women Writers and Old Age in Great Britain, 1750–1850* (Baltimore, MD: Johns Hopkins University Press, 2008), pp. 75–96; Maggie Lane, *Growing Older with Jane Austen* (London: Robert Hale, 2014). See also Devoney Looser, 'Age and Aging Studies, from Cradle to Grave', *Age Culture Humanities*, 1 (2014), https://ageculturehumanities .org/WP/age-and-aging-studies-from-cradle-to-grave/.

45. Thomas Hardy, *Jude the Obscure* (London and New York: Penguin, 1998), pp. 342–3.

46. Edward W. Said, *On Late Style* (London: Bloomsbury, 2006), pp. 135–6. For a critical appraisal of what is meant by such a style, see Linda and Michael Hutcheon, 'Late Style(s): The Ageism of the Singular', *Occasion: Interdisciplinary Studies in the Humanities*, 4 (2012). https:// arcade.stanford.edu/occasion/late-styles-ageism-singular.

When Charlotte Brontë wanted to criticize Austen's fiction to George Henry Lewes, she argued that it showed the wrong kind of face to its readers. In *Pride and Prejudice*, Brontë saw only 'an accurate daguerrotyped portrait of a commonplace face' with 'no glance of a bright, vivid physiognomy' (Lewes responded that Brontë had an 'almost contemptuous indifference to the art of truthful portrait painting').[47] For those who had known Jane Austen personally, disputes about the face of her work had a natural reference to the face of their author. Might one be a likeness or reflection of the other? Austen's niece Anna Lefroy was puzzled to think how all of her aunt's separately attractive features did not quite add up to a woman you could call 'handsome':

> A mottled skin, not fair, but perfectly clear & healthy in hue; the fine naturally curling hair, neither light nor dark; the bright hazel eyes to match, & the rather small but well shaped nose. One hardly understands how with all these advantages she could yet fail of being a decidedly handsome woman. (*Memoir*, p. 158)

This appraisal falters into something less than 'decidedly handsome' before it pauses to say as much. 'Mottled skin' that is 'not fair'; hair that is 'neither light nor dark'; a nose that is 'rather small': these are perhaps not unmitigated 'advantages'. Still, it seems to be the failure of her separate, individually attractive facial features to cohere that makes Jane Austen something other than 'a decidedly handsome woman'; something that 'One hardly understands'. It is as if the onlooker, distracted into anatomizing the constituent parts of her face—each of which has its own distinctive appeal—cannot then quite reconcile them into a whole. Austen's face seems to incarnate the irresolution of diversity and unity. That her face was in some sense difficult to summarize—which may be one reason for the many disputed likenesses of her—must have been the impression of more than one member of the Austen family.

James Edward Austen-Leigh, her nephew, had his own qualified praise to bestow:

> In person she was very attractive; her figure was rather tall and slender, her step light and firm, and her whole appearance expressive of health and animation. In complexion she was a clear brunette with a rich colour; she had full round cheeks, with mouth and nose small and well formed, bright hazel

---

47. *The Critical Heritage*, vol. 1, pp. 126, 160–61.

eyes, and brown hair forming natural curls close round her face. If not so regularly handsome as her sister, yet her countenance had a peculiar charm of its own to the eyes of most beholders. (*Memoir*, p. 70)

His sister, Caroline Austen, on whom Austen-Leigh's *Memoir* often drew, wrote that:

> As to my Aunt's personal appearance, her's was the first face that I can remember thinking pretty, not that I *used* that word to myself, but I know that I looked at her with admiration—Her face was rather *round* than long—she had a *bright*, but not a *pink* colour—a clear brown complexion and very good hazle eyes—She was not, I beleive, an absolute beauty, but before she left Steventon she was established as a very pretty girl, in the opinion of most of her neighbours. [...] Her hair, a darkish brown, curled naturally— it was in short curls round her face. (*Memoir*, p. 169)

Jane Austen's brother Henry left this impression of her face:

> Her features were separately good. Their assemblage produced an unrivalled expression of that cheerfulness, sensibility, and benevolence, which were her real characteristics. Her complexion was of the finest texture. It might with truth be said, that her eloquent blood spoke through her modest cheek. ('Biographical Notice of the Author' (1817), in *Memoir*, p. 139)

Jane Austen's features, considered individually, were good; considered together, they needed to be summarized in terms other than those of physical attractiveness. One by one, they worked; as a composite, they did not quite amount to the face of a beautiful woman. Was this aspect of her embodied self one reason why Austen excelled at the description of bit-parts, and played games with zeugma, whereby one verb governs two different, incongruous objects, inner and outer? '[I cannot flourish in this east wind] which is quite against my skin & conscience', as she wrote; 'I will not boast of my handwriting; neither that, nor my face have yet recovered their proper beauty' (? late Feb.– early March 1815, *Letters*, p. 302; 27 May 1817, *Letters*, p. 357). The face, as a whole, did not quite add up.[48] Its inverse or mirror image, as it were, would be that of Muriel Spark's Chief Inspector Mortimer in *Memento Mori* (1959)—someone

---

48. On discussions of Austen's face see also Tomalin, *Jane Austen*, pp. 110–11.

with individually unattractive features which nevertheless combine to form a beguiling total impression:

> At the sides and back of his head his hair grew thick and grey. His eyebrows were thick and black. It would be accurate to say that his nose and lips were thick, his eyes small and his chin receding into his neck. And yet it would be inaccurate to say he was not a handsome man, such being the power of unity when it exists in a face.[49]

One of the valuable things about Cassandra Austen's pencil and watercolour sketch of her sister, probably in her mid-thirties—described by Chapman as a 'disappointing scratch'—is that it depicts a woman whose face somehow lacks 'the power of unity'. This is Jane Austen captured just before the age by which William Hogarth thought that a person's character might be 'written' in his or her face:

> It is by the natural and unaffected movements of the muscles, caused by the passions of the mind, that every man's character would in some measure be written in his face, by that time he arrives at forty years of age, were it not for certain accidents which often, tho' not always prevent it. [. . .] It is strange that nature hath afforded us so many lines and shapes to indicate the deficiencies and blemishes of the mind, whilst there are none at all that point out the perfections of it beyond the appearance of common sense and placidity.[50]

In the only authenticated likeness of her face, Jane Austen is neither decidedly handsome nor decidedly unhandsome, but rather a not entirely coherent mixture of sweet and sour, softness and angularity, the light brown curls and round pinkish cheeks offset by a sharp straight nose and small, thin-lipped, unsmiling mouth.[51] David Piper, echoing Chapman's suggestion that '*the way of destruction*' might have been the best for Austen's early writings, described the portrait as 'a bad job; unfortunately [Cassandra] neglected to tear it up and now it must be preserved forever to salve the consciences of historians'.[52]

---

49. Muriel Spark, *Memento Mori* [1959] (Harmondsworth: Penguin, 1961; repr. 1996), p. 140.

50. William Hogarth, *The Analysis of Beauty. Written with a view of fixing the fluctuating ideas of taste* (London: for the author, 1753), pp. 126, 131.

51. R. W. Chapman, *Jane Austen: Facts and Problems* (Oxford: Clarendon Press, 1948), p. 214.

52. David Piper, *Shades: An Essay on English Portrait Silhouettes* (New York: Chilmark Press; Cambridge: Rampant Lions Press, 1970), p. 51.

FIGURE 1. Jane Austen by Cassandra Austen, pencil and watercolour (c. 1810). NPG 3630, National Portrait Gallery, London.

It is a face that, suggesting a certain acerbic vitality as well as stiffness, looks somewhat at odds with itself. One explanation for its slightly pinched or strained aspect—perhaps recalled in that 'sharp & anxious expression of her face' that is ascribed to Mrs Robert Watson, and which detracts from her beauty, in 'The Watsons' (*JAFM*, vol. 4, p. 139)—could be that Austen often endured episodes of neuralgia, or excruciating 'face-ache'.[53] Lizzie Knight recalled her aunt walking 'with head a little to one side, and sometimes a very small cushion pressed against her cheek, if she were suffering from face-ache, as she not unfrequently did in later life'.[54] Diary entries made by Fanny Knight record (on 18 July 1813) that Austen had 'a bad face ache'; on 2 August, she observes that her aunt 'slept here and suffered sadly with her face'.[55] The following month, Austen wrote to assure her sister that she had had 'no pain in my face since I left you' (15–16 Sept. 1813, *Letters*, p. 230). This was evidently a family complaint. In the same letter in which she reported her own recovery from face-ache, Henry Austen, whom his younger sister Jane (at least in early life) resembled,[56] is said to have been 'suffering from the pain in the face which he has been subject to before. He caught cold at Matlock, & since his return has been paying a little for past pleasure.—It is nearly removed now,— but he looks thin in the face—either from the pain, or the fatigues of his Tour' (*Letters*, p. 227). In an earlier letter to Cassandra, Austen wrote that Henry had sent 'the welcome information of his having had no face-ache since I left them' (26 June 1808, *Letters*, p. 140). (The term 'face-ache', according to the *OED*, is first recorded by the Hampshire naturalist Gilbert White in a journal entry of 1784; it could mean either the agony endured by victims of neuralgia or, in a facetious later use, the agony inflicted on an observer by the sight of a hideous visage).[57]

Like the later examples of Austen's teenage writing (especially 'Kitty, or the Bower'), and like those stories summed up as 'betweenities', Cassandra's portrait may capture rival impulses in the originator to produce a likeness and a caricature, a novel and a burlesque. Perhaps the sitter presented herself to the artist as a combination of satire and sentiment. These are not mutually

---

53. The description of Mrs Robert Watson originally read: 'the expression of her face, sharp & anxious in general' (*JAFM*, vol. 4, p. 139).

54. *Fanny Knight's Diaries: Jane Austen through Her Niece's Eyes*, ed. Deirdre le Faye ([Winchester]: The Jane Austen Society, 2000), p. 27. See also Annette Upfal, 'Jane Austen's Lifelong Health Problems and Final Illness: New Evidence Points to a Fatal Hodgkin's Disease and Excludes the Widely Accepted Addison's', *Medical Humanities*, 31 (2005), 3–11.

55. *Fanny Knight's Diaries*, p. 27.

56. 'She is to be Jenny and seems to me as if she would be as like Harry as Cassy is to Neddy'. See letter from Rev. George Austen to his sister, 17 Dec. 1775, in *Austen Papers 1704–1856*, pp. 32–3.

57. 'face-ache n. *(a)* pain in the face, *esp.* that caused by trigeminal neuralgia; (also) an instance of this; *(b) slang* (chiefly *British*) an ugly or miserable-looking person (frequently as a form of address)' (*OED*).

exclusive possibilities, and something of their mixed constituents is captured in the verbal portrait of another 'sweet Sister' in her mid-thirties, also called Jane, in young Austen's 'Collection of Letters'. The correspondent hails the 35-year-old Miss Jane, whom she has known 'above fifteen Years' (a key threshold, period of time, and age in these early writings), as charming and physically lovely: 'in spite of sickness, Sorrow and Time', she is 'more blooming than ever I saw a Girl of 17. [...] There is something so sweet, so mild in her Countenance, that she seems more than Mortal' (*TW*, p. 136). The glaring implausibility of Miss Jane's sweet, mild face defying the years is matched by the cracks that swiftly appear in her sweet, mild conversation. When the letter-writer proves incapable of expressing her adoration and can only stammer out 'How do you do?', Miss Jane comes to her aid with a barbed comment: 'My dear Sophia be not uneasy at having exposed Yourself—I will turn the Conversation without appearing to notice it' (*TW*, p. 137). In this story, as in Cassandra Austen's sketch, a face and a character emerge that are at once appealing and disarmingly spiky.

One way of resolving the undecidedness of Cassandra Austen's version of her sister would be to make it more sentimental—younger, prettier, softer, and sweeter—as in the engraving that was produced for the 1869 frontispiece of Austen-Leigh's *Memoir*.[58] Another way of resolving the original sketch would be to make it more satirical—older, uglier, harder, bitchier—in the manner of an eighteenth-century caricature. This would bring it into line with the countenance of Elizabeth I, as depicted by Cassandra in 'The History of England', and sharply contrasted with the sweet, red-cheeked image of Mary, Queen of Scots, that sits alongside it—an illustration that has been interpreted as a likeness of the young Jane.[59] The two monarchs are presented alongside one another, in parallel, as if they might be twin aspects of a single character (no other portraits are paired in this manner in the 'History of England').

Cassandra's view of her sister in or around 1810 contains the potential for both Victorian and Augustan readings of Jane Austen's face. It marries (to borrow Mary Russell Mitford's terms) the skittish young 'butterfly' to the

---

58. On the sketch of Austen and its Victorian adaptations, see Claudia L. Johnson, *Jane Austen's Cults and Cultures* (Chicago: University of Chicago Press, 2012), pp. 30–38.

59. On the identification of Cassandra's medallion portraits with members of the Austen family, see *Jane Austen's 'The History of England' & Cassandra's Portraits*, ed. Annette Upfal and Christine Alexander (Sydney: Juvenilia Press, 2009), pp. xix–xxxvii.

JANE AUSTEN.

LONDON: RICHARD BENTLEY, 1870

FIGURE 2. Engraving of Jane Austen, after Cassandra Austen, commissioned by James Edward Austen-Leigh for the frontispiece to the *Memoir of Jane Austen* (1869, dated 1870). NPG D13873, National Portrait Gallery, London.

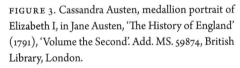

FIGURE 3. Cassandra Austen, medallion portrait of Elizabeth I, in Jane Austen, 'The History of England' (1791), 'Volume the Second'. Add. MS. 59874, British Library, London.

FIGURE 4. Cassandra Austen, medallion portrait of Mary, Queen of Scots, in Jane Austen, 'The History of England' (1791), 'Volume the Second'. Add. MS. 59874, British Library, London.

ferocious middle-aged 'poker'.[60] The relatedly questioning appraisal of Emma Woodhouse also revolves around the 'handsome', and invites us to consider how such a term does and does not cohere with other items in a list of qualities that 'seemed to unite'—but which might, on further inspection, be under less than perfect management or subject to a less unified impression than they appear to be:

> Emma Woodhouse, handsome, clever, and rich, with a comfortable home and happy disposition, seemed to unite some of the best blessings of existence; and had lived nearly twenty-one years in the world with very little to distress or vex her. (*Emma*, vol. 1, ch. 1, p. 3)

Once the state of unity or individual coherence is called into question by 'seemed', a story comes into being.

---

60. *The Life of Mary Russell Mitford [...] related in a selection from her letters to her friends*, ed. Rev. G. A. L'Estrange, 3 vols. (London: Richard Bentley, 1870), vol. 1, pp. 305–6 (3 April 1815). On Mitford's description of Austen, see ch. 3.

In a review of *Camilla: or, A Picture of Youth* (1796), the *British Critic* saw Frances Burney's high-life characters as probable or realistic, while casting her low-life characters as farcical, suggesting that two widely divergent strains of fiction or characterization here co-existed, side by side, in a single work (the same might be said of *Evelina, or The History of a Young Lady's Entrance into the World* (1778) and the satirical handling of its French and Scottish characters, by comparison with the sentimental treatment of others).[61] More recent biographers and critics of Burney have tended to present the satirical side of her authorial character as one that was rejected as she grew older: her keenly observed playlet *The Witlings* (written and revised 1778–80), suppressed at the wish of Charles Burney and another beloved father-figure, Samuel Crisp, is on this view of things evidence of a direction the novelist might have taken—but did not.[62] Jane Austen's career has often been interpreted in proximate terms: following the abandonment of an early strain of improbability or satire or caricature, she committed herself to sober, everyday truth to nature. Such is the family reading of her life and writing, portrayed as that aspect of growing up which permitted the novelist to flourish. Even a modern critic such as Margaret Anne Doody, far more sympathetic to young Austen's works than was Caroline Austen or James Edward Austen-Leigh, once construed the early writing as evidence of a choice Austen might have made, had she not been compelled to recognize that the market called for triple-decker novels of sentiment rather than for hectic spoofs. Glossing Chesterton's introduction to the juvenilia, Doody wrote:

> That Austen can—and should—be placed on a line which runs from Rabelais to Dickens seems to me right. Or at least, Chesterton's statement points to the line to which Austen *could* have belonged—had the world and the publishers allowed such a thing.[63]

This is the narrative of a career that changed tack, moved on, or recognized that the satirical impulse must be subdued to the demands of the reading public. But Austen's might also be a career that is understood as a perpetual

---

61. 'Her characters of a higher stamp are usually drawn with exact propriety and truth; but those either of lower life, or of a ridiculous cast, are, for the most part, strong caricatures. They are related more to farce than to comedy'. 'ART. XIII. *Camilla: or, A Picture of Youth*', *British Critic, A New Review*, VII–VIII (1796), 527–36 (p. 528).

62. See Frances Burney, *The Witlings and the Woman-Hater*, ed. Peter Sabor and Geoffrey Sill (Peterborough, Ontario: Broadview Press, 2002), 'Introduction', pp. x–xxxv.

63. *Catharine and Other Writings*, p. xxxiv.

attempt to adjust the rival claims of satire and sentiment, Gothic and realism, a combination of young and old in which the early quixotic strain is not necessarily rejected or chastened but rather encouraged to live on, alongside other ways of seeing the world. To do justice to Doody, she has herself recently embraced something akin to this view of Austen's works, rejecting her earlier lament for the lost exuberance of a teenage comedian. In 2015, looking back to her 1993 introduction to the adolescent writings, Doody found that her attitude to their author's development had itself developed into something else:

> Jane Austen, so it seemed to me, had sacrificed a great deal not only of her original humour and wit but of her vision of the world, in order to please the circulating libraries and get published at last. [...] At that point I had not realized the full magnificence of Austen's achievement. She had not let go of the surreal and fantastic and edgy elements so wonderfully present in the first works. Instead, she combined these elements with the decorum and concerns of the courtship novel. Her daring pretence to be *only* realistic is as good as a masquerade.[64]

Another way to think about the persistence of the early works into the published fictions is to consider Austen's plots. Her novels are often concerned with what it means to relinquish (or try to relinquish) the past, to reject a first love, embrace a new direction or pursue a second thought. First impressions—the original title of *Pride and Prejudice*—are proverbially wrong, but Austen's last completed novel, *Persuasion* (1817), might be read as a cautionary tale of the opposite kind: it suggests that first impressions are the right ones, and not to be easily given up (William Godwin observed that one lesson he had learnt from Mary Wollstonecraft was 'a minute attention to first impressions, and a just appreciation of them').[65] A marginal note beside the early-but-late passage in *Persuasion*—'Dear, dear Jane! This deserves to be written in letters of gold'[66]—suggests how deep the feeling of and for continuity might run. It also provides a clue to Jane Austen's personal and artistic development:

64. Margaret Anne Doody, *Jane Austen's Names: Riddles, Persons, Places* (Chicago: University of Chicago Press, 2015), pp. 387–8.

65. Mary Wollstonecraft, *A Short Residence in Sweden, Norway, and Denmark*, and William Godwin, *Memoirs of the Author of A Vindication of the Rights of Woman*, ed. Richard Holmes (Harmondsworth: Penguin, 1987), *Memoirs*, p. 273.

66. This pencil note in the margin next to the passage beginning 'How eloquent . . .', in Cassandra Austen's copy of *Persuasion*, is thought to be in her hand. See R. W. Chapman, 'Jane

How eloquent could Anne Elliot have been,—how eloquent, at least, were her wishes on the side of early warm attachment, and a cheerful confidence in futurity, against that over-anxious caution which seems to insult exertion and distrust Providence!—She had been forced into prudence in her youth, she learned romance as she grew older—the natural sequel of an unnatural beginning. (*Pers*, vol. 1, ch. 4, p. 32)

If Cassandra Austen was indeed the person who wrote the pencil note beside this passage of *Persuasion*, what did she mean by it? The comment about Anne's muted eloquence might be read in terms of a private sisterly relationship in which both older and younger Austen girls had suffered the loss of an 'early warm attachment'. At the time Anne Elliot is described in this way, she has no hope or prospect of reconciliation with Wentworth. So the 'romance' that she has 'learned [. . .] as she grew older' is not that of reciprocated love, but of devotion—perhaps akin to that of Cassandra to her dead fiancé, Tom Fowle—that endures with no prospect of return. As Anne puts it towards the end of the book: 'All the privilege I claim for my own sex (it is not a very enviable one, you need not covet it) is that of loving longest, when existence or when hope is gone' (*Pers*, vol. 2, ch. 11, p. 256). Equally striking is the commitment to authorship that is quietly but forcefully intimated in the passage from chapter 4: both 'sequel' and 'romance' are literary terms, implying that what Anne or her narrator has learnt is in some sense bound up with the life of writing, and that a woman who commits herself to such a life is posing a direct challenge to the conventions of gender, development, and chronology. ('The author' is employed in a similarly ambiguous way, to comic effect, in *NA*, vol. 1, ch. 14, p. 113.)[67]

Romance is the genre with which girls including the Austen sisters might have been expected to 'begin' their experience of literature, even if the results of such early reading were allegedly dire, and even if the realistic novel had, from its beginnings, deployed 'romance' as a catch-all term for everything that the new genre was supposed to have outgrown. It was certainly not meant to be something learned or acquired in maturity. Zak Sitter sums up the progressive or developmental history of the novel as it was understood by many

---

Austen's Text: Authoritative Manuscript Corrections', *Times Literary Supplement*, 13 Feb. 1937, p. 116); *Pers*, pp. 348–9, n. 9.

67. Compare Anna Lefroy's reference to 'installments' as a way of measuring units of breath in her continuation of 'Evelyn' (*TW*, p. 207), and Austen's to 'volumes' in her comment about protracted courtship in a letter to Cassandra (5 Sept. 1796, *Letters*, p. 9).

readers and authors from the mid-eighteenth century onwards, a history that itself involves construing romance as simultaneously early and late:

> Romance was at once 'older than' and a 'juvenile' form of the novel because the history of cultural forms was understood developmentally (or, alternately, providentially), and thus the past could contain only incomplete forms, prefigurations on their way to fulfillment in the present. [. . .] From the beginning, then, romance has served the novel as both adversary and uncanny reminder of its own origins.[68]

Charlotte Lennox, shoring up her anti-romance credentials as the author of *The Female Quixote* (1752), included in the first number of *The Lady's Museum* (1760) a translation from the French which argued that: 'There is a scarcely a young girl who has not read with eagerness a great number of idle romances, and puerile tales, sufficient to corrupt her imagination and cloud her understanding'.[69] The sequel of such an immersion in 'unnatural' plots was, so girls were repeatedly warned, a way of living and thinking that had lost contact with reality and with morality. Read thus, the presentation of Anne's character in the fourth chapter of *Persuasion* is akin to an anti-conduct book in which the heroine's early submission to prudence yields to a mature rejection of such dictates in favour of romance. The woman reverts to the teenager. This is not the only such moment in Austen's fiction. The surface-level interpretation of *Sense and Sensibility* as a work in which Elinor's prudence is shown to be superior to the conduct of romantic Marianne—who loses her first love, Willoughby, and is hastily married off to Colonel Brandon—is confounded, as Tomalin notes, 'by Elinor's acknowledgement to herself that [Willoughby] would have been the right husband for her sister, in spite of his misdemeanours'.[70] The moral of the story, if there is one, appears not to be that prudence trumps romance, but that sisterly love constitutes a great part of the happiness of life.[71] If we may assume that, as Teresa Michals has recently argued, the

68. Zak Sitter, 'On Early Style: The Emergence of Realism in Charlotte Brontë's Juvenilia', in *Charlotte Brontë from the Beginnings: New Essays from the Juvenilia to the Major Works*, eds. Judith E. Pike and Lucy Morrison (London and New York: Routledge, 2017), pp. 30–43 (p. 33).

69. [Charlotte Lennox], 'Of the Studies Proper for Women. Translated from the French', in *The Lady's Museum. By the author of The Female Quixote*, 2 vols. (London: J. Newbery and J. Coote, 1760–61) vol. 1, no. 1, p. 13.

70. Tomalin, *Jane Austen*, p. 159.

71. The closing words of the novel are: 'among the merits and the happiness of Elinor and Marianne, let it not be ranked as the least considerable, that though sisters, and living almost

novel throughout Austen's lifetime was pitched at a mixed-age audience rather than—as tends now to be assumed—at adults, it seems entirely apt to the form that it should freely revert from a grown-up to an adolescent reading of the world and that its emphasis should fall in the end not upon marital bliss but on the lasting affection of siblings.[72]

This model of progress—from prudence to romance—entirely reverses the trajectory bestowed on Austen's career by her younger relatives, in which spoof romance is represented as passing away in favour of judicious, sober imitation of real life. It also counters the conventional model of female growth, whereby an early exposure to romance will vitiate character. But perhaps Cassandra and Jane Austen continued to imagine, in their sisterly realm, a quite different view of female progress. To judge by the teenage writings, Cassandra was always someone who understood the rules of the game—however nonsensical it might appear to others—as she is shown to do in the early tale that she commands, 'The beautifull Cassandra'. This tiny circular quest narrative, or 'novel in twelve Chapters', is set in central London and may therefore be dated to some point soon after summer 1788, when the Austen sisters travelled with their parents to enjoy what an early letter to Cassandra calls 'this Scene of Dissipation & vice' (23 Aug. 1796, *Letters*, p. 5). The number of chapters may reflect the author's age, since in 1788 Austen was twelve (turning thirteen on 16 December of that year).

'The beautifull Cassandra' might also be subtitled 'the romance of a bonnet', since it is with that alluring accessory that the heroine chances to 'fall in love'— rather than with 'the Viscount of—a young Man, no less celebrated for his Accomplishments & Virtues, than for his Elegance & Beauty' (*TW*, pp. 37–9). The profession of 'a celebrated Milliner' ascribed to 'that worthy Woman', mother of the beautiful Cassandra, has a whiff of impropriety and resistance

---

within sight of each other, they could live without disagreement between themselves, or producing coolness between their husbands' (*S&S*, vol. 3, ch. 14, p. 431).

72. 'The first commercially significant age-specialized publishing appeared with the rise of a distinct market for children's literature in the middle of the eighteenth century. These children's books contrasted with novels intended for a mixed-age audience—not with novels intended for adults. Specialization by age for adults occurred only much later in the history of the novel. Through most of the nineteenth century, the novel's core readership remained mixed-age. If we think of children's literature as emerging out of "adult reading", and as changing "adult" conventions of form and content to make them suitable for children, we reverse the order in which fiction was in fact age-leveled'. Teresa Michals, *Books for Adults, Books for Children: Age and the Novel from Defoe to James* (Cambridge: Cambridge University Press, 2014), p. 2.

to convention about it, too (*TW*, p. 38). It may even hint at a family embarrassment: the Rev. George Austen's sister Philadelphia had been apprenticed in 1745 to a Covent Garden milliner, Mrs Cole. The same name, as Tomalin notes, is given to the '"middle-aged discreet sort of woman", ostensibly a milliner, actually a bawd' in John Cleland's *Fanny Hill*, 'published in 1748–9, exactly the period of Philadelphia's employment by Hester Cole'.[73] In the young Austen's miniature novel, the heroine neatly and serenely dodges two conventional outcomes of an eighteenth-century sentimental novel: falling for a handsome and eligible bachelor, and meeting with disaster in her solitary adventures. Having run away from home with a stolen hat, and having committed further acts of theft and violence, Cassandra simply returns 'to her paternal roof', is 'pressed to her Mother's bosom' and 'smiled & whispered to herself "This is a day well spent"' (*TW*, p. 40).[74] A great deal has happened, and on the other hand nothing at all has changed.

In a sense, Cassandra and Jane Austen might themselves be said not to have grown up: they continued to live with their parents, remained unmarried, and never had children. Their father referred to them, long into their adulthood, as 'the Girls'—a habit which struck his little granddaughter as 'so very odd'.[75] Writing to that granddaughter when Anna was herself no longer a child but an aspiring novelist, Austen advised that 'One does not care for girls till they are grown up' (9–18 Sept. 1814, *Letters*, p. 288). But growing up did not have to mean a renunciation of girlhood, and the Austen sisters learned romance as they aged. We might perhaps say of them, as V. S. Pritchett said of Italo Svevo's characters, that it was

> their curious fate to learn the lesson of life backwards, becoming younger and more apt for life as they grew older; so that if they were to look back

---

73. Tomalin, *Jane Austen*, pp. 14–15. Tomalin is careful to add that 'we are not entitled to conclude anything about Philadelphia from Cleland's fiction. The two Mrs Coles of Covent Garden remain no more than a striking coincidence'. It is nevertheless the case that millinery was 'a trade that was only on the border of respectability' (p. 15).

74. See also Jane Austen, *The Beautifull Cassandra: A Novel in Twelve Chapters*, ed. Claudia L. Johnson (Princeton, NJ: Princeton University Press, 2018).

75. Anna Lefroy: 'Children do not think of Aunts, or perhaps of any grown up people as young; yet at the time to which I refer my Aunts must have been very young women—even a little later, when I might be 9 or 10 y^rs. old I thought it so very odd, to hear Grandpapa speak of them as "the Girls". "Where are the Girls?" "Are the Girls gone out?"' (*Memoir*, p. 157). Anna was born in April 1793, when Jane Austen was 17.

upon their youth, and even their middle age, these would seem to them like a puzzling sleep from which, little by little, they have been permitted to awake.[76]

That Jane Austen died without having had children or grown old—the fact of her lifelong girlhood—affects in turn how she has been conceived as a figure in literary history, to her 'age' in the larger, contextual sense of that word. As Mary Favret observes,

> Without the culturally visible markers of marriage and motherhood, the unattached female's relationship to her period remains unmarked, its dating open to question: is [Jane Austen] the daughter of Samuel Johnson and his age; the mother of Henry James, E. M. Forster and the modernist novel; or always the maiden aunt, surveying the family legacy from a loving but detached perspective?[77]

Clara Tuite, investigating 'relations of continuity and discontinuity' in the history of Jane Austen's reception, notes the 'ritual invocation' in mid-twentieth-century literary criticism of an 'Augustan Austen' whose writings are repeatedly aligned with the style and morality of her eighteenth-century predecessors, especially Johnson. Tuite, pointing out the limits of such an approach, suggests that we might prefer to construe Austen as a 'Romantic'.[78] One way of doing so would be to consider the 'centrality of the loss and gain motif' that has long been recognized in the early and later works of Austen's contemporary, William Wordsworth (he was five years her senior, and lived almost twice as long as she did).[79] A process involving loss and gain is equally discernible in his compulsion to revise earlier work in line with his latest thoughts, feelings, and convictions. Thematically and formally essential properties of his compositions in their multiple versions, loss and gain have also governed critical responses to Wordsworth's revisions. For better and for worse, Wordsworth could not leave his texts alone. That he acted in this way testifies partly to the need to register

---

76. V. S. Pritchett, *Books in General* (London: Chatto & Windus, 1953), p. 26.

77. Mary A. Favret, 'Jane Austen's Periods', in *A Companion to Jane Austen*, ed. Claudia L. Johnson and Clara Tuite (Malden, MA, and Oxford: Wiley-Blackwell, 2009), pp. 402–12 (p. 403).

78. Clara Tuite, *Romantic Austen: Sexual Politics and the Literary Canon*. Cambridge Studies in Romanticism, no. 49 (Cambridge: Cambridge University Press, 2002), pp. 2–3.

79. Stephen Gill, *William Wordsworth: A Life*, 2nd edition (Oxford: Oxford University Press, 2020), p. 370.

changes in himself as he aged; stronger still, however, was his sense of 'affinities preserved / Between all stages of the life of man'.[80]

This book argues for an equally deliberated preservation of affinities between all stages of the life of woman, from young to middle-aged Jane Austen, from the teenage satirist to the adult moralist and back again. She is both Augustan and Romantic in her authorial allegiances. While it may have been the endeavour of nineteenth-century biographers and twentieth-century critics of her first writing to suggest or contrive a yawning vacancy between her mature and younger self, this book sees those two consciousnesses as 'indissolubly bound / Together'.[81] Like Wordsworth's poetry, Austen's fiction repays a critical interpretation that is not driven primarily by chronology, or by the view that early work necessarily yields to later, better things.

80. Lines relating to 'Michael' (1800), in *The Poetical Works of William Wordsworth*, ed. E. de Selincourt and Helen Darbishire, 5 vols., 2nd edition (Oxford: Clarendon Press, 1954), vol. 2, p. 481.

81. Lines relating to 'Michael', in *The Poetical Works of William Wordsworth*, vol. 2, p. 481.

1

Developing

UNWITTINGLY OR with conscious intent, editions of literary works create narratives of authorial growth. They may do so by organizing their contents chronologically, according to dates of composition or publication. They may choose instead to replicate collections or volumes of texts in the form in which they appeared in the author's lifetime. Or they may gather their subjects' works into categories invented by the author or editor that seem appropriate to discrete stages or phases of literary development, perhaps to the interests and approaches that governed such works at their point of origin: 'Novels of Character and Environment', say, as distinct from 'Romances and Fantasy' and 'Novels of Ingenuity' or 'Experiments'. In the Wessex Edition of his complete works (1912–20), Thomas Hardy welcomed the 'opportunity of classifying' his novels in this way, while recognizing the necessary limitations of any such scheme. Grouping his works of fiction under three 'heads' could at best 'show approximately the author's aim, if not his achievement, in each book of the series at the date of its composition'.[1]

---

1. *The Works of Thomas Hardy in Prose and Verse, with Prefaces and Notes*, 23 vols. (London: Macmillan, 1912–20), 'General Preface to the Novels and Poems', vol. 1, p. vii. Hardy's categorization had lasting effects; the first group of fictions, 'Novels of Character and Environment', was accorded pre-eminence over the rest for decades to come. Almost a century before the Wessex Edition appeared, Walter Scott did not avail himself of a comparable opportunity to subdivide or categorize his novels (also interchangeably referred to as tales and romances) in the Waverley Edition. In his 'General Preface', Scott offered the reader an autobiographical, chronologically ordered account of 'my advance towards romantic composition', explaining that 'to preserve the traces of these is in a great measure the object of this Essay'. Walter Scott, *Waverley Novels*, 48 vols. (Edinburgh: Robert Cadell; London: Simpkin and Marshall, 1829–33), vol. 1: *Waverley* (1829), p. xvi. In the 'Advertisement', discussing his revisions, Scott describes the 'occasional pruning' to which he had subjected the dialogues, and (like Hardy) he offers encouragement

The sense that such classifications should reflect the impulse that animated the author at the beginning of his work, rather than his settled judgement of its character at the end, had influenced William Wordsworth, too. He chose to organize his own collected shorter poetic works of 1815 'with reference to the powers of mind *predominant* in the production of [poems]; or to the mould in which they are cast; or, lastly, to the subjects to which they relate'. Hence the subdivision of these works into such groups as 'Poems Founded on the Affections', 'Poems of Sentiment and Affection', 'Poems of the Fancy', and 'Poems of the Imagination'. The arrangement neither wholly adheres to nor entirely rejects the chronological progress of an individual lifespan, as Wordsworth went on to explain:

> From each of these considerations, the following Poems have been divided into classes; which, that the work may more obviously correspond with the course of human life, for the sake of exhibiting in it the three requisites of a legitimate whole, a beginning, a middle, and an end, have been also arranged, as far as it was possible, according to an order of time, commencing with Childhood, and terminating with Old Age, Death, and Immortality.[2]

'An order of time' hedges its bets, allowing for more than one such order, and more than one conception of time, to govern the ensuing sequence 'as far as it was possible'. The first category in the list of contents is 'Poems Referring to the Period of Childhood'—in other words, poems concerned with that period, rather than poems which derive from it—while the second is 'Juvenile Pieces', or poems that date from the early part of the author's life. Towards the end of the collection the close of life is represented by 'Poems Referring to the Period of Old Age', followed by 'Epitaphs and Elegiac Poems', and culminating in the 'ODE.—Intimations, &c.' which occupies a separate category all by itself, a category that is unnamed but which (judging by the 'Preface', and by the poem's full title) is to be described as 'Immortality'. Two columns occupy the right-hand margin of the contents page, the first giving the date on which the poem in question was 'Composed', the second its date of being 'Published'

---

to the reader who seeks to establish the 'real' basis for his fictions (pp. iii–iv). See also *Works of Thomas Hardy*, vol. 1, p. xi.

2. *Poems by William Wordsworth: including Lyrical Ballads, and the Miscellaneous Pieces of the Author. With additional poems, a new preface, and a supplementary essay*, 2 vols. (London: Longman, Hurst, Rees, Orme, and Brown, 1815), vol. 1, 'Preface', pp. xiii–xiv.

(only fourteen poems, out of a total of nearly 250, are given dates in both columns).

That this complicated presentation and sequence of his works, nervously accompanied by caveats and exceptions, did not entirely meet with the author's satisfaction is evident from the way that he continues to worry at it in 'Preface':

> But, as I wish to guard against the possibility of misleading by this classification, it is proper first to remind the Reader, that certain poems are placed according to the powers of mind, in the Author's conception, predominant in the production of them; *predominant*, which implies the exertion of other faculties in less degree. Where there is more imagination than fancy in a poem it is placed under the head of imagination, and vice versâ. Both the above Classes might without impropriety have been enlarged from that consisting of 'Poems founded on the Affections;' as might this latter from those, and from the class 'Proceeding from Sentiment and Reflection.' The most striking characteristics of each piece, mutual illustration, variety, and proportion, have governed me throughout.[3]

Wordsworth's classification does not attribute or imply anything like fixed status or immutable character for the works he has just classified, and poems listed under one category might well be moved into another. He seeks 'to guard against [. . .] misleading', but he is just as concerned not to be trapped—by categories of his own contrivance, as by anyone else's. His desire to impose control on his past is met by an equiponderant desire to elude rigorous definition; to retain the power to change and reshape his own work—and indeed to challenge any assumptions or conventions regarding the relationship of youth to age. This is hardly surprising in a collection whose opening stanza includes the celebrated line 'The Child is Father of the Man!'[4]

Samuel Taylor Coleridge may have recommended—'After all you can say'—the chronological presentation of a poet's works as the best and most interesting method available, but he too failed to pursue it in volumes of his own writing.[5] Many other authors have resisted arranging their own works

3. *Poems by William Wordsworth*, vol. 1, 'Preface', p. xv.

4. 'My heart leaps up', *Poems by William Wordsworth*, vol. 1, p. 3.

5. 'After all you can say, I still think the chronological order the best for arranging a poet's works. All your divisions are in particular instances inadequate, and they destroy the interest which arises from watching the progress, maturity, and even the decay of genius'. *Table Talk*

according to this pattern, one likely reason being that nobody enjoys observing in himself or herself what Coleridge called 'the decay of genius'. Another reason, in Coleridge's case, may have been that he felt something akin to what his friend and collaborator Wordsworth did: that his works were 'emanations of a mind which needed to register its evolution not only in new work but in active communion with old'.[6] In other words, while the author remained alive, the early work could always be revisited and re-written so as to accord with present conceptions and expressions (and in Coleridge's case, as Jack Stillinger suggests, so as to respond to Wordsworth's published statements regarding his own principles of classifying and categorizing his poetry).[7]

The title as well as the contents of Wordsworth's *Poems, Chiefly of Early and Late Years* (1842) exhibits an overtly double character, looking backwards and forwards. While some of these works are indeed early and some by contrast are late (that is, recent), there are also some poems that must be classified, like Austen's teenage writings, as both early and late, or as neither one nor the other. In the 'Advertisement' to 'Guilt and Sorrow; or, Incidents upon Salisbury Plain', a work that is presented in *Poems, Chiefly of Early and Late Years* in its most recent form of 1842 but which exists in multiple versions and whose origins date back to 1793, Wordsworth suggests that he, like Austen, generates patchworks and motley productions that are never quite of a piece or belonging to one time alone:

> Not less than one-third of the following poem, though it has from time to time been altered in the expression, was published so far back as the year 1798, under the title of 'The Female Vagrant.' The extract is of such length that an apology seems to be required for reprinting it here; but it was necessary to restore it to its original position, or the rest would have been unintelligible. The whole was written before the close of 1794, and I will detail, rather as matter of literary biography than for any other reason, the circumstances under which it was produced.
>
> During the latter part of the summer of 1793, having passed a month in the Isle of Wight, in view of the fleet that was then preparing for sea off Portsmouth at the commencement of the war, I left the place with

---

(1837), 1 Jan. 1834, in *The Collected Works of Samuel Taylor Coleridge*, vol. 14: *Table Talk*, part 2, ed. Carl Woodring, part 2 (Princeton, NJ: Princeton University Press, 1990), p. 271.

6. Gill, *William Wordsworth: A Life*, p. 81.

7. Jack Stillinger, 'The Multiple Versions of Coleridge's Poems: How Many "Mariners" Did Coleridge Write?', *Studies in Romanticism*, 31 (1992), 127–46 (p. 144).

melancholy forebodings. The American war was still fresh in memory. The struggle which was beginning, and which many thought would be brought to a speedy close by the irresistible arms of Great Britain being added to those of the allies, I was assured in my own mind would be of long continuance, and productive of distress and misery beyond all calculation. This conviction was pressed upon me by having been a witness, during a long residence in revolutionary France, of the spirit which prevailed in that country. After leaving the Isle of Wight, I spent two days wandering on foot over Salisbury Plain, which, though cultivation was then widely spread through parts of it, had upon the whole a still more impressive appearance than it now retains.

The monuments and traces of antiquity, scattered in abundance over that region, led me unavoidably to compare what we know or guess of those remote times with certain aspects of modern society, and with calamities, principally those consequent upon war, to which, more than other classes of men, the poor are subject. In those reflections, joined with some particular facts that had come to my knowledge, the following stanzas originated.

In conclusion, to obviate some distraction in the minds of those who are well acquainted with Salisbury Plain, it may be proper to say, that of the features described as belonging to it, one or two are taken from other desolate parts of England.[8]

In both the introductory 'Advertisement' and the poem that it announces, Wordsworth rehearses the joining of disparate parts. Literary biography combines with the circumstances of composition, as well as with the fragmentary nature of the author's creative instincts. To write is to disperse and unite, and his 'Salisbury Plain' verses seek both to aggregate and to separate their constituent elements. As a single composition, the poem must remain unstable in the sense that it may always come to assume new guises, to be pressed into new combinations: first, by its creator; later, by editors seeking to achieve cohesion or a single authoritative version of the text. As published in 1842, the poem depends on the restoration 'to its original position' of a substantial portion that was composed decades earlier, in 1793–4. In this form, the work as a whole exhibits a richly varied sense of the antique and the modern in relation

---

8. William Wordsworth, *Poems, Chiefly of Early and Late Years; including The Borderers, A Tragedy* (London: Edward Moxon, 1842), 'Advertisement', pp. 3–4.

to the volume's titular combination of 'early' and 'late'. Motivated 'unavoid-ably' in its earliest guise by the compulsion 'to compare what we know or guess of [. . .] remote times with certain aspects of modern society', the 1842 text is itself an embodiment of a remote time combined and compared with a mod-ern one. It is also populated by characters who seek, often in vain, to trace continuities between their older and their younger selves—to make of the vio-lent abruptions of past from present, present from past, something that is of a piece, enduring and cohesive: something individual, in short, that survives. In a sense, the poem revolves around the strange relationship of its older self to its newer one: a sailor enters a ruin in which he hopes to sleep; he finds there a woman who is terrified by him because she has heard a prophetic story of this very arrival happening (stanzas 18–21). It is as if the protagonist of the old poem fears encountering and being supplanted by a later version of her own text—a future telling of her own story about which she already knows or has intimations that are half-correct. But the tale the woman has in mind is not quite the right one, or quite the same as what she finally encounters; there is no perfect match of anticipation and event. The story she has prepared herself to experience concerns a murderer, but the murderer of a horse and not of a traveller (as we already know, from stanza 8, that the sailor is). So the parallels don't quite fit, but were the woman to communicate them to the visitor they would be disturbing enough—perhaps enough to make him kill her. Instead, a 'natural sympathy' is forged between the two (stanza 22), and telling her own life history to him seems to make her more 'youthful' (stanza 36), even if it involves memories of that 'fearless youth' that has been lost forever (stanza 49). 'Joy's second spring' is invoked, albeit only as something of which the sailor does not speak and probably cannot feel (stanza 51). The third strand of the narrative tells of the death of the sailor's wife, and the confession and ex-ecution of the sailor himself. The last word is a date, '1793–4'; 1793 was also the year in which Austen copied the last of her teenage writings into 'Volume the First' dating it 'June 3^d 1793' (*TW*, p. 66).[9]

Discussing the third edition (1827) of Wordsworth's collected works, Henry Crabb Robinson told him that, in Charles Lamb's view, there was 'only one good order' in which to present poems:

And that is the order in which they were written—That is a history of the poet's mind—This would be true enough of a poet who produced

9. *Poems, Chiefly of Early and Late Years*, p. 42.

everything at a heat—Where there is no pondering and pausing and combining and accumulating and bringing to bear on one point the inspirations and the wise reflections of years [. . .] In the last of the author's own editions intended for future generations the editor will say to himself [. . .]— How shall I be best understood and most strongly felt? By what train of thought and succession of feelings is the reader to be led on—his best faculties and wisest curiosity be most excited? The dates given to the table of contents will be sufficient to inform the inquisitive reader how the poet's mind was successively engaged.—Lamb disapproves (and it gave me pleasure to find I was authorised by his opinion in the decided opinion I had from the first) of the classification into poems of fancy, imagination and reflection—The reader who is enjoying for instance [. . .] the magnificent Ode which in every classification ought to be the last, does not stay to ask nor does he care what faculty has been most taxed to the production. This is certain that what the poet says of nature is equally true of the mind of man and the productions of his faculties. They exist not in 'absolute independent singleness'. To attempt ascertaining curiously the preponderance of any one faculty in each work is a profitless labour—[10]

Crabb Robinson himself would have rather seen the poems arranged in order best to reflect not the prevailing tendencies of the mind that produced them but 'the great objects of human concern'. The list of those objects, as he contrives it, retains the vestiges of chronology as it moves from infancy to old age, but also seeks to place that individual lifespan within a global frame: 'Nature— Infancy and Youth—Active Life—Old Age—Social Relations—the Contemporary World'.[11] Wordsworth had no truck with either Lamb's or Crabb Robinson's opinion on the matter, arguing that Lamb's proposed order was 'the very worst that could be followed' and going so far as to remove 'from the contents page such information as had previously been given about the chronology of his poems'.[12] As he explained:

in my judgement the only thing of much importance in arrangement is that one poem should shade off happily into another—and the contrasts where

10. *Correspondence of Henry Crabb Robinson with the Wordsworth Circle*, ed. Edith Morley, 2 vols. (Oxford: Clarendon Press, 1927), vol. 1, pp. 151–2 (26 Feb. 1826).

11. *Correspondence of Henry Crabb Robinson*, vol. 1, pp. 151–3 (26 Feb. 1826).

12. Wordsworth to Crabb Robinson (27 April [1827]), *Letters*, vol. 4, part 1, p. 444; Gill, *William Wordsworth: A Life*, p. 428.

they occur be clear of all harshness or abruptness—I differ from you and Lamb as to the classification of Imagination etc—it is of slight importance as matter of Reflection, but of great as matter of *feeling* for the Reader by making one Poem smooth the way for another—if this be not attended to classification by subject, or by mould or form, is of no value, for nothing can compensate for the neglect of it.—When I have the pleasure of seeing you we will take this matter up, as a question of literary curiosity—I can write no more.[13]

Wordsworth had, as the reader might expect, a great deal more to say 'on the subject of arrangement'—not only as 'a question of literary curiosity', but also as a 'general principle [...] affecting all the Arts, in individual composition'.[14] What emerges from his view of the matter in the exchange with Crabb Robinson, as also from parts of the 1815 'Preface', is that the juxtaposition of individual works, and the smooth transition from one to the next, are more important than anything else when deciding on a sequence.

Christopher Ricks has pointed out that 'to print poems in order of individual composition may be to illuminate the development of art and of the artist, but must obscure the ways in which particular volumes have their own sequences, their imaginative rationale or reason for existing'. He asks a related question: 'Where within a chronological sequence do you place a poem that was drafted by a young poet and completed by the old poet that he had become?'.[15] Considering that question, and its implications—should such a poem be presented and understood as the work of the younger or of the older writer, when in truth it belongs to both of them?—reveals the territory which the editor shares with the critic on the score of authorial development. Barbara Everett observes of what she calls 'orthodox' critical studies of Keats that:

The image or 'portrait' of the poet to be found there is essentially of a career more or less exemplary in its development and progression. The writer matures triumphantly but steadily from Sensation into Thought, discovering how to make a true philosopher out of a mere poet [...] one whom fatal illness cut off as he was producing his most perfect and brilliant work[.][16]

13. William Wordsworth to Crabb Robinson (6 April [1826]), *Letters*, vol. 4, part 1, p. 440.
14. Wordsworth to Crabb Robinson (27 April [1827]), *Letters*, vol. 4, part 1, p. 444.
15. Christopher Ricks, 'Neurotic Editing', *Essays in Criticism*, 62 (2012), 474–82 (p. 477).
16. Barbara Everett, 'Keats: Somebody Reading', in *Poets in Their Time* (London: Faber and Faber, 1986), pp. 140–58 (p. 145).

To this stock trajectory Everett opposes the suggestion that Keats's powers
were on the wane before his final sickness; that the last poems betray defeat;
and that 'there is something terminal in the perfection of "To Autumn"', which
at times 'seems "good" in the way that a child will be called "good", when what
is really meant is that its spirit is broken'.[17] Whatever you think of this argument in regard to Keats, it usefully calls attention to a prevalent cast of mind
about authors and their progress. Metaphors of development and improvement are so pervasive in editorial theory and practice, as well as in literary
criticism and biography, as to pass all but unnoticed. Anyone who has edited
a literary text will have considered the implications of choosing a manuscript
version over a printed edition, or a first edition over a last authorially sanctioned revision, but how far does that thought extend into the effect of such
choices on the critical evaluation and reception of a writer's creative life from
youth to old age? Should we even construe a career in such terms—as moving
from start to finish, from A to Z, when in truth many authors begin something,
drop it, and return to it? How should an editor or a critic respond to the fact
that some authors—Jane Austen included—apparently revert, in later life, to
a mode that characterized their earliest compositions? What about those
authors—Thomas Love Peacock, for instance—who show very little change
in their style and subject matter across decades, whose signal virtue (or vice)
is consistency? Can they be said to develop at all, and, if not, is that a mark of
failure? H. W. Garrod's view of Austen was of a writer who 'shows no development', and this perceived inability to grow and change is a key element of his
'Depreciation' (1928): 'She began at twenty, and stopped almost at once; and
she began again at thirty-eight exactly where she had left off'. The nature of her
alleged artistic failure is bound up with Austen's gender, and with a life that
seemingly lacked incident: it is, in other words, a reading entirely dependent
on biography. Garrod announced that Austen was 'as incapable of having a
story as of writing one—by a story I mean a sequence of happenings, either
romantic or uncommon'.[18]

17. Everett, *Poets in Their Time*, pp. 146–7.
18. H. W. Garrod's 'Jane Austen: A Depreciation' was originally delivered at the Royal Society for Literature in May 1928 and published in *Essays by Divers Hands: Transactions of the Royal
Society of Literature*, 8 (1928), 21–40; it has been frequently reprinted elsewhere. The version
quoted here is from William W. Heath, ed., *Discussions of Jane Austen* (Boston: Heath and Company, 1961), pp. 32–40.

In the first published volume of his works to appear in his lifetime, the *Poems* of 1817, Keats included a prefatory note pointing out that 'The Short Pieces in the middle of the Book, as well as some of the Sonnets, were written at an earlier period than the rest of the Poems'.[19] He was not reacting against a contemporary tendency to organize such collections by date—since no such tendency yet existed—but he *was* being strategically vague about which poems might incur dislike on the basis of the author's immaturity. Suggesting that the early material falls somewhere or other 'in the middle of the Book' and that it comprises 'some', but not all, 'of the Sonnets' is designed to make it harder to read the collection chronologically. The clearest possible chronological arrangement, however, gradually began to be imposed on posthumous collections of Keats's works, in line with a growing emphasis on his biography. By the time of Monckton Milnes' edition of 1876, it had become a headline claim in the title that Keats's poems were 'Chronologically arranged and edited, with a memoir'.[20] For both Austen and Keats, who died young and in a period in which biography was becoming more and more popular, the life of writing and the personal history were and are 'extraordinarily interdependent'.[21] There may be all the more reason, in these cases, to imagine what it might be like to read their works in an anti-linear, non-chronological way. Such a reading might allow for the kind of temporary escape from biography and teleology—sidestepping the ineluctable—that is afforded only by suicide in Jane Austen's riddle about a girl who is sewing:

> When my 1st is a task to a young girl of spirit
> And my second confines her to finish the piece
> How hard is her fate! but how great is her merit
> If by taking my whole she effect her release!

'My first' is 'hem'; 'my second' is 'lock'; 'my whole' is therefore 'hemlock', the means of 'release' from confinement—and in an odd sense, too, a ducking of

---

19. *21st-Century Oxford Authors: John Keats*, ed. John Barnard (Oxford: Oxford University Press, 2017), p. 18.

20. The *Atlantic Monthly* noted of the American edition of this text (1877) that 'The chronological arrangement [. . .] is of service in showing the change and wonderful growth of the poet's mind up to the time of his death' (vol. 40 (1877), p. 117). Compare *The Poems of John Keats; Arranged in Chronological Order with a Preface by Sidney Colvin*, 2 vols. (London: Chatto & Windus, 1909); Barnard presents 'Keats's writings chronologically as his contemporary readers first encountered them' (*21st-Century Oxford Authors: John Keats*, p. xlv).

21. Everett, *Poets in Their Time*, p. 145.

the remorseless advance from '1st' to 'second', or indeed from 'Augustan' to 'Romantic', younger to older Austen.[22] Combining the two halves of the word into their complete form is tantamount to escaping the onus of completion. While the idea of suicide as an act of 'great [. . .] merit' is clearly a bold joke at the expense of over-wrought, Werther-ish fiction, Austen's fellow-feeling for 'a young girl of spirit', confined against her will to finish the task she has been set, seems genuine. Bearing in mind the author's own impatience with endings, and her tendency as an adolescent to leave her own compositions incomplete, 'the piece' of work in question could even be understood as something written as well as something stitched: both of them might make the business of ending feel akin to an imposition.[23] To consider the matter of Austen's authorial development naturally involves attention to how she her-self understood and chafed against the various duties of and restrictions placed upon women. As Sandra M. Gilbert and Susan Gubar point out, she 'began to define herself as a writer by self-consciously satirizing not only the female tradition in literature but also its effects on the growth and develop-ment of the female imagination'. Viewed in these terms, her earliest writings may be her boldest statement of all.[24]

Between June 1941 and spring 1944, Q. D. Leavis published four essays in *Scrutiny* under the umbrella title 'A Critical Theory of Jane Austen's Writings' (there was a longer gap between the third and fourth parts than between the others, all of which appeared in vol. 10 (1941–2)).[25] The serial form of this criticism means that it was, and still is, properly understood as a developing

22. *Collected Poems*, p. 18. In Keats's 'Ode to a Nightingale' (1819), hemlock may signal libera-tion from 'the egoism of pain' to 'some good outside the self'. Everett, *Poets in Their Time*, p. 144.

23. Austen's writing surfaces themselves incorporate needlework; on the manuscripts of *Persuasion* and 'Sanditon' as stitched gatherings, possibly sewn by the author herself, see for example *JAFM*, vol. 1, p. 22; Jane Austen, *Sanditon: An Unfinished Novel: reproduced in facsimile from the manuscript in the possession of King's College, Cambridge*, ed. Brian Southam (Oxford: Clarendon Press, 1975), p. v.

24. Sandra M. Gilbert and Susan Gubar, ed., *The Norton Anthology of Literature by Women* (New York: Norton, 1985), p. 207.

25. Q. D. Leavis, 'A Critical Theory of Jane Austen's Writings', reprinted in *A Selection from Scrutiny*, compiled by F. R. Leavis, 2 vols. (Cambridge: Cambridge University Press, 1968), vol. 2, pp. 1–80. Decades later, D. W. Harding published a lecture on 'Two Aspects of Jane Austen's Development', *Theoria: A Journal of Social and Political Theory*, 35 (1970), 1–16. Some substantial objections to Leavis's argument are outlined in Marvin Mudrick, *Jane Austen: Irony as Defense and Discovery* (Princeton, NJ: Princeton University Press, 1952), pp. 260–63. Brian Southam's response is comprehensively sceptical: 'Mrs. Leavis and Miss Austen: The "Critical Theory"

work of commentary—never revised or re-published by its author in the form of a book—as well as being a commentary on development. An evolving context of this kind partly determines the value attributed to growth as both the object and medium of literary criticism. Leavis's highly influential theory also led to R. W. Chapman's presentation of Austen's early writings as directly preparatory for the later novels when he finally came to publish a full edition of the juvenilia in 1954.[26]

Q. D. Leavis's essays were not the first discussions of Austen to appear in *Scrutiny*; her work is, among other things, a response to and elaboration upon D. W. Harding's notorious 'Regulated Hatred: An Aspect of the Work of Jane Austen', which had been published in March 1940 and is cited with approval in Leavis's initial essay.[27] Taking Jane Austen as 'a uniquely documented case of the origin and development of artistic expression' and countering (among other things) Garrod's view of her as a writer who 'shows no development', Leavis handles and appraises Austen's works as 'geological structures', revealing to the careful observer irrefutable proofs of 'an evolutionary process of composition'.[28] The two characteristics of this body of criticism—as developing works of commentary and as commentaries on development—are further related to one another in that Leavis's own speculations about how the novels grew into themselves themselves grow into conjectures increasingly unmoored from any evidence discernible in or recoverable from the primary texts. Such a critical approach is not unlike the attitude of an Austen heroine whose ingenious conjectures and suppositions quickly lose touch with reality. As Southam puts it: 'Mrs. Leavis is compelled to construct a hypothesis out of speculation rather than fact', extracting as much as possible not only from what remains, but from a great deal of imagined authorial activity and composition.[29] Works that Leavis herself admits are very different—'The Watsons' and *Emma*; 'Lady

---

Reconsidered', *Nineteenth-Century Fiction*, 17 (1962), 21–32, partially reprinted as an appendix to *JALM* (pp. 141–53).

26. The dust jacket of *Minor Works*, the last volume to appear in the Clarendon edition of Austen, summarizes in the passive voice Q. D. Leavis's claim that 'The Watsons', an unfinished novel in manuscript, 'has been thought a sketch for *Emma*'.

27. 'As Mr. Harding has suggested in his valuable essay on Jane Austen, we can often sense an outbreak of irritation or nervous tension in features of the novels, but in addition I believe we can see the writer exploring her own problems by dramatizing them, or in this way giving them relief'. *A Selection from Scrutiny*, vol. 2, p. 19.

28. *A Selection from Scrutiny*, vol. 2, pp. 1, 5.

29. Southam, 'Miss Leavis and Miss Austen', p. 25.

Susan' and *Mansfield Park*—are also claimed to be, self-evidently, far more than loosely continuous with one another. Everything, Leavis argues, is connected (a claim which is indisputably novelistic, but perhaps not entirely critical), and every late work must derive from an early original.[30] Where there is no longer any manuscript material for us to consider, its existence is not only hypothesized but its assumed form—usually epistolary—asserted with an extraordinary confidence.[31]

The plausible general contention that animates Leavis's four compelling essays is that Austen's novels are 'palimpsests through whose surface portions of earlier versions, or of other and earlier compositions quite unrelated, constantly protrude, so that we read from place to place at different levels.'[32] The protrusion of one phase or period of life into another can be discerned at the level of her chosen forms, characters, plots, or styles of writing. The 'different levels' perceived by Leavis, for which she provides little in the way of direct evidence, might account for (say) a strange joke in the third sentence of *Northanger Abbey*: 'Her father was a clergyman, without being neglected, or poor, and a very respectable man, though his name was Richard—and he had never been handsome' (vol. 1, ch. 1, p. 5). Is this the family idiom, transposed into print, combining disputes about the 'very respectable' or dastardly character of Richard III (such as feature in the early 'History of England' (1791) and 'Kitty, or the Bower' (1792), *TW*, pp. 124, 198) with a reference to the fabled good looks of Austen's father, a clergyman?[33] There is undoubtedly

---

30. See the celebrated epigraph to E. M. Forster's *Howards End* (London: E. Arnold, 1910): 'Only connect . . '.

31. So, for instance, while Q. D. Leavis claims to have found in the juvenilia ur-texts for all the Austen novels other than *Persuasion*, the apparent absence of a teenage prototype for Austen's last completed work of fiction means that the prototype must have been lost. Southam rightly takes issue with this argument, as with other 'mistaken assumptions, ignorance of certain important facts, and hypotheses pressed beyond the bounds of reasonable development' ('Mrs. Leavis and Miss Austen', p. 26).

32. *A Selection from Scrutiny*, vol. 2, pp. 4–5.

33. Compare Austen's letter to Cassandra: 'Mʳ Richard Harvey's match is put off, till he has got a Better Christian name, of which he has great Hopes' (*Letters*, p. 10); 'Mr. Austen was a remarkably good-looking man, both in his youth and his old age. During his year of office at Oxford he had been called "the handsome Proctor," and at Bath, when more than seventy years old, he attracted observation by his fine features and abundance of snow-white hair' (*Memoir*, p. 15; see also *Family Record*, p. 136). See also *Collected Poems*, p. 80, n.; Doody, *Jane Austen's Names*, p. 89. The Rev. George Austen's beauty and bright eyes may be one origin of young

something odd about the way this apparently private or semi-private joke is left hanging in the air—but then *Northanger Abbey* was published posthumously. Would Austen, had she been alive to revise it once again, have explained or removed the cryptic reference? Perhaps she would have done so; or maybe the persistence of earlier into later material, as well as a willingness to leave some things unexplained, characterizes her native style in print as in manuscript (Southam discerns a comparable 'family joke' in one of the cancelled passages of *Persuasion*, *JALM*, p. 96; Michelle Levy comments on Austen's 'public confidences' and 'playfulness with confidentiality in the print novels').[34]

Leavis's most daring claims yield the presumably unintended effect of an impoverished view of Austen's imagination. In order to write her celebrated novels, we are told, she could only have quarried things she had already written, could only have depicted characters she met in life or took from other novels, and could only come up with plots deriving from events in her own family.[35] The more speculative and mysteriously over-determined the criticism becomes, the further it diminishes its subject's powers of invention. The critic here comes to seem as much an assailant upon as a champion of the novels she had set out to rescue from the imputations of miraculous brilliance on the one hand and a tiresome lack of scope on the other. Leavis's evolutionary critical argument leads, strangely, to an absence of perceived development: Austen's novels 'as a whole' cannot be said to be 'the work of any given date'.[36] If what seems to be new in her writing is also and always in some sense old, how do we set about construing her career? It is as if everything she ever wrote exists in all states at all times. Transformation is also, oddly, equivalence. One thing that perhaps designedly falls by the wayside in this type of analysis is character *Bildung*: as criticism, this takes no interest in how heroines move from ignorance to knowledge. Characters are rather functions transposed from one context to another, from early to later Austen. Authorial success is judged, as is

---

Austen's startlingly gorgeous Charles Adams in 'Jack & Alice': 'so dazzling a Beauty that none but Eagles could look him in the Face' (*TW*, p. 10); to her brother Frank, Austen wrote on 6 July 1813: 'I hope you continue beautiful' (*Letters*, p. 226).

34. Michelle Levy, 'Austen's Manuscripts and the Publicity of Print', *ELH*, 77 (2010), 1015–40 (p. 1033).

35. For Southam's rebuttal of these claims, see 'Mrs. Leavis and Miss Austen', pp. 23–5.

36. *A Selection from Scrutiny*, vol. 2, p. 5.

authorial development insofar as it can be said to exist, by the increasing so-
phistication with which the same ingredients are combined and deployed in
new settings. If we approached every author's work in this way, it could never
be assigned a secure date of composition (as opposed to a date of publication);
it would never have been decisively begun but always continued from some
other known or unknown ur-text.

In R. W. Chapman's edition of Austen's novels, the chronology pursued is
that of dates of publication rather than of composition. *Northanger Abbey* and
Persuasion, early and late novels (but first published together in the same year,
1817, five months after Austen's death), therefore occupy the fifth volume and
serve as makeweights for one another as they did when they originally appeared in print. No matter that *Northanger Abbey* may have been one of the
earlier book-length fictions, at least in terms of when it was begun. Many critical studies of Austen continue to be organized according to a presumed compositional chronology of the six published novels—despite the uncertainty
and speculative nature of any such timeline, and despite the fact that Austen
was often writing and revising more than one work at a time. Such an orga-
nizational principle also involves, typically, neglecting Austen's first and last
prose compositions, and her letters, although these might be considered at
least equally informative aspects of her authorial development.

Thus W. A. Craik omits Austen's fragments and juvenilia from her study of
the novelist, feeling compelled to assert that the early, unpublished or unfinished work shows a marked inferiority to the later, complete and published
fiction. For Craik, the inferiority derives from the fact that 'None of these
fragments and juvenilia has the serious moral *impulse* which is so essential to
the six major novels (even though a moral *attitude* is generally implicit in
them); and one cannot observe a writer's principles of selection and organ-
ization when the work is unfinished and one is not sure of her intentions'.[37] To
this we might object that *Northanger Abbey* was not considered finished
enough by its author to have been published in her lifetime, and that it concludes with a joke about morality which suggests something other than a 'serious moral *impulse*' might be in play. *Persuasion*, also unpublished in its author's
lifetime, may also for that reason be considered unfinished. Mary Augusta
Austen-Leigh writes thoughtfully on this score: 'The book, though called
"ready for publication," in the sense, perhaps, that its final page had been written, does not seem to have been ready for perusal'. She asks her readers to

37. W. A. Craik, *Jane Austen: The Six Novels* (London: Methuen, 1965), p. 5.

remember that *Emma* was 'the last novel put forth' by Austen 'as a completely finished work of art'.[38]

Craik's approach, which is representative of tendencies in twentieth-century criticism of Austen, causes her immediate difficulties. 'Lady Susan' was not published in the author's lifetime, but it appears to be a complete and polished work; however, as it turns out, it 'is complete only in so far as the story is complete; it is very summarily brought to its end, and looks like an experiment: writing in letters is a form Jane Austen rejected for finished work when she revised *Elinor and Marianne* into *Sense and Sensibility*.[39] But we have only cursory reference to this epistolary ur-text for *Sense and Sensibility* (*Memoir*, p. 185), and we cannot know that Austen associated letters with unfinished writing. They continue to feature, after all, in her published novels (even if those works are not entirely epistolary). *Northanger Abbey*, too, is brought 'very summarily' to a close with the narrator's reference to 'the tell-tale compression of the pages' (vol. 2, ch. 16, p. 259), and there is a quality of summary execution to the endings of all the novels. Craik has to admit that *Northanger Abbey* communicates what she calls 'an air of incompleteness' and is close in spirit to the juvenilia; it does not deserve, she argues, to be put alongside 'the finest and most finished works' by Austen, but it allegedly shows her 'working with the materials most congenial to her, in what is coming to be her characteristic way'. A great deal of unacknowledged critical freight is being carried in that sentence by 'what is coming to be': it describes, in hindsight, what is unlikely to have been recognized by the author or at the time as 'her characteristic way' (a similar function is performed by 'already' in such claims as that *Northanger Abbey* 'shows already Jane Austen's liking for a steady passage through a short time', and that *Sense and Sensibility* 'shows how Jane Austen already organizes her work').[40] In other words, because *Northanger Abbey* can be made to anticipate the superior achievements of the later work, it is to be included where other, less malleable works, must be omitted as not 'to my purpose'. It has been placed at the start of Craik's book because to put it anywhere else in the sequence of chapters and therefore of Austen's novels would be 'inconvenient and misleading', interrupting 'a perceptible line of development'.[41] Craik here comes very close to saying that what the author

38. *Personal Aspects of Jane Austen*, p. 126.
39. Craik, *Jane Austen*, p. 5.
40. *Jane Austen: The Six Novels*, pp. 4, 24, 36.
41. *Jane Austen: The Six Novels*, pp. 4–5.

wrote (and when) may be out of line with how the critic wishes to interpret it, and that the novels will be reshuffled so as to keep the critic's reading predominant.

In the same year that Craik's study appeared, A. Walton Litz published *Jane Austen, A Study of Her Literary Development*, drawing substantially upon the work of Mary Lascelles in *Jane Austen and Her Art* (1939).[42] Far more space is given to the teenage writings in Litz's appraisal of Austen's career than is the case in Craik's—the first 54 pages of *Jane Austen, A Study of Her Literary Development* document the juvenilia and 'Lady Susan', whereas Craik cites Austen's early works only in the introduction. Litz's discussion construes them as 'stages in a process of exploration', a 'search for congenial subjects and a comprehensive moral outlook', and 'a quest for stylistic and narrative techniques adequate to express them'. What emerges from this analysis is that the young Austen was not exploring subjects or characters that she later rejected, but which she subsequently chose to handle in different ways. A year earlier, in 1964, Brian Southam had published the first edition of *Jane Austen's Literary Manuscripts: A Study of the Novelist's Development through the Surviving Papers*, of which the first three chapters are devoted to the juvenilia and *Lady Susan*. Southam here reiterates the standard opinion that most of the early works are 'mere trifles'; at the same time, however, 'in outlook and method the novels are intimately related to the juvenilia'. Like Litz, Southam exhibits some anxiety about whether and how to pursue the meanings that seem to lie below the surface of many of the teenage Austen's spoofs; like Lascelles and many other critics, he diagnoses lost biographical details and local observation not only as the engines of a comedy we can no longer wholly understand, but also as subjects which it is neither the duty nor the province of literary criticism to consider:

> Perhaps these are the living dramas of the parish, the history of her neighbours, now recorded and re-created for all the family to remember and laugh over. But to a large extent this historical content has passed away with the memory and lives of the Rectory audience. Its recovery is a task for the historian and biographer. For our purpose it is enough to be aware of this stratum of lost or hidden meaning. (*JALM*, p. 7)

42. The study by Lascelles is not organized chronologically or novel-by-novel; she includes discussion of the juvenilia in her opening chapter, 'Biography'. See Mary Lascelles, *Jane Austen and Her Art* (Oxford: Oxford University Press, 1939; repr. 1961), pp. 8–10.

Various models of development are in play in these different critical studies, as in other works about Austen which do not so explicitly demarcate their concern with authorial growth. Such models may involve attending to the shape of the novelist's career; the move from the eighteenth into the nineteenth century, and hence from the Augustan to the Romantic; the plot of development (as in *Emma*); or the repudiation of the burlesque and epistolary modes in favour of other, more technically complex narrative forms. Emphasis is in most cases placed upon a perceived refinement in Austen's compositional method, and a deepening of her insight into character.

The past two centuries of Austen studies have been shaped by familial and critical disputes over where her novels came from and where, at her death, they might have been going. For Southam, 'Curiosity over about the origins of such finished works of art seems to belong to the historian, the biographer, or the literary psychologist, rather than to the critic' ('finished' here seems designed to mean 'over and done with').[43] But for many subsequent readers, the recovery of Austen's earliest compositional methods and sources of inspiration must be the foundation of any worthwhile response to the novels. There is something peculiarly squeamish about Southam's insistence on the one hand that the beginnings of art cannot be of interest or use to the critic (an insistence belied by his own attention to Austen's manuscripts); on the other hand, Leavis's discovery in Austen's juvenilia of an antecedent for almost every work of her maturity seems to impose an equally restrictive reading of the opposite kind.

The developmental or evolutionary model of an authorial career, attempted in various ways by Q. D. Leavis, W. A. Craik, A. Walton Litz, and Brian Southam—and which is implicit or explicit in countless critical treatments of the rise or growth of the novel—is in Austen's case made far more difficult to establish thanks to the dubious chronology of her works.[44] Even if we leave to one side the possibility that her earliest writings might also be thought of as in some sense her latest—they were the last to appear print, and her final incomplete novel, 'Sanditon' (untitled in manuscript, also known as 'The Brothers', *JAFM*, vol. 5, pp. 1–2), seems far closer to her early style than to her later—Cassandra Austen's chronology of the published novels' composition, in trying to be clear, provokes as many questions as it answers about the

43. 'Mrs. Leavis and Miss Austen: The "Critical Theory" Reconsidered', p. 21.

44. D. W. Harding, 'Two Aspects of Jane Austen's Development', 1–16; Q. D. Leavis, *Scrutiny*, 10 (1941), 61–90, 114–42; (1942), 272–94; 12 (1944), 104–19.

origins of texts and the working patterns of their author. This is partly because her list shows signs of adhering both to dates of initial composition and to dates of completion or publication.[45] While some novels are said to have begun on a particular day or in a particular month or year, the point of initiation for others is tricky to establish:

> First Impressions began in Oct 1796
> Finished in Augt 1797. Publishd
> afterwards, with alterations & contractions
> under the Title of Pride & Prejudice.
> Sense & Sensibility begun Nov. 1797
> I am sure that something of the
> same story & characters had been
> written earlier & called Elinor & Marianne
> Mansfield Park, begun somewhere
> about Feb^ry 1811—Finished soon after
> June 1813

45. It also overlaps with another incomplete note which Chapman and Southam ascribed to Jane Austen (*Plan of a Novel* [. . .] *and Other Documents* [ed. R. W. Chapman] (Oxford: Clarendon Press, 1926), p. 35; *JALM*, p. 53). Sutherland outlines the case for ascribing it to Cassandra: 'The hands of the sisters are difficult to distinguish. [. . .] not only does it set out some of the same information in the same phrasing as the longer memorandum, it also includes the title "Persuasion", assumed to be a posthumous attribution. From the arrangement of information on this scrap (with the eleventh line deleted and dates for *Persuasion* and *Emma* presented in reverse chronological order), it would appear to be an early attempt at the fuller chronology of the signed memorandum' (*JAFM*, vol. 5, p. 297). Southam dates Cassandra Austen's longer memorandum to a period between March 1817 (before which point Austen was still referring to *Northanger Abbey* as 'Catherine') and December 1817, when *Northanger Abbey* and *Persuasion* were published (at which point, Southam argues, Cassandra Austen would have been unlikely to have spelt the title of the earlier novel as she does in the memorandum). He further observes that 'the most probable date within this period would be soon after her sister's death, in July 1817, when Cassandra may have recorded these details for the benefit of the family' (*JALM*, pp. 53–4). Sutherland adds that 'Cassandra Austen, the executrix and chief beneficiary of Jane Austen's will, may have made her list of the composition dates of the six major novels soon after her sister's death, as an aid to memory, and perhaps to assist Henry Austen in editing the final works for the press and compiling his brief "Biographical Notice of the Author" (dated in print 13 Dec. 1817). The fact that she refers to the two posthumously published novels not by their working titles of "Catherine" and "The Elliots" but by those credited to Henry, *Northanger Abbey* and *Persuasion*, offers some confirmation for this dating' (*JAFM*, vol. 5, p. 297).

Emma begun Jan^{ry} 21st 1814, finishd
March 29th 1815
    Persuasion begun Augt 8th 1815
finished Augt 6th 1816
North-hanger Abbey was written
about the years 98 & 99

C.E.A. (JAFM, vol. 5, pp. 298–9)

We do not know when this chronology of Jane Austen's published novels was written. Although it is all about dates, the memo fails to abide by its own rationale and is itself undated. There are other peculiarities about the note. Why, for instance, is so little information given about *Northanger Abbey*, a novel for which Jane Austen herself—in her authorial 'Advertisement'—provides the detail that it was 'finished in the year 1803, and intended for immediate publication' (*NA*, p. 1)? Why is this early work placed at the end of the list? Does the strange form of the title—'North-hanger'—show traces of a Hampshire accent ('hanger' is a term widely used in the county, as in Sussex, to denote a steep, wooded hillside; Jane Austen's older brother James wrote a poem called 'Selbourne Hanger' in 1812)?[46] Does it perhaps indicate how the name of the abbey might have been spelt in the no-longer-surviving manuscript of the novel? Or might it reveal a lack of easy familiarity with that name when used as a title, one which was not given to the novel by Jane Austen herself? What relationship does the text of 1798–9 have to that of 1803, or indeed to that which was eventually published after Austen's death in 1817?

As what seems to be the first novel to be drafted (from October 1796), it is perhaps appropriate that 'First Impressions' has a different form of the verb 'to begin' from that given to the other novels in this list. 'First Impressions began in Oct 1796' itself sounds like the opening of a story: one that narrates an author's career. That story immediately becomes more complicated if we take into account Austen-Leigh's remark that '"Pride and Prejudice," which some consider the most brilliant of her novels, was the first finished, if not the first begun' (*Memoir*, p. 43). 'If not' is manifestly hedging its bets, making it hard to determine whether this work of fiction really was or was not 'the first begun'.

---

46. See *OED* 'hanger, *n.¹*', which cites Gilbert White and William Cobbett on Hampshire hangers. 'Selborne Hanger' is included in *The Complete Poems of James Austen, Jane Austen's Eldest Brother*, ed. David Selwyn (Chawton: Jane Austen Society, 2003), pp. 46–50.

Austen-Leigh intimates later in the same paragraph that the earliest novel could have been the one that provided the groundwork for *Sense and Sensibility*, but that suggestion does not rule out another lost work, or indeed the early draft of a different novel that went on to be published in later years.

As a title, 'First Impressions' is a highly effective announcement of an author's arrival in the world, not only because it starts with the word 'First'. The term 'Impressions' belongs to the language of published authorship as well as to that of a romantic plot, and is therefore nicely poised between the novelist's ambitions and the experiences of her characters. In his *Dictionary* (1755), Samuel Johnson (son of a bookseller) defined an impression as 'one course of printing' and 'hence, the aggregate of copies thus printed'.[47] It is a shame that Austen had to abandon her preferred title (it had been used by a different author in the meantime) when the novel finally appeared in print.[48] 'First Impressions' implies a decisively successful step into a life of writing and publishing—one for which she had been rehearsing since she was a child. It asks to be understood as the preferred choice of a print-savvy, cash-hungry novelist, someone who could write to her brother after the publication of two works of fiction that:

> You will be glad to hear that every Copy of S.&S. is sold & that it has brought me £140—besides the Copyright, if that sh^d ever be of any value.—I have now therefore written myself into £250.—which only makes me long for more.—I have something in hand—which I hope on the credit of P.&P. will sell well, tho' not half so entertaining. (6 July 1813, *Letters*, p. 226)

The work that was once called 'First Impressions' (Jane Austen also referred to it in the lowercase form, as 'first impressions') is evidently not quite the same as that which was published 'afterwards', both revised and bearing another title.[49] Cassandra's phrasing, 'alterations & contractions', suggests that she remembered the nature of the changes made to the first version of the novel; as Austen wrote to her sister on 29 January 1813, more than 15 years after she had ostensibly 'finished' it and the day after it was at last published: 'I have lopt &

---

47. 'impression, *n.*', 3.c. (*OED*).

48. The title 'First Impressions' had to be changed to *Pride and Prejudice* when the novel was published in 1813. In the meantime, Margaret Holford had published a novel called *First Impressions* (1801).

49. 'first impressions' (to Cassandra, 8–9 Jan. 1799, *Letters*, p. 36); 'First Impressions' (to Cassandra, 11 June 1799, *Letters*, p. 46).

cropt so successfully however that I imagine it must be rather shorter than S. & S. altogether' (*Letters*, p. 210). No such detail is offered for the process by which 'Elinor & Marianne' became the published *Sense and Sensibility*, although the novel in print must be quite different from the suggested epistolary ur-text, even if '*something* of the same story & characters' existed 'earlier'. A far more radical process of revision seems to have been involved here—traditionally understood as the translation of an epistolary work into a novel written in the third person. (The story of its epistolary origins derives from Jane Austen's niece Caroline, who recalled to her brother that 'Sense and Sensibility was *first* written in letters, & *so* read to [the] family', *Memoir*, p. 185.)

Later in Jane Austen's compositional life—when she had become a published author—she and Cassandra developed a much sharper sense of when the fictions began and ended, down to the very day. The precise closing dates given in the chronology for *Emma* and *Persuasion* are reminiscent of Austen's occasional practice of noting the date in manuscript at the end of her work (or the point at which the work has been suspended), a practice that is discernible across three decades of her career, from the teenage writings to 'Sanditon' (*JAFM*, vol. 5, p. 287): exact closing dates are given at the end of 'Volume the First', 'Love and Friendship', and 'The History of England' (*TW*, pp. 66, 95, 133). But what about the equally precise opening dates provided for those two novels in Cassandra Austen's list?

Tomalin speculates that 'Jane Austen kept a diary, as other women in the family did, in which she entered the starting and finishing dates of her last two books; enabling Cassandra to draw on her entries before she destroyed them'.[50] Whether or not that is true, it was perhaps a mark of Jane Austen's creative maturity to have given a definite beginning and period to each of her compositions: an indication of growing confidence in her authorship.[51] We know that exactness, or the first impression of it, mattered to her as far as days of the week, months, seasons, and years were concerned. Many critics have

50. Tomalin, *Jane Austen*, p. 244. Tomalin further speculates that Austen may have destroyed some earlier diaries herself—and with them, perhaps, the exact opening and closing dates of other novels. She also notes that such diaries might have helped Austen to establish an internal or working chronology for her novels (*Jane Austen*, p. 334).

51. 'Sanditon' is an oddity in having multiple dates included in the manuscript, possibly a sign of Austen's repeatedly having to stop before rallying and attempting once again to proceed with her final work of fiction. It also means that that text is a little like a letter in that successive portions are precisely dated (this format contributes to the mysterious sense it communicates of adventitiousness and deferral).

taken this to mean that she wanted to follow and reflect the passage of real, historical time in her works of fiction. In an appendix to volume 2 of his Clarendon Edition of the novels, R. W. Chapman, building on a suggestion first made by Sir Frank MacKinnon, argued that Austen must have used an almanac while writing *Pride and Prejudice* (and when composing other novels, too). He thought so because the weekdays, holidays, and dates provided throughout that work demonstrate what he called a 'punctilious observance of the calendars of 1811 and 1812', and that

> The indications of time in *Pride and Prejudice* are frequent and precise; and though only three complete dates are given (that is with the day of the week and month), and one of those is certainly wrong, it is none the less possible to date almost every event with precision and with virtual certainty.[52]

What can it mean to say that one of the dates supplied in a work of fiction 'is certainly wrong'? As Julia Grandison has recently pointed out, Chapman's approach to Austen's work—a very common one among her fans and readers—derives from the belief or assumption that specific dates and places are not there solely in order to create the effect of reality, but consistently and intentionally to reproduce it.[53] On this view of things, reading Austen is a matter of working back from or out of the novels into the real world; from what is only a lightly disguised or partially obscured version of history into its truer manifestation as fact. (As Chapman put it in regard to an apparent slip in the chronology of *Pride and Prejudice*: 'in the end we were able to get at the truth from other indications, and finally to correct the error'.[54]) Brian Southam could therefore expect to be taken entirely seriously when he proposed of *Mansfield Park* that 'Although no dates are given in the text, there is a strict and very detailed internal chronology which enables us to work backwards and forwards in the story from a central marker: Fanny's possession, in chapter 16, of a volume of Crabbe's *Tales*'.[55]

---

52. *The Works of Jane Austen*, ed. R. W. Chapman, 6 vols. (Oxford and New York: Oxford University Press, 1923–54), vol. 2: *Pride and Prejudice*, 3rd edition, revised (1988), 'Chronology of *Pride and Prejudice*', pp. 400, 406.

53. Julia Grandison, 'Jane Austen and the Almanac', *Review of English Studies*, 70 (2019), 911–29 (pp. 911–3).

54. R. W. Chapman, 'Chronology of *Pride and Prejudice*', p. 400.

55. Brian Southam, *Jane Austen and the Navy* (London and New York: Hambledon and London, 2000), p. 187. For a response to Southam, see J. A. Downie, 'The Chronology of *Mansfield Park*', *Modern Philology*, 112 (2014), 427–34.

By 'internal chronology' Southam meant the timeframe within the novel—
which, whatever he says, cannot be made entirely consistent, or to conform
with a particular historical period, simply because George Crabbe's *Tales* were
published in 1812. Several ingenious variations on and extensions of his and
Chapman's approach to the novels have resulted in such extreme manifestations of date-related fetishism as Ellen Moody's claim that *Northanger Abbey*
is the only one of Austen's 'longer finished novels' in which Tuesday is not
'pivotal'.[56] This does not in itself get us very far in critical terms. But Southam's
phrase, 'internal chronology', is a felicitous one if we choose to apply it to the
people in these stories, and to the ways in which they live through, experience,
and respond to time.

The forms in which dates are recorded and understood as points of reference in Austen's works are determined, as is everything else, by her characters.
Fanny Price's mournful thought, in *Mansfield Park*, that 'Easter came—
particularly late this year' does not necessarily mean (as some critics have argued) that Austen here departed, in error, from faithfully representing the
calendar of 1808–9 and slipped into that of 1813—when, as John Wiltshire
notes, 'Easter was indeed very late' (*MP*, vol. 3, ch. 14, pp. 498, xxxi; he also
observes that Easter was late in 1811 and 1812 (p. 730 n.)).[57] Fanny's perception
cannot be tantamount to evidential value for the timing of Easter in any particular year, since it is uttered in the course of a work of fiction. At most, it
might suggest the distinction between what Elizabeth Bishop called 'my own
time pattern' and the 'idea of the world's time'.[58] To Fanny, stuck in Portsmouth and missing Edmund, Easter does seem very far off. But we have no
way of knowing whether it *really* was in the world outside the novel, because
there is no real Easter against which to check her perception.

Perhaps the only thing we can say on this score is that, braced sympatheti-
cally against Fanny's view of things, is that of the narrator, who often suggests,
with delicate comedy, that her heroine's downcast responses may be prematurely sober, serious, or unhappy—in which case 'this Easter', whenever it is

56. Ellen Moody, 'A Jane Austen Event Calendar' (10 Jan. 2001), https://janeausten.co.uk
/blogs/jane-austen-life/jane-austen-event.

57. On Easter in *Mansfield Park* and the distinction between personal and communal time,
see Grandison, 'Jane Austen and the Almanac', pp. 913–4. See also A. Walton Litz, 'Chronology
of Mansfield Park', *Notes and Queries*, 8 (June 1961), 220–21.

58. Elizabeth Bishop, 'Time's Andromeda' (1933), in *Poems, Prose, and Letters*, ed. Robert
Giroux and Lloyd Schwartz (New York: Library of America, 2008), pp. 643–4.

or was, may well not be 'late' at all. Free indirect style, the mingling of first- and third-person perspectives, operates in the realm of narrative time as well as elsewhere in Austen's work. If we accept that possibility, we might also accept that indications of a date or season may conflate the heroine's 'time pattern' with the narrator's implicit or explicit 'idea of the world's time'. But 'the world' in this instance is as fictional as the heroine.

It might also be said of Cassandra Austen's chronology that it hints at a personal 'time pattern' while appearing neutrally to record a beloved sister's authorial life; their two lives were, after all, intertwined. As far as the dating and placing of *Northanger Abbey* are concerned, Cassandra's fiancé Tom Fowle died in 1797; she might therefore be hazy on what exactly happened in 1798 and 1799 (*Memoir*, p. 28 and n.), and perhaps even construe that period as marking an endpoint in her own life. No letters from Austen survive from the period between 8 November 1813 and 1 March 1814 (during which time *Emma* was begun) or for August 1815 (when she started to write *Persuasion*). Were the sisters together on some of those days, or in that month? Does Cassandra's spatiotemporal word 'somewhere', used to time the beginning of *Mansfield Park*, suggest that the novel was begun when Austen was, in fact, elsewhere, in a different place from her sister?[59]

The most likely reason for *Persuasion* and the oddly styled 'North-hanger Abbey' being grouped together at the close of the list is that they were published alongside one another after Austen's death. In terms of chronology, it would perhaps make better sense to place *Northanger Abbey* between *Sense and Sensibility* and *Mansfield Park*—but only if we agree that such a chronology should be governed by the dates on which the novels were begun (October 1796, November 1797, and some time in 1798) rather than by the dates on which they were completed or published. It may seem odd that Cassandra provides no completion or publication date for *Sense and Sensibility*, or indeed a publication date for *Pride and Prejudice*—despite the fact that she writes of the latter 'Publishd afterwards . . . under the Title of . . .'. Is such information as that of the date of publication assumed to be a matter of general record and therefore unworthy of being listed here?

Whatever motivates the omission, the primary effect of leaving these details out of the list is that a gulf appears to exist between Jane Austen's first pair

---

59. For what evidence there is of the sisters' locations and activities during the periods in question, see Deirdre le Faye, *A Chronology of Jane Austen and Her Family* (Cambridge: Cambridge University Press, 2006), pp. 467–73, 512–4.

of novels and the next group of three (*Mansfield Park, Emma,* and *Persuasion*). Cassandra's way of ordering and presenting the fiction has had far-reaching and potentially misleading effects. It has encouraged the critical and biographical view that the years Jane Austen spent in Bath (from 1801 to 1806) were largely unproductive in authorial terms—despite the fact that she revised and then sold 'Susan' to Benjamin Crosby & Co. in 1803, and despite the survival of 'The Watsons', an unpublished manuscript work dating from this period—and that it was not until she returned to Hampshire and a settled home in Chawton that she was able to write fiction again.[60] But we have no firm evidence to support such an interpretation of the compositional record, and she may well have been writing and revising all the time.

Cassandra's list, by omitting dates of publication, further gives the sense that her sister's first two novels are eighteenth-century works, while the next three are Regency masterpieces. This is partly true, but if her chronology included the date of publication for *Pride and Prejudice* (28 Jan. 1813) and for *Sense and Sensibility* (30 Oct. 1811), we would be encouraged to see the relationship of all the novels to one another quite differently.[61] It should change our own first impressions of Austen's career to know that *Mansfield Park* was begun in the year in which *Sense and Sensibility* finally appeared in print (having been accepted for publication by Thomas Egerton in 1810), and that it was finished in the year in which *Pride and Prejudice* was published to immediate acclaim. In just one month of that landmark year, October 1813, there was a second impression of both *Pride and Prejudice* and *Sense and Sensibility*, prompting Egerton to snap up *Mansfield Park*. A few months later, Austen had begun work on *Emma*. A reader would not guess at that degree of proximity or indeed overlap from the way in which Cassandra's list is presented.

The arrangement of the texts in this timeline—two novels within two years (1796–7), then three novels in five years (1811–6), then a final one at the end, albeit out of chronological order (1798–9)—is faintly reminiscent of the distribution of the Austen children's births. Three boys arrived within three years (1765–7), followed four years later by four more children within a period of four

---

60. See for example *Family Record*, pp. 127–8, 164. Le Faye remarks of Austen's return to Hampshire that 'it cannot be known exactly when Jane returned at last to literary composition, nor how it was that she summoned up enough courage to offer another novel for publication after the discouragement received in this respect in regard to *First Impressions* and *Susan*' (*Family Record*, p. 164). Compare Tomalin, *Jane Austen*, pp. 169, 175, 211.

61. See for example *Family Record*, pp. 173–7, 164–9.

years (1771–5), and, three and a half years after that, a final son. Austen's creative fertility—in the version of her career that is presented by Cassandra—resembles that of their mother, making it look as if there were discrete bursts of novelistic gestation and production, with years of inactivity in between. The comparison of the novelist to the parent is not entirely fanciful: Jane Austen herself, referring to *Sense and Sensibility*, told Cassandra on 25 April 1811 that 'I can no more forget it, than a mother can forget her sucking child' (*Letters*, p. 190). She called *Pride and Prejudice*—or, to be specific, the first copy of the book that she received— 'my own darling Child' (29 Jan. 1813, *Letters*, p. 210). Tomalin notes that 'When Jane Austen wrote the first draft of *Pride and Prejudice*, she was twenty, the same age as Elizabeth Bennet. By the time it was published in 1813 she was thirty-seven: almost old enough to be Elizabeth's mother'.[62]

If we recognize that, far from completing one piece of fiction and then moving on to the next, Austen must often have been occupied with two or three novels in varying states and working on them alongside one another, it may help to elicit another aspect of her fiction. Her novels are dramas of adjacency, simultaneity, displacement, and substitution. She famously suggested to her novel-writing niece Anna that '3 or 4 Families in a Country Village' were 'the very thing to work on' (9–18 Sept. 1814, *Letters*, p. 287). We might build on that observation; perhaps three or four novels about three or four families were the very thing to work on, and at the same time. Each Austen novel might be said to contain the same essential cast-list and to be set in more or less the same location, only different members of the cast are brought into the foreground in different works. In *Emma*, Jane Fairfax seems ideally qualified to be the heroine, if not of this work then certainly of another; indeed, that is one reason why Miss Woodhouse finds her so irritating (Richard Cronin and Dorothy Macmillan observe that *Emma* is the non-novel that surrounds the true novelistic plot, that of Jane Fairfax and Frank Churchill, *Emma*, pp. liv–lv). Many readers have observed of *Mansfield Park* that Mary Crawford seems better qualified than Fanny Price to fulfil the lead female role, resembling in her charm and wit the heroine of *Pride and Prejudice*. Might Fanny Price perhaps represent, among other things, an attempt to take Mary Bennet of *Pride and Prejudice* seriously? Fanny is herself supplanted at the end of that novel by her younger sister, a girl said to become even more of a favourite with Lady Bertram than the heroine we have been reading about. That new favourite's name is Susan, a name she shares with an earlier Austen novel which was itself

62. Tomalin, *Jane Austen*, p. 156.

supplanted—first, by the name 'Catherine' (because, in a familiar turn of events, the name 'Susan' had been taken by another novel in 1809), and then—after Austen's death—by the title *Northanger Abbey*.[63]

Austen's striking tendency to re-use names already suggests a native fondness for duplication and adaptation rather than for wholesale rejection or re-invention. Perhaps the same technique applies to dates and ages. Anne Elliot in *Persuasion* is the same age as Charlotte Lucas in *Pride and Prejudice*—twenty-seven—a point in life at which all hope of romance is widely understood to be long over and done with. Each woman, to her own great surprise, lands a husband—but although each of them might feel what Charlotte calls her 'good luck' (*P&P*, vol. 1, ch. 22, p. 138), what differences there are between Mr Collins and Captain Wentworth.

Northanger Abbey is the only work of fiction in Cassandra Austen's chronology not to be explicitly referred to in terms of when it was begun or finished, but we may assume from the way the rest of the list is organized that she means it was started in 1798 and finished in 1799 (however, Austen-Leigh writes assuredly that *Northanger Abbey* was 'certainly first composed in 1798'; that is, presumably, both begun and ended in one and the same year). If the dates on which the novels were begun supply the organizing principle of the list, should all the novels in question not then be referred to by their names at the point of inception: 'First Impressions', 'Sense and Sensibility' (if the novel begun in 1797 had, at this stage, its new title), 'Susan', and 'The Elliots' (apparently leading contender for the title of *Persuasion*)?[64] No modern critical study or edition of Austen endeavours to pursue this chronology or to defend this

---

63. In 1803, via her brother Henry's agent, Austen sold a novel called 'Susan' to the firm of Benjamin Crosby & Co. for £10. But as she explains in the 1816 'Advertisement' to a revised version of this novel, Crosby inexplicably failed to publish her work as promised. In 1809, another novel called *Susan* was published, necessitating a change to the title of Austen's. In a letter of 13 March 1817, she referred to it as 'Catherine' (to Fanny Knight, *Letters*, p. 348). See *NA*, pp. xxvi–xxix. The lengthy gaps between the first completion of this work in 1798 or 1799, its acceptance for publication in 1803, and Austen's return to it in 1816, mean that substantial revisions and additions may have been made to the text in the course of nearly two decades.

64. Mary Augusta Austen-Leigh writes of the title of *Persuasion*—which she considers to have been 'unfinished' at Austen's death at least partly because 'it had received no name'—that 'Younger generations of the family learnt subsequently, through their Aunt Cassandra, that this question had been a good deal discussed between Jane and herself, and that among several possible titles, the one that seemed most likely to be chosen was "The Elliots." Nothing, however, was finally settled, and Henry Austen, to whose care it had been bequeathed, brought it out under the name of "Persuasion," re-naming at the same time her other work left in MS.,

particular method. But one author did begin to imagine in 1880 what it would be like to do so, and rated the matter of compositional chronology even more highly than textual completeness. Introducing her one-volume selection of Austen's radically abridged works, Sarah Tytler (a pseudonym for the Scottish novelist Henrietta Keddie) argued that

> My intention in this book is to present in one volume to an over-wrought, and in some respects over-read, generation of young people the most characteristic of Jane Austen's novels, together with her life. I think the tales and the life are calculated to reflect light on each other; I think, also, that the arrangement of the tales—which I have selected as the author wrote them, and not as they happened to be published, particularly in reference to the fact that the two which I have given first were written more than ten years before 'Emma' and 'Persuasion'—is an advantage, in permitting the growth of the author's mind and taste to be recognised.[65]

Tytler presents an extremely lopped, cropped, and paraphrased version of *Pride and Prejudice*, not so much an abridgement as a précis interspersed with commentary, followed by comparably extreme yet discursive redactions of *Northanger Abbey*, *Emma*, and *Persuasion*. Her book has few discernible merits other than a single and substantial one: it is an experiment in how to arrange a writer's works in the likeness of her life, and in how best to represent 'the growth of the author's mind'. Tytler's exceptional self-consciousness in regard to sequence and development can tell us a good deal about the history of how Austen's texts have been presented and received.

'Books on Jane Austen', as Peter Sabor remarks, 'often begin with a chapter on the early writings before proceeding, with an almost palpable sigh of relief, to the mature fiction'.[66] But which novel should come first? Is all the 'mature fiction' equally mature? The *Cambridge Edition* understandably dodges the issue by not numbering its volumes. Few editions or studies choose to begin, as Cassandra Austen and Sarah Tytler do, with 'First Impressions' (or *Pride and Prejudice*), mostly because it was published two years after *Sense and Sensibility*. Chapman duly made *Sense and Sensibility* the first volume of his Oxford

---

which she had called "Catherine," but which he published as "Northanger Abbey." *Personal Aspects*, p. 126.

65. Sarah Tytler [Henrietta Keddie], *Jane Austen and Her Works* (London: Cassell, Petter, Galpin, [1880]), 'Preface', p. vii.

66. Juliet McMaster, *Jane Austen, Young Author* (Farnham: Ashgate, 2016), Peter Sabor, 'Foreword', p. ix.

Austen edition, as the earliest of her novels to appear in print; in *Jane Austen, Feminism and Fiction* (1983), Margaret Kirkham also places it before *Northanger Abbey* in her contents list.[67] But Craik puts *Sense and Sensibility* second in line, after *Northanger Abbey* and before *Pride and Prejudice*.

For many other critics who organize their book-length studies of Austen novel-by-novel, whether or not those studies have a developmental agenda, *Northanger Abbey* comes first—despite the fact that on Cassandra Austen's list it is the third in chronological order, and last on the list, and was published after Austen died. Presumably, they do so because it was intended and sold for publication in 1803 (although that text may have been quite different from the one that was eventually published in 1817), and because this novel seems closest in tone and spirit to the parodic teenage writings. Marilyn Butler and Claudia L. Johnson, for instance, bracket the juvenilia with *Northanger Abbey*; John Hardy, whose chapters are named after the heroines, moves sequentially from *Northanger Abbey* through to *Persuasion*; and Jocelyn Harris, Robert P. Irvine, Vivien Jones, Marvin Mudrick, and Tony Tanner all follow a version of this order.[68] Critics who choose to proceed differently include Alistair Duckworth, who in *The Improvement of the Estate* (1971) begins with *Mansfield Park* as the novel that best exemplifies his argument; Peter Knox-Shaw, who in *Jane Austen and the Enlightenment* (2004) places his chapter on *Pride and Prejudice* before successive chapters on *Northanger Abbey* and *Sense and Sensibility*; and Michael Suk-Young Chwe, who in *Jane Austen, Game Theorist* (2013) also puts *Pride and Prejudice* first—followed by the appealingly scrambled sequence of *Sense and Sensibility, Persuasion, Northanger Abbey, Mansfield Park*, and *Emma*.[69]

————

67. Margaret Kirkham, *Jane Austen, Feminism and Fiction* [1983] (London and Atlantic Highlands, NJ: Athlone, 1997).

68. Marilyn Butler, *Jane Austen and the War of Ideas* (Oxford: Clarendon Press, 1975); Claudia L. Johnson, *Jane Austen: Women, Politics and the Novel* (Chicago and London: Chicago University Press, 1988); John Hardy, *Jane Austen's Heroines* (London: Routledge, 2011); Jocelyn Harris, *Jane Austen's Art of Memory* (Cambridge: Cambridge University Press, 1989); Robert P. Irvine, *Jane Austen* (London and New York: Routledge, 2005); Vivien Jones, *How to Study a Jane Austen Novel* (Basingstoke: Macmillan, 1987); Marvin Mudrick, *Jane Austen: Irony as Defense and Discovery*; Tony Tanner, *Jane Austen* (Basingstoke: Macmillan, 1986).

69. Alistair M. Duckworth, *The Improvement of the Estate: A Study of Jane Austen's Novels* (Baltimore, MD, and London: Johns Hopkins, 1971; Peter Knox-Shaw, *Jane Austen and the Enlightenment* (Cambridge: Cambridge University Press, 2004); Michael Suk-Young Chwe, *Jane Austen, Game Theorist* (Princeton, NJ: Princeton University Press, 2013).

Conjectures on Original Composition (1759)—a book completed by an author named Young who was then in his mid-seventies, and which opens by contrasting the 'the Follies of Youth' with those of 'Age'—distinguishes between two kinds of genius:

> an Earlier, and a Later; or call them *Infantine,* and *Adult.* An Adult Genius comes out of Nature's hand, as *Pallas* out of *Jove's* head, at full growth, and mature: *Shakespeare's* Genius was of this kind: On the contrary, *Swift* stumbled at the threshold, and set out for Distinction on feeble knees: His was an Infantine Genius; a Genius, which, like other Infants, must be nursed, and educated, or it will come to nought: Learning is its Nurse, and Tutor; but this Nurse may overlay with an indigested Load, which smothers common sense; and this Tutor may mislead, with pedantic Prejudice, which vitiates the best understanding[.][70]

Which of these terms, 'Earlier' or 'Later', '*Infantine*' or '*Adult*', better applies to Jane Austen? G. K. Chesterton hailed her as 'born, not made [. . .] she simply was a genius'.[71] Young's distinction between the adult and infantine genius strongly implies that the former is a more impressive phenomenon than the latter (Shakespeare being far greater than Swift), as Giorgio Vasari had also suggested in his appraisal of Andrea del Verrochio,

> at once a goldsmith, a master of perspective, a sculptor, a woodcarver, a painter, and a musician. It must be admitted that the style of his sculpture and painting tended to be hard and crude, since it was the produce of unremitting study rather than of any natural gift or facility.[72]

Such comments show that the distinction between immediate, natural facility and slow, diligent application has a long history.[73] Jane Austen seems, however, to have possessed both, proving Vasari's subsequent point that the perfection of art in fact requires 'a union of study and natural power'. She was composing

70. Edward Young, *Conjectures on Original Composition. In a Letter to the Author of Sir Charles Grandison* (London: for A. Millar, and R. and J. Dodsley, 1759), pp. 1, 31–2.

71. *Love and Freindship*, 'Preface', p. xiii.

72. Giorgio Vasari, *Lives of the Artists*, trans. George Bull, 2 vols. (Harmondsworth: Penguin, 1987), vol. 1, p. 232.

73. See also William Godwin's summary of the painter Henry Fuseli's opinion on this subject, an opinion imbibed by Mary Wollstonecraft: 'the first essays of a man of real genius are such, in all their grand and most important features, as no subsequent assiduity can amend'. Godwin, *Memoirs*, p. 234.

sophisticated burlesques and parodies from at least the age of eleven or twelve, with no evidence of stumbling at the threshold. She could also impersonate at the same young age another kind of genius—the infantine sort gone wrong, vitiated by prejudice and lacking in common sense—as in the figure of her 'partial, prejudiced & ignorant historian', although to be 'ignorant' is not incompatible with Austen's sense of genius, and may even be a positively good thing, as Darcy tells Elizabeth in *Pride and Prejudice* (vol. 3, ch. 16, p. 409). Like the infantine genius Pindar, as invoked in Young's *Conjectures*, Austen could make a boast of her 'No-learning', even if she did not quite call herself 'the Eagle' on account of her 'Flight above it'.[74] In two letters of 1815, the Prince Regent's librarian James Stanier Clarke praised her 'Genius' (*Letters*, pp. 309, 320); Austen replied to the first in such a way as to endorse the diagnosis, while not agreeing with Clarke's suggestions as to how she should direct it: 'I think I may boast myself to be, with all possible Vanity, the most unlearned, & uninformed Female who ever dared to be an Authoress' (11 Dec. 1815, *Letters*, p. 319). In letters, as in fiction, she prided herself on possessing a talent that could make much of little, or indeed of nothing: 'Expect a most agreable Letter; for not being overburdened with subject—(having nothing at all to say)—I shall have no check to my Genius from beginning to end' (to Cassandra Austen, 21–22 Jan. 1801, *Letters*, p. 78). The dearth of materials was nothing to fear; quite the opposite, it cleared the way.[75]

What has recently been termed a 'juvenile tradition' meant something different for a would-be novelist from what it meant to a young poet. In the late eighteenth century, 'juvenilia' or 'juvenile' works tended to mean poems by young people: Milton and Chatterton were the heroes in this category. A shift in the application of terms saw 'juvenilia' come to mean the earlier works of a writer collected after his or her rise to fame, perhaps posthumously, while 'juvenile poems' was the preferred name for works published by young authors. Furthermore, 'juvenilia' might define the 'origin of [an] individual career' or serve as a 'metonym for a recast tradition'.[76] The metaphors and trajectories whereby we capture literary genres or periods of history—the rise

---

74. Young, *Conjectures*, p. 30.

75. On the various conceptions of 'genius' in Austen's lifetime, and its role in her posthumous fame, see Deirdre Lynch, 'Austen and Genius', in *A Companion to Jane Austen*, pp. 391–401.

76. Laurie Langbauer, *The Juvenile Tradition: Young Writers and Prolepsis, 1750–1835* (Oxford: Oxford University Press, 2016), p. 77. See also Langbauer, 'Leigh Hunt and Juvenilia', *Keats-Shelley Journal*, 60 (2011), 112–33.

of the novel, say; the decline and fall of the Roman Empire—may or may not help to make sense of individual literary lives, which considered separately might assume the form of a linear progression, or which might be cast as a series of rises and falls, gains and losses, or indeed take the shape (as in Coleridge's projected reissue of the *Friend*) of something at once 'compleat and circular'.[77]

In the twentieth century, when literary juvenilia began to win serious critical attention, the interest and value of an author's early work were typically conceived in terms of what it might show us about his or her mature achievement. What it showed us tended to be that the child or teenage writer embodied whatever the mature writer was not. Juvenilia represented the first steps in a career that became great at least partly because the author judiciously rejected his or her early style. First writings apparently exist primarily in order to be outgrown, and reward our notice only when they are understood on those terms. Although some critics (Stephen Parrish on William Wordsworth, Zak Sitter on Charlotte Brontë) have subsequently argued for the value of such works considered separately from later compositions by the same author, the general consensus has been that we rightly look on a child's or teenager's writings in terms of the greater things that they anticipate.[78] (Writers who die as children or teenagers, or who survive but write nothing in adulthood, must be considered as a separate category of author.) Views on the superiority or inferiority of later to earlier work—or indeed the position that eschews such value judgements and asserts the equality of the two—have implications for editorial theory and practice and will produce very different texts of the writers in question. These questions bear not only upon the issue of authorial maturation, but also upon revision and the editorial preference for first or last versions of texts. In Zachary Leader's summary of the modern editorial landscape, pluralism has triumphed:

---

77. Samuel Taylor Coleridge to Joseph Cottle, 10 (11) March 1815, *Collected Letters of Samuel Taylor Coleridge*, ed. E. L. Griggs, 6 vols. (Oxford: Clarendon Press, 1956–71), vol. 4, pp. 551–2.

78. Stephen M. Parrish, 'The Whig Interpretation of Literature', *Text*, 4 (1988) challenges the view of all rejected compositional drafts and discarded variants 'as false starts, misjudgments', mistaken versions 'happily rectified' en route to a work's 'final form' which represents the poet's 'final intention' (pp. 344–5). The early version of a literary work, Parrish says, is to be 'valued not for what it contributed to the late versions, not as a step in an inevitably flowing design, but for its own sake, as an achievement separate from the later history of the text' (p. 345).

Once upon a time, authors were believed to improve their work in revision. Then editorial theory fell in love with first versions, stigmatising second thoughts as impositions. The old dispensation, in which rejected drafts and variants were seen as false starts happily rectified on the road to a work's final form, which was an incarnation of the author's final intention, became 'The Whig Interpretation of Literature'. [...] Today, a third position is in ascendance. Editors [...] no longer talk of best and worst: instead, the equal validity of all versions is asserted. This third or pluralist position grows out of and reflects several recent developments: the triumph of history in the study of literature in the universities, the much-heralded new dawn of hypertext, and a near universal reluctance on the part of literary academics to make judgments of value.[79]

The 'Whig Interpretation of Literature' might, in this context, be subdivided along Burkean lines into old and new Whiggism. The old Whig interpretation of literature favours continuity, and accordingly promotes a view of authorial character and composition that is consistent; a clear line may be traced from early to late work. The task of an editor or critic of this bent is to recover aspects of the writer that have always somehow been there. But for an editor or critic of the new Whig persuasion, authorial progression necessarily entails a decisive, revolutionary break with the past, and therefore with earlier writings, and the works he or she edits will be presented accordingly: with sharp divisions elicited between individual phases of life. Some authors have positively encouraged the new Whig interpretation of their own lives and writings; others have equally strenuously resisted it. Despite carefully preserving her own early works, and returning to supplement those first inventions into her twenties, Charlotte Brontë, a new Whig of sorts concealing old Whig sympathies, described them in a preface to *The Professor* (1857) as 'crude' and pretended they had been 'destroyed almost as soon as composed'. They were, she claimed, unwelcome reminders of a false taste for 'the ornamented and redundant in composition' that had to be rejected in favour of 'what was plain and homely'.[80]

---

79. Zachary Leader, 'Daisy Packs Her Bags', *London Review of Books*, 22 (2000), 13–5 (p. 13). The essay draws on arguments made in Leader's *Revision and Romantic Authorship* (Oxford: Clarendon Press, 1996).

80. *The Clarendon Edition of the Novels of the Brontës*: [Charlotte Brontë], *The Professor*, ed. Margaret Smith and Herbert Rosengarten (Oxford: Oxford University Press, 1987), 'Preface', p. 3.

In *The Improvement of the Estate*, Duckworth argues that 'the estate as an ordered physical structure' serves in this novelistic context as 'a metonym for other inherited structures—society as a whole, a code of morality, a system of language', and that '"improvements," or the manner in which individuals relate to their cultural inheritance', are a means for Austen 'of distinguishing responsible from irresponsible action and of defining a proper attitude toward social change'.[81] Excluding Austen's teenage writings from consideration, he has an overt thematic concern with continuity and progression. His work is built on the assumption that Austen is constitutionally averse, like Burke, an old Whig, to change. Burke's repeated call is for 'reference to the antecedent state of things' and respect for existing institutions. It follows that 'The subversion of a government, to deserve any praise, must be considered but as a step preparatory to the formation of something better'. Whoever chooses to break with the past must bear in mind that all such change 'contains in it something of evil', and that it can therefore be considered a good only with reference to futurity, not to the present. When thinking of posterity, we should regard it as a child in our care and not 'attempt an improvement of his fortune' which puts 'the capital of his estate to any hazard'.[82] This argument about preserving the estate—and therefore judiciously rather than wantonly setting out to change it through sudden revolution—has been applied by Duckworth and others, for obvious reasons, to *Mansfield Park*. But it has broad implications for Austen's literary estate, too; for editions of all her published and unpublished writings. If the status of her six great novels is perceived to be threatened by editorial and critical attention to her early experiments in satire—experiments often glossed as the subversion of established forms—then the only way in which such efforts may be presented to the public is (as Chapman and Leavis would have it) in terms of their preparatory status. They exist in order to lay the ground for something better, something which comes later. Other critics, Southam included, have argued for as decisive a break between young and mature Austen as to render critical interest in the early writings unwarranted.

The dominant modern conception of development (authorial or otherwise) as a progression from imperfection to mature achievement would have puzzled

81. Duckworth, *The Improvement of the Estate*, 'Preface', p. ix.

82. Edmund Burke, 'Appeal from the New to the Old Whigs' (1791), in *The Writings and Speeches of Edmund Burke*, vol. 4: *Party, Parliament, and the Dividing of the Whigs: 1780–1794* (Oxford: Oxford University Press, 2015), pp. 382–3.

many eighteenth-century readers, for whom the word and its cognates primarily indicated a stripping away of complication, disguise, or pretence. Two senses of development came into widespread use in the eighteenth century: the earlier one, coined in the mid-seventeenth century, describing the revelation of a truth; the later one, the experience or promotion of growth and change. One stresses the fuller view of what is perpetually the same; the other, the gradual or successive improvement of something or someone. As a result, we have two ways of conceiving an author: on the one hand, someone of whom it could be said that 'Every thing came finished from her pen' (Henry Austen on his sister, 'Biographical Notice', *Memoir*, p. 140); on the other, someone who described her novels as 'the little bit (two Inches wide) of Ivory on which I work with so fine a Brush, as produces little effect after much labour' (16–17 Dec. 1816, *Letters*, p. 337), gradually and painstakingly improving them until they were ready for public view, and herself gradually improving across her career. We could map this distinction onto Austen's heroines, too: Fanny Price and Anne Elliot remain essentially unchanged in the course of their fictions, while Catherine Morland, Elizabeth Bennet, and Emma Woodhouse move from ignorance to knowledge. *Sense and Sensibility* might be said to contain both kinds of heroine: Elinor, who does not change, and Marianne, who does.

While these two senses of the world involved in the two senses of development are not mutually exclusive, they are fruitfully competitive with and hostile to one another throughout Austen's lifetime. The persistence of the first sense of development (public disclosure of an unchanging truth) alongside the rise of the second (private growth, change, emergence, or evolution) tells us something potentially useful about the age of Jane Austen; about apprehensions of history, literature, authorship, and selfhood. Both these conceptions of human life are needed, and each of them might be said to embody or enact its own definition only while braced against the other. That Austen herself thought in these terms is evident from the title of *Sense and Sensibility*: two abstractions that are, like the two sisters onto whom they partially map, at once interdependent and independent. If you subject the first sense of development (the revelation of a truth) to the view of things that is embodied by the second, you might say that a conception of the world as an unchanging state of affairs, revealed to the observer who may or may not come to understand it, matures into a more advanced or elaborate conception of human life as perpetually altering and improving. The development of one sense into the other is itself evidence of the ascendancy of the second view. But this is the proverbial Whig conception of history and morality, and in any case it is not always possible to distinguish between the two senses of development and its cognates. When in 1808 Charles Thomson translates Job 19.29 as 'Stand in awe, I beseech you, of the developing scene', does 'developing' indicate a scene that is itself changing and growing as the human viewer looks on, or a scene that is being progressively unfurled to view by a supra-human deity while not itself changing at all?[83] Such questions become especially charged in the context of divine omniscience, according to which there can be no such thing as growth or change because everything is already fully seen and understood. But within the merely human perspective, apprehensions of reality are necessary partial and successive, unfolding in time if they unfold at all. In the realm of fiction, the equivalent of the divine perspective on events is that of the narrator, and here there may be something of the same toying with a distinction between development as the revelation of sameness and development as the emergence of a changing, maturing character. Emma Woodhouse experiences her feelings for Knightley as a shocking revelation of something entirely new, but to the author and narrator—as, perhaps, to the reader—they have been evident throughout the novel.

A person or non-human agent of development shares qualities with the novelist; he, she or it may be a 'developer of the human heart'; a 'great developer of imposition'; 'the developer of [. . .] darkest schemes'.[84] To the modern eye these claims look as if they are stating something very different from what is in fact the case: such developers are all being praised for the display of what would otherwise remain hidden from view. The late eighteenth-century 'developer' of something fraudulent or evil is not secretly promoting its growth, but publicly arresting it through laying it open to everyone—a sense that is retained in the title of Martin M'Dermot's triple-decker *The Mystery Developed. A Novel* (1825). Jane Austen fits into this picture as the clear-headed exponent of muddy truths. She is an unmasker of character—a 'developer' in the old sense of the word—some of whose fictional people might be shown to change.

To view the matter of development another way, Austen is a writer whose works may be cast in terms of a progression from early childhood experiments in wild burlesque to a mature novelist who embraced sober reality—or, equally persuasively, as one who remained perpetually wedded to romance and caricature, aspects of which continue to break out of (or into) all her

---

83. Charles Thomson, trans., *The Holy Bible, containing the Old and New Covenant, commonly called the Old and New Testament* (Philadelphia: Jane Aitken, 1808), Job 19.29.

84. *OED* examples under 'developer' dating from 1772 (earliest citation), 1784, and 1796.

novels. Her last two works, 'Sanditon' and the poem on Winchester Races, are both about the origins of places or customs. 'Sanditon' concerns itself with growth and change, the emergence of new territory and the abandonment of old practices—yet its characters are also drawn up according to their respective dominant enthusiasms, so that they appear to demonstrate an older conception of selfhood and a reversion in their creator to her first instincts about literary composition. Are they personifications rather than people? Are they the rudimentary sketches of characters who would have been made more three-dimensional in revised form?

The burden of eighteenth-century novelistic character development typically lies with the reader or upon the observer within the story, rather than with or within the character himself or herself. Hence, perhaps, the many ways in which fiction of the period—especially that of Henry Fielding and Laurence Sterne—associates itself with the dramatic mystery of *Hamlet*. Readers have always been willing enough to admit that Sterne's writing goes nowhere; perhaps what has been less frequently considered is that his own characters do not grow either. The *OED* cites him as the only example of 'development' in the sense of 'supplement', suggesting that he writes accretively, not purposively. As W. W. Robson noted of Byron, 'development' is both exemplified in an author's career and itself a feature or preoccupation of the work he or she produces. The reader, encountering Byron,

> must be prepared to recapitulate, in his experience of Byron's poetry, something of that general process of maturing, often painfully and with loss as well as gain, which parts of *Don Juan* itself unforgettably record; a development necessarily implying the renunciation of much that delighted our youth.[85]

Jerome McGann has subsequently described *Don Juan* as an anti-developmental work—the word 'development' and its cognates are never used in the poem, he observes, while 'add' and 'adding' appear on numerous occasions.[86] Like *The*

---

85. W. W. Robson, 'Byron as Poet', in *Critical Essays* (London: Routledge & Kegan Paul, 1966), pp. 148–88 (p. 151).

86. '*Don Juan* attacks the organic concept of *development*—a word which never appears, in any form, in the poem. The words *add*, *added*, and *adds*, on the other hand, appear with great frequency, and they locate a crucial quality in the form and style of the *Don Juan* manner'. Jerome McGann, *Don Juan in Context* (Chicago: University of Chicago Press, 1976), p. 60. See also Leader, *Revision and Romantic Authorship*, p. 95.

Life and Opinions of Tristram Shandy, Gentleman (1759–67), and like 'Sanditon', *Don Juan* works acquisitively, digressively, and cumulatively—rather than progressively—racking up circumstances, characters, and encounters.[87] In place of growth and the sense of individual change might be felt rather the shoring up of experiences, and this could be one of those 'painful' recognitions of maturity to which Robson alludes: that ageing may in fact be a counter- or non-developmental process. Peter Cook, remembering *Beyond the Fringe*, remarked that 'I may have done some other things as good but I am sure none better. I haven't matured, progressed, grown, become deeper, wiser, or funnier. But then, I never thought I would'.[88]

We see very little of Jane Austen's characters before their late teens. In the equivalent period of her own authorial life, as Frances Beer notes, she was not remotely interested in the possibility of her characters changing; rather, the heroines of the early works are governed by ruling passions which render them inherently incapable of escaping the dispositions with which they are born and for the display of which Austen creates them.[89] Even in the works of her maturity, we get to know many characters, including her own as a writer, in ways that might be summed up by the eighteenth-century verb 'develope'. That spelling suggests the word's association with opening and revealing the contents of an envelope, hence also its proximity to the obsolete verb 'disvelop',[90] as in the first chapter of *Pride and Prejudice*:

> Mr. Bennet was so odd a mixture of quick parts, sarcastic humour, reserve, and caprice, that the experience of three and twenty years had been insufficient to make his wife understand his character. *Her* mind was less difficult to develope. She was a woman of mean understanding, little information, and uncertain temper. When she was discontented she fancied herself nervous. The business of her life was to get her daughters married; its solace was visiting and news. (vol. 1, ch. 1, p. 5)

87. On 'Sanditon' as a work of addition rather than of development see *JAFM*, vol. 5, pp. 5–6.

88. Alan Bennett, Peter Cook, Jonathan Miller, and Dudley Moore, *The Complete Beyond the Fringe*, ed. Roger Wilmut (London: Methuen, 1987), p. 159.

89. *The Juvenilia of Jane Austen and Charlotte Brontë*, ed. Frances Beer (Harmondsworth: Penguin, 1986), 'Introduction', pp. 9–10.

90. '†disvelop, *v.* 1. *transitive*. Originally *Heraldry*. To display or unfurl (a banner or flag). [. . .] 2. *transitive*. To uncover or reveal; to bring to light or make known' (*OED*).

Both Mr and Mrs Bennet are here considered as the objects, potentially, of 'development', but the matter is complicated in that Mrs Bennet is the one who is depicted as failing to understand her husband's character. Whether *we* will come to understand it, in time, is unclear. His oddity may signal the inaccessibility of Mr. Bennet's truly reserved self, perhaps not only because his wife is too stupid or incurious to pursue it. She, on the other hand, is 'less difficult' for *anyone* 'to develope'. However long Mrs Bennet existed in the fictional realm, she would not and could not be improved or extended—she does not belong in a *Bildungsroman*. Her limitations are immoveable in the novel; she never changes, other than by offering new embarrassments and fresh affronts to decorum (these will be 'developed' or 'discovered' later on, in terms of being revealed to us more fully, and in a variety of scenarios). This resistance to change makes her a lesser character who serves as a foil not only to Lizzy and Darcy—both of whom learn from their mistakes and change as a result—but also to other marginal characters such as Kitty Bennet, of whom we are told at the end of *Pride and Prejudice* (vol. 3, ch. 19, p. 428) that 'her improvement', once she is removed from her mother, 'was great'. The faultline between novelistic characters such as these is perhaps better expressed not so much in terms of their ability or inability to change as in terms of their major or minor status.[91] Bernard Richards may be suggesting this distinction when he proposes that 'one of the mainsprings of Jane Austen's humour' is 'a species of *apartheid*' separating 'characters who have an intimate connection with the world of abstract morality from those who are inexorably trapped in the world of material contingency'.[92]

The opposite of a character who is easy to develop (in the older sense of that verb) is one that is not immediately comprehensible. But it is a serious error to assume that the complex or changeable character is better than the simple unchanging one; the shortcomings of such an assumption comprise the moral of *Emma*. Perhaps Austen realized as much when she had Elizabeth say to Bingley 'It does not necessarily follow that a deep, intricate character is more or less estimable than such a one as yours'; it is just that 'intricate characters are the *most* amusing. They have at least that advantage' (vol. 1, ch. 9,

91. For a reading of Austen in terms of her minor characters, see Alex Woloch, *The One vs. the Many: Minor Characters and the Space of the Protagonist in the Novel* (Princeton, NJ: Princeton University Press, 2003), pp. 43–124.

92. Bernard Richards, 'George Eliot's GSOH', *Essays in Criticism*, 69 (2019), 399–421 (p. 404).

p. 46). The capacity to amuse is what matters more than anything else for most of this novel, at least to Elizabeth Bennet and her father, while Emma Wood-house is punished for making a joke that exposes a simple woman's limitations to sophisticated company (vol. 3, ch. 7, p. 403). Her appetite for amusement, hence for creating plots where there are none (only to ignore the true mystery under her nose) is a moral disadvantage. Another way of construing the op-posite of a character that is easy to develop would be in terms of the character that reveals changes and growth to the careful onlooker. Elizabeth says to Darcy that 'people themselves alter so much, that there is something new to be observed in them forever' (vol. 1, ch. 9, p. 47). In other words, it is not just a matter of waiting to pick up on traits that the observer might initially have missed; the object of his or her observation will also, always, be changing. This might seem an obvious thing to say, but it is not self-evident to novelists of the eighteenth century that their characters should or could themselves alter. Some fictions are structured on quite different assumptions—that characters are progressively revealed to us, rather than necessarily making any progress themselves. There is a theatrical aspect to such an idea of character or scenario, in the sense of its denouement on a stage and as in the 'development' which strikes Sir Thomas Bertram on his return home:

> Fanny was left with only the Crawfords and Mr. Yates. She had been quite overlooked by her cousins; and as her own opinion of her claims on Sir Thomas's affection was much too humble to give her any idea of classing herself with his children, she was glad to remain behind and gain a little breathing time. Her agitation and alarm exceeded all that was endured by the rest, by the right of a disposition which not even innocence could keep from suffering. She was nearly fainting: all her former habitual dread of her uncle was returning, and with it compassion for him and for almost every one of the party on the development before him—with solicitude on Edmund's account indescribable. She had found a seat, where in exces-sive trembling she was enduring all these fearful thoughts, while the other three, no longer under any restraint, were giving vent to their feelings of vexation, lamenting over such an unlooked-for premature arrival as a most untoward event, and without mercy wishing poor Sir Thomas had been twice as long on his passage, or were still in Antigua. (vol. 2, ch. 1, pp. 206–7)

The 'development before him' is a revelation of how things are to Sir Thomas, but it also strikes him as a revelation of how much things have changed (if only from what he expected to find, or thought they were). Emma's feelings for Knightley don't so much change as become progressively revealed (or discovered) to her. She has not become a different person, but finally recognized the person she was and still is: 'A few minutes were sufficient for making her acquainted with her own heart [. . .] It darted through her, with the speed of an arrow, that Mr. Knightley must marry no one but herself!' (vol. 3, ch. 11, p. 444).

Further instances of a character being 'developed' in late eighteenth- and early nineteenth-century fiction reveal a common novelistic vocabulary—that of interest, endeavour, and observation—associated with such an activity.[93] Across the century, what it means to develop yourself moves from the public embarrassment of self-revelation to a private moral imperative to change and grow. Initially, development is something to fear and shun, as the antiquary William Cole bitchily indicated in a letter to Horace Walpole of 1774: 'Your rencounters at Thornbury were really comic, and Mr Holwell's development

---

93. See for example Mary Barker, *A Welsh Story*, 3 vols. (London: Hookham and Carpenter, 1798): 'she caught herself endeavouring to develop his character several times. [. . .] She was induced to think it worthy of her observation' (vol. 1, p. 165); *Elizabeth Percy; A Novel, Founded on Facts*, 2 vols. (London: A. Hamilton, 1792): 'Lucy Bouchier possessed a quick discernment, which led her to develop Stephen's character with uncommon precision' (vol. 1, p. 20); [John Moore,] *Mordaunt. Sketches of Life, Characters, and Manners, in Various Countries*, 3 vols. (Dublin: W. Watson and son, 1800): 'Whatever relates to human nature, and tends to develop character, is interesting to me' (vol. 1, p. 22); Eliza Parsons, *Women as they are. A novel*, 4 vols. (London: William Lane, 1796): 'I have often, when endeavouring to develop his character, felt surprised to account for the general predilection of the women in his favour' (vol. 2, p. 177); Mary Wollstonecraft, advertisement to *Mary, A Fiction* (London: J. Johnson, 1788): 'In delineating the Heroine of this Fiction, the Author attempts to develop a character different from those generally portrayed. This woman is neither a Clarissa, a Lady G—, nor a Sophie' (p. 3). In Edward Morris's *False Colours, A Comedy* (Dublin: P. Byrne, W. Jones, J. Jones, and J. Rice, 1793), the novelistic convention of developing a character is held up as hackneyed (and as an implicit competitor with the onstage presentation and evolution of character): Lady Panick mentions her 'last new novel' and proceeds to list its aims and contents: 'to develop the character of the heroine, whose exquisite feelings cannot be brought to comprehend—how any woman of delicacy can submit to the indecorum of premeditated marriage;—and so I make her elope with her father's footman;—and then follows a description of the family in all the eloquence of woe; the silent despair of the mother;—the impetuous ravings of the father;—the uncle forgetting his gout;—no, stay;—the father—the uncle—I protest, Sir Harry, I don't recollect which has the gout' (pp. 19–20). Elements of this sketch resemble Austen's 'Plan of a Novel, according to hints from various quarters' (*JAFM*, vol. 4, pp. 343–52), as well as her teenage plots.

of himself after so much bearishness must have been a very laughable scene.'[94] In the history of the novel, implications of a character's growth and change for the better remain bound up with some excruciatingly awkward revelations of self, but such development is not only necessary. It becomes the purpose of fiction.[95]

94. *Horace Walpole's Correspondence with the Rev. William Cole*, ed. W. S. Lewis and A. Dayle Wallace, 2 vols. (London: Oxford University Press; New Haven, CT: Yale University Press, 1937), vol. 1, p. 346.

95. The photographic sense of 'development' retains the primary, seventeenth-century sense of the noun, since it concerns faithfully capturing something in static form and making it public. In the second decade of the eighteenth century, Johann Heinrich Schulze, experimenting with silver nitrate, photographed cut-out letters on a bottle of a light-sensitive slurry, but was apparently unable to make the result durable. By 1800, Thomas Wedgwood and Humphry Davy had produced more substantial shadow images on coated paper and leather, but they could not render them permanent either. The eighteenth century had the technological means to generate photographs, but no way of making those images last. See R. B. Litchfield, *Tom Wedgwood, the First Photographer: An Account of His Life, His Discovery and His Friendship with Samuel Taylor Coleridge, Including the Letters of Coleridge to the Wedgwoods and an Examination of Accounts of Alleged Earlier Photographic Discoveries* (London: Duckworth & Co., 1903).

2

Effusions of Fancy

IN 1793, a slim miscellaneous volume was published in London. *Effusions of Fancy by a very young lady, consisting of tales in a style entirely new* contained a dozen capsule novels (epistolary and third-person), several dramatic skits, parodic sketches, and verses, a couple of spoof descriptions and a few moral fragments. The very young author remained, for some years, unknown beyond her immediate circle; she was the seventh child and second daughter of a Hampshire clergyman, and would go on to identify her first full-length novel to appear in print only as 'BY A LADY'.[1] *Effusions of Fancy* launched her career in satirical fiction with 'a degree of savagery' that persisted into subsequent works, from *Northanger Abbey* to 'Sanditon'.[2] Her last known piece of literary invention, some comic verse dictated three days before she died, was, like her first known experiments in satire, 'replete with fancy and vigour' (*Memoir*, p. 138).

Effusions of Fancy by a very young lady, consisting of tales in a style entirely new does not exist—or rather, not quite. Austen's teenage writings were not published in their entirety until the twentieth century. With good reason, these works have long been primarily understood and represented in critical discussion not as draft materials awaiting their final form in print, but as 'limited private or confidential publications' that were outgrown by their author (*JAFM*, vol. 1, p. 51). However, their appearance in the shape of a book and in the author's lifetime—edited, perhaps, but retaining much of their power to shock and surprise—may not be as unlikely as her family and first biographers made it sound. Mary Gaither Marshall, reviewing the appearance of Austen's

---

1. The original title page of *Sense and Sensibility*, as noted in the introduction, states that the novel is 'BY A LADY'.

2. Chapman, *Jane Austen: Facts and Problems*, p. 208.

'Volume the First' and the revisions made to that text, thought it possible that the author 'was using the volume [. . .] as a working manuscript for future publication.'[3] Austen may have been thinking about publication even before any revisions were made. 'Effusions of Fancy / by a very Young Lady / consisting of Tales / in a Style entirely new' is written in pencil on the inside cover of 'Volume the Third'. The lines are a confection of titles and subtitles given to a heterogeneous but distinct group of works published by young men and women (especially women) throughout Austen's lifetime. The pencilled inscription has traditionally been understood as the Rev. George Austen's, although it could with equal plausibility have been written by Jane or Cassandra Austen.[4] George Austen had bought his seventh child at least one of the bound stationer's notebooks in which her early writings were transcribed.[5] On 1 November 1797, he further endorsed her authorial ambitions by writing in a somewhat peremptory and innocent fashion to the publisher Thomas Cadell, offering his 'respectable' firm Cadell and Davies—which had, a year earlier, published Burney's *Camilla*, to which Austen was a subscriber—an unnamed novel. The work in question is often said to be 'First Impressions', later revised and published as *Pride and Prejudice*, although we cannot be certain on that score. George Austen asked for it to appear 'at the Author's risk' (in other words, Austen or her father would take the financial gamble of producing the book and retain copyright, while the publisher would help to market her work and earn commission on sales). Cadell, unsurprisingly, rejected it 'by Return of Post' and without sight of the manuscript (*Memoir*, p. 105).

Several years earlier than this, could Austen's father—or whoever wrote 'Effusions of Fancy . . .' on the inside cover of 'Volume the Third'—have been trying out a possible title for the juvenilia, in whatever form they might feasibly be prepared for publication? Given that *Effusions* by young ladies were, by the late eighteenth century, an established genre, such a title potentially locates Austen's teenage writings somewhere beyond the realm of what Donald

3. Mary Gaither Marshall, 'Jane Austen's Manuscripts of the Juvenilia and *Lady Susan*: A History and Interpretation', *Jane Austen's Beginnings*, pp. 107–21 (p. 115).

4. 'It is not clear on whose authority the hand has been identified as that of JA's father. Sotheby's *Catalogue* (1976) describes the hand as "unidentified"; but in *Catalogue* (1988) as "in the hand of Jane Austen's father, the Rev. George Austen". The identification is repeated in the British Library Manuscript Catalogue entry; in *Family Record*, p. 78; and in *Juvenilia*, p. xxvi' (*JAFM*, vol. 3, p. 8, n. 8).

5. The head of the contents page in 'Volume the Second' contains the words '*Ex dono mei Patris*' in Jane Austen's hand (*JAFM*, vol. 2, p. 12).

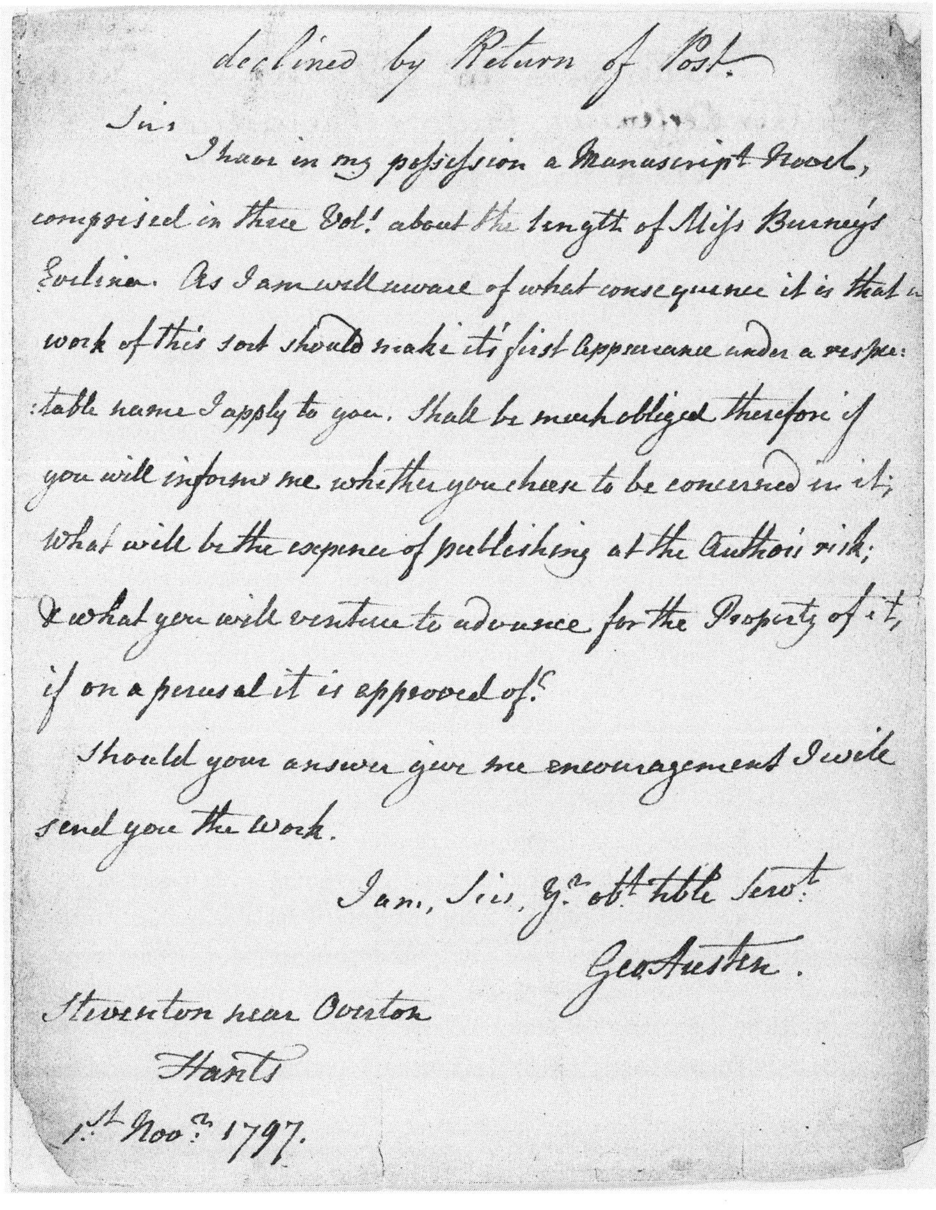

declined by Return of Post.

Sir

I have in my possession a Manuscript Novel, comprised in three Vol.ˢ about the length of Miss Burney's Evelina. As I am well aware of what consequence it is that a work of this sort should make its first Appearance under a respectable name I apply to you. Shall be much obliged therefore if you will inform me whether you chuse to be concerned in it; What will be the expence of publishing at the Author's risk; & what you will venture to advance for the Property of it, if on a perusal it is approved of.

Should your answer give me encouragement I will send you the work.

I am, Sir, &.ᶜ ob.ᵗ hble Serv.ᵗ

Geo Austen.

Steventon near Overton
Hants
1.ˢᵗ Nov.ᵉ 1797.

FIGURE 5. Letter from George Austen to Thomas Cadell (1 Nov. 1797). MS 279—Letter 1. St John's College, Oxford.

Reiman identified as 'confidential publication', in which otherwise unpublished work is read by and within a defined group that is personally known to the author.[6] As Sutherland puts it, the pencilled inscription 'reads like a semi-public endorsement' (*JAFM*, vol. 1, p. 40). Perhaps it even resembles something like a modern dust jacket puff, albeit not within the realm of print—but not far from it, either. The generic label 'Effusions of Fancy . . .' moves Austen's early work one step closer to the literary marketplace, suggesting that the material it summarizes might not be confined to private circulation, but could instead be on its way to a printed, published text. The book imagined in my first paragraph combines ingredients from all three of the notebooks, bearing in mind that Austen did not write her material into those books in chronological order. The title 'Effusions of Fancy . . .', whether it was placed at the start of the 'Volume the Third' or 'Volume the Second' (the book which was a gift from her father), might be looking backwards or forwards, summarizing the contents of one or two previous notebooks or heralding the contents of the present one. It seems far more aptly to describe the shorter miscellaneous offerings of 'Volume the First' and 'Volume the Second' than 'Volume the Third', which contains only the two longer pieces of unfinished fiction 'Evelyn' and 'Kitty, or the Bower'. Could the pencilled title even have been designed, at some stage, as a cover for a newly edited version of those two first volumes of juvenilia? Is it retrospective rather than prospective?

Effusions of various kinds appeared throughout the eighteenth and early nineteenth centuries, including those ascribed to 'a Lady'.[7] J. Douglas Kneale has 'come across approximately one hundred' publications of the period bearing some variation on the title; he notes that Samuel Taylor Coleridge's first collection of poems (1796) included thirty-six designated 'effusions' that were accorded their own half-title page as such, because 'the terms in which Coleridge thought about his "Effusions" have as much to do with questions of genre as with emotional content and tone'.[8] The years in which Coleridge

6. Donald H. Reiman, *The Study of Modern Manuscripts: Public, Confidential, and Private* (Baltimore, MD, and London: Johns Hopkins University Press, 1993), p. 39; *JAFM*, vol. 1, p. 34.

7. 'As a distinct genre, however, the effusion was relatively short-lived, becoming more common as a "lady's" genre, suitable for the expression of delicate feelings and sensibilities, though occasionally lending itself to more "heroic" sentiments by military men'. J. Douglas Kneale, *Romantic Aversions: Aftermaths of Classicism in Coleridge and Wordsworth* (Montreal; Kingston; London; and Ithaca, NY: McGill-Queen's University Press, 1999), p. 49.

8. *Romantic Aversions*, pp. 165 n. 30, 29; S. T. Coleridge, *Poems on Various Subjects* (London: G. and G. Robinson; Bristol: J. Cottle, 1796).

was experimenting with this kind of writing (1788–96), a form which is bound up with the public-private epistle in prose or verse, 'a literary structure of address and aversion', approximate the years of Austen's teenage writings (c. 1787–93).[9] Kneale sees Coleridge as the most accomplished explorer of the 'betweenness' of effusions, poetic and non-poetic, formal and informal. But had a selection of Austen's teenage works been published in the 1790s, it too would have sanctioned, in its own distinctive fashion, the effusive mode as one 'both public and private—that is, personal and familiar in its content, but public in its literally being published'.[10]

The *OED* has traced back the profession of 'effusionist' (that is, a writer of effusions) to no earlier than 1842, but the term might conceivably be applied to Austen as a teenage 'novelist', and (given its coupling with 'fancy') even form something of a counterpart to Emma Woodhouse the 'imaginist' (*Emma*, vol. 3, ch. 3, p. 362). Anna Maria Porter, born in 1778 (three years after Austen), began at the age of thirteen a series of miniature sentimental novels which subsequently appeared in print as *Artless Tales, by Anna Maria Porter, ornamented with a frontispiece, designed by her brother, R. K. Porter* (1793). A second volume, subtitled *Romantic Effusions of the Heart*, was published in 1795. Within a few years, Porter had finished two triple-decker novels, her teenage compositions inaugurating a three-decade career in fiction and historical romance.[11] Effusions were in this period associated with youth—the derogatory generic label was affixed in a review to Lord Byron's *Hours of Idleness* (1807), whose full title indicated that he was *a Minor*[12]—as well as with miscellaneousness and the first steps from manuscript and coterie circulation into print. Hence the frequent appeals of such works to the reader's candour. As Kneale argues, Coleridge expected an intimate, familiar, even 'painful subject' to occupy the centre of an effusive 'description'—and he considered in various texts the propriety or otherwise of sharing such feelings or subjects with an audience; Austen plays with this private-public, proper-improper mixture in

9. *Romantic Aversions*, p. 36.

10. *Romantic Aversions*, pp. 49, 36.

11. See Eric Quayle, 'Porter, Anna Maria', in *Oxford Dictionary of National Biography*, https://doi.org/10.1093/ref:odnb/22559.

12. *Hours of Idleness, A Series of Poems, original and translated, by George Gordon, Lord Byron, a Minor* (Newark: S. and J. Ridge; London: B. Crosby and Co.; Longman, Hurst, Roes, and Orme; F. and C. Rivington; and J. Mawman, 1807); [Henry P. Brougham], *Edinburgh Review*, 11 (Feb. 1808), 285–9, repr. in *Lord Byron: The Critical Heritage*, ed. Andrew Rutherford (London: Routledge, 2010), p. 27.

one of her 'Detached peices' in 'Volume the First', 'A beautiful description of the different effects of Sensibility on different minds' (1793) (*TW*, pp. 63–4). Coleridge also defended the passionately egotistical writer who in the context of effusions is allowed to speak in the first person; the 'partial, prejudiced & ignorant Historian' in Austen's 'Volume the Second' is one of several comic trial runs of this kind of persona in her early writing (*TW*, p. 120).[13]

Austen might have known about the precocious first appearance in print of a novelist she admired: *Poems on Several Occasions* (1747) by Charlotte Ramsay (later Charlotte Lennox) was issued by subscription when the author was sixteen or seventeen years old.[14] The volume included overtly parodic and satirical content (much of it echoing Pope) as well as rapturous pastoral effusions, odes, songs, and epistles, and announced itself on the title page as the work of a *Young Lady*, one who was subsequently championed in a verse tribute in the *Gentleman's Magazine* as a 'very young lady'.[15] Ramsay could have offered the child or teenage Austen one precedent for a kind of female authorship characterized by confidence, cheek, opportunism, and a degree of aggression, qualities also reflected in the subject matter and attitudes rehearsed in both these young ladies' works. In such verses as 'The Rival Nymphs. A Tale' and 'Envy. A Satire', Charlotte Ramsay announced an unapologetic interest in competition.[16]

Adolescents were, from the 1740s, beginning to emerge as a distinct group of readers and writers with their own designated categories of publication. Katharine Kettredge, who has 'identified 125 books of poetry that were published between 1770 and 1830 by authors under the age of twenty-one' argues that 'in the United Kingdom at the end of the eighteenth century, a number of factors came together to create an environment in which young writers could

13. *Romantic Aversions*, pp. 36–8.

14. [Charlotte Ramsay], *Poems on Several Occasions. Written by a Young Lady* (London: S. Paterson, 1747). For Austen's admiration of Lennox's *The Female Quixote* (1752), see *Letters*, 7–8 Jan. 1807, p. 120.

15. In the November 1750 issue of the *Gentleman's Magazine*, a poem by 'E.N.' praising Lennox is followed by two of her own—a reprinting of 'The Art of Coquettry' which had first appeared in her *Poems on Several Occasions*, and a new piece, 'An Ode on the Birth Day of Her Royal Highness the Princess of Wales'. 'To Mrs Charlotte Lennox, upon seeing her Poems, and Proposals for printing them', *Gentleman's Magazine*, 19 (June 1749), p. 278; E.N., 'To Mrs. Charlotte Lennox. On reading her Poems, printing by Subscription, in one Vol. 8vo, price 5s.', *Gentleman's Magazine*, 20 (Nov. 1750), p. 518. On youth as an identifying marker that was 'strategic, not demeaning' to female authors, who 'claimed their youth to try to sidestep the hurdles that gender placed before their writing', see Langbauer, *The Juvenile Tradition*, p. 187.

16. [Ramsay], *Poems on Several Occasions*, pp. 7–10, 20–23.

find early recognition and frequent publication'.[17] Summarizing the period from 1750 to 1835, Laurie Langbauer remarks that:

> Writing by young people, which until then might have seemed independent and unrelated, coalesced in this period in large part because of the historically unprecedented number of young people; their critical mass made anything they did more noticeable. [. . .] Shifts in education, along with an exploding periodical press that required copy, also allowed young people to write and find audiences.[18]

Viewed in this light, the title of Agnes Maria Bennett's five-volume *Juvenile Indiscretions* (1786) might be said to describe, amongst other things, a whole genre of fiction produced by and for 'the young novel readers of the age'.[19] (Edward Young, too, speaks of 'years of *Indiscretion*' as a conventional phase of the writing life—one in which we cease to be originals, instead submitting to the destruction of our individuality).[20] Addressing the reviewers, Bennett refers to her own 'Juvenile Indiscretions' without italics, suggesting that they might—like Austen's 'First Impressions'—constitute a recognized stage in any authorial life or career; perhaps a known variety of composition or category of fictional subject matter, as well as the focus of this particular novel. Such a descriptive label-cum-title as 'Juvenile Indiscretions' exerts a strong biographical pull (is the author both juvenile and indiscreet?) as well as encouraging a pedagogical or pseudo-pedagogical interpretation (is this the kind of work that will teach young readers how to avoid making such mistakes?). Popular miscellanies designed for the education and entertainment of young people at home flourished alongside this kind of fiction throughout the late eighteenth century.[21] There was a further proliferation of

17. Katharine Kettredge, 'Early Blossoms of Genius: Child Poets at the End of the Long Eighteenth Century', *Looking Glass: New Perspectives on Children's Literature*, 15 (2011), http://www.the-looking-glass.net/index.php/tlg/article/view/274/271.

18. Laurie Langbauer, *The Juvenile Tradition*, p. 1.

19. Mrs. Bennett, *Juvenile Indiscretions. A novel*, 5 vols. (London: W. Lane, 1786), vol. 1, 'To the reviewers', pp. i–ii. The novel is misattributed to Burney in a French translation of 1788, *Les imprudences de la jeunesse, par l'auteur de Cécilia; traduit de l'anglois, par Madame la Baronne de Vasse*, 4 vols. (London [Paris?]: Buisson, 1788).

20. Young, *Conjectures*, p. 42.

21. See for example John Aikin, *Evenings at Home; or, the Juvenile Budget Opened. Consisting of a variety of miscellaneous pieces, for the amusement and instruction of young persons*, 6 vols. (London: J. Johnson, 1792–6 and reprinted).

anecdotal works by and about prodigious young authors themselves, and these must have encouraged many teenagers to venture into print.[22]

Effusions flowed from the provinces as well as from London; one subgenre had distinctly satirical (sometimes political) associations.[23] One encouraging precedent for the young Austen, had she come across it, might have been a work published anonymously by a female author in a neighbouring county: *Flights of Fancy, or Poetical Effusions, by a Lady, Late of Mitcham, in the County of Surry* (1791). Like many other effusive collections, this one was published by subscription and prefaced by a claim that the author did not originally intend her works to appear in print; 'but her friends having been pleased to think that they contain some degree of merit, she has therefore ventured to publish them, and humbly solicits the candor of those generous friends and the public'.[24] Two distinct categories of audience are kept in play: 'generous friends' and 'the public'. The borderline inside-outside territory occupied by the effusion is here avowedly occasional. *Flights of Fancy* includes riddles, acrostics, games, and jests (particularly involving names and surnames) akin to those composed and relished by the Austen family, and which retain when printed the quality of speaking to a group of intimates or initiates.[25] This context gives the writer permission to exercise a degree of effrontery, a satiric temperament. Whoever she was, 'Mrs Knight', if that is the name of the author of *Flights of Fancy* (as one annotated title page suggests), tackled with gusto many of the same subjects as

22. See for example *Juvenile Poems, by the late John Courtenay, jun. With an elegy on his death* (London: J. Jones, 1795); J. Donoghue, *Juvenile Essays in Poetry* (Barnstaple: L. B. Seeley; London: J. Owen, 1797); Miss J. Griffiths, *A Collection of Juvenile Poems, on Various Subjects* (Warwick: for the author, [1784]); *The Blossoms of Early Genius and Virtue; containing a great variety of juvenile memoirs and anecdotes* (Burslem: J. Tregortha, 1800); John Evans, *Juvenile Pieces: Designed for the Youth of Both Sexes* (London: B. Crosby, [1797]). Many further examples are discussed in Langbauer, *The Juvenile Tradition*.

23. See for example *Royal Magnificence; or the Effusions of Ten Days: A Descriptive and Satirical Poem, in three cantos. On the subject of His Majesty's late visit to Worcester, on the sixth of August, 1788* (London: for the author, 1788).

24. [Mrs Knight?], *Flights of Fancy, or Poetical Effusions, by a Lady, Late of Mitcham, in the County of Surry* (London: J. Long, 1791), preface, [p. 1]. In a copy held by the Bodleian Library (Vet. A5 e.6793), the name 'Mrs Knight' is inked into the text on the title page, between the line 'By a LADY' and the line 'Late of MITCHAM, in the County of SURRY', in handwriting that is designed to look exactly like a printed font.

25. For riddles and charades composed by the Austens, see *Charades &c. Written a Hundred Years Ago by J. Austen and Her Family* (London: Spottiswoode & Co., 1895); *Collected Poems*, pp. 35–9.

appear in Austen's teenage works: double engagements, female declarations of love to men, and disparities in age between lovers. Some of her devices are reminiscent of young Austen, too: she plays with mock-pastoral; she inserts the odd footnote; she makes human bodies indecorous and sweaty; she teases men from Oxford. Could Mrs Knight even have been related to the Knights of Surrey, cousins of the Rev. George Austen who adopted Jane's brother Edward in 1783 and gave him their own name?

Whoever wrote the inscription on the inside cover of 'Volume the Third' appears to be claiming for Jane Austen that she wrote works of fiction in a strikingly unprecedented way. The author of that inscription was further relating, in the manner of Samuel Johnson's *Dictionary* definition of 'NEW' ('Not old; fresh; lately produced, made or had; novel. It is used of things: as *young* of persons'), the 'very Young' to the 'entirely new'. But to celebrate the novelty of what this teenage writer does must also involve recognizing that it is a return to well-worn territory, to many other fictions and effusions written by many other young ladies. The title appeals and applies with equal force to the originality and the triteness of what follows; it announces 'An easy commerce of the old and the new'.[26] Novels are generically newer than any other kind of writing—it is their central business, after all, to be 'Not old; fresh; lately produced, made, or had'; to be, in fact, 'novel'—but by the time of Austen's apprenticeship they had come to seem very old hat indeed. In a letter of 1814 to her niece Anna, she describes the phrase 'vortex of dissipation' as 'thorough novel slang' that is 'so old, that I dare say Adam met with it in the first novel he opened' (*Letters*, p. 289). As a group of fictional writings, *Effusions of Fancy* were enough of a cliché by the turn of the nineteenth century to be invoked in *Northanger Abbey*, in the course of the narrator's celebrated defence of the novel: 'Let us leave it to the Reviewers to abuse such effusions of fancy at their leisure, and over every new novel to talk in threadbare strains of the trash with which the press now groans' (vol. 1, ch. 5, p. 30). On the next page, novels are collectively described as vehicles for 'the liveliest effusions of wit and humour' (*NA*, vol. 1, ch. 5, p. 31). These remarks suggest how keenly Austen kept up with the critical description and reception of novels, and therefore with the journals by which she was herself hoping to be noticed and praised. In the year of Austen's death, the *Edinburgh Review* opened its article on Maria Edgeworth's *Harrington* and *Ormond* by praising the latter's writing as nothing like the standard

---

26. T. S. Eliot, *Four Quartets*, 'Little Gidding', 5, line 7, in *The Poems of T. S. Eliot*, ed. Christopher Ricks and Jim McCue, 2 vols. (London: Faber & Faber, 2015), vol. 1, p. 208.

'effusions of fancy', works of fiction that are here associated with accident or chance, and with immaturity:[27]

> Miss Edgeworth belongs to a class of writers who are less liable to failures than most of those who adventure in the public pursuit of excellence or distinction. Her works are not happy effusions of fancy, or casual inspirations of genius. There is nothing capricious or accidental about them; but they are the mature and seasonable fruits of those faculties that work the surest and continue the longest in vigour,—of powerful sense and nice moral perception, joined to a rare and invaluable talent for the observation and display of human character,—tempered, in its wholesome exercise, with far more indulgence to its less glittering qualities than usually falls to the lot of those who are gifted with so quick a sense of its weakness and folly.[28]

Compliments are extended here to a satirical instinct that is baited or held in check by an author who nevertheless retains her 'vigour' (the word used by Henry Austen of his sister's verses on Winchester Races) and who secures her longevity through tempering her wit. The reviewer discerns satirical reserves in Edgeworth, an ability to be far sharper in print than she is, to deploy her 'quick sense' with harsher implications for her characters than are in fact allowed to develop.

Austen had abandoned her last novel, 'Sanditon', in March 1817; as late as 1948, it continued to provoke anxiety about its 'harshness of satire' and 'coarse strokes'.[29] The *Effusions of Fancy* category of publication brings into focus a late eighteenth- and early nineteenth-century tussle between satire and fiction, and the necessary subduing of one to the other (especially in the case of female authors). When Austen began as a writer, it may well have seemed possible for her to publish novels with a ferocious parodic and observational bite; by the time of her death, that possibility seems to have weakened. We cannot know how she would have 'tempered' her last work of fiction, or how much of its

---

27. Austen sent a copy of *Emma* to Maria Edgeworth; see *Bibliography*, p. 71. For Austen's admiration of Edgeworth's novels, see *Letters* (28 Sept. 1814), p. 289.

28. 'ART. VI. *Harrington a Tale, and Ormond a Tale; in Three Volumes*. By MARIA EDGEWORTH, Author of Comic Dramas, Tales of Fashionable Life, &c. &c. 12mo. London, 1817', *Edinburgh Review*, 28 (Mar.–Aug. 1817), 390–413 (p. 390). On the reception of novels in Austen's lifetime, and on the interrelated 'processes of criticism and creation', see Olivia Murphy, *Jane Austen the Reader: The Artist as Critic* (Basingstoke: Palgrave Macmillan, 2013), pp. 1–29 (p. 2).

29. Chapman, *Jane Austen: Facts and Problems*, p. 208.

'savagery' is attributable to her fatal illness, but in order to remain a marketable novel by a lady in 1817 'Sanditon' would, it seems, have had to rein itself in. Perhaps it is appropriate that *Northanger Abbey* and *Persuasion* appeared in December 1817, the same month in which William Hone went before the court in the so-called parody trials.[30]

If the proposed title 'Effusions of Fancy / By a very Young Lady / Consisting of Tales / In a Style entirely new' is itself not 'entirely new'—but rather, like the novel as a genre at this stage, nothing new at all—then perhaps the familial and critical divisions between various phases of Austen's career begin to look questionable, as might the traditional distinction between her unpublished and published works. Is the elaborate formal and paratextual apparatus of the early writing—the tables of contents, titles, dedications, printer's rules, and chapter divisions—not necessarily a comic impersonation of a published book that would only later come to fruition with the novels, but the draft, plan, or anticipation of an early satirical printed miscellany, combining spoof prose with verse? Sonnets are often called 'effusions' in the eighteenth century (and therefore styled a kind of poetic training ground or workshop for young authors), but as a literary category the effusion originates in prose. John Langhorne's well-received *Effusions of Friendship and Fancy. In Several Letters to and from Select Friends* was published in two volumes by T. Becket and P. A. De Hondt in 1763; a second edition, 'with large additions and improvements', came out in 1766.[31] In this decade, the same publishers saw into print volumes 5–9 (1761–7) of Laurence Sterne's *Life and Opinions of Tristram Shandy, Gentleman* and his *Sentimental Journey* (1768). Langhorne's work, featuring both male and female letter-writers, is as abrupt, exclamatory, capricious, and varied as you might expect from the connection with Sterne; his *Effusions*, which went on to inspire many imitations, is not really a correspondence so much as a gathering of conversational essays or pronouncements on various themes including fame, literary criticism, benevolence, and brotherhood. Portions of

---

30. For an account of the trials and the contested definitions of parody that they involved, see for example Mark Jones, 'Parody and Its Containments: The Case of Wordsworth', *Representations*, 54 (1996), 57–79 (pp. 57–9).

31. [John Langhorne], *The Effusions of Friendship and Fancy. In Several Letters to and from Select Friends. The Second Edition, with Large Additions and Improvements*, 2 vols. (London: T. Becket and P. A. De Hondt, 1766). For a comparison of the first with the second ('more serious') edition, see 'Art. 14. *The Effusions of Friendship and Fancy*', *The Monthly Review or Literary Journal Enlarged*, vol. 34 (1766), 313–4.

verse are often included within individual letters, giving a heterogeneous fla-vour to his work and to future *Effusions*.

Novels were originally understood to be something short as well as some-thing new: sometimes no more than a brief, eye-catching experiment or inter-lude. The young Austen's training as a 'novelist' asks to be understood within, on the one hand, this older conception of the genre; on the other, within the more recent Richardsonian tradition of hugely protracted, minutely observed epistolary narratives spanning multiple volumes (and their numerous senti-mental imitators). As a teenager, Austen set out to reduce and accelerate Rich-ardson's kind of novel, so that it became curiously spliced with the other, earlier variety of the form. Favouring the older sense of the word, Lord Chesterfield defined the novel as 'a little gallant history, which must contain a great deal of love, and not exceed one or two small volumes. [...] A Novel is a kind of ab-breviation of a Romance';[32] Johnson's *Dictionary* definition of 'NOVEL' is, similarly, 'A small tale, generally of love'. As late as 1834, the idea retained some currency: 'Tieck's novels [...] are a set of exquisite little tales, novels in the original meaning of the word'.[33] So a gathering of brief or abbreviated prose works, such as we might now call short stories or novellas, possibly interspersed with verses, dramatic skits, descriptions, and riddles, and published under the headline *Effusions*, would have been a marketable publication in the late eigh-teenth century. One published collection's full title could in fact serve to sum-marize the various contents of Austen's earliest works, including the author's lip service to their morally improving function. Here, the 'novelist' is the dedi-cated provider and hawker of all kinds of professedly new things: *The Sentimen-tal Connoisseur: or, Pleasing and Entertaining Novelist. Being an elegant and new assemblage of lively effusions of fancy, polite tales, diverting essays, droll adventures, pleasing stories, entertaining novels, comic characters, facetious histories, affecting examples, striking remarks, pointed satires, &c. &c. Entirely calculated to form in the Mind the most Virtuous Sentiments: and Adapted to promote a Love of Virtue and Abhorrence of Vice* (London: R. Newton, etc., 1778).

Austen's teenage writings have rightly been said to anticipate in their formal and paratextual properties 'a standard contemporary novel format'; further-more, they 'gesture in their generic virtuosity to books beyond their covers:

---

32. *Letters written by the Late Right Honourable Philip Dormer Stanhope, Earl of Chesterfield, to his son, Philip Stanhope, Esq.,* 4 vols., 6th edition (London: J. Dodsley, 1775), vol. 1, p. 126.

33. *The Correspondence of John Lothrop Motley,* ed. George William Curtis, 2 vols. (London: John Murray, 1889), vol. 1, p. 35.

play-texts, novels, conduct books for young ladies, schoolroom textbooks' (*JAFM*, vol. 1, p. 39). But there was one genre in the 1780s and 1790s that already welcomed all such forms within its covers, and which might therefore have been Austen's direct model in the gathering and presentation of her early works. The category of 'effusions', freely accommodating short fictions, essays, histories, character sketches, and satires, evidently licensed all manner of 'Detached peices', 'Miscellanious Morsels', and 'Scraps' such as those contrived by the young Jane Austen (*TW*, pp. vii, viii, 63, 67, 151). These apparently self-deprecating generic labels may therefore serve not to ring-fence the kinds of writing that are separable from novels proper or to be kept back from publication, but rather indicate works to be presented alongside her short fictions, and with which she once intended to make her debut in print. It may well be the case that these teenage compositions, like 'Lady Susan', exhibit 'a sense of publishable authorship' (*JAFM*, vol. 1, p. 36).

When Mr Elton's charade is copied by Emma Woodhouse into 'Miss Smith's collection' of such writings, the heroine is careful to reassure him that she has 'not transcribed beyond the eight first lines' (the last two comprise an admiring and therefore private compliment to the female recipient). Elton is 'confused', partly by the 'honour' of his gallant riddle being copied out in even this redacted form—and hence 'not [. . .] confined to one or two' readers (one of Austen's private comic quatrains underwent comparable editing so that it could be circulated beyond her immediate family).[34] His manuscript communication to Emma has not only been entirely misconstrued by her as directed towards Harriet; Emma is also, as the amorous and socially awkward clergyman now discovers, planning to share his lines with other female friends. 'He may be sure of every woman's approbation', she reassures him, 'while he writes with such gallantry'. At this point, 'looking at the book again' and on the brink of its becoming less private, more public, Elton refers to his charade—a form of puzzle that Austen composed and included in her teenage works—as 'a little effusion' (*Emma*, vol. 1, ch. 9, pp. 87–8; *TW*, p. 132). That term, 'effusion', implying spontaneous, intimate communication of the spoken or written variety, is appropriate to the kinds of extempore performance and composition

34. See Jane Austen to Martha Lloyd, 29–30 November 1812: 'The 4 lines on Miss W. which I sent you were all my own, but James afterwards suggested what I thought a great improvement & as it stands in the Steventon Edition' (*Letters*, p. 205 and n. 7). The 'great improvement' is a change in the first name of 'Miss W.' from 'Camilla' to 'Maria', thereby concealing the subject's identity; in this form, the poem appears in the *Memoir* (p. 74). *Collected Poems*, pp. 16–7, 68, 84.

in which families including the Austens and their friends routinely engaged. Such productions often incorporated charades, of which the most successful examples might be transcribed and circulated, like Elton's, sometimes by way of prelude to their appearance in semi-private or printed collections. In a letter of 1808, Austen mentions 'riddles, conundrums, and cards' as some of the amusements enjoyed by the family party; she seems to have copied out charades and mentions them in her letters. She praised her sister's compositions in this line, and deprecated her own: 'We admire your Charades excessively, but as yet have guessed only the 1st. The others seem very difficult. There is so much beauty in the Versification however, that the finding them out is but a secondary pleasure' (*Letters*, pp. 156, 223, 238, 210–11).[35]

When 'a tour of pleasure' is proposed to her, Elizabeth Bennet exclaims delightedly to her aunt Gardiner: 'Let *our* first effusions be less insupportable than those of the generality of travellers' (*P&P*, vol. 2, ch. 4, p. 175). Pat Rogers rightly glosses these 'effusions' as 'Frank and eager expression (of emotions)' (*P&P*, p. 498, n. 11), but there is a further implication of their potential for bookish form. Travellers' effusions were, after all, a recognized variety of publication, the most celebrated being Sterne's *A Sentimental Journey*, although Austen probably has in mind William Gilpin's numerous picturesque tours (earlier in the novel, Elizabeth invokes his theories to comic effect in order to get away from Darcy and his companions, *P&P*, vol. 1, ch. 10, p. 58). Could there be a sly glance at the ur-text of the novel we are reading, perhaps at even earlier works than that, in the reference to '*our* first effusions'? 'First Impressions' did not appear in print as *Pride and Prejudice* until 1813. It would be in character for the author to enclose an allusion to her own earlier work in this way, so as to gesture only to those very few privileged readers in the know.

Of the twenty-seven pieces in Austen's teenage notebooks, eight are in the form of letters: 'Amelia Webster an interesting & well written Tale' and 'The Three Sisters a novel' in 'Volume the First'; 'Love and Friendship a novel in a series of Letters', 'Lesley Castle an unfinished Novel in Letters', 'A Collection of Letters', 'The female philosopher.—a Letter', 'A Letter from a Young Lady, whose feelings being too strong for her Judgement led her into the commission of Errors which her Heart disapproved', and 'A Tour Through Wales—in a Letter from a young Lady' in 'Volume the Second'. Each of the two stories in 'Volume the Third', 'Evelyn' and 'Kitty, or the Bower', is a narrative in the third

---

35. On 'scribal culture', 'the dangers of publication', and 'confidential writing' in relation to Elton's charade, see Levy, 'Austen's Manuscripts and the Publicity of Print', pp. 1030–33.

person, but the majority of 'Volume the Second' is written in letters and each
of the six epistolary tales in that volume announces its generic affiliation in
its full title. Two of these compositions are explicitly the work of 'a Young
Lady'; all of them involve young ladies as characters and correspondents. Did
Austen perhaps reserve this notebook chiefly for epistolary fiction, as a distinct category of her 'Effusions' by a 'Young Lady'? And might 'Elinor &
Marianne', emerging from these experiments as well as (possibly) from that
of 'Lady Susan', have begun as a more overtly satirical epistolary treatment of
sense and sensibility than the third-person novel it became? A 'faithless' Willoughby and two Dashwoods appear in the second of Austen's 'Collection of
Letters', titled 'From a Young lady crossed in Love to her freind', where the
mere performance of sentiment in the letter-writer suggests a harsher, funnier
version of the Marianne-Willoughby plot in the later novel (*TW*, pp. 135–6).
There are further hints to that effect in letters that appear to have survived the
transition from 'Elinor & Marianne' to *Sense and Sensibility*. Lucy Steele's
blandly conventional 'My paper reminds me to conclude' (vol. 3, ch. 2, p. 315)
echoes the vacuity of Amelia Webster in the teenage writings. Having managed
to compose only one sentence to Maud Hervey—containing the redundant
news that 'I did not stop at your house in my way to Bath last Monday'—
Amelia promptly comes to a halt: 'but my Paper, reminds me of concluding'
(*TW*, p. 42). This is what it means to write a bad letter about nothing.

'Susan', later *Northanger Abbey*, was (as Austen put it in her 'Advertisement'
to that novel) 'finished in the year 1803, and intended for immediate publication. It was disposed of to a bookseller, it was even advertised, and why the
business proceeded no farther, the author has never been able to learn' (*NA*,
vol. 1, p. 1). Begun (according to Cassandra Austen) in or about 1798,
Northanger Abbey should have been among the first of Austen's full-length
fictions to appear in print, but ended up being published two decades later.
The fact that it appeared in public so long after it was begun can serve to obscure its proximity (in time, and in terms of subject matter) to the unpublished
juvenilia. Young Austen's Kitty Petersen, of 'Kitty, or the Bower' in 'Volume
the Third', has been described as a 'heroine-in-training', a tag that positions her
as the unripe forerunner of another unripe heroine, Catherine Morland.[36] The
characters have a resemblance to one another that goes beyond the immediate
kinship of their first names. Each is introduced to the reader on the cusp of

---

36. Barbara Britton Wenner, *Prospect and Refuge in the Landscape of Jane Austen* (Aldershot:
Ashgate, 2006), p. 38.

adulthood (Kitty's story itself having been styled one of Austen's 'betweeni-ties', as if it were generically pubescent). Both Kitty and Catherine show some naivety, coupled with genuine kindness and a fondness for reading, although in the later novel Kitty's enjoyment of history is given to Eleanor Tilney and not to Catherine herself. Bearing in mind its satirical and parodic elements (perhaps especially its overt consciousness of what a heroine and a novel should be and do), as well as its chronological proximity to the unpublished writings, we might say of *Northanger Abbey* that it is both an early and a late work—as indeed are *Pride and Prejudice* and *Sense and Sensibility*. The first has a gap of seventeen years between its beginning as 'First Impressions' and its date of publication under another name; the second, a comparable hiatus of fourteen years.

A plausible case might be made in quite the opposite direction to the one I have just been pursuing: for thinking about the kinship of *Northanger Abbey* with *Persuasion*. On this view of things, *Northanger Abbey* is not an early work, but a late one. In December 1817 readers had a chance to compare the young and middle-aged Austen side by side in the simultaneous publication in one volume of *Northanger Abbey* and *Persuasion* (begun in 1815 and completed in 1816). The tales, if we separate them according to the initial composition date of *Northanger Abbey*, are a generation apart, and they are often viewed as radi-cally opposed imaginative visions, the one depicting a silly, ignorant girl, the other a sober, chastened heroine. But are they really so different? Austen may well have been revising *Northanger Abbey* while completing *Persuasion*, given that 'Susan' was bought back from Crosby in 1816.[37] Each work is partly set in Bath and centres on persuadability—with the heroine yielding to, or resisting, what other people tell her to do. *Northanger Abbey* contains twenty-four ex-amples of 'persuasion' or its cognates to *Persuasion*'s thirty-two.[38] Both novels

---

37. The pattern of revision might have been more extensive, had Austen's health not been deteriorating. On 13 March 1817, she wrote to her niece Fanny Knight that 'Miss Catherine [that is, *Northanger Abbey*] is put upon the Shelve for the present, and I do not know that she will ever come out; but I have a something ready for Publication, which may perhaps appear about a twelvemonth hence. It is short, about the length of Catherine' (*Letters*, p. 348).

38. For example, from vol. 1 of *Northanger Abbey*: 'you should not persuade me' (ch. 6, p. 34); 'This brother of yours would persuade me out of my senses' (ch. 7, p. 40); 'persuade your brother how impossible it is' (ch. 8, p. 53); 'this persuasion did not incline her to a very gracious reply' (ch. 8, p. 54); 'you must persuade her to go' (ch. 11, p. 84); 'nothing should have persuaded her to go out with the others' (ch. 9, p. 66); 'She felt almost persuaded' (ch. 12, p. 90); 'to be so easily persuaded by those she loved' (ch. 13, p. 98); 'you were not used to be so hard to persuade'

further concern themselves with maturity and immaturity, with natural and unnatural behaviour. In volume 1, chapter 14, of *Northanger Abbey*, Catherine is 'most unnaturally able to fulfil her engagement' (this is a social appointment rather than a commitment to marriage, although the two are linked and a series of the first will often lead to the second), phrasing which anticipates the differently unnatural *in*ability of Anne Elliot to fulfil her own engagement to Wentworth (*NA*, vol 1, ch. 14, p. 107). Each novel centres on a heroine who is passionately committed to reading—*Persuasion* begins and comes close to ending with a reference to other books (vol. 1, ch. 1, pp. 3–4; vol. 2, ch. 11, pp. 254–5); *Northanger Abbey* is saturated in Gothic fiction and the narrator's consciousness of and pride in a novelist's vocation. Each work considers a conventional view of female progress as (at least potentially) a form of retardation. Both of them offer by way of conclusion or near-conclusion what the narrator of *Persuasion* admits is, on one view of things, 'bad morality'; on the other, 'truth' (*Pers*, vol. 2, ch. 12, p. 270): namely, the superior wisdom of youthful rebellion to parental or pseudo-parental authority. The final sentence of *Northanger Abbey* ends as follows:

> I leave it to be settled by whomsoever it may concern, whether the tendency of this work be altogether to recommend parental tyranny, or reward filial disobedience. (*NA*, vol. 2, ch. 16, p. 261)

Parts of the cancelled closing sections of *Persuasion* that survive in manuscript have been heavily deleted as well as densely revised; one mysterious erased portion, as deciphered by Kathryn Sutherland, runs as follows:

> Bad Morality again. A young Woman proved to have ^had^ more discrimination of Character than her elder—to have seen in two Instances more clearly what ~~a Man was~^it was about^ than her Godmother! But on the point of Morality, I confess myself almost in despair after understanding_^myself^ to have_^already^ given a mother offence (having already appeared weak exactly in the point where I thought myself most strong) and shall_^therefore^ ~~leave it~^leave the present matter^ to

---

(ch. 13, p. 100); 'I could not be persuaded into doing what I thought wrong' (ch. 13, p. 101); 'I do not think you would have found me hard to persuade' (ch. 13, p. 105); 'Catherine endeavoured to persuade her, as she was herself persuaded' (ch. 15, p. 121). All four of Austen's other published novels contain more examples than either *Northanger Abbey* or *Persuasion* of the word 'persuasion' or its cognates. This can be partly accounted for by the fact that the two novels published in 1817 are shorter than the others.

the mercy of Mothers & Chaperones & Middle aged Ladies in general—
(*JAFM*, vol. 4, p. 269)[39]

'Bad Morality *again*' because, in this first or earlier version of *Persuasion*, there
has already been one such reference: 'This may be bad morality to conclude
with, but I beleive it to be Truth' (*JAFM*, vol. 4, p. 261). In the final, published
phrasing of volume 2, chapter 12 (originally ch. 11), this single reference to the
bad morality with which the novel concludes is the only one to survive. In
manuscript, the second reference to 'Bad Morality' seems to be worrying, as
ever, at the whole business of conclusions. It also appears to be partly in Lady
Russell's voice (as she confronts her mistake in preventing Anne Elliot and
Captain Wentworth's marriage when they were young), and partly in that of
the narrator-author who is talking to herself about the story she is writing.
Who or what is meant by 'a mother' here—or is this a slip for 'another'? If 'a
mother' is intentional, is that offended maternal figure the deceased Lady
Elliot, and is Lady Russell thinking of her own failures as a substitute parent
in promoting the happiness of Anne Elliot, her daughter? Brian Southam
thought that the reference to having 'given a mother offence' was evidence of
'a family joke [. . .] allowed to creep in', as it did in the opening sentence of
Northanger Abbey (*JALM*, p. 96). Leaving 'the present matter' to be resolved
by others, or hoping to do so, echoes the end of *Northanger Abbey*, but the
'mistake' and 'offence' at issue in *Persuasion* must be primarily Lady Russell's.
The weakness identified in the passage appears to be shared by both the narrator and Lady Russell, but quite what that weakness (previously construed
as a strength) might be is unclear: the misapprehension of character, or the
difficulty of wrapping things up, or both (it may be relevant that Austen referred, in the final months of her life, to her condition as a 'weakness' of body
and nerves; *Letters*, pp. 354, 356).

Like the author's punctuation in manuscript, sometimes combining (say)
an exclamation mark with a semi-colon in a way that seems at once to urge a
pause *and* a continuation, and which cannot be reproduced in print (in 'Jack
& Alice' and 'Lesley-Castle', *TW*, pp. 22, 96, 97, 222, 229),[40] the cancelled passage in *Persuasion* hovers uncertainly between two intentions and two consciousnesses regarding the best way forward. Does the 'again' that appears
straight after 'Bad Morality' signal not only conscious repetition of the phrase

39. See also *JAFM*, vol. 1, p. 64; *Pers*, appendix 1, p. 301.
40. See *JAFM*, vol. 1, p. 45.

itself, but the author's recognition that, when faced with an ending and 'almost in despair', she is constitutionally tempted to reverse or ignore the usual moral of the story? The apprehension at this stage of weakness and strength, or the possibility of having mistaken one for the other, shows an authorial temptation to reverse or change tack at the last gasp. The wisdom of age, in *Persuasion*, cedes to the superior wisdom of youth—and such a process might be discovered in the minutiae of revision as well as in the movements of the story.

All this perhaps serves only to show that arguments can be made for thinking of Austen's early work as late, her late work as early, and at the same time. None of her published novels is quite as early *and* late as her very first compositions, however, which 'were the last to be brought to public notice and the last to appear in full in print'—almost two centuries after they had first been transcribed by their author (*JAFM*, vol. 1, p. 18). The long hiatus between that transcription and their full publication ensured that, in the meantime, the Victorian family biographers' account of the first writings of their famous aunt had come to predominate. Evidence and inclination to contradict such a prejudicial and protective account were hard to find; Austen's earliest surviving letter postdates the years in which she wrote her teenage works, and the twentieth-century editors who championed her mature fiction were never as captivated by her authorial beginnings, or as concerned to find value in them.

Despite vivid accretions of evidence and suggestion in the early writings, Southam argues that

> The manuscripts reveal that the entries are mere copying, automatic transcription. The verbal omissions, repetitions, and inconsistencies are the errors commonly associated with this kind of work. They are not the mistakes of a writer who is thinking critically about her material. [. . .] The most important signs of later revision are cancellations, modifications rather than improvements. (*JALM*, p. 18)

This is needlessly discouraging (as well as inaccurate). It shuts the door on critical enquiry into the teenage works by suggesting that the best action Austen took was to eliminate things.[41] But even the most casual slips bear traces of the author and her audience, suggesting how the work is put together and why we respond to it as we do. In the case of manuscripts, rather than allow mistakes to prevent us from asking questions, we might look at them as James Joyce's Stephen famously insisted we should when he said that mistakes are

41. *JALM*, p. 19.

'the portals of discovery'.[42] Take one small example, from the beginning of the first of Austen's stories in 'Volume the First'—probably written c. 1787—which suggests a few of the continuities that may fruitfully be traced between the early and the late writer, and which again involves a mother. The correction of 'Mother' to 'Father' in the first sentence of 'Frederic & Elfrida' seems no more than a basic, obvious business:

> The Uncle of Elfrida was the ~~Mother~~ Father of Frederic; in other words, they were first cousins by the Father's side. (*TW*, pp. 3, 220)

As Austen was transcribing the story, she made a mistake. But it is a strange mistake to make, even if your mind isn't wholly on the job (which seems unlikely at the very start of the tale, and of the notebook). How could an 'Uncle' also be a 'Mother' of anyone? Is it relevant that this is a tale in which the hero's and heroine's names are imperfect anagrams of one another? Or that 'Frederic & Elfrida' begins by asserting an absolute identity of male and female, recalling *Twelfth Night* and hence romance plots involving male-female twins and women disguised as men?

In the manuscript deletion of 'Mother' and insertion of 'Father' that opens 'Frederic and Elfrida', we have a trace of the same wilful confusion of male and female that is going on at the level of plot (such as it is). A boy and a girl, we are told, are born on the same day and go to the same school. This is laughable because it is impossible; but perhaps for Austen, who had recently left school, it may also have been wishful thinking. Other instances of a clearly deliberate gender-switching occur in the teenage works, in her adult letters, and in *Mansfield Park*.[43] In 'Frederic & Elfrida', a boy looks almost exactly the same as a girl, 'so much alike, that it was not every one who knew them apart' (this appears to give the lie to, among other things, Young's claim in *Conjectures on Original Composition* that 'No two faces, no two minds, are just alike, but all bear Nature's evident mark of Separation on them'.)[44] Only look again: in fact, we can, and we must, tell them apart because, on second glance, here are all

42. James Joyce, *Ulysses* [1922], ed. Jeri Johnson (Oxford: Oxford University Press, 2008): 'Bosh! Stephen said rudely. A man of genius makes no mistakes. His errors are volitional and are the portals of discovery' (ch. 9, p. 182). The effrontery with which this is uttered sounds very like that of young Austen; compare 'an artist cannot do anything slovenly' (to Cassandra Austen, *Letters*, 17–18 Nov. 1798, p. 21).

43. See for example *TW*, p. 124; to Cassandra Austen, 23–4 Sept. 1814, *Letters*, p. 238; *MP*, vol. 3, ch. 14, p. 499.

44. Young, *Conjectures*, p. 42.

the discrepancies between the two (descending, for propriety's sake, no lower than the head): 'the shape of the face, the colour of the Eye, the length of the Nose & the difference of the complexion' (*TW*, p. 3). We might accept the first, perhaps even the second of these items, and think the initial assertion of likeness still just about holds. But two more counter-instances defeat us. Is the same kind of process in which we are involved here—adjudication of likeness and difference, the progress or lack of it from one to the other, the shift from first to second impressions—applicable to how we try to read and discriminate between early and late Austen?

Time and again, the teenage writings work—like a child repeatedly asking 'are we there yet?'—by pushing at something until it gives way. We think we have established a rule, only to find it boisterously engulfed by the sheer number and force of contrary examples, assertions, or impressions. The blanket assertion of sameness eventually cancelled by itemized differences can be made to work in the opposite direction: apparent differences or distinctions turn out, beyond a certain point, to amount to the same thing. The 'inflexibly cool' Lady Williams of 'Jack & Alice', the next story to be transcribed in 'Volume the First', is a mistress of this art; instructed 'in the Paths of Virtue' and having 'nearly attained perfection', she has very little to say and do. She is introduced accordingly: 'Tho' Benevolent & Candid, she was Generous & sincere; Tho' Pious & Good, she was Religious & amiable, & Tho, Elegant & Agreable, she was Polished & Entertaining' (*TW*, pp. 14, 13–4, 10–11).

In the teenage writings, at moments like these, the more that is said the less it tends to mean. Pedagogical guides to language such as John Trusler's *The Distinction Between Words Esteemed Synonymous* (1776)—the first English thesaurus—and Hester Lynch Piozzi's *British Synonymy* (1794), suggest, as Austen's writing does, the necessity of choosing between words that might appear to be identical but conceal vital differences (on this activity, Henry Tilney in *Northanger Abbey* has his own point-scoring joke to make: 'I use the verb "to torment," as I observed to be your own method, instead of "to instruct," supposing them to be now admitted as synonimous' (vol. 1, ch. 14, p. 111)). The ways in which these authors, on their title pages, style the proper art of speaking as a form of learned discrimination, propriety, and regulation have obvious and immediate application to social and moral spheres—as they do in Austen's early mock-conduct books, and in Maria Edgeworth's contemporaneous spoof 'Essay on the Noble Art of Self-Justification' (written in 1787, published in 1795). What Edgeworth says here echoes Johnson's advice to Boswell about clearing his mind of 'cant' while continuing both freely and necessarily to deploy it in conversation, only Edgeworth's description of such a practice as 'laudable' makes her treatment of the subject even more barbed than Johnson's:[45]

> Distinguish then between sensibility and susceptibility; between the anxious solicitude not to give offence, and the captious eagerness of vanity to prove that it ought not to have been taken; distinguish between the desire of praise and the horror of blame: can any two things be more different than the wish to improve, and the wish to demonstrate that you have never been to blame?
>
> Observe, I only wish you to distinguish these things in your own minds; I would by no means advise you to discontinue the laudable practice of confounding them perpetually in speaking to others.[46]

We might categorize Austen's description of Lady Williams in 'Jack & Alice' as reversing the aims of Trusler's thesaurus in eliciting the synonymity between words esteemed distinct; where we expect clarity, she follows the advice of Edgeworth's satirical essay and deliberately, laudably, confounds. Elsewhere in this story, things that are forgotten are simultaneously recalled, and things that don't matter suddenly loom large: 'remember it is all forgot', says Lady Williams to Alice; to Lucy, she recommends with equal force both marrying and rejecting a Duke, and both returning home and staying away (*TW*, pp. 16, 22). But *Sense and Sensibility* takes us back to Trusler again, dwelling on the need to distinguish between 'like', 'esteem', and 'love', terms which Mrs Dashwood prides herself on confounding:

> 'It is enough,' she; 'to say that he is unlike Fanny is enough. It implies everything amiable. I love him already.'

45. 'JOHNSON. "My dear friend, clear your *mind* of cant. You may *talk* as other people do: you may say to a man, 'Sir, I am your most humble servant.' You are *not* his most humble servant. You may say, 'These are sad times; it is a melancholy thing to be reserved to such times.' You don't mind the times. You tell a man, 'I am sorry you had such bad weather the last day of your journey, and were so much wet.' You don't care six-pence whether he was wet or dry. You may *talk* in this manner; it is a mode of talking in Society: but don't *think* foolishly." *Boswell's Life of Johnson*, ed. G. B. Hill, rev. and enlarged L. F. Powell, 6 vols. (Oxford: Clarendon Press, 1934–50), vol. 4, p. 221.

46. Maria Edgeworth, 'An Essay on the Noble Science of Self-Justification' (1795), in *Letters for Literary Ladies to which is added An Essay on the Noble Science of Self-Justification*, ed. Claire Connolly (London: Everyman, 1993), p. 73.

'I think you will like him,' said Elinor, 'when you know more of him.'

'Like him!' replied her mother with a smile. 'I can feel no sentiment of approbation inferior to love.'

'You may esteem him.'

'I have never yet known what it was to separate esteem and love.' (*S&S*, vol. 1, ch. 3, p. 19)

Mrs Dashwood thinks it a positive virtue in herself not to distinguish between esteem and love. But her author, like her eldest daughter, regards it as evidence of linguistic, emotional, and moral confusion; not to know how 'to separate' different things is to live in a wilfully muddled state. (The 'yet' implies that Mrs Dashwood, like Mrs Bennet and Mary Bennet in *Pride and Prejudice*, and like Sir Walter Elliot in *Persuasion*, remains in a protracted state of infancy—she should, by now, realize how and when to separate one feeling and word from another—but that 'yet' also suggests that she may still have the chance to learn her lesson.) Differences in vocabulary stand for differences of feeling and call for appropriate differences in conduct. In other words, Elinor's mother should recognize and act on the distinctions between 'like', 'esteem', and 'love'.

In his thesaurus, Trusler does in fact elicit a distinction between 'religion' and 'piety'—two of whose cognates are applied to Lady Williams, suggesting that no such distinction exists ('Tho' Pious & Good, she was Religious & amiable'); Trusler says that '*Religion*, is more internal; *piety* is both internal, and external'.[47] But it is entirely the point of most characters in the teenage writings that they lack 'internal' selves; they tend to be one-dimensional, outward-facing, publicity-seeking creations. The kind of opposition we might expect between a novelistic character who appears to be pious or virtuous, but who is secretly quite the opposite, does not generally apply in these works (Austen creates such a character in Lady Susan, but that is another and a later story). The joke of Lady Williams lies in our expectation of being pushed towards acknowledging the difference between two things, the kind of expectation created by a didactic manual such as Trusler's, and the glaring lack of difference with which that expectation is met. In later life, Austen continued to relish these moments of studied let-down, or comically achieved dead ends. Writing to her niece Anna, she mentioned Cassandra's fear that, in Anna's novel,

---

47. John Trusler, *The Distinction between words esteemed synonymous in the English language, pointed out, and the proper choice of them determined. Useful to all who would either write or speak with Propriety and Elegance*, 2nd edition (London: for the author, 1783), p. 128.

'circumstances will be sometimes introduced of apparent consequence, which will lead to nothing.—It will not be so great an objection to <u>me</u>, if it does' (*Letters*, p. 281). As John Bayley remarked, 'anticlimax is for [Austen] much more full of comic potential than any number of big scenes'. This preference is clear in the earliest works, littered as they are with big scenes that go no-where and with 'quotidian dullness' on which 'an unexampled vitality' has been lavished.[48] Thus we find 'a Mother to her friend' in 'A Collection of Letters' trembling with apprehension at her daughters' imminent 'appearance in the World'. Threatened with a realm of 'wonderfull Things'—vices, seduc-tive examples, and contaminating follies—the quivering pair of girls survive their trial of tea-drinking with a neighbour and her daughters, 'the World, its Inhabitants, & Manners' amounting to no more than the span of 'Mrs Cope's parlour' (*TW*, pp. 134–5). Coming out, we learn, has an awful lot in common with staying in.

48. John Bayley, 'Characterization in Jane Austen', in *The Jane Austen Handbook*, ed. J. David Grey (London: Athlone, 1986), pp. 24–34 (pp. 31, 30).

3

Reading and Repeating

SAMUEL JOHNSON is said to have refused to meet Hugh Kelly, the 'drunken staymaker' turned dramatist, because he wouldn't talk to a man who had written more than he had read. According to Claude Rawson, Samuel Richardson came nearest of all major authors to embodying that joke for real.[1] Jane Austen, however 'unlearned, & uninformed' she was, cannot plausibly rival either Richardson or Kelly on this score (*Letters*, 11 Dec. 1815, p. 319).[2] Perhaps she habitually claimed to have read less than she truly had; however little the sum total was, it must add up to more than the equivalent of six novels plus her teenage writings and letters (even if many of those were lost or destroyed). Still, it is worth taking seriously a message that Austen reportedly sent her niece Caroline from her deathbed in Winchester, to the effect that 'if I would take her advice, I should cease writing till I was 16, and that she herself often wished she had *read* more, and written *less*, in the corresponding years of her own life' (*Memoir*, p. 174).

This advice impressed her young niece. It shows, apart from anything else, that Austen envisaged for herself a quite different sort of induction into authorship from the one we have on record—the one on record being that of someone who, from a very early age, avidly wrote and re-wrote her own work.

---

1. 'When some one asked him whether they should introduce Hugh Kelly, the author, to him—"No sir", says he, "I never desire to converse with a man who has written more than he has read". *Boswell's Life of Johnson*, vol. 2, p. 48, n. 2; Samuel Beckett, *Human Wishes*, in *Disjecta: Miscellaneous Writings and A Dramatic Fragment* (London: John Calder, 1983), p. 162; Claude Rawson, *Satire and Sentiment, 1660–1830: Stress Points in the Augustan Tradition* (Cambridge: Cambridge University Press, 1994), p. 221.

2. 'If she had no personal help from her contemporaries, she cannot be said to have derived much from books. The record of her studies is brief' (Richard Simpson in *Critical Heritage*, vol. 1, p. 242).

Young Jane Austen exhibited symptoms of what Hannah More termed 'the frightful facility' of novel-writing, no sooner having begun to read fiction than being 'tempted to fancy that she can also write'.[3] 'From reading to writing', as the Austen brothers' alter ego Mr Loiterer observed in 1789, 'it is but one step'; and thence, 'to keep our Talent any longer wrapt in the Napkin would be equal injustice to our writings, the world, and ourselves'.[4] Such reading as Austen undertook in her childhood appears to have been intensive, governed by the family itch to re-write it. Saul Bellow thought that 'many of my books, in retrospect, are comedies of wide reading'.[5] Had Austen ventured a retrospective judgement of this kind on her early works, she might have called many of them comedies of narrow reading. There is perhaps an exaggeration of her own case in one teenage character summary: 'she never reads any thing but the letters she receives from me, and never writes any thing but her answers to them' ('Lesley-Castle', *TW*, p. 104). This frenetically myopic author, like the fifteen-year-old spoof historian for whom 'the recital of any Events (except what I make myself) is uninteresting to me', feasts on and responds to an absurdly slender range of material ('The History of England', *TW*, p. 133). 'What I make myself' is what compels her attention. Intense or accelerated repetition seems, for Austen, to have been a quality associated with books and what to do with them (a question often considered in terms of whose property they are). Having achieved a good price for her copy of Robert Dodsley's *Collection of Poems in Six Hands* (1758), she told Cassandra, with hard-nosed absurdity, 'I do not care how often I sell them for as much. When Mrs Bramston has read them through I will sell them again' (21–22 May 1801, *Letters*, p. 92). In a mirror image of this impossible scenario, Edward Ferrars says of Marianne Dashwood that, had she a large fortune at her command, she would purchase the works of Thomson, Cowper, and Scott 'over and over again; she would buy up every copy [...] to prevent their falling into unworthy hands' (*S&S*, vol. 1, ch. 17, p. 107).

3. Hannah More, *Strictures on the Modern System of Female Education*, 2 vols. (London: T. Cadell Jun. and W. Davies, 1799), vol. 1, p. 170.

4. *The Loiterer, A Periodical Work*, 2 vols. ([Oxford]: for the author, 1790), no. 1, vol. 1, p. 7. This journal was edited and largely written by James and Henry Austen. See also *The Loiterer: A Periodical Work in Two Volumes Published at Oxford in the Years 1789 and 1790 by the Austen Family*, ed. Robert L. Mack (Lewiston, NY; Queenstown, Ontario; and Lampeter: Edwin Mellen Press, 2006).

5. Saul Bellow, 'The Civilized Barbarian Reader', *New York Times* (8 March 1987), section 7, p. 1.

The female correspondent of 'Lesley-Castle' is perversely echoing Hester Chapone's *Letters on the Improvement of the Mind* (1773), whose author suggests in the opening epistle that her niece 'pay me the compliment of preserving my letters' in order that 'you may possibly reperuse them at some future period'.[6] Burney, another writer whose works were familiar to the teenage Austen, has one character (Dr Gabriel Marchmont) in *Camilla: or, A Picture of Youth* recommend to a younger acquaintance (Edgar Mandlebert) that he read his letter twice, and then act on the result of that second reading; in the event, the recipient reads the letter three times. Having initially rejected its contents on a too-hasty perusal, Edgar next dwells (first inadvertently, then deliberately) on one sentence and proceeds slowly to digest the whole epistle, rejoicing at its close at having mastered himself and newly resolved on winning the heroine. In this determination, he proves to be excessively confident; we are, after all, in the early stages of the second of five hefty volumes.[7] Readers of the novel can plainly see that, as yet, there is no tell-tale compression of the pages to herald imminent matrimony. Austen, who subscribed to *Camilla*, seems to have found Marchmont's protracted meddling in the hero and heroine's courtship both irksome and funny (his name, combining a march with a mountain, fittingly suggests a laborious climb united with obstruction). It is a formal requirement of eighteenth- and nineteenth-century romantic fiction that difficulties continually impede a marriage which is also, generically speaking, inevitable; that requirement will often generate, at ground level, oddities and implausibilities of conduct in the characters made responsible for contriving such impediments. Those contrivances may also provoke a reader. As one generally admiring reviewer of *Camilla* put it in 1796: 'The story is doubtless spun out to an immoderate length; many dialogues, and many adventures, might well be spared'.[8] Marchmont's advice is repeatedly, and apparently baselessly, no more or less than not to do anything. 'Why?', as Edgar quite reasonably objects, 'will he thus obtrude upon me these fastidious doubts and causeless difficulties?'[9] In order to fill up the pages, is (at least from a reader) the most

6. Mrs. [Hester] Chapone, *Letters on the Improvement of the Mind, Addressed to a Young Lady*, 2 vols., 2nd edition (London: J. Walter, 1773), vol. 1, p. 2.

7. [Frances Burney], *Camilla: or, A Picture of Youth*, 5 vols. (London: T. Payne, T. Cadell Jr., and W. Davies, 1796), vol. 2, book 3, ch. 2, pp. 42–5.

8. 'ART. XIII', *British Critic*, p. 536.

9. Burney, *Camilla*, vol. 2, book 3, ch. 2, p. 43.

obvious reply. Reflecting belatedly on his interference, Dr Marchmont is himself compelled to acknowledge 'its injustice, its narrowness, and its arrogance'.[10] There is no obvious authorial irony to be detected in that admission of 'narrowness'—no glimmer of apology for the fact that it has yielded such physical breadth, so much prose.

Burney might not have chosen to do so, but many eighteenth-century novelists wove into their protracted fictions the writer's knowledge or apprehension that readers might find, at various stages and for various reasons, matter not to their taste or devoid of interest and relevance. Some of Henry Fielding's chapter titles, heralding '*what the Reader may perhaps expect to find in it*', even '*little or nothing*' by way of ensuing content, offer an early, wry awareness of books and their subdivided portions of text as cases, niches, or containers—perhaps of a predetermined size—for material no more than makeweight in a triple-decker, four- or five-volume novel ('makeweight' in the figurative sense of 'insignificant' is itself a mid-eighteenth-century term).[11] The teenage Austen's response to all this was to write contracted, very fast stories that, far from deferring satisfaction or withholding conclusions, often supply an excess of both in short order. It may reflect badly upon the unpleasant Mr Watts of 'The three Sisters' that 'he wont be kept in suspense', but the early tales themselves tend not to keep anyone waiting for long (*TW*, p. 54). While Burney in *Evelina* suspends the completion across three letters of a recognition scene involving a father and his daughter, in 'Love and Friendship' Austen closes the gap between anticipation and event, supplying within two paragraphs and 'in the space of 3 minutes' one grandchild after another, such that her 'venerable Peer' looks 'fearfully' towards the door, enquiring 'have I any other Grand-Children in the House?' Having disbursed some banknotes, he next beats a hasty retreat (*TW*, pp. 81–2, 288 n.). (Such jokes about suddenly expanding families and dependents springing out of nowhere may owe something to what Jane Austen's uncle disapprovingly

10. Burney, *Camilla*, vol. 5, book 10, p. 556.

11. *The Wesleyan Edition of the Works of Henry Fielding, The History of Tom Jones, A Foundling*, ed. Fredson Bowers and Martin C. Battestin, 2 vols. (Oxford: Clarendon Press, 1974), vol. 1, book 1, ch. 12; vol. 1, book 3, ch. 1 (chapter headings), pp. 69, 116; 'makeweight, 2. *fig.* A person or thing of insignificant value introduced to make up a deficiency or fill a gap' (1750), *OED*. On Austen as a satirist's in Fielding's line, see for example Sutherland, *English Satire*, 116–22.

referred to as 'the violent rapid increase' of George and Cassandra Austen's brood.[12])

For Fielding and his imitators, whether taking up novel-readers' time in burgeoning volumes of pricey fiction amounted to treating them with respect or to imposing on their good will occupied a fair amount of extra prose in itself. By the time Austen began to write, what constituted various kinds of 'respect' (and its cognates) was a recognizable part of the novelist's armoury. Most definitions of the 'respectable' supplied by the *OED* have been traced back to no earlier period than the mid- to late eighteenth century, a period in which they are discussed, tested, and rehearsed in domestic fiction. In 'Lady Susan', the villainous heroine refers to Mr. Johnson as 'a Man to whom that great word "Respectable" is always given' (*JAFM*, vol. 3, p. 332); in 1808, Austen remarked sardonically to Cassandra that 'I wrote without much effort; for I was rich—& the Rich are always respectable, whatever be their stile of writing' (*Letters*, pp. 135–6). As is suggested by its use in Robert Bage's *Hermsprong; or Man as he is not* (1796), another novel owned by Austen, 'respectable' amounted by the end of the eighteenth century to a cant literary term, pregnant with social comedy and social criticism.[13] In Thomas Love Peacock's *Melincourt*, Mr. Desmond makes passing sardonic reference to 'what the world calls respectable people', the adjective defined by the author as implying 'arrogance, ignorance, and the pride of money'; in *Crotchet Castle* (1831), Lady Clarinda sums things up: 'Respectable means rich, and decent means poor'.[14] In a letter of 1796, also the year of *Camilla*'s publication, Austen wrote to Cassandra: 'Give my Love to Mary Harrison, & tell her I wish whenever she is attached to a young Man, some <u>respectable</u> Dr Marchmont may keep them apart for five Volumes' (*Letters*, p. 9). The underlining implies some consciousness of this word's recent novelistic deployment; perhaps, too, of how the 'respectable' summons up pretensions, social climbing, and inequality of the

12. Tysoe Saul Hancock to Philadelphia Hancock, 23 September 1772, in *Austen Papers 1704–1856*, pp. 65–6. At the time at which this letter was written, the Austens had four children and another (who would be named Cassandra, for her mother) on the way.

13. On Austen's copy of *Hermsprong*, see *Bibliography* K3, pp. 437–8; on the 'respectable art' of agreeing to everything pronounced by a man of wealth and power, see Robert Bage, *Hermsprong; or Man as he is not*, 3 vols. (London: William Lane, 1796), vol. 1, ch. 21, p. 229.

14. [Thomas Love Peacock], *Melincourt*, 3 vols. (London: for T. Hookham, Jun., and Co., and Baldwin, Cradock, and Joy, 1817), vol. 1, p. 193; *The Cambridge Edition of the Novels of Thomas Love Peacock: Crotchet Castle*, ed. Freya Johnston and Matthew Bevis (Cambridge: Cambridge University Press, 2016), p. 30.

type that, later in the year, Austen began to investigate in 'First Impressions' (*Hermsprong* is one possible source for the published title of *Pride and Prejudice*).[15] There is an additional joke in the implied social distancing of 'five Volumes': the sheer physical bulk of the books is made synonymous with a kind of decorum that has no real purpose other than to keep itself going and therefore to keep two people from one another, delaying the inevitable for as long as possible.

Austen's emphasis to Cassandra on 'respectable' may indicate a family joke, combined with a reference to the opening of *Camilla*—where the heroine is said to reside 'In the bosom of her respectable family'.[16] There is a comment, most likely Austen's, pencilled at the bottom of the last page of her own copy of *Camilla*, above and below the '**FINIS.**' line and now almost entirely erased as well as partially cut off at the bottom (the letters are so faint on the original that reproducing them in photographic form is no longer possible). It suggests her sardonic appreciation of the sheer length of time that novels spun out in this way could end up taking:

> Since this work went to the
>> **FINIS.**
> Press, a circumstance of some
> Importance to the happiness of
> Camilla, has taken place, namely
> that Dr Marchmont has at last

Here Austen is cut off, most likely in the act of cutting off Marchmont. For we may assume, with R. W. Chapman, that the missing word or words at the bottom of the page refer to the busybody doctor's having shuffled off his mortal coil and finally left the young couple in peace (*Letters*, p. 9, n. 14). If so, it would not be the last time that Austen speculated about the death of a character after the formal close of a work of fiction.[17] The pseudo-authorial note to *Camilla*, concerned as it is with the old and querulous making way for the young and the new, chimes with a memory recorded by Austen's nephew. Reporting on

---

15. See Knox-Shaw, *Jane Austen and the Enlightenment*, pp. 100–103.

16. Burney, *Camilla*, vol. 1, book 1, ch. 1, p. 3. On the comically disconcerting association of bosoms with respectability, compare 'The beautifull Cassandra': 'She [...] was pressed to her Mother's bosom by that worthy Woman' (*TW*, p. 40).

17. On Austen's copy of *Camilla* and the mutilated inscription, see *Bibliography* K7, pp. 439–40.

the fate of her own characters after the end of the novels in which they appeared, and on obstructions to their marital happiness, the novelist apparently told her family that 'Mr. Woodhouse survived his daughter's marriage, and kept her and Mr. Knightley from settling at Donwell, about two years' (*Memoir*, p. 119).

As a subscriber to *Camilla*, 'Miss J. Austen' makes an appearance in print (the only such named appearance in her lifetime) very near the front of the first volume; with her concluding comment, she was stamping her identity on and supplementing the end of the fifth and final volume, too.[18] Unlike the remarks she inserted in ink into William Robertson's 'Character' of Mary, Queen of Scots, and David Hume's 'Character' of Elizabeth I, both included in Vicesimus Knox's *Elegant Extracts: or Useful and Entertaining Passages in Prose*, and unlike her equally virulent contradictions (in pencil) of Oliver Goldsmith's *History of England, from the Earliest Times to the Death of George II*, 4 vols. (1771), this observation (and extension of the plot) is in the voice of the author rather than in that of the annotator.[19] Austen's contribution to *Camilla* thus amounts to an epilogue, over- and under-writing '**FINIS.**' and pursuing the action beyond the point at which what we have just finished reading 'went to the Press'. Here, in this note, more than one kind of 'circumstance' might be said to have 'taken place'.

It sounds odd to describe a circumstance rather than (say) an occurrence as 'taking place'—Austen may well be using the word as a euphemism for death, although to treat a circumstance as an event appears to be something of a habit throughout her writing life. That habit may locally express the way in which her novels make plots out of what struck and continues to strike many readers as non-events. Yoon Sun Lee has recently described how 'events take on a different nature in Austen's plots: conventionally scaled cause-and-effect relations are considerably, sometimes surprisingly, downplayed even at the level of social events'.[20] In the teenage writings, as in the mature works, there are curious conceptions of what it means for something to pass the threshold of having happened, as of having been completed. In

18. Burney, *Camilla*, vol. 1, p. x; vol. 5, p. 556. Bodleian Library Arch. A. e. 108 / 1.

19. On marginalia as a form of co-authorship, see H. J. Jackson, *Romantic Readers: The Evidence of Marginalia* (New Haven, CT, and London: Yale University Press, 2005), pp. 142–3; Jason Snart, 'Recentering Blake's Marginalia', *Huntington Library Quarterly*, 66 (2003), 134–53.

20. Yoon Sun Lee, 'Austen's Swarms and Plots', *European Romantic Review*, 30 (2019), 307–14 (p. 308).

a letter to Cassandra (21–22 May 1801), Austen reports that 'The friendship between Mrs Chamberlayne & me which you predicted has already taken place, for we shake hands whenever we meet' (*Letters*, p. 91). Why has this friendship 'taken place', rather than (say) 'begun'? More than a decade earlier, in 'Henry & Eliza' (one of her earliest surviving compositions), Austen informed her reader that 'A mutual Love took place', phrasing which transforms a condition or state of affairs into what sounds like a sudden, disreputable act (*TW*, p. 29). It does, indeed, have immediate consequences (illegal marriage, flight to the continent), since results are generally 'easy to be effected' in this teenage realm (*TW*, p. 29).

To refer to what are usually conceived as processes as one-off events—to write 'A mutual Love took place', thereby in effect summarizing in five words the whole plot of a later Austen novel, rather than to say something like 'a mutual attachment was in progress' (*Memoir*, p. 188)—implies a preference for the fully-fledged occurrence, the completed action, the done-and-dusted, even in the realm of feelings. For a teenager to write like this further suggests impatience with any conception of adolescence as a transitional phase of life. That such a period was recognized as a separate stage, despite the absence of the noun 'teenager' from the eighteenth-century and Romantic lexicon, is evident from works such as Isaac Taylor's *Advice to the Teens; or, Practical Helps towards the Formation of one's own Character* (1818).[21] The more decisive Austen's authorial voice, the less incomplete or unformed its adolescent originator might seem to be. The fairy-tale atmosphere, or something like it, of a circumstance or process being translated into an accomplished, one-off occurrence, persists into later novels and their phrasing. In *Emma*, the 21-year-old heroine says: 'Yes, Harriet, just so long have I been wanting the very circumstance to happen which has happened' (vol. 1, ch. 9, p. 78). Here, 'circumstance' again appears to be magically synonymous with event; crucially, however, Emma (a deluded reader of other people) has misapprehended what that event might be. If we understand a 'circumstance' to capture the 'condition or state of affairs' materially surrounding and affecting a text (Burney's 'FINIS.', say), or, more conventionally, an agent (Marchmont's death, for example), we might further say that it encompasses the mark one

---

21. Isaac Taylor, *Advice to the Teens; or, Practical Helps towards the Formation of one's own Character* (London: Rest Fenner, 1818). See also *OED* 'teen, n.²', sense 1.a.(a), with examples dating from 1596 onwards; 'teen' 1.a.(b) (first example 1789); 'teen' 1.b. (first example 1818); 'teening' (first example 1818); 'teenish' (first example 1811).

author has made on another version of events.[22] For something to 'take place' is a spatiotemporal construction that can involve moving into the role once filled by another, as when Fanny Price's place at the centre of Mansfield Park is, at the end of that novel, occupied by her sister Susan—who is said, 'gradually to become, perhaps, the most beloved of the two' (*MP*, vol. 3, ch. 17, p. 547). Might Austen, supplementing the end of *Camilla* with her own 'circumstance', have imagined a comparable role for herself as Burney's successor? The *OED* contains a fudged description of 'circumstance' as a second-order 'event', which may well be confused because the phenomenon under examination is shirking definition, being uncertainly classified as something 'properly [. . .] subordinate' but assuming a status that is (perhaps temporarily, and perhaps improperly) central:

> 10. An event viewed as a detail of some narrative, or history, or of the general course of events; an incident, an occurrence; a matter or fact (properly of a secondary or subordinate kind).
>
>   In this use 'circumstance' tends to be entirely emptied of its etymological meaning, and to become merely a vaguer expression for 'fact', 'event'.

Emma's great failing—hence the plot of the novel in which she appears—is to work up details of her own narratives concerning friends and neighbours into what she regards as facts and events. But they do not merit that status, and her authorship of circumstance is unwarranted. A committed 'imaginist [. . .] on fire with speculation and foresight' and 'a ground-work of anticipation', Emma's wresting and arrogating of 'the general course of events' into her preferred line of narration may well be a mature, chastened portrayal of how Austen had coaxed her younger authorial self into being (*Emma*, vol. 3, ch. 3, p. 362).

———

An early reader of *Pride and Prejudice*, the Earl of Dudley, asked a correspondent whether she had come across the book, singling out for her attention Mr Collins as 'a parson in it quite admirable'.[23] What Dudley probably meant was that Collins was an admirably drawn character (in other words, it is the author rather than the character who deserves admiration); but there is the additional

---

22. See 'circumstance', sense 4a., *OED* (incorporating Johnson's *Dictionary* definition).

23. S. H. Romilly, *Letters to 'Ivy' from the First Earl of Dudley* (London: Longman, 1905), p. 194.

ironic implication that Collins is 'admirable' in the same way that Marchmont is 'respectable': not at all. This is the attitude which allows Mr Bennet himself perversely to admire Collins—a man whose consummate absurdities, as teased out by Austen, make him (unlike Burney's Marchmont) an admirably executed character as far as her readers are concerned. Therein lies the skill of the novelist, and the deficiency of Mr Bennet, who should not always be treating the people he meets as if they are in a work of literature, to be savoured without consequences.[24] 'Quite', as in Dudley's 'quite admirable', may mean anything from 'fairly' to 'consummately'. Like other words of social placement and judgement, the 'admirable' and the 'respectable' are acutely susceptible to pressure, liable to slip up or down the scale of 'quite' when subjected to the most delicate conversational suspicion or gossipy insinuation. Austen made full use of this vulnerability from the start of her career. The opening sentences of *Northanger Abbey*, invoking the 'respectable', suggest the same appeal to a small group of related initiates as that of Austen's '<u>respectable</u>' letter about *Camilla*: 'Her father was a clergyman, without being neglected, or poor, and a very respectable man, though his name was Richard—and he had never been handsome' (*NA*, vol. 1, ch. 1, p. 5).

Focusing on one word such as 'respectable' reveals Austen's tendency to return to, quarry, and investigate single socially or privately charged terms and names, which, like epigraphs, may become a sort of carapace—or, to cite one of her letters, 'a Nest of my own': at once self-expressive and self-protective.[25] We see her, from the teenage years onwards, revisiting the same contracted verbal and social terrain, her affection and mockery being directed towards the same targets. Some of her fictional people (Mr Knightley, Elinor Dashwood, Henry Tilney), like their author, exhibit a heightened sense of individual words as indices of national or personal character and taste. 'Respectable' is at once an outward-facing literary joke about novel slang and an inward-facing family gag about intimacy and disrespect or the margins of respectability.

The teenage writings come into being as a form of backchat with earlier writers and genres, whether overtly—as in the case of 'The History of England', which flaunts a structural and stylistic relationship with Goldsmith's work of

---

24. See, for instance, vol. 3, ch. 15, where Mr Bennet's ill-timed 'wit' is capped by his sardonic comment that 'It is admirable!' (*P&P*, p. 402).

25. On epigraphs as 'an actual or pretended way of disguising [the author's] identity from the uninitiated', see Anne Ferry, *The Title to the Poem* (Stanford, CA: Stanford University Press, 1996), p. 232; Austen to James Edward Austen, 16–17 December 1816 (*Letters*, p. 337).

the same name—or indirectly, as when the author parodies the conventions of sentimental novels without seeming to have any particular author or work of fiction in mind. The ethics of reading in Austen are governed by sceptical attitudes towards passion as a guiding impulse or impetus. But even when she is ironizing her characters' misguided responses to the books they read, and apparently maintaining a certain distance from their views, Austen is affectionately—impudently—familiar with the texts and genres that are the objects of her satire. She never enters fully into, or seems fully persuaded by, Charlotte Lennox's and Maria Edgeworth's brand of female anti-quixotry. Although her reworking of tired tropes and characters is often sharply parodic, she is not only criticizing novels and their readers, but rather compiling a sophisticated defence of the genre in which she and they have collectively and often happily become ensnared.

Family accounts of or summary references to Jane Austen's reading therefore do not seem quite right.[26] They tend to make it sound less dynamic, supple, and competitive—more inert—than Austen herself does. Reading was a group activity as well as a private one, shared with friends and relatives. It was also a pursuit in which Austen was professionally, jealously, interested. She often poked fun at books and authors, and at her own relationship to literary tradition. She was self-conscious about not knowing enough, and on the other hand about knowing plenty to be going on with. Those two kinds of comment are flipsides of each other. Her assertions that she must get hold of a particular book can become a mock-insistence that she won't read anything else from now on. Some decisive remarks about reading concern books she has yet to see. She determines not to be pleased with Walter Scott's fiction, but fears she must; she refuses to like Jane West's historical novel *Alicia de Lacy: An Historical Romance* (1814), without having read it (to Anna Austen, 28 Sept. 1814, *Letters*, p. 289). In similar vein, we find her in 1813 professing 'I detest a Quarto'; this is no random detestation, since a trim octavo announces the type of author who 'condenses his Thoughts' into a smaller compass than that of the 'great stupid thick Quarto' (*Letters*, p. 215). Long before the celebrated pronouncements that her own work took the form of a nest or little bit of ivory,

---

26. See for example 'she followed the old guides'; 'the native good taste of herself and of those with whom she lived'; 'looking on the author quite as an abstract idea'; 'she seldom changed her opinions either on books or men'; 'Her reading was very extensive in history and belles lettres' (Austen-Leigh and Henry Austen in *Memoir*, pp. 71, 141).

Austen was toying with the sheer heft or bulk of a long book and weighing that superficial claim to notice against its real or spurious intelligence.

Isobel Grundy, Gillian Dow, Katie Halsey, and Olivia Murphy have all noted the exuberant judgements involved in Austen's reading.[27] Francis O'Gorman, stressing the centrality of adjudication to readers of a slightly later period, argues that

> in the critical prose of the mid-nineteenth century, it is hard to find a sense of the mobility of reading; a recognition that a text may look different when it is read again; that one reading is not all a text can or even must accommodate. [. . .] The preference for certainty in rereading was primarily, for the literary-critical writing of the period, to do with evaluation.

He cites Austen in support of his argument:

> Jane Austen shared that view, it seems, when she wrote in 1813 of Mary Brunton's *Self Control: A Novel* (1811): 'I am looking over Self-Control again, & my opinion is confirmed of its' being an excellently-meant, elegantly-written Work, without anything of Nature or Probability in it.' An arch judgement indeed.[28]

Austen's brother Henry seems to chime in anticipation with O'Gorman when he says that 'she seldom changed her opinions either on books or men' (*Memoir*, p. 141). But both assertions are strange, if only in view of the plots of Austen's novels, which so often involve false initial impressions yielding to second thoughts. 'It is particularly incumbent on those who never change their opinion, to be secure of judging properly at first', says Elizabeth Bennet to Darcy, but the joke is on both of them since each is compelled to change an opinion

---

27. Isobel Grundy, 'Jane Austen and Literary Traditions', in *The Cambridge Companion to Jane Austen*, ed. Edward Copeland and Juliet McMaster, 2nd edition (Cambridge: Cambridge University Press, 2011), pp. 192–214; Gillian Dow and Katie Halsey, 'Jane Austen's Reading: The Chawton Years', *Persuasions On-Line*, vol. 30 (2010), [n. p.], http://www.jasna.org/persuasions /on-line/vol30no2/dow-halsey.html; Katie Halsey, *Jane Austen and Her Readers, 1786–1945* (London: Anthem, 2012); Olivia Murphy, *Jane Austen: The Reader as Critic*. On the possible range of Austen's reading, see too recent attempts to create a digital version of the library at Godmersham Park, home of Austen's brother Edward Knight: https://www.readingwithausten .com/.

28. Francis O'Gorman, 'Matthew Arnold and Rereading', *Cambridge Quarterly*, 41 (2012), 245–61 (pp. 245–6). The passage quoted from Austen is in *Letters*, p. 244 (with 'Self Control' rather than 'Self-Control').

formed hastily and wrongly of the other (*P&P*, vol. 1, ch. 18, p. 105). In Austen's fictional landscapes, 'Very few things cannot be undone. Very few events turn out to be irreversible. Second chances seem to abound. Macro-effects can be erased, or simply not occur (think how different it is, for example, in a Hardy novel)'.[29] As for their author, we would not expect someone who rarely changed her mind to return to her early and late texts and alter them as frequently as Austen seems—from the manuscript evidence that survives—to have done. Henry Austen cannot be right, on that basis alone, to claim that 'Every thing came finished from her pen' (*Memoir*, p. 141).

Whatever her motives for doing so, Austen read the same books over and over again. Her earliest writings are full of characters returning to people, places, and stories, repeating themselves and others. Laura's account of her own life is produced at the instigation of her friend Isabel's 'repeated intreaties', and itself includes repeated acts of enquiry, fainting, frenzy, and snoring ('Love and Friendship', *TW*, p. 69). A joke in 'Lesley-Castle' about hearing a story many times is potentially both heartfelt and tart on the joys of repetition: 'I return you many thanks', says Charlotte to Peggy, 'for the account [. . .] of Lesley's acquaintance, Love & Marriage with Louisa, which has not the less entertained me for having often been repeated to me before' (*TW*, p. 103). Alice is 'provoked' by Lady Williams' fondness for 'reviving old stories'; in particular, the 'renewal of the old story' that is Alice's drunkenness ('Jack & Alice', *TW*, p. 16). However maddening it may be, a tale returned to or repeated is never quite the same as it was before, since repetition also elicits differences between one version or experience of a story and another. In the passage quoted by O'Gorman, Austen talks of 'looking over' *Self-Control* again, an activity not exactly synonymous with re-reading. She refers to something done alone rather than in company, and could be describing a less than thorough-going read, possibly just a quick refresher, against which she is measuring and assessing her own work.

A contrasting sort of activity is described to Cassandra Austen in 1799, in a letter that circles around acts of sisterly re-reading, with reference to the work Austen here calls 'first impressions'. For an author to give her novel a title including the word 'first' could be taken as a sign of its provisional status, or of its likely revision. First impressions are proverbially mistaken, after all; like first drafts, they invite another, more mature and considered version of themselves—even if, as the first number of the Austen brothers' Oxford

29. Yoon Sun Lee, 'Austen's Swarms and Plots', p. 308.

periodical, *The Loiterer*, anxiously pointed out: 'first impressions are seldom affected by subsequent alteration.'[30] There is an aptness to the fact that the only two references to the novel by this title in Austen's surviving letters describe a second reading of it: 'I do not wonder at your wanting to read first impressions again, so seldom as you have gone through it, & that so long ago'; 'I would not let Martha read First Impressions again upon any account, & am very glad that I did not leave it in your power.—She is very cunning, but I see through her design;—she means to publish it from Memory, & one more perusal must enable her to do it' (*Letters*, 8–9 Jan. 1799, 11 June 1799, pp. 36, 46).[31] Cassandra's re-reading will be at once a repetition, and an other experience from the first, built on the confident hope that her sister paid very close attention to her work (in 1814, Austen expected her to recognize a casual allusion to 'Love and Friendship', completed more than two decades earlier; *Letters*, p. 282). A niece remembered Austen reading 'first impressions' to Cassandra at a time when 'the composition of the story was still a secret kept from the knowledge of others.'[32] So by 1799, Cassandra had heard the book read to her, and perhaps taken part in recitals or performances of it (hence 'gone through'); but she now wanted to read it for herself. (After the work appeared in print, the Austens read *Pride and Prejudice* aloud to a Miss Benn, not entirely to the author's satisfaction: 'I beleive something must be attributed to my Mother's too rapid way of getting on—& tho' she perfectly understands the Characters herself, she cannot speak as they ought', 4 Feb. 1813, *Letters*, p. 211.) Bearing in mind her early sensitivity to print conventions, it is striking that Austen, in her previous reference to the novel, uses lowercase letters to refer to its working title (she does not do this, as far as we know, with her other fictions). Does 'first impressions' rather than 'First Impressions' suggest a title that is in some sense waiting to be superseded, or that has not yet made its way into print? Claire Tomalin proposes that the 'denial of initial capital letters in the title is like a lowering of the voice' and that it signals a possible reluctance to mention the book, at

---

30. *The Loiterer*, no. 1 (31 Jan. 1789), vol. 1, p. 5. There are some rare examples in Austen of a first impression being correct: 'I have a very good eye at an Adultress' (to Cassandra, 12–13 May 1801, after seeing a well-known demirep at the Pump Room in Bath), 'for tho' repeatedly assured that another in the same party was the *She*, I fixed upon the right one from the first' (*Letters*, p. 88).

31. See also Austen's aunt, Jane Leigh Perrot, on her second reading of *Emma*, cited in *A Goodly Heritage*, pp. 94–5.

32. William and Richard Arthur Austen-Leigh, *Jane Austen: Her Life and Letters* (London: Smith Elder, 1913), p. 73.

least in public.[33] But is Austen perhaps gesturing towards the subject matter or territory of her novel, rather than quoting its confirmed title?[34] This would make sense, given that (as Brian Southam notes) susceptibility to first impressions—typically, love at first sight—amounted to a cliché of sentimental fiction, and that the topic had already been handled in the Austen brothers' periodical. It might therefore be a satirical target, or motivating impulse, of the novel that became *Pride and Prejudice*, the idea of 'first impressions' perhaps affecting its young author in the same way that, a few years earlier, it had affected Mary Wollstonecraft—who was celebrated by her husband William Godwin for her 'minute attention to first impressions', but whose *Vindication of the Rights of Woman* (1792) attacked the 'habitual slavery to first impressions' that she discerned in girls.[35] Perhaps 'first impressions' are also related to the lowercase '<u>first veiw</u>' of a new acquaintance that Austen mentions in a letter of 18 September 1796: 'I will not pretend to say that on a <u>first veiw</u>, she quite answered the opinion I had formed of her' (*Letters*, p. 12). This comment also concerns the nature of an initial impression, and a necessary revision of preconceptions.[36] The underlining may suggest that first views were another kind of in-joke or part of the family idiom.

Austen does not use the verb 're-read' in her surviving correspondence or fiction (when she does use verbs of this 're-' form, her favoured one is 're-establish'). But she makes it clear in the letters when she has returned to a text,

33. Tomalin, *Jane Austen*, p. 145.

34. Compare the various names by which Keats's 'On First Looking into Chapman's Homer' is known in its earliest manuscript and print manifestations; some of these names are descriptions of the subject rather than titles as such, or halfway between the two: 'On the first looking into Chapman's Homer'; 'The SONNET ON CHAPMAN'S HOMER'; 'that noble sonnet on first reading Chapman's Homer'. For a discussion of these titles, see John Barnard, 'The Harvard Manuscript of Keats's "On First Looking into Chapman's Homer"', Joseph Severn, Leigh Hunt, and its Transmission into Print', *Romanticism*, 25 (2019), 157–68.

35. *JALM*, pp. 11, 59–60; Southam quotes Mrs Shirley's confession in one of Austen's favourite works, Richardson's *History of Sir Charles Grandison* (1753): 'I had very high ideas of first impressions: eternal constancy: of Love raised to a pitch of idolatry'. Samuel Richardson, *The History of Sir Charles Grandison*, 6 vols. (Oxford: B. Blackwell, 1931), vol. 6, p. 223. Mary Wollstonecraft, *A Vindication of the Rights of Woman: with Strictures on Political and Moral Subjects* (1792), in *The Works of Mary Wollstonecraft*, 7 vols., ed. Janet Todd and Marilyn Butler (London: Pickering & Chatto, 1989), vol. 5, p. 113. On Godwin's view of 'first impressions', see introduction, p. 27.

36. For other instances of a 'first veiw' and disappointed expectations, see letters to Cassandra of 17 May 1799 and 5–6 May 1801 (*Letters*, pp. 41, 86).

and seeks to differentiate a second experience from the first and potentially from a third. The plural 'we' that often governs her reading also influences the nature of the experience she describes. In February 1807, she wrote to Cassandra that: 'We are reading *Clarentine*, & are surprised to find how foolish it is. I remember liking it much less on a 2^d reading than at the 1st & it does not bear a 3rd at all. It is full of unnatural conduct & forced difficulties, without striking merit of any kind' (*Letters*, pp. 125–6).[37] So this third, shared reading offers a 'surprise' which might not be a confirmation of first impressions, though it is affected by the memory of a disappointing second reading. The prepositions attending each stage of reading are delicately differentiating, too: 'at the 1st' and 'on a 2^d'. There is something unique, hence the definite article, about the first reading, but it can be broken 'on' the occasion of 'a 2^d' reading, such that 'a 3^d' might be attempted but cannot be supported until the end.

In the teenage works, reading is sometimes presented as garishly inadequate. There are deplorable and magnificent people who read to fuel their prejudices, or self-love, or both (this is also true of Sir Walter Elliot in *Persuasion*).[38] As is often the case in *Pride and Prejudice*, reading may be a female affectation: 'Lady Jane Grey [. . .] has been already mentioned as reading Greek. Whether she really understood that language or whether such a Study proceeded only from an excess of vanity for which I beleive she was always rather remarkable, is uncertain' ('The History of England', *TW*, p. 128; *P&P*, vol. 1, ch. 2, p. 7; ch. 5, p. 21; ch. 11, p. 60). Or it is a chore, ranked alongside other kinds of 'work' in 'Lesley-Castle' (*TW*, p. 97). In 'The History of England', re-reading is similarly presented as a 'task':

> It would be an affront to my Readers were I to suppose that they were not as well acquainted with the particulars of this King's reign as I am myself. It will therefore be saving *them* the task of reading again, & *myself* the trouble of writing what I do not perfectly recollect, by giving only a slight sketch of the principal Events which marked his reign. (*TW*, p. 126)

37. Compare 'Your Letter gave pleasure to all of us, we had all the reading of it of course, I three times—as I undertook to the great releif of Lizzy, to read it to Sackree, & afterwards to Louisa' (to Cassandra, 11–12 Oct. 1813, *Letters*, p. 243).

38. 'Sir Walter Elliot, of Kellynch-hall, in Somersetshire, was a man who, for his own amusement, never took up any book but the Baronetage; there he found occupation for an idle hour, and consolation in a distressed one [. . .] he could read his own history with an interest which never failed' (*Pers*, vol. 1, ch. 1, p. 3).

These versions of reading are likely to reflect Austen's youth and schoolroom learning by rote of works presented as improving, but whose weaknesses she discerned and exposed at a very early age. Writing, by contrast, is often presented as a relief and a facility, something by which authors vent their feelings and coerce the audience into accepting their views. Reading, on this view of things, is a duty exacted by a tyrannical writer whom the audience cannot hope to escape: 'The Possibility of being able to write, to speak, to you of my losst Henry will be a Luxury to me, & your Goodness will not I know refuse to read what it will so much releive my Heart to write' ('Lesley-Castle', *TW*, p. 114). Only rarely is writing depicted as the kind of nuisance or 'trouble' mentioned in 'The History of England'; it is, apparently, what the young Austen longed to escape reading in order to do.

Like her mock-epic predecessor Alexander Pope, Austen appears to have been galvanized by the twin constraints of littleness and vacuity:

> The intensity of focus provided by the small booklets and the challenge of setting down her vision in the narrowest scope may have been vital spurs to creativity: the constrained space of the little page tightly filled to its very edges, the single draft worked over and over, may have been requisite conditions for her own spare art. (*JAFM*, vol. 1, p. 45)

Writing within the limits and up to the margins of small notebooks, electing as a young writer the forms of radically contracted letters, playlets, and capsule novels populated by characters who exhibit very little in terms of internal self-hood or three-dimensional motivations, Austen's imagination took flight. Beyond their hunger for acquisition, characters in many of the early stories appear to be motiveless. They feast, binge-drink, steal, get engaged, married, or imprisoned, insult one another, and charge through people's houses and across the countryside with seeming impunity, armed with a ready stock of literary conventions and blithe compliments, as well as with a large helping of self-regard—and that, apparently, is enough for most of them to survive anything. Even those who don't get away with murder seem oddly and comically impervious to events. They lack mental furniture. These creatures are vivid in the way that caricatures or cartoons are vivid.

In 'Frederic & Elfrida', the excessively (and eventually fatally) obliging Charlotte goes to visit a new friend, Rebecca. She finds her plastering make-up all over her face in a doomed attempt to conceal her ugliness. This passage includes one of the young Austen's most glaring literary allusions:

As to the lovely Charlotte [. . .] she determined to accept the invitation & in consequence of it walked to Mrs Fitzroys to take leave of the amiable Rebecca, whom she found surrounded by Patches, Powder, Pomatum & Paint with which she was vainly endeavouring to remedy the natural plainness of her face.

'I am come my amiable Rebecca, to take my leave of you for the fortnight I am destined to spend with my aunt. Beleive me this separation is painfull to me, but it is as necessary as the labour which now engages you.'

'Why to tell you the truth my Love, replied Rebecca, I have lately taken it into my head to think (perhaps with little reason) that my complexion is by no means equal to the rest of my face & have therefore taken, as you see, to white & red paint which I would scorn to use on any other occasion as I hate art.'

Charlotte, who perfectly understood the meaning of her freind's speech, was too goodtemper'd & obliging to refuse her, what she knew she wished,—a compliment; & they parted the best freinds in the world. (*TW*, pp. 5–6)

'Vainly' is brilliantly positioned, two-facedly capturing the personal conceit and universally acknowledged futility of Rebecca's war against nature. (Charlotte and her friends have already recoiled, loudly and in unison, from what they describe as Rebecca's 'forbidding Squint, [. . .] greazy tresses & [. . .] swelling Back, which are more frightfull than imagination can paint or pen describe'—although they immediately add their 'raptures, at the engaging Qualities of your Mind, which so amply atone for the Horror with which your first appearance must ever inspire the unwary visitor', *TW*, p. 5). Rebecca's 'Patches' were initially 'Rouge'. In substituting one word for the other when she re-read the story, Austen made the link with Pope's *Rape of the Lock* (1712–17) more explicit than it had been in her initial transcription. Belinda's dressing table is famously garlanded with 'Puffs, Powders, Patches, Bibles, Billet-doux', and that one-liner, a list which is itself parodying Milton, among others, is perhaps among the 'set of phrases' lodged in Austen's mind from childhood.[39] (The reference in *Northanger Abbey* to Catherine Morland's reading of Pope

---

39. *The Twickenham Edition of the Poems of Alexander Pope*, vol. 2: *The Rape of the Lock and Other Poems*, ed. Geoffrey Tillotson (London: Methuen & Co.; New Haven, CT: Yale University Press, 1940; repr. 1966), *The Rape of the Lock*, canto I, l. 138. On the line as a parody of Milton, see p. 402.

suggests that he was one of a handful of poets to supply girls with 'quotations which are so serviceable'; vol. 1, ch. 1, pp. 7–8). Here, a version of Pope's cele-brated poetic inventory is inserted into a new scene of a woman arming and beautifying herself for social combat, or trying her best to do so.

Austen's revision to her original wording—the change from 'Rouge' to 'Patches'—brings out a further echo of the *Rape* in this scene: the 'necessary [. . .] labour', as Charlotte refers to it, 'which now engages' Rebecca. That phrasing probably glances back again to Pope's dressing table: we are told in the final line of Canto I that '*Betty*' is 'prais'd for Labours not her own'.[40] Jokes about 'labour' as dirty, undignified, or just plain stupid appear many times in Austen's early works (she would later famously refer to her own writing as a form of 'labour', *Letters*, 16–17 Dec. 1816, p. 337).[41] She makes such jokes partly in order to confound expectations of lady-like behaviour, partly as a more general and structural affront to class distinctions. Wealthy people who shouldn't be toiling or sweating are shown doing just that. High life soils itself below stairs and above the shop.

We can conjecture Austen's knowledge of Pope from a sprinkling of refer-ences to him in her writing, and we can in any case feel confident that a girl in the 1780s from a bookish family would have known *The Rape of the Lock* well.[42] There is a Popean application of the verb 'take'—and taking is a key activity in these tales of sometimes futile, often illicit acquisition—which moves from internal to external properties of the female head, from mind to face, in that passage from 'Frederic & Elfrida'. Rebecca says 'I have lately taken it into my head' and 'I [. . .] have therefore taken [. . .] to red & white paint'. The technique is repeated in other stories. The young Austen sometimes em-ploys overt forms of zeugma, incongruously splicing inner and outer realms, as in 'Jack & Alice', where the impossibly handsome 'cruel Charles' is said 'to wound the hearts & legs of all the fair' (*TW*, p. 18). In a strange piece of simul-taneous disaggregation and collocation, the beautiful Charlotte is reported to

40. *The Rape of the Lock*, canto I, l. 148.

41. On such authorial labour, see also for example Richard Simpson: 'What [Jane Austen] wrote was worked up by incessant labour into its perfect form. She did not cast her statues in one jet, nor mould them with a few strokes on the anvil. She had no Cyclopean force of poetical production. She was patient as Penelope at her web, unpicking at night much that she had la-boriously stitched in the day' (*Critical Heritage*, vol. 1, p. 253).

42. Pope is mentioned, alluded to, or quoted in *NA* (vol. 1, chs. 1 and 5, pp. 8, 31), *S&S* (vol. 1, ch. 10, p. 57), and *Pers* (vol. 2, ch. 3, p. 156); *The Essay on Man* is slightly misquoted in a letter to Cassandra of 20 October 1813 (*Letters*, p. 256).

have thrown both 'her sweet Body & her lovely face' into a deep stream, in order to escape a 'double engagement' (*TW*, p. 7). Since they are favoured techniques of Pope's, these zeugmatic habits of conjoining so as to enforce, comically, an equally compelling sense of separation were probably learnt from *The Rape of the Lock*, in which (in the most celebrated example of eighteenth-century zeugma) Queen Anne's dignity is vaguely but mischievously compromised when she is said to 'take' both 'Counsel' and '*Tea*'.[43]

Such compositional techniques can only have been encouraged by the fact that, in the eighteenth century, people were so often described or construed in terms of their individual 'parts'. Heralding someone as a man or woman 'of parts' invites attention to their separate limbs and features as well as to their roles in the world, a form of attention that came naturally to Austen and her family.[44] In *Northanger Abbey*, a large gaggle of children (ten to the Austens' eight) is introduced and accounted for in terms of the sheerly adequate number of individual limbs that it comprises: 'A family of ten will always be called a fine family, where there are heads and arms and legs enough for the number' (vol. 1, ch. 1, p. 5). However, as the narrator goes on to tell us, focusing next on their facial features, 'the Morlands had little other right to the word, for they were in general very plain, and Catherine, for many years of life, as plain as any'.

The 'Puffs, Powders' allusion to Pope suggests a little of what Austen might have been trying to achieve when at various stages in her life she returned to and revised her teenage volumes, and of what her attitude to such allusive practices was. In the initial transcription she had already eliminated the reading material—'Bibles' and 'Billets-doux'—from Pope's original dressing table scene, in order to make her own list home in on nothing but beauty kit. In a move that is typical of her second thoughts about the early works, she then makes her own alliteration more extreme. Although, in doing that, she creates a more obvious, screechier resemblance between her own prose and Pope's verse, she also heightens our sense of what she might be doing differently, or might go on to do differently. The most vital of those differences is that she is writing spoof sentimental fiction, not mock-epic verse, but within the conventions of that form she has a very sharp sense of what constitutes 'serviceable'

---

43. *The Rape of the Lock*, canto III, l. 8.

44. See *OED* 'part, *n.¹*', sense 15: 'A personal quality or attribute, esp. of an intellectual kind; an ability, gift, or talent. Usually in *plural*. Now *rare* except in man (also woman, lad, etc.) of (many) parts n. a man, etc., who is talented or accomplished in many respects'.

female allusion.[45] When she burlesques a line from *The Essay on Man* (1733–4)—'Laugh where we must, be candid where we can'—in her teenage 'Collection of Letters', as 'Ride where you may, Be Candid where You can', she does so in full knowledge of the fact that she is the latest in a very long line of impersonators. Hence the pre-emptive, sarcastic gloss of that parodic line as 'extempore' (that is, learned off by heart) '& equally adapted to recommend both Riding & Candour' (in other words, equally useless to both) (*TW*, pp. 137, 312 n.).

Unlike other women who blithely, blandly parrot bits of Pope, Austen will re-make her source while showing in such acts of re-making that she knows many others have gone before her. The gorgeous Belinda, through labour and make-up lavished on her by others, becomes—layer by layer, allusion upon allusion—ever more beautiful. The unfortunate Rebecca's toil, by contrast, is at once necessary, and entirely her own, and useless. There seems to be a bigger joke lurking in here about contrasting models of writing and behaviour; about gender (and gender reversals); about authors; and about the relationship of nature to artifice in life and in fiction. The mature Austen's surviving criticism of books suggests that she officially deplored but also rather enjoyed the absence of nature in the works of rival female novelists.[46] *The Rape of the Lock* delicately celebrates, as well as laughs at, the capacity of art to decorate and improve on reality. In the forced, slapstick marriage of life and art that is on show in 'Frederic & Elfrida', we are made to look at the seam between them. 'I hate art', says Rebecca, pretending not to be keen on hiding her defects. She fails to conceal for a second how she looks or what she feels from Charlotte, or from us. So nature triumphs over artifice, but in such a way as to render that triumph absurdly pyrrhic. That moment anticipates a long history of critical discussions about Austen's renowned truth to nature, of which James Stanier Clarke's comment that 'there is so much nature' in *Emma* is among the earliest (?21 Dec. 1815, *Letters*, p. 320).

But Austen's early works also mock any attempts to pin down such perceived differences between the natural and the artificial, and indeed to identify many of her sources. These stories are garlanded with blanks in place of names,

---

45. Richard Cronin and Dorothy McMillan remark on Austen's preference for 'hackneyed' and clichéd sources: 'It is as if Austen takes a perverse pride in the tediousness of her quotations' (*Emma*, p. xlii).

46. See *Letters* (to Cassandra, 11–12 Oct. 1813): 'an excellently-meant, elegantly-written Work, without anything of Nature or Probability in it' (p. 244).

with whispered conversations that cannot be fully heard or perfectly understood, and with in-jokes wholly accessible only to a small group of Hampshire friends and relatives, or perhaps only to Cassandra Austen. In these compositions, we encounter the superlatively accomplished treatment of surfaces. Such 'surfaces' include the physical appearance of the teenage writings—their division into three volumes in order to resemble a triple-decker novel; their title-pages and dedications; the puffed-up importance and anonymity of the writer (Austen does not name herself, but repeatedly signs off her dedications as 'The Author'). Then there is her precociously expert sense of the cant of fiction; and the curious flattening effects she practises at the local level of what her sentences are doing and being.

'What mighty Contests rise from trivial Things'.[47] When she revises numerical counts in these stories, the figures get bigger—twelve months become twelve years; £12,000 becomes £18,000—expanding their outrageous claims on our attention within an increasingly, comically suffocating and closeted realm (*TW*, pp. 223, 235). Some forms of her punctuation are so compacted as to defy representation in print (*TW*, p. 222 n.). If it is impossible to transfer such an idiosyncratic symbol as the combined exclamation mark and semicolon from manuscript into print, the habitual expansion, in twentieth-century editions of the juvenilia, of Austen's '&' into 'and' can and should be avoided. Her habitual use of the ampersand in place of 'and' offers one local, crucial hint of the space-saving, thrifty disposition of the author, a disposition that combines in these tales with a spirit of gleeful, hurtling experimentation. What she takes in by way of source material she swiftly redeploys in arrestingly contracted, accelerated form, and many of her characters are engaged in the parallel activities of grabbing things (cash, jewels) and people (husbands, relatives) before quickly moving on.

Identity, sameness, or duplication can be hysterically funny in itself—perhaps especially to two sisters, Cassandra and Jane Austen, of whom their mother apparently said, recalling the seven-year-old Jane's insistence on accompanying her older sibling to boarding school in 1782, 'Jane was too young to make her going to school at all necessary, but it was her own doing; she *would* go with Cassandra; "if Cassandra's head had been going to be cut off, Jane would have her's cut off too"' (*Memoir*, p. 160). The beheading scenario is staged again for laughs in the teenage writings, when one of several irksomely perfect Janes in Austen's fictional world—this time, Lady Jane Grey,

---

47. *The Rape of the Lock*, canto I, l. 2.

who had died aged sixteen, at almost the same age as the author—is depicted as second in line to the scaffold:

> she preserved the same appearance of knowledge, & contempt of what was generally esteemed pleasure, during the whole of her Life, for she declared herself displeased with being appointed Queen, and while conducting to the Scaffold, she wrote a Sentence in latin & another in Greek on seeing the dead Body of her Husband accidentally passing that way. ('The History of England', *TW*, p. 128)

In nine words ('being appointed Queen, and while conducting to the Scaffold'), to encompass the mere nine days of her reign, Lady Jane has passed from coronation to execution—but it is made to sound as if she does so while coolly surveying her own life from a stage-coach window. True novelists as well as true poets write about things before they happen to them—and, in Austen's case, to her family.[48] This is one of those claims for which proof is in necessarily short supply (unless, perhaps, your name is Cassandra); however, three years after 'The History of England' was written, Austen's cousin Eliza de Feuillide, who features more than once in the teenage notebooks, would learn that her French husband had been guillotined for conspiracy against the republic. Putting to one side that future 'accident' involving 'the dead Body' of a husband, the association of learning with beheading—stuffing your head full of things, only to lose it—fuels both Mrs Austen's anecdote and her daughter's brutal reimagining of Lady Jane's final display of precocity. Cassandra's head takes on a weird agency of its own, as if already operating independently of her body, when it is described as 'going to be cut off' ('going' is on the edge of meaning 'a-going', as well as something that might be about to happen).

The oddity of this phrasing, another aspect of the Austen family idiolect, has to do with the individual's perfect or imperfect control of his or her constituent body parts (a joke that may also govern the titular designation of some of the earliest works as 'Detached peices' and 'Scraps', swept up towards the end of 'Volume the First' and 'Volume the Second', *TW*, pp. 63–5, 151–7). The Austens were, as their younger daughter pointed out, 'great Novel-readers & not ashamed of being so' (to Cassandra, 18–19 Dec. 1798, *Letters*, p. 27). One of the

---

48. T. S. Eliot told William Empson 'that the test of a true poet is that he writes about experiences before they have happened to him'. William Empson, 'Donne the Space Man', *Kenyon Review*, 19 (1957), 337–99 (p. 398).

things they would have come across in fiction of the eighteenth and early nineteenth centuries was an emphasis on endurance, self-command, or self-control—as in Mary Brunton's 1811 novel of that name—in stories in which virtue and physical survival were tested well beyond the limits of plausibility. Ronald Paulson has referred to a 'breaking and remaking' aesthetic in eighteenth-century literature, Margaret Anne Doody to the young Austen as one who '"disassembles" the English novel'.[49] Read in this light, Austen's earliest writing might be understood as continuous, in its very breakages, with Swift's. Austen's fragmented novels, like Swift's satirical prose—full of hiatuses, lacunae, and interruptions—show how apparent cohesiveness can suddenly transform into sundering and wreckage, only to suffer repair once again, or at least the intention to be reassembled into something 'compleat': 'the Professor shewed me several Volumes in large Folio already collected, of broken Sentences, which he intended to piece together, and out of those rich Materials to give the World a compleat Body of Arts and Sciences'.[50]

Austen's teenage works show us a writer whose powers were engrossed by junking and rebuilding the Augustan satirical tradition, the tropes and conventions of sympathy and sensibility—and of the creakiest epistolary and sentimental fiction—as well as the upstairs-downstairs social comedy of eighteenth-century drama, the clichés of pastoral and picturesque landscape, and the poorly concealed biases of history-writing. Illness, death, and mourning are material for jokes; accidents, theft, loss, and breakage are forms of play both ruinous and law-abiding (the laws in question being those of the sentimental novel). Austen's iconoclasm flourished within a framework of domestic and familial routine. Her early writings bear out the truth of what Chesterton said of childhood, that it has 'a callousness, a carelessness, a curious combination of random and quite objectless energy with a readiness to accept conventions'.[51] Jane Austen possessed, too, an acute sense of being one of a pair—with her accomplice and only sister, Cassandra—and was keen to perform the role of duplicate or second fiddle to that older sibling as well as to stake her

49. Ronald Paulson, *Breaking and Remaking: Aesthetic Practice in England, 1700–1820* (London: Rutgers, 1989), pp. 3–5; Margaret Anne Doody, 'Jane Austen, That Disconcerting "Child"', in *The Child Writer from Austen to Woolf*, p. 112.

50. *The Cambridge Edition of the Works of Jonathan Swift*, vol. 15: *Gulliver's Travels*, ed. David Womersley (Cambridge: Cambridge University Press, 2012), vol. 3, section 5, p. 269.

51. *The Collected Works of G. K. Chesterton*, 35 vols. (Charlottesville, VA: InteLex, 2002), vol. 16: *The Autobiography of G. K. Chesterton* (1936), p. 61.

claim to originality. Assertions of sameness and difference govern her earliest surviving letters, taking fictional characters as well as friends and relatives into the fold: 'To-morrow I shall be just like Camilla in Mr. Dubster's summer-house. [...] My situation, however, is somewhat preferable to hers, for I am very happy here' (*Letters*, 1 Sept. 1796, p. 6). How to stand out from as well as blend in with a crowd might well be a question to occur to the penultimate child of a big family, especially to the younger of two sisters, born to be 'a present plaything for her sister Cassy and a future companion'[52]—or 't'other Miss Austen', as she identified herself to the superior claimant to that title in December 1798 (the two teenage stories dedicated to Cassandra address her as 'Miss Austen'; another letter to Cassandra (14–16 Jan. 1801) begins by hailing her as 'Poor Miss Austen!', *Letters*, pp. 31, 75). This keen sense of individual position within a large family in which the two girls had their own distinct relationship and identity persisted into subsequent generations; Austen's niece Catherine Hubback launched her novelistic career with a book called *The Younger Sister* (1850), dedicated 'TO THE MEMORY OF HER AUNT, THE LATE JANE AUSTEN.'[53]

The state or condition of infancy might be said to last a matter of months, or a great deal longer. It can mean 'the earliest period of human life, early childhood, babyhood' (*OED*, 'infancy', sense 1); or the legal condition of being a minor (in the eighteenth century, and in Johnson's *Dictionary*, this meant that anyone under the age of twenty-one was an 'infant'); or the second childhood that is old age (whenever that is understood to begin). For Chapone, her niece's 'fifteenth year' marked the point at which childhood ended, or ought to end: 'it is high time to store your mind with those principles, which must direct your conduct, and fix your character'. The oldest female pupil in Mrs Teachum's academy for girls is also fourteen.[54] The opposite of Baby Jane, young Austen was by her fifteenth year already an old hand at parodying such adult advice. She seems to have known and understood from a very early age what grown-ups at their worst could be and do; unlike William Wordsworth, she never showed much interest in writing about children—although she was very good at telling them stories—or in considering their experiences as

52. Rev. George Austen to his sister, 17 December 1775, in *Austen Papers 1704–1856*, pp. 32–3.

53. Mrs Hubback, *The Younger Sister: A Novel*, 3 vols. (London: Thomas Cautley Newby, 1850).

54. Chapone, *Letters on the Improvement of the Mind*, vol. 1, p. 2; Sarah Fielding, *The Governess or, Little Female Academy* [1749] (London: Oxford University Press, 1968), p. 5.

formative.[55] She had a ruthlessly foreshortened perspective in her early tales, and not only because the tales are brief. In this fictional world, things tend to happen suddenly and for no apparent reason; many people are impulsive, criminal, reckless, or violent; others are horribly ill; some of them die. Perhaps the closest that the very earliest works (in 'Volume the First') come to an analysis of motivation is in the case of 'the lovely Charlotte', who finds herself agreeing to marry a handsome stranger within moments of having consented to become the wife of a rich old man. The next day, 'the reflection of her past folly, operated so strongly on her mind, that she resolved to be guilty of a greater, and to that end threw herself into a deep stream which ran thro' her Aunts pleasure Grounds in Portland Place' ('Frederic & Elfrida', *TW*, p. 7). The combination of a suggested mental disorder (folly operating strongly on the mind) and cool calculation ('she resolved [. . .] to that end') is characteristic of a period in which fictional heroines, self-destructive or not, are presented by turns as helpless lunatics and rational agents. The first view makes them not responsible for their actions; the second renders them potentially culpable.

If the end of childhood meant, as Chapone told her niece, that character must become fixed—that the possibility of development and change was from now on to be ruled out—then in a sense for the eighteenth-century adolescent, as for Young Hamlet, '"growing up" is also growing dead'.[56] Even its richest and strangest transformations might be understood as forms of progressive immobility, as Catherine Fanshawe, that 'designer in almost every style', imagined in her parody of Wordsworth.[57] Austen may have known this poem in manuscript, since a copy of Fanshawe's 'Charade by a Lady' survives in her hand.[58] The 'Fragment in Imitation of Wordsworth' is undated and was unpublished until 1876, but its inspiration is evidently *Lyrical Ballads* (1798). The speaker, a fond father and lover of nature, rapturously envisages his young son's metamorphosis into a tree:

---

55. 'she would tell us the most delightful stories, chiefly of Fairyland, and her fairies had all characters of their own. The tale was invented, I am sure, at the moment, and was continued for two or three days, if occasion served' (*Memoir*, p. 72).

56. Barbara Everett, *Young Hamlet: Essays on Shakespeare's Tragedies* (Oxford: Clarendon Press, 1989), p. 33.

57. Mary Russell Mitford, *Recollections of a Literary Life; or, Books, Places, and People*, new edition, 2 vols. (London: Richard Bentley, 1857), vol. 1, p. 205.

58. Winchester College MS 128 A.

And I have said, my little Will,
Why should he not continue still
    A thing of Nature's rearing?
A thing beyond the world's control—
A living vegetable soul,—
    No human sorrow fearing.

It were a blessed sight to see
That child become a willow tree,
    His brother trees among
He'd be four time[s] as tall as me,
And live three times as long.[59]

Ovid's Baucis and Philemon are transformed in death into intertwining trees; Daphne becomes a laurel as the only defence against Apollo's rape. Such terrible metamorphoses have now become a fate to aspire to. The brilliant, touching absurdity of this 'Fragment' springs from the speaker's heartfelt paternal wish to see the son outstrip his father—as a tree, this child of nature would indeed escape certain kinds of control, grow taller and live longer than his sire. But who in his right mind would hope for his child to become a 'thing' or a 'vegetable'? At least one person is known to have read this poem straight: a 'distinguished friend and admirer of Wordsworth' thought the lines 'beautiful, and wondered he had never shown them to her'.[60]

Young Will, idealized among his brother trees, is one of many late eighteenth-century model children, the nature of whose exemplarity is a decidedly mixed bag. The status of a vibrant yet thing-like child of nature flourished alongside the continuing popularity of works such as *The History of Little Goody Two-Shoes* (first published in 1765), a copy of which Jane Austen owned and passed on after her death.[61] Margaret Meanwell, later known as Little Goody, embodies everything that the child of nature does not: she learns to read, becomes a teacher, escapes poverty, shares her wealth, and ends up with a fine estate and social position. Both the wild, uncultivated young protagonist 'beyond the world's control' and the dutiful, obedient child eventually

---

59. *The Literary Remains of Catherine Maria Fanshawe, with notes by the late Rev. William Harness* (London: Basil Montagu Pickering, 1876), p. 71.

60. *Literary Remains of Catherine Maria Fanshawe*, p. 71.

61. On Austen's signed copy, which is of uncertain date (possibly 1780), see *Bibliography* K13, p. 442.

crowned with worldly success present themselves as fodder for parody. But perhaps the chief distinction between Little Goody Two-Shoes and little Will is that the first tale, a *History*, is narrated in the past tense, while the second moves from the present tense to expressing, in the final stanzas, a hope for the future. The older story is analeptic, the newer one at once conditionally and boldly proleptic. This means that Fanshawe's parody is voiced in the same tense and idiom as that of Austen's dedication to Cassandra (whose name itself bears a prophetic character) of 'Kitty, or the Bower': 'the following Novel, [...] I humbly flatter myself, possesses Merit beyond any already published, or any that will ever in future appear, except such as may proceed from the pen of Your Most Grateful Humble Servant' (*TW*, p. 169).

Catherine Fanshawe was a friend of Mary Russell Mitford, whose *Recollections of a Literary Life* (1852) included many extracts from Fanshawe's verse as well as numerous reflections of her own on childhood and adolescence. Perhaps, Mitford thought, this period of life was different for girls; they were far more changeable than boys:

> It is not merely growing, boys grow;—it is positive, perplexing and perpetual change: a butterfly hath not undergone more transmogrifications in its progress through this life, than a village belle in her arrival at the age of seventeen. [...] It would be well if a country girl could stand at thirteen. Then she is charming. But the clock will move forward, and at fourteen [...] her next appearance is in the perfection of the butterfly state, fluttering, glittering, inconstant, vain,—the gayest and gaudiest insect that ever skimmed over a village green. [...] If woman be a mutable creature, man is not.[62]

Writing to Cassandra in 1811, Jane Austen's brief natural history of their eighteen-year-old niece seemed to endorse this view of the stages of 'perpetual change' in young women: 'She is quite an Anna with variations—but she cannot have reached her last, for that is always the most flourishing & shewey—she is at about her 3d or 4th which are generally simple & pretty' (*Letters*, p. 192). If all girls pass through 'a butterfly state', a period in which they are 'most flourishing & shewey', then Mitford's notorious appraisal (or rather, her mother's) of the young Austen may not be quite as damning as it appears:

---

62. Mitford, *Our Village*, vol. 2, pp. 70–73.

I have discovered that our great favourite, Miss Austen, is my countrywoman; that mamma knew all her family very intimately; and that she
herself is an old maid (I beg her pardon—I mean a young lady) with
whom mamma before her marriage was acquainted. Mamma says that she
was then the prettiest, silliest, most affected, husband-hunting butterfly
she ever remembers; and a friend of mine, who visits her now, says that
she has stiffened into the most perpendicular, precise, taciturn piece of
'single blessedness' that ever existed, and that, till 'Pride and Prejudice'
showed what a precious gem was hidden in that unbending case, she was
no more regarded in society than a poker or a fire-screen, or any other thin
upright piece of wood or iron that fills its corner in peace and quietness.
The case is very different now; she is still a poker—but a poker of whom
every one is afraid.[63]

What sort of 'case' are we encountering in this spiky, curious study of one
author by another? Mitford's appraisal of her countrywoman is built on a series of reversed expectations. Butterflies are hunted, not hunters (of husbands,
or anything else). 'That unbending case'—evoking the kind of reversion
whereby a butterfly has folded itself up into a chrysalis, or indeed 'an old maid'
has turned back into 'a young lady'—seems to refer to the external Austen, the
case or carcass (often, in this period, spelt 'carcase') that encloses a secret.
(Mitford writes elsewhere of a shoemaker's daughter, aged between fourteen
and a half and sixteen years old and 'a notable exemplification of the develope-
ment which I have already noticed amongst our young things', that 'she is in
the real transition state, just emerging from the chrysalis'.)[64] The second 'case'
mentioned in *The Life of Mary Russell Mitford* places Miss Austen within a set
of circumstances, makes of her a different kind of case, according to which she
has become public property.

Austen's transformation from butterfly to poker, from teenage years to
middle age, from a restless living creature to a static and lifeless domestic uten-
sil, is followed by another change—consequent on the discovery of her authorship, and according to which her own unmasking is bound up with her
novelistic unmasking of others. The just reward for her apparent revelation to
the world of otherwise obscure villagers—people understood as individual

---

63. *The Life of Mary Russell Mitford*, vol. 1, pp. 305–6. Mitford does immediately strike a note
of caution: 'I do not know that I can quite vouch for this account'.

64. Mitford, *Our Village*, vol. 1, pp. 281–2.

cases, and not as general fictional types—is to lose her own obscurity. The feeling that Austen had portrayed the truths of everyday life, and ordinary people as they really existed, was pervasive years before she died. For her contemporaries, as for many more recent critics, a natural extension of sensing about her characters that 'you actually <u>live</u> with them' was the belief that, in fact, she *did* live with them. Miss Isabella Herries, so Austen recorded, was 'convinced that I had meant M^rs. & Miss Bates for some acquaintance of theirs—People whom I never heard of before' ('Opinions of Mansfield Park and Opinions of Emma' (1816–7), *JAFM*, vol. 4, pp. 327, 333). Mitford, another home counties writer who herself composed 'the history, half real, and half imaginary, of a half imaginary and half real little spot on the sunny side of Berkshire', was a local competitor on this score (they also shared a birthday), one who had good reason to reduce the scope of Austen's naturalism to mere unscrupulous copying of her immediate environment.[65] From having been a poker that is merely ignored, Austen therefore becomes cast as a poker that is noticed only because it is feared. She does not screen the fire: she stokes the flames. The sense of Jane Austen or her writing as quite another kind of object—one that might be found in Thomas Gray's *Elegy Wrote in a Country Churchyard* (1751)—is raised, but left undeveloped. It is that of 'a precious gem [. . .] hidden':[66]

> This Hampshire parson's daughter had found the philosopher's stone of the novel: and the very pots and pans, the tongs and pokers of the house, could be turned into novel-gold by it.[67]

65. *Our Village*, vol. 5, p. 3.

66. 'Full many a Gem of purest Ray serene, / The dark unfathom'd Caves of Ocean bear: / Full many a Flower is born to blush unseen, / And waste its Sweetness on the desart air'. [Thomas Gray], *Elegy Wrote in a Country Churchyard* (London: R. Dodsley, 1751), ll. 53–6 (p. 8).

67. George Saintsbury, *The English Novel* (London: J. M. Dent & Sons Ltd; New York: E. P. Dutton & Co., 1913), p. 201.

4

Dying with Laughter

REVIEWING JAMES EDWARD AUSTEN-LEIGH's *Memoir* of his aunt in 1870, Richard Simpson discerned in Jane Austen 'the highest exercise of the critical faculty' matched by 'a notable deficiency in the poetical faculty'. 'Perhaps', he ventured to suggest, 'there is no author in existence in whom so marvellous a power of exhibiting characters in formation and action is combined with so total a want of the poetical imagination'. This seemingly lopsided combination of strength and weakness he later modified into the claim that Austen 'was just so far a poet as a critic might be expected to be'; on this view of things, the critical aspect of her genius would have been compromised by a more developed or equiponderant poetic talent (had she chosen, or indeed been able, to cultivate it).[1] Hence her relatively successful efforts in the genres of short, pointed epigrams, charades, and jests, forms of writing which her contemporary novelist Thomas Love Peacock might have denominated 'critico-poetical'. Peacock is the only source given in the *OED* for this portmanteau term—his triple-decker fiction of 1817, *Melincourt*, contains a reference to 'The members of the criticopoetical council'—but he did not in fact coin it.[2] Volume 66 of the *Gentleman's Magazine* (1789) includes a letter from 'SPICILE-GUS' referring sardonically to the 'critico-poetical' character of Dr Joseph Warton. The label is given by way of preliminary castigation for Warton's 'sins of partiality, [. . .] ignorance, carelessness, and error' in his *Essay on the Genius*

---

1. Richard Simpson in *Jane Austen: The Critical Heritage*, vol. 1, pp. 243–4.

2. 'critico-, *comb. form*' (*OED*). 'Critico-poetical' is the earliest of the combined forms noted here; 'critico' is also said to be a 'base for nonce-words'. All the examples given in the *OED* date from the nineteenth century, but there are combinations with 'critico-' which clearly pre-date these texts. See for example the '*Critico-comical Reflections*' in *A History of the Ridiculous Extravagancies of Monsieur Oufle* (London: J. Morphew, 1711), pp. 100, 163, 164.

and Writings of Pope (1756–82), sins wilfully cultivated by Austen the teenage historian.[3] 'Critico-' denominates a narrowly specialist, pedantic, and blinkered kind of writer, someone who (like Samuel Johnson's Dick Minim in *The Idler* (1758–60)) is both vain and professionally nice: accurate within an extremely contracted sphere, and ignorant of the world beyond it.[4] Such a character description sounds overwhelmingly negative, but Austen might be said to have claimed it as her own and made it triumph. Her novels, like her earliest writings, are a form of local history. They occasionally make a virtue of ignorance, and they both exemplify attention to detail and send up pedantry—as in the opening scene of *Persuasion*, in which Sir Walter is shown reading the Baronetage's dates and information about his own family, and enters his corrections 'most accurately' into the prized book (vol. 1, ch. 1, p. 3).

Had Simpson been able to read more of Austen's unpublished manuscripts in 1870, it is doubtful that he would have revised his opinion of the distribution of critical and poetical talents in his subject. But he would at least have had a much greater sample of evidence on which to base his judgement, and he might have considered it worth mentioning that Austen's last known composition was a poem. Henry Austen had included in his 1817 biographical notice of his sister what their family considered an unlucky incidental reference to Jane Austen's deathbed lines on Winchester Races (*Memoir*, p. 138). Despite this reference, Austen's twentieth-century editor R. W. Chapman considered the verse unlikely to be hers.[5] He may have been misled in part because, by

3. The *Gentleman's Magazine*, 66 (1789), p. 890. Warton published *An Essay on the Writings and Genius of Pope* in 1756; a second volume appeared, and was published alongside the first, in 1782. In some editions the title is given as *An Essay on the Genius and Writings of Pope*.

4. See *Idler* nos. 60 and 61, in *The Yale Edition of the Works of Samuel Johnson*, vol. 2: *The Idler and the Adventurer*, eds. W. J. Bate, John M. Bullitt, and L. F. Powell (New Haven, CT, and London: Yale University Press, 1963), pp. 184–93.

5. Chapman gave the poem the title 'Venta'. He noted 'a presumption that the verses are [Austen's]', but remarked that 'it does not seem probable that she could have composed four-and-twenty lines of verse within three days of her death. There is a possibility that the lines are in the hand of James Austen and were composed by him. [. . .] The authors of *Jane Austen's Sailor Brothers* (1906, p. 272) published the verses as hers. But it may be significant that the authors of the 1870 *Memoir* and of the *Life*, 1913, all of whom had access to this collection, ignored them'. In a subsequent postscript, Chapman remarked that 'In writing this note I strangely overlooked the evidence of Henry Austen's *Biographical Notice*. [. . .] That no doubt settles the question'. *The Works of Jane Austen*, ed. R. W. Chapman, vol. 6: *Minor Works. Now first collected and edited from the manuscripts*, rev. edition (1987), p. 451.

1833, allusion to the Winchester poem had been excised from Henry Austen's revised notice, probably at the instigation of James Austen's children James Edward and Caroline. Why did this final work cause such disquiet that it remained unpublished until 1906?

Jane Austen's very last composition is also something of a fresh start. Both retrospective and prophetic, the poem has an overdetermined initial line: 'When Winchester races first took their beginning'.[6] This conversational pleonasm ('first' as well as 'beginning') has endured: people continue habitually to refer to having 'first started' something. 'Took their beginning', though, sounds odd to a modern ear: while 'making a start' remains a common figure of speech, 'taking a beginning' does not. But there are many eighteenth-century precedents for Austen's way of putting it, especially in historical and antiquarian accounts of the origins of certain disciplines, customs, and institutions: 'Vitruvius tells us, that Architecture took its Beginning from wooden Porticoes'; 'As to the original of this ancient Order [. . .] it took its beginning from a bright cross in Heaven'; 'Then it was those famous Factions first took their Beginning'.[7] If Austen had read John Milner's *History Civil and Ecclesiastical, & Survey of the Antiquities, of Winchester* (1798–1801)—it is the kind of book she sometimes liked to read—she would have come across the same wording there: 'It will be asked, Where then is this celebrated post from which the kingdom of West Saxons took its beginning?'[8] Perhaps 'took' further suggested itself to her because the 'beginning' that is narrated in the poem is something akin to taking a liberty. This mode of beginning further implies

6. Quotations from the poem are from the text as reproduced in *The Cambridge Edition of the Works of Jane Austen: Later Manuscripts*, ed. Janet Todd and Linda Bree (2008), p. 255, which takes as its copytext the fair copy in Cassandra Austen's hand now held by the Jane Austen Memorial Trust at Chawton. I also refer to variant readings in another manuscript of the poem, held by the Henry W. and Albert A. Berg collection at the New York Public Library.

7. James Anderson, *The Constitutions of the Antient and Honourable Fraternity of Free and Accepted Masons* (London: Brother J. Scott, 1756), p. 153; Hugh Clark, *A Concise History of Knighthood*, 2 vols. (London: W. Strahan, J. F. and C. Rivington, T. Payne, etc. 1784), vol. 1, p. 123; John Bancks, *The History of the House of Austria, and the German Empire: containing the Germanick constitution, and an account of all their emperors* (London: [n. p.], 1743), p. 16.

8. Rev. John Milner, *The History Civil and Ecclesiastical, & Survey of the Antiquities, of Winchester*, 2 vols. (Winchester: Jas. Robbins; London: Cadell and Davies, etc., 1798–1801), vol. 1, p. 66. On Austen's reading of civil and religious history, see for example her letter to Martha Lloyd (12–13 Nov. 1800) on Robert Henry's *History of Great Britain* (1771–93), and to Cassandra (24 Jan. 1813) mentioning the 'extraordinary force and spirit' of C. W. Pasley's *Essay on the Military Policy and Institutions of the British Empire* (1810), *Letters*, pp. 61–2, 207. See also chapter 5.

speed: taking off, as in a race, before time runs out; perhaps also an element of choice (as in 'took its origin from').

Winchester Races, the poem announces, were rashly instituted. In their haste to enjoy themselves, 'the good people' of the town 'forgot' to beg 'the leave of St Swithin' to do so (Austen was always interested in proper versus inadequate preparations). The fourteenth-century bishop of Winchester to whom they did remember to apply, William of Wykeham, offers approval that is no more than 'faint' (ll. 1–4). The races proceed regardless, and all seems well: 'The company met & the weather was charming / The Lords & the Ladies were sattin'd & ermin'd / And nobody saw any future alarming' (ll. 6–8). But St Swithin, 'informed of these doings', bounds from his shrine to the top of the ruined bishops' palace, from which elevation he castigates his 'subjects rebellious' for their sin and vice, and pronounces a 'curse' on their 'pleasures' (ll. 9–19). The races will never be dry: 'The curse upon Venta is July in showers' (l. 24). In a letter to Cassandra of 11–12 October 1813, as the Cambridge editors of her *Later Manuscripts* note, Austen had expressed a related concern about weather conditions at the races:[9]

> Monday, Nov:ʳ 15ᵗʰ is the day now fixed for our setting out.—Poor Basingstoke Races!—there seem to have been two particularly wretched days on purpose for them;—& Weyhill week does not begin much happier. (*Letters*, p. 243)

The oddly pathetic terms ('Poor', 'particularly wretched', 'not . . . much happier') in which she describes that weather are suggestive of the origins of the idea that governs the Winchester Races poem. Rain is in both cases conceived as being unleashed 'on purpose'—by someone, or something—to spoil enjoyments that, in the last poem, are directly presented as 'rebellious' and therefore rightly incurring punishment (perhaps Basingstoke was at the back of Austen's mind when she described the feckless gambler Tom Bertram leaving home to watch a horse he has running in 'B—races': 'Much was said on his side to induce [Miss Crawford] to attend the races, and schemes were made for a large party to them, with all the eagerness of inclination, but it would only do to be talked of' (*MP*, vol. 1, ch. 5, p. 56).[10] In fiction, court depositions, and at least one jest book of the late eighteenth century, Winchester Races figure as the

9. *Later Manuscripts*, p. 738.
10. John Wiltshire points out that, if Austen is thinking of towns 'within reasonable distance of Northampton', she could mean Banbury, Bedford, or Buckingham (*MP*, p. 651 n.).

backdrop to flirtation, elopements, teenage marriages, crude jokes, and carousing. It is easy to see why Austen might have associated such a scene with illicit pleasure.[11] Other phrasal resemblances between her letter of 1813 and her last composition suggest a particular cast of mind, too: 'the day now *fixed* for our setting out' before the turn to 'Poor Basingstoke Races!' anticipates the last poem's shift from 'The races however were *fix'd* & determin'd' (l. 5) to 'The curse upon Venta is July in showers' (l. 24) (my emphases).

This last poem is about remaining firm on the one hand and giving way on the other: St Swithin, standing aloof, may resist 'dissolute measures', but he also determines to 'Let them stand'. The lines are both historical and mock-historical, made up like a composite of bits and pieces of evidence and hearsay about Winchester past and present, and taking off from that realm into differently 'made up' terrain, that of fantasy. This is also in more than one sense an occasional poem, taking its cue from a specific date, place, and event (the steeplechase races at Worthy Down, three miles outside Winchester, were advertised in the *Hampshire Chronicle and Courier* on Monday, 14 July 1817; by the time they began, just over two weeks later, Austen was dead).[12] Because of the circumstances in which the text came into being, it is charged with mysterious import. The lines survive in two manuscript versions, neither of them in Jane Austen's hand (although her initials are at the bottom of one text). It is not certain which version was written down first or by whom. Prime candidates for having completed the transcription now held in the Berg Collection and reproduced here must be Cassandra and Mary Austen (formerly Mary Lloyd, by now wife of James Austen), both of whom attended Jane Austen in her last days, but the large writing does not look like that of either woman. Nor would Cassandra have been likely, even in a state of exhaustion and distress, to misspell 'William' or to have twice put an 'r' on the end of 'Venta' (as if to anglicize the Latin name for Winchester, deriving from the Celtic word for 'market', into a place akin to the Isle of Wight resort town of Ventnor). The Cambridge editors of Austen's later manuscripts suggest that a friend rather than a relative might have taken down the lines at her dictation,

11. See for example [William Jackson], *The New and Complete Newgate Calendar; or, Villany* [sic] *Displayed in All its Branches*, 6 vols. (London: Alex. Hogg, [1795]), vol. 5, p. 198; Marmaduke Momus, *The Jolly Jester; or The Wit's Complete Library* (London: W. and J. Stratford, 1794), p. 23; *The Posthumous Daughter: A Novel*, 2 vols. (London: G. Cawthorn, 1797), vol. 1, p. 155.

12. 'WINCHESTER RACES', *Hampshire Chronicle and Courier* (Monday, 14 July 1817), p. 1, column 2.

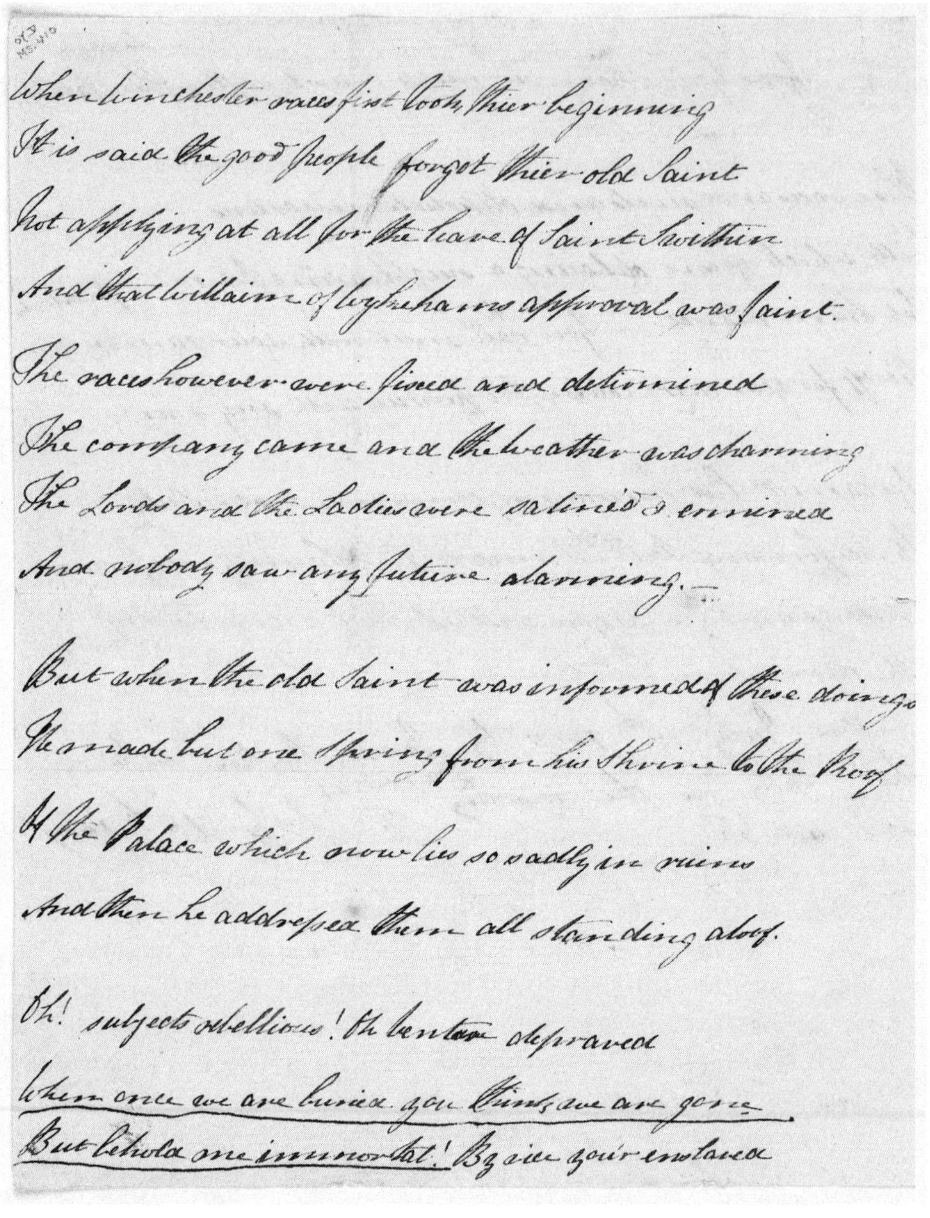

When Winchester races first took thier beginning
It is said the good people forgot thier old Saint
Not applying at all for the leave of Saint Swithin
And that William of Wykehams approval was faint.

The races however were fixed and determined
The company came and the weather was charming
The Lords and the Ladies were satine'd & ermined
And nobody saw any future alarming.—

But when the old Saint was informed of these doings
He made but one Spring from his shrine to the roof
Of the Palace which now lies so sadly in ruins
And then he addressed them all standing aloof.

Oh! subjects rebellious! Oh Venta depraved
When once we are buried you think we are gone
But behold me immortal! By vice you're enslaved

FIGURE 6. Jane Austen, Lines on Winchester Races. MS 209715B (No. 410–12). The Henry W. and Albert A. Berg Collection of English and American Literature, The New York Public Library, Astor, Lenox, and Tilden Foundations.

he said

Your Your'e have sinned & must suffer, Then farther

These baus and revels and dissolute measures
With which you're debasing a neighbouring Plain
Let them stand — You'll meet with your curse in your
pleasure
Set off for your curse course, I'll pursue with my rain.

Ye cannot but know my command o'er July
Henceforward I'll triumph in shewing my powers
Shift your race as you will it shall never be dry
The curse upon Venta is July in showers —

written July 15th 1817. by Jane Austen who
died early in the morning (12 rent 4)
aged 41 yrs. of July 18th 1817

and that 'Ventar' could have been 'written by someone ignorant of Latin listening to a speaker with a Hampshire accent which would lengthen and soften the last syllable'.[13] Other mistakes in the transcription include 'thier' for 'their', 'you'r' for 'you're', and 'You've' for 'You'. Perhaps the lines were written down by another member of the Winchester household—a servant or housekeeper?—rather than by a friend or relative, while Cassandra and Mary Austen were temporarily absent. The date of the poem and its ascription to Jane Austen at the end of the manuscript are written in another hand, different from that of the poem itself. This may or may not be the same hand as that which underlined one and a half lines in the verse.

We do know that the poem was composed in College Street, Winchester, on St Swithin's Day, Tuesday, 15 July 1817, three days before Austen died, when she was presumably too weak to do anything other than dictate her composition. St Swithin or Swithun was Anglo-Saxon bishop of Winchester from 852 until his death in 863 and subsequently patron saint of Winchester Cathedral, where Austen like Swithin was buried. It is the place of his interment, rather than horse racing (which began in Winchester in the seventeenth century), that is proverbially said to have caused the rain.[14] Swithin had insisted in no uncertain terms that he be buried outside, in front of the west door of the Saxon Old Minster, exposed to the footsteps of the townspeople and to the elements. When, in the next century, his remains were dug up and taken indoors, it was the first of several such removals into ever grander settings. Perhaps it was the striking mobility of his bones that led Austen to imagine him jumping from one ecclesiastical abode to another.[15] A great storm was apparently provoked on the date of his shrine's consecration—15 July—by Swithin's anger at the contravention of his wishes. Hence, according to tradition, if it rains on Saint Swithin's bridge in Winchester on his feast day, it will continue to do so for forty days.[16]

---

13. 'Introduction', *Later Manuscripts*, p. cix.

14. As the Cambridge editors note, the proverb is itself in the form of verse, which may have prompted Austen's elected form: 'St Swithin's day, if thou dost rain / For forty days it will remain; / St Swithin's day, if thou be fair / For forty days 'twill rain nae mair' (*Later Manuscripts*, p. 740).

15. John Milner writes of St Swithin that his remains were 'so often translated and moved'. *The History . . . of Winchester*, vol. 2, p. 68.

16. See A. R. Wright, *British Calendar Customs*, ed. T. E. Jones, 3 vols. (London: William Glaisher Ltd; Glasgow: John Wylie & Co. for the Folk-Lore Society, 1936–1940), vol. 3: *Fixed*

The disconcerting Winchester lines have several things in common with at least one other *jeu d'esprit* by Jane Austen. First, a newspaper article as the likely trigger to composition; second, a tripping, anapaestic measure; third, an utterly irreverent attitude both to aristocracy and to mortality; and, fourth, a joke about jumping (which Austen seems throughout her life to have found hilarious). Five years earlier, she had written a verse quatrain in response to an announcement of the forthcoming nuptials of the middle-aged Miss Urania Catharine Camilla Wallop (the order of her first names varies in different accounts, but she was one year older than Austen) and an elderly clergyman, the Rev. Mr Wake:

> Camilla, good humoured, & merry, & small
> For a Husband was at her last stake;
> And having in vain danced at many a Ball
> Is now happy to jump at a Wake.[17]

'At her last stake' suggests gambling, and that this marriage is Miss Wake's final roll of the dice. Camilla was a popular name among what Austen referred to in a letter of 1805 as 'the Wallop Race', Wallop being the surname of the earls of Portsmouth (*Letters*, 8–11 April 1805, p. 106). The name Camilla may have been associated in her mind not only with Burney's novel of that title, but also with a speedy and possibly 'dissolute' poetic 'measure' (if so, the fact that *Camilla* is such a long and slow-moving book would be a joke in itself). In the *Essay on Criticism*, Alexander Pope's example of how fast a poetic line might be made to go is exemplified by 'swift *Camilla*', who 'scours the plain, / Flies o'er th'unbending corn, and skims along the main'.[18]

'Her looks altered', wrote Cassandra Austen of her sister's last days, '& she fell away' (*Letters*, 20 July 1817, p. 359.) The feminine ending, Christopher Ricks argues, 'naturally evokes a dying fall or courage in the face either of death or loss, something falling poignantly away'.[19] In the lines on Winchester Races, dictated by a dying woman, there is in the use of rhymed and softly half-rhymed

---

Festivals (1940), pp. 33–5; John Milner, *The History . . : of Winchester*, vol. 2, pp. 7–12; *Later Manuscripts*, pp. 739–40

17. *Collected Poems*, pp. 16–17 (and p. 85). See also *Letters*, p. 205 and n. 7.

18. *The Twickenham Edition of the Poems of Alexander Pope*, vol. 1: *Pastoral Poetry, and, An Essay on Criticism*, ed. E. Audra and Aubrey Williams (London: Methuen & Co.; New Haven, CT: Yale University Press, 1961), *Essay on Criticism*, ll. 372–3.

19. Christopher Ricks, *Dylan's Visions of Sin* (London: Viking, 2003), p. 222.

unstressed final syllables ('beginning' / 'Swithun'; 'charming' / 'alarming'; 'doings' / 'ruins'; 'measures' / 'pleasures'; 'powers' / 'showers') a comparable effect to that identified by Ricks. At once bracing, jaunty, and forgiving, these endings are compounded by the gerunds—and their dying fall—that occur within lines: 'Not applying', 'debasing', 'shewing', and (as an adjective) 'neighbouring'. Austen's brother Henry rightly discerned the author's 'fancy and vigour' rather than any fading inventiveness or loss of energy in the composition (*Memoir*, p. 138). But it is also true that St Swithin—whose name probably derives from the Old English word for 'strong'—has 'powers' that are eventually expressed in nothing more devastating than the mild form of 'showers'. The formidable threat to sinners declared in the poem is dissipated at its close into what might even be tears of remembrance, a penance exacted for having 'forgot' the 'old Saint' (l. 2). In the annual return of rain or shower, St Swithin and Jane Austen will be called back to mind.

Did Austen perhaps know at this point, or suspect, that she would be buried in Winchester Cathedral, 'a Building she admir'd so much' (Cassandra Austen, *Letters*, 20 July 1817, p. 361)?[20] If so, could she already have been identifying herself with its patron saint as a soon-to-be neighbour? Saint Swithin was bound up with the beginning and middle of her life, as well as with its ending: in 1764, her parents were married at St Swithin's Church in Walcot, Bath, and her father was buried there in 1805. David Selwyn, editor of Austen's poems, remarks of the lines on Winchester Races that

> The shift in tone from the mock-social ('the weather was charming') to the comically melodramatic leads to a resolution of the old Saint's curse in nothing more terrible than 'July in showers'. Is it possible that something else was being resolved here? Those who, 'by vice . . . enslaved', have 'sinn'd . . . must suffer'; yet the 'curse' they will meet 'in [their] pleasures' is only rain—'the gentle rain from heaven', perhaps?[21]

Selwyn is presumably discerning in the poem Austen's sense of her own sin and suffering; the possibility of her being forgiven for the former and released from the latter. We might indeed approach this poem as a sort of verse

---

20. 'College Street, where she died, was in the parish of St Swithun-upon-Kingsgate, which had no burial ground of its own; but as this little church was associated with the nearby Cathedral, its parishioners would be buried in either the Cathedral graveyard or in the Cathedral itself' (*Letters*, p. 361 n. 6).

21. *Collected Poems*, p. 85.

autobiography, a feminine ending of another kind, according to which Austen's literary career could be understood as a race conducted without due preparation and exhibiting that 'latent strain of impetuosity' noted in her family.[22]

Whoever roughly underlined the words (in the version of the Winchester poem held in the Berg Collection) '<u>When once we are buried you think we are gone / But behold me Immortal!</u>' is likely to have thought of them as an authorial reference to Jane Austen's afterlife—perhaps in manuscript and print, as well as in heaven. Someone who has left evidence of his or her life in the form of imaginative composition, after all, is not 'gone' in the same way that other people are, and that person's immortality may accordingly be construed in terms other than—or as well as—the Christian. A further striking aspect of that word 'gone' is that it is used in place of the fair copy's 'dead'. 'Dead' is what the rhyme with 'said', two lines later, appears to call for. So is that word in the fair copy a correction of what was originally, when Austen dictated it, the more periphrastic, euphemistic 'gone'? Was that word 'gone', as the Cambridge editors suggest, 'a black joke between dying author and amanuensis'?[23] If so, what kind of joke would it be? Even if 'dead' works as a rhyme, it is also redundant in terms of sense. We would naturally assume that someone who is buried is also dead, and the next line does not contradict that assumption. You can die, and then prove to be immortal. So the meaning of the Berg version of the line— 'You think the buried are <u>gone</u>, but you're wrong'—is superior to that of the fair copy: 'You think the buried are <u>dead</u>, but they aren't'. For the author to be chasing a rhyme with 'said' would be a bit odd, too, given that the half-line that concludes with that word is itself a kind of padding: 'Then further he said' is scarcely climactic. But perhaps the erosion of strength, the loss of power, is itself partly the point. It would make sense to consider the poem as a series of rallies and relapses.

A related question concerns how we should read the line 'And nobody saw any future alarming', when three days later its author was dead. Is this too a joke of some sort, or did Austen think at this point that her future might not be as alarming as had been feared? To entertain such questions about her last known work of imagination is also to ask about her first. Might this last work be returning to the atmosphere of her earliest writings, in which characters who behave badly—who take 'dissolute measures' and live wholly for their own 'pleasures'—are repeatedly let off the hook? Several critics have discerned

---

22. On 'the latent strain of impetuosity in the Austens', see *Family Record* (p. 128).

23. 'Introduction', *Later Manuscripts*, p. cix.

in the freakish and satirical elements of Austen's teenage compositions resemblances to her final writings—'Sanditon', as well as this poem. In the early works, characters throw themselves, their clothes, or their children into streams, out of windows, and in front of other people. Are these inventions the ancestors of Austen's Swithin, and of his 'one spring from the shrine to the roof'? There is a sudden defiance of convention and authority common to first and last things. In a letter from her Winchester lodgings to her nephew James Edward, claiming that 'I am gaining strength very fast', Austen is already working this vein. If the doctor cannot restore her to health, she writes, she will protest to the Cathedral authorities: 'Mr Lyford says he will cure me, & if he fails I shall draw up a Memorial & lay it before the Dean & Chapter, & have no doubt of redress from that Pious, Learned & disinterested Body' (to James Edward Austen-Leigh, 27 May 1817, *Letters*, p. 357). By a 'Memorial' Austen ostensibly means a petition or remonstrance, submitted to the Dean and Chapter of Winchester. But the dark joke here is that she will only need to present such a document if she is not cured. In that case, she will die, and the proposed Cathedral 'Memorial' takes on a different meaning entirely, shifting from the combative to the pitiful. The word possesses a special charge in the context of a letter addressed to the relative who would decades later compose a *Memoir* of his aunt.

The gallows humour that Austen delighted in showing off in her early tales and correspondence was honed at the Abbey School in Reading, as she recalled on 1 September 1796, telling Cassandra: 'The letter which I have this moment received from you has diverted me beyond moderation. I could die of laughter at it, as they used to say at school. You are indeed the finest comic writer of the present age' (*Letters*, p. 5). But there was a deeply felt point in their screaming with laughter about dying from a joke. It was bound up with the Austen sisters' consciousness of being two unmarried girls and then two prematurely middle-aged spinsters, as well as with the lurid scenarios of love and loss contained in the teenage works, when marriage and (possibly fatal) childbirth loomed as prospects for the author and her sibling collaborator. Deathbed skits and dramatic final lines of advice such as appear in tales including 'Love and Friendship' and 'A beautiful description of the different effects of Sensibility on different Minds' are in a sense trial runs for dying. These writings are both very early (the works of a teenager) and very late (imagining the end of a life). At the age of forty-one, in Winchester, Jane Austen lay both punning and expiring, nursed by her sister-in-law and her sister. Cassandra Austen wrote that, after she had nipped into town to complete an errand, 'I sat close to her with a pillow in my lap to assist in supporting her head, which was almost off the bed, for six hours' and 'When I asked her if there was any thing she wanted, her answer was she wanted nothing but death' (*Letters*, 20 July 1817, pp. 360–1; see also *Memoir*, p. 138). The teenage Austen had imagined her own version of that scene:

> The lovely Sisters are much to be pitied. Julia is ever lamenting the situation of her friend, while lying behind her pillow & supporting her head—Maria more mild in her greif talks of going to Town next week, and Anna is always recurring to the pleasures we once enjoyed when Melissa was well.—I am usually at the fire cooking some little delicacy for the unhappy invalid—Perhaps hashing up the remains of an old Duck, toasting some cheese or making a Curry which are the favourite dishes of our poor friend.—In these situations we were this morning surprized by receiving a visit from Dr. Dowkins; 'I am come to see Melissa,' said he. 'How is She?' 'Very weak indeed,' said the fainting Melissa—'Very weak,' replied the punning Doctor, 'aye indeed it is more than a very *week* since you have taken to your bed—How is your appetite?' 'Bad, very bad,' said Julia. 'That *is* very bad'—replied he; 'Are her spirits good, Madam?' 'So poorly, Sir, that we are obliged to strengthen her with cordials every Minute.'—'Well then she receives *Spirits* from your being with her. Does she sleep?' 'Scarcely ever.'—'And Ever Scarcely, I suppose, when she does. Poor thing! Does she think of dieing?' 'She has not strength to think at all.' 'Nay, then she cannot think to have Strength.' (*TW*, pp. 63–4)

The kind of set-piece 'description' that young Austen is spoofing was meant to present the reader with a striking and engaging tableau, typically one that involved extreme states of emotional and physical suffering. The genre was designed to cultivate the sensibility and sympathy of those who encountered it. Her authorial, housekeeping 'I' stands a little to the side, cooking and observing the scene of composed loveliness that is virtue in distress, along with all the mundane duties and dreams of another world—full of clothes shops, rather than of salvation—that accompany human suffering. The varieties of repetition and rehashing that occur at the culinary level, even in this short sketch or 'beautiful description', play out with equally skilled economy on the literary plane. Take that reference to 'making a Curry' for the ailing Maria. The culinary aspect of the quip is that this spicy dish will hardly suit the delicate stomach of an invalid. But like Dr Dowkins, who enjoys reversing the order of words for a cheap thrill ('Scarcely ever' / 'Ever Scarcely'; 'strength to think' /

'think to have Strength'; you can hear the strained laughter in the sick chamber), Austen is also flipping a joke made in another of her early works, 'The Visit' (c. 1789–90), in which a soothing drink, fit for a querulous invalid such as *Emma*'s Mr Woodhouse, is served up to a young, healthy woman (*TW*, p. 47). Such deft reversals show how quickly she learnt the formulas of comic writing. They also underline the aptitude of Austen's last composition, at death's door, having been a joke.

Doubling, and doubling up with laughter, may be acts of solicitude and kindness; they can shield friends and relatives from blows, or take on the burden of their grief. An excruciating pun is, in these circumstances, palliative treatment of sorts. Cassandra's letter to her niece Fanny Knight about the death of Jane Austen begins 'My dearest Fanny—doubly dear to me now for her dear sake whom we have lost' (*Letters*, 20 July 1817, p. 359), before going on to thank that niece for writing funny letters when she did not feel like being funny at all. The repeated 'dear', uniting the dead and the living, combines with the identification, in Fanny, of a new 'double' for Jane or perhaps for Cassandra, until now for most of her life one of two sisters and almost always either with or writing to the younger and sillier one. In this letter, Cassandra goes on to say:

> I <u>have</u> lost a treasure, such a Sister, such a friend as never can have been surpassed,—She was the sun of my life, the gilder of every pleasure, the soother of every sorrow, I had not a thought concealed from her, & it is as if I had lost a part of myself. I loved her only too well, not better than she deserved, but I am conscious that my affection for her made me sometimes unjust to & negligent of others, & I can acknowledge, more than as a general principle, the justice of the hand which has struck this blow. (*Letters*, 20 July 1817, pp. 359–60)

Before dismissing the argument that divine justice killed Jane Austen at forty-one in order to teach her sister Cassandra how to be a better person, we might recall the death of Sophia in another letter, a fictional one from 'Love and Friendship', which contains a version of the same moral:

> Alas! my fears were but too fully justified; she grew gradually worse—& I daily became more alarmed for her.—At length she was obliged to confine herself solely to the Bed allotted us by our worthy Landlady—. Her disorder turned to a galloping Consumption and in a few Days carried her off. Amidst all my Lamentations for her (& violent you may suppose they were) I yet received some consolation in the reflection of my having paid every

Attention to her that could be offered, in her illness. I had wept over her every Day—had bathed her sweet face with my tears & had pressed her fair Hands continually in mine—. 'My beloved Laura (said she to me a few Hours before she died) take warning from my unhappy End & avoid the imprudent conduct which had occasioned it . . . Beware of fainting-fits. . . . Though at the time they may be refreshing & Agreable yet beleive me they will in the end, if too often repeated & at improper seasons, prove destructive to your Constitution . . . My fate will teach you this . . . I die a Martyr to my greif for the loss of Augustus . . . One fatal swoon has cost me my Life . . . Beware of swoons Dear Laura. . . . A frenzy fit is not one quarter so pernicious; it is an exercise to the Body & if not too violent, is I dare say conducive to Health in its consequences—Run mad as often as you chuse; but do not faint—'.

These were the last words she ever addressed to me . . . It was her dieing Advice to her afflicted Laura, who has ever most faithfully adhered to it. (*TW*, pp. 89–90: ellipses in the original)

'My fears were but too fully justified', says Laura; 'I can acknowledge, more than as a general principle, the justice of the Hand which has struck this blow', says Cassandra. Cassandra Austen's letter is concerned with the mysteries of non-human justice, whereas Laura's is (as ever) entirely concerned with justifying herself. But in their own ways both letters observe the 'daily' and rapid decline of a beloved friend, and try to tell someone else what it might mean and how that death could serve as an example to the living. To borrow the terms suggested by 'Sanditon', one version of this scene is 'very amusing', while the other is 'very melancholy, just as Satire or Morality might prevail' (*JAFM*, vol. 5, p. 153). Laura consoles herself with fantasies of having tenderly cared for her friend by watering her face with tears and pressing her hands; Cassandra Austen was able more rationally to reflect on having performed a genuine service of love: 'I thank God that I was enabled to attend her to the last & amongst my many causes of self-reproach I have not to add any wilfull neglect of her comfort' (20 July 1817, *Letters*, p. 360).

After the last words, there is a body to deal with—one of those inconvenient truths about people and their remains that the sublime Laura simply ignores, side-stepping Sophia's darling corpse just as she has championed, earlier in the tale, the view that love need not descend to the material niceties of eating and drinking (*TW*, p. 75). Cassandra, by contrast, tells her niece what will happen to what is left of Jane Austen:

The last sad ceremony is to take place on Thursday morning, her dear remains are to be deposited in the Cathedral—it is a satisfaction to me to think that they are to lie in a Building she admird so much—her precious soul I presume to hope reposes in a far superior Mansion. May mine one day be reunited to it.—(*Letters*, 20 July 1817, p. 361)

The question what to do with remains preoccupies several loony yet mundane characters in the teenage writings. It is something that Charlotte Luttrell, heroine of 'Lesley-Castle', cannot stop thinking, talking, and writing about:

I have a thousand excuses to beg for having so long delayed thanking you my dear Peggy for your agreable Letter, which beleive me I should not have deferred doing, had not every moment of my time during the last five weeks been so fully employed in the necessary arrangements for my sisters Wedding, as to allow me no time to devote either to you or myself. And now what provokes me more than any thing else is that the Match is broke off, and all my Labour thrown away: Imagine how great the Dissapointment must be to me, when you consider that after having laboured both by Night and by Day, in order to get the Wedding dinner ready by the time appointed, after having roasted Beef, Broiled Mutton, and Stewed Soup enough to last the new-married Couple through the Honey-moon, I had the mortification of finding that I had been Roasting, Broiling and Stewing both the Meat and Myself to no purpose. Indeed my dear Freind, I never remember suffering any vexation equal to what I experienced on last Monday when my Sister came running to me in the Store-room with her face as White as a Whipt syllabub, and told me that Hervey had been thrown from his Horse, had fractured his Scull and was pronounced by his Surgeon to be in the most emminent Danger.

'Good God! (said I) you dont say so? why what in the name of Heaven will become of all the Victuals! We shall never be able to eat it while it is good. However, we'll call in the Surgeon to help us—. I shall be able to manage the Sir-loin myself; my Mother will eat the soup, and You and the Doctor must finish the rest.' (*TW*, pp. 98–9)

Laurie Langbauer has observed of juvenile writings that they 'at one and the same time anticipate growth and signal loss. [. . .] Juvenile prolepsis harnesses for the present a futurity it cannot completely articulate'.[24] This vivid passage

24. Langbauer, *The Juvenile Tradition*, p. 77.

from 'Lesley-Castle' dives into the business of accelerated consumption within a context of human damage. It also happens to anticipate the reality of Cassandra Austen's fiancé's sudden death, five years after 'Lesley-Castle' was written, and the loss of Jane Austen's beloved older friend Anne Lefroy, thrown from a horse and killed on Austen's birthday in 1804 (*Memoir*, pp. 28, 48). Unlike the Homeric simile, which often takes us out of the immediate realm of battle and back onto the dying hero's home turf, the point of Charlotte's foody comparisons and frame of reference is that she simply cannot or will not remove herself, or her thoughts, from the pantry. She is only ever losing her mind more and more deeply within the provisions. Her first thought about the surgeon is not that he might cure or support the dying Hervey, but that he should be called to help the living by stuffing his face. Sustenance has become a burden. Panic sets in, and not only because there is no refrigerator. What can be done with what is left on the shelf? We retain a sense throughout this passage of how the scene that is being described to us from one radically compromised, singular perspective could also be presented in a wholly contrasting way, as a human tragedy, if narrated (say) by Charlotte's sister. It is that contrasting possibility, and Charlotte's complete failure to countenance it, that generates the laughter.

The Austen sisters, after the death of Cassandra's fiancé, became, so their family put it, 'everything to each other' (*Memoir*, p. 198). They adopted what struck their younger relatives as a prematurely dowdy style of dress and seem to have professed themselves grateful for whatever compliments they might still be lucky enough to get (*Memoir*, p. 169). To remember this is not to diminish Jane or Cassandra Austen. If we fail to acknowledge the ridicule of grief that was evidently part of the sisters' conversational and epistolary routine (not necessarily a sign of desperation or regulated hatred), and which fitfully surfaces in the letters that Cassandra did not destroy, we miss part of what was lost and bequeathed to the Austen tribe when their great chronicler died.[25] This is a patter about things and people going off, perishing, or scraping by, about leftovers, a patter that comes closest of all Austen's characters' speech habits to those of Miss Bates.

Failure to pay the respect that is due to someone's remains, whether bodily or textual or culinary, is the engine not only of Austen's 'Plan of a Novel' (c. 1816), the little outline of an otherwise unwritten mock-fiction. The teenage

25. See D. W. Harding, 'Regulated Hatred: An Aspect of the Work of Jane Austen', *Scrutiny*, 8 (1940), 346–62 (and often reprinted).

works are, collectively, exercises in stockpiling and consuming that stock as rapidly as possible once it has been gathered in, so that many stories read as if they have concluded in virtually the same breath as that in which they began. The sense of an ending is virtually synonymous or simultaneous with that of an opening, and the story appears to be dead almost as soon it starts. In Austen's unfinished novella 'Evelyn', for instance, the magical reciprocity of Mr Gower's wants with the world that his desires encounter—of demand with supply—affronts the rules of fiction as well as the reality of life beyond it. Such a situation can last 'For some months', but not forever (*TW*, p. 164). While it persists, the hero cannot suffer, because he cannot meet any resistance to his wishes; quite the opposite, since the family whose house he invades not only give him a banquet and resign their property and daughter to him, they also insist on giving him money that he has not even asked for (*TW*, pp. 162–4). Having 'tasted something of all, and pocketed the rest' (*TW*, p. 163), Mr Gower finds himself 'perfectly happy' and married to a wealthy seventeen-year-old heiress within a few pages rather than at the close of a three-, four-, or five-volume novel of courtship; 'could he have a wish ungratified?' (*TW*, p. 164).

Perhaps the structure of this tale expresses Austen's amusement and occasional frustration with protracted novels and implausible impediments to marriage; by making life go so absurdly smoothly for Mr Gower, she has answered one kind of improbability with its mirror image. The narrator's question—'could he have a wish ungratified?'—indicates the challenge posed by the tale. How do you tell a story about someone for whom everything not only always goes exactly as he wants it to, but even better than that? The beginning-as-ending trope is related to jokes about the rules of the picturesque. Perfect symmetry in trees or cattle, exact regularity in the disposition of a house within its grounds such as characterizes the setting of 'Evelyn' (*TW*, p. 162), breaks with William Gilpin's well-known strictures on landscape, according to which a group of three is always preferable to a group of four.[26] The only way out of the stasis created at top speed by the story is to engineer another plot through the hero's having forgotten something: namely, his sister. She dies from his neglect—but is swiftly resurrected in a continuation of the tale written by Austen's nephew James Edward; in this version of events, however, Maria (Mr Gower's wife) has died (*TW*, pp. 205–6). James

26. See *TW*, p. 321 n. Compare *P&P*: 'The picturesque would be spoilt by admitting a fourth' (vol. 1, ch. 10, p. 58 and p. 482 n.).

Edward's contribution to 'Evelyn' is in the spirit of the original in that it takes death and life as reversible at a moment's notice. Since reports of a death, especially within a work of fiction, are just that—reports—why should they be taken as reliable? Why can't the movement from life to death, death to life, be repeated ad infinitum?

Jane Austen's life did not end, like Felicia Hemans', with a 'deathbed hymn of agonized affection', but with humorous verse.[27] The Winchester poem was left out of the first and second editions of Austen-Leigh's *Memoir*, and when Lord Stanhope expressed disappointment at its absence from the revised and expanded text of that work, Caroline Austen (as one of many close and competing guardians of her aunt's reputation) explained to James Edward her own conviction that the poem should remain private:

> Tho' there are no reasons *ethical* or orthodox against the publication of these stanzas, there are reasons of taste—I never thought there was much point in them—they were good enough for a passing thought, but if she had lived she would probably soon have torn them up—however there is a much stronger objection to their being inserted in any memoir, than a want of literary merit—If put in at *all* they must have been introduced as the latest working of her mind—*They* are dated July 15ᵗʰ—her death followed on the 18ᵗʰ—*Till* a few hours before she died, she had been feeling much better, & there was hope of amendment at least, if not of recovery—she amused herself by following a harmless fancy suggested by what was passing near here—but the joke about the dead Saint, & Winchester races, all jumbled up together, would read badly as amongst the few details given, of the closing scene—If I were to meet with it in any other biography, it would jar at once on my feelings, & I should think the insertion *then* & there of such light words, a sad incongruity—(*Memoir*, p. 190)

'Fancy' has been degraded here from what it means in Henry Austen's brief allusion to the Winchester Races poem in 1817, where he unites it with 'vigour' (*Memoir*, p. 138). Her persisting comic and imaginative powers, for those of her own generation, were evidence of Austen's astonishing strength, even at the last, a feature of their sister's final days on which Cassandra also remarked to Fanny

---

27. [Harriet May Owen], 'Memoir of Mrs Hemans', in *The Works of Mrs Hemans; with a Memoir of her Life*, 7 vols. (Edinburgh: William Blackwood and Sons; London: Thomas Cadell, 1839), vol. 1, p. 5.

Knight.[28] But to Caroline, her niece, fancy of this kind was 'harmless' and 'passing'. So the lines on Winchester Races are not, in themselves, objectionable (however lacking in 'point' they might be); it is the biographical context of 'the closing scene' in which they would have to appear that would render their effect jarring. Lord Stanhope, discovering that the 'light & playful nature' of the poem was the source of the family's disquiet, pointed out to Richard Bentley (publisher of the *Memoir*) that 'a similar mood at such a time [that is, near death] has been held not only excusable but admirable in some high ornaments of our Country, & of others too'—but his words had no effect. Fresh material was added to the second (1871) edition of the *Memoir*, but that material did not include the verses on Winchester Races.[29] Caroline was not the last of Austen's relatives or editors to express the wish that more of her literary relics could have been destroyed. But the much-feared incongruity between 'the latest working of her mind' and 'light words'—between a deathbed and a joke, an ending and a beginning—is in truth only the same kind of odd mixture, native to Jane Austen, that Caroline had found in her early writings.

––––––

Both the physical appearance in manuscript of Austen's last work of fiction, known as 'Sanditon', and the story it narrates possess a stop-start motion that appears to embody the author's determination to go on and the equally compelling, conflicting need to have done. Sanditon is itself an early-late environment. A place of growth, development, experiment, fashion, and transition, its snug old houses are being abandoned for elegant new villas, but not without a regretful backward glance at least from Mrs Parker, who misses her former 'very comfortable House' (*JAFM*, vol. 5, p. 100). The same movement from old to new (and back again) characterizes the way in which we can see the text emerging as a construction on the page and simultaneously disintegrating. By the time she began to write 'Sanditon', it is possible that Austen had apprehended that her illness was fatal; indeed, that she may have thought so for some time. As early as spring 1816, it was observed that 'she went about her old haunts, and recalled old recollections connected with them in a particular

28. 'I perceived no material diminution of strength & tho' I was then hopeless of a recovery I had no suspicion how rapidly my loss was approaching' (20 July 1817, *Letters*, p. 359).

29. Lord Stanhope to Richard Bentley (3 May 1870), cited in Deirdre le Faye, 'Jane Austen's Verses and Lord Stanhope's Disappointment', *Book Collector*, 37 (1988), 86–91 (pp. 87–8).

manner, as if she did not expect ever to see them again' (*Memoir*, p. 120).
Would it have been possible for Jane Austen to complete 'Sanditon'—an unfinished novel built on sand, a speculative piece of mushrooming growth that
is suddenly cut off—even if she had been physically well enough to do so?

The work itself, a fiction about imaginary illness by a woman who really was
dying, is as brave or foolhardy a venture as the resort whose fortunes it begins
to chart, the success of both being vulnerable to accident and disorders of
mind and body, as well as to perceptions of the world that may be feverishly
distorted. Diana Parker, one of two sisters, is a representative of sorts for the
novelist, suffering as she says from 'my old greivance'—which is very close to
Austen's own—'Spasmodic Bile' and therefore 'hardly able to crawl from my
Bed to the Sofa' (*JAFM*, vol. 5, p. 119). Three days before dating the first page
of 'Sanditon' Austen had written to Alethea Bigg: 'I think I understand my own
case now so much better than I did, as to be able by care to keep off any serious
return of illness' (*Letters*, p. 341). Yet in the mouth of Diana Parker, such claims,
subject to a little exaggeration, are presented as absurd: 'we must trust to our
own knowledge of our own wretched Constitutions for any releif' (*JAFM*, vol.
5, p. 111). It is further implied in 'Sanditon' that letters may constitute dubious
evidence as far as health is concerned. The initial claim 'that either Susan,
Diana or Arthur had been at the point of death within the last month' has been
revised to 'that either Susan, Diana or Arthur w^d. appear by this Letter to have
been at the point of death within the last month' (*JAFM*, vol. 5, p. 117). Was
Austen making a joke at her own expense about the relationship of health to
epistolary testimony? In 1805 she voiced, at length, a marked scepticism about
Cassandra's claim, by letter, to be well; the persistence with which she questions her sister's account suggests a habitual suspicion that people make themselves out to be either better or worse than they really are:

> I am heartily glad that you can speak so comfortably of your own health &
> looks, tho' I can scarcely comprehend the latter being really approved [that
> is, improved?]. Could travelling fifty miles produce such an immediate
> change?—You were looking so very poorly here; everybody seem'd sensible
> of it.—[. . .] Jenny is very glad to hear of your being better, & so is Robert,
> with whom I left a message to that effect   as my Uncle has been very much
> in earnest about your recovery.—I assure you, you were looking very ill
> indeed, & I do not beleive much of your being looking [sic] well already
> People think you in a very bad way I suppose, & pay you Compliments to
> keep up your Spirits. (*Letters*, 8–11 April 1805, pp. 104–6)

Critics have found it exceptionally difficult to work out where 'Sanditon' might have been going or intended to go. Mary Lascelles thought that, while it represented in some ways 'an advance beyond its predecessors, none of them would, if broken off short at the eleventh chapter, have left us in such uncertainty as to the way in which it was going to develop'.[30] Did Austen have a sense of this uncertainty herself, and if so would she have been troubled by it? The second chapter opens by considering the status of something 'thus oddly begun'; its tentative conclusion, expressed (like so much else in this story) by negation, is that it is 'neither short nor unimportant' (*JAFM*, vol. 5, p. 47). The prevalence of the passive voice contributes to a lack of clarity or singularity of direction; it is hard to know if that is deliberate, or something that might have changed in subsequent revision. The excision of agency, combined with indefinite articles, creates some very dislocated constructions: 'a Prospect House, a Bellevue Cottage, & a Denham Place were to be looked at by Charlotte with the calmness of amused Curiosity' (*JAFM*, vol. 5, p. 111). 'Were to be looked at' suggests that the point of the passive voice is that Charlotte is being directed, by Mr Parker, as to what she should notice. Yet 'with the calmness of amused Curiosity' informs us that the act of looking in fact remains entirely her own. It is as if the governing perspective has silently shifted, under the auspices of an expertly performed female obedience, from guide to visitor, from older man to younger woman. The act of looking is then passed on to Mr Parker in his turn: 'to be looked at [...] by M^r. P. with the eager eye which hoped to see scarcely any empty houses' (*JAFM*, vol. 5, p. 111). The use of indefinite articles in 'a Prospect House, a Bellevue Cottage, & a Denham Place'—not unique to 'Sanditon'—contribute to the sense that we might be reading something like a recipe or list of ingredients for a novel; that these are names and places that could at any time be substituted or removed, rather than being features in the simulation of an actual landscape.[31]

As a writer who seems to have allowed her stories to change direction as she went along (apparently debating with Cassandra, while composing *Mansfield Park*, whether Fanny Price would marry Henry Crawford), perhaps Austen did not herself know where 'Sanditon' would end up.[32] The text shows an

---

30. Mary Lascelles, *Jane Austen and Her Art* (Oxford: Clarendon Press, 1939), p. 39.

31. Compare 'a Harriet Smith' (*Emma*, vol. 1, ch. 4, p. 25), 'an Anne Elliot' (*Pers*, vol. 2, ch. 1, p. 135).

32. The narrator herself tells us: 'Would [Henry] have persevered, and uprightly, Fanny must have been his reward—and a reward very voluntarily bestowed—within a reasonable period

appetite for finitude, reminiscent of the juvenilia, competing with distraction by local colour whose potential is disquietingly infinite: 'the miscellaneous foreground' on which Charlotte gazes from her window consists of 'unfinished buildings', among other items of interest (*JAFM*, vol. 5, p. 113). That 'unfinished' is a hint that attention to such miscellaneity threatens the progress of the story, and that time is running out: 'Charlotte was glad to see as much, & as quickly as possible, where all was new' (*JAFM*, vol. 5, p. 129).

In its hectic accretion of proximate detail and consciousness of a past that is disappearing before the author's eyes, 'Sanditon' might be construed in Byronic terms as possessing the character of 'mobility'. His 1823 note on Adeline's temperament describes such a quality as 'an excessive susceptibility of immediate impressions—at the same time without *losing* the past'.[33] Just as the opening page of the first story in 'Volume the First' shows a keen desire to get to the end, so various references to completeness and conclusiveness rush in from the first page of 'Sanditon' onwards. On the last line of the first page, Austen has written the sentence with which the first booklet in fact closes: 'that Loveliness was complete' (*JAFM*, vol. 5, p. 17). Later on, Mr Parker (whose departure from home in a bustle of hurry and confusion makes him sound rather like the Rev. George Austen)[34] laments that 'One is never able to [...] complete anything in the way of Business you know till the Carriage is at the door' (*JAFM*, vol. 5, p. 31). It is a mark of Sanditon's desirability as a resort that it lies 'one complete, measured mile nearer than East Bourne' to London, and of Mr Parker's ruling passion that he is 'a complete Enthusiast'; Clara Brereton's 'appearance so completely justified M^r. P's praise' and she is associated with 'the idea of a complete heroine' (*JAFM*, vol. 5, pp. 41, 49, 137).

---

from Edmund's marrying Mary' (*MP*, vol. 3, ch. 17, p. 540). Henry Austen, having felt confident how it would turn out, then 'changed his mind as to foreseeing the end—he said yesterday at least, that he defied anybody to say whether H. C. would be reformed, or would forget Fanny in a fortnight' (2 March and 5 March, 1814, *Letters*, pp. 255, 258); John Plumptre 'had not an idea till the end which of the two w^d marry Fanny, H. C. or Edm^d' ('Opinions of Mansfield Park', *JAFM*, vol. 4, p. 325). Austen's niece and god-daughter Louisa Knight reported that 'Miss Austen's sister Cassandra tried to persuade her to alter the end of Mansfield Park and let Mr. Crawford marry Fanny Price. She [Louisa] remembers their arguing the matter but Miss Austen stood firmly and would not allow the change' (*Family Record*, p. 181).

33. *Lord Byron: The Complete Poetical Works*, ed. Jerome J. McGann, 7 vols. (Oxford: Clarendon Press, 1980–93), vol. 5, p. 769.

34. James Edward Austen-Leigh writes of his paternal grandfather that he 'was always rapid in forming his resolutions and in acting on them' (*Memoir*, p. 50).

These frequent and occasionally premature or odd references to the 'complete' mark a return to the instincts that produced the teenage writings. 'Sanditon' begins with a hastily conceived, ill-advised undertaking—a journey uphill—in search of someone who is not there. Even without the accident of an overturned carriage (also a feature of 'Love and Friendship'), this journey could not have been successful, since Mr Parker in his search for a surgeon has confused two places, and his rightful destination is not Willingden but its neighbour Great Willingden, or Willingden Abbots (*JAFM*, vol. 5, p. 31).[35] Still, in risking his own and his spouse's life and health, and in suffering a sprained ankle, he has triggered another plot.

Perhaps more than any other aspect of 'Sanditon', the nature of the opening scenario suggests that Austen was exhausted. No other novel begins with a scene of quite such impeded progress, although *Northanger Abbey* presents a version of the same stop-start dynamic by telling us in no uncertain terms that its elected heroine is singularly unqualified for that role. If it were not known for certain that Austen composed 'Sanditon' between January and March 1817, aspects of its style, pace, characterization, and language, as well as its physical appearance in the form of three notebooks, might lead it to be classed as one of the teenage works. Mr Parker's lame pun about not being '<u>down</u> in the Weald' sounds very like the doctor's excruciating wordplay in 'A beautifull description' (*JAFM*, vol. 5, p. 31; *TW*, pp. 53–4). The joke about Charlotte, a vigorous young woman taken on a spa break, having to try 'with excellent health, to bathe & be better if she could' revisits a similar moment in the teenage writings when an invalid's drink is offered to a girl who manifestly has no need of it (*JAFM*, vol. 5, p. 63; *TW*, p. 47).

There are other throwback elements to this last, unfinished novel which make it seem close to early Austen: references to Richardson's *Clarissa. Or, The History of a Young Lady* (1748) and Burney's *Camilla*, alongside inclusion of the more recent Burns and Wordsworth (*JAFM*, vol. 5, p. 133). The tendency in authorial revisions to exaggerate numerical jokes (on second thoughts, Diana Parker rubs a coachman's ankle for six hours rather than four, and six leeches

---

35. On overturned carriages, see also Jane Austen's parodic letter to Anna Austen (29–31 Oct. 1812), which ends: 'Miss Jane Austen cannot close this small epitome of the miniature abridgment of her thanks & admiration without expressing her sincere hope that Mrs Hunter is provided at Norwich with a more safe conveyance to London than Alton can now boast, as the Car of Falkenstein which was the pride of that Town was overturned within the last 10 days' (*Letters*, pp. 203–4).

are applied to Susan Parker for ten days in place of a week, *JAFM*, vol. 5, pp. 119, 123) is in line with changes made to the teenage writings, where such quips are intensified when Austen returns to them. Jokes about food (not eating anything versus overeating, or eating incessantly) associate this story with 'Lesley-Castle' (*TW*, pp. 98–100). Wordplay such as 'whether he were risking his fortune or spraining his ancle' revisits the zeugmatic humour of 'Jack & Alice' ('cruel Charles to wound the hearts & legs of all the fair' *TW*, p. 18). References to haymakers and the 'snug' house or room suggest a link with 'Henry & Eliza' (*TW*, pp. 27, 30). There are echoes of Laura in 'Love and Friendship' in Sir Edward's deriving 'only false Principles from Lessons of Morality, & Incentives to Vice from the History of its Overthrow (*JAFM*, vol. 5, pp. 182–3). The 'ruling passion' attitude to character in 'Sanditon' also resembles that of the teenage works.[36] Then there is a meta-literary alertness to handling the same episode from different perspectives, which suggests a certain detachment in the author from her material even as it is being created and evolving.

Readers have long been divided as to whether 'Sanditon' is looking backwards or forwards; whether it represents a bold new direction for the novelist's style, or a reversion to her earlier hyberbolic mode (*JAFM*, vol. 5, pp. 5–6). It suited the Austen family's purposes to depict her authorial career as a gradual ascent to the heights of the published novels, followed by a sudden, drastic waning of her powers that is purportedly attested by the weakening of her hand in the 'Sanditon' manuscript. But there is in fact no physical evidence in that manuscript to support the idea of any such weakness.[37] Austen's mysterious complaint took the form not of a consistent decline, but of a series of debilitating episodes from which she rallied until the last day or two of her life.

In 'Sanditon', Austen revised one epithet conferred on the ludicrous Sir Edward Denham, changing it from 'sagacious' to 'anti-puerile'. Sir Edward is busy condemning what he takes to be trashy popular novels in terms of their childish character ('those puerile Emanations [. . .] those vapid tissues of ordinary occurrences', *JAFM*, vol. 5, p. 177), and celebrating by contrast fiction of the high-blown, sentimental, and seductive kind:

> 'These are the Novels which enlarge the primitive Capabilities of the Heart, & which it cannot impugn the Sense or be any Dereliction of the character, of the most s̶a̶g̶a̶c̶i̶o̶u̶s̶ ^anti-puerile^ Man, to be conversant with.' (ch. 8, *JAFM*, vol. 5, p. 179)

36. See *The Juvenilia of Jane Austen and Charlotte Brontë*, 'Introduction', pp. 9–10.
37. See *Memoir*, p. 181; *JAFM*, vol. 5, p. 4.

'Sagacious', the adjective initially chosen to pair with 'Man', looks back to *The History of Tom Jones, A Foundling* (1749), possibly refracted through Charlotte Lennox's *Henrietta* (1758), which like *Tom Jones* refers with heavy irony to '*the sagacious Reader*'.[38] Sir Edward is a patently daft novel-reader without a trace of sagacity in his mind; that, however, is the quality he is first made to pride himself upon. As a character, he is a throwback to the villainous male anti-heroes of Richardson; he fancies himself a Lovelace, but his threat to Clara is entirely spurious. He cannot even frame his dastardly designs in the active voice: 'Her seduction was quite determined on' (*JAFM*, vol. 5, pp. 183–5). In any event, she 'saw through him, & had not the least intention of being seduced' (*JAFM*, pp. 184–5). Sir Edward speaks not only the cant of sentimental fiction, but of its critical reception throughout the latter half of the eighteenth century; arguments about and parodies of Richardson (including Fielding's *Apology for the Life of Mrs. Shamela Andrews* (1741) and *The History of the Adventures of Joseph Andrews and of his Friend Mr. Abraham Adams* (1742)) often involved claims about the effects of immersion in his works upon a reader's sense and, relatedly, about the derelict or exemplary character of his heroes and heroines.[39] The word 'anti-puerile' was and is very unusual, indeed cutting-edge (it does not appear in the *OED*), and it is part of Sir Edward's absurdly fruity yet vacuous armoury of hard words; in the same discussion of novels, he refers to an

38. See *The Wesleyan Edition of the Works of Henry Fielding, The History of Tom Jones, A Foundling*—for example vol. 1, book 1, ch. 6, p. 47; book 1, ch. 8, p. 57; book 5, ch. 10, p. 258; book 7, ch. 12, p. 377; book 8, ch. 3, p. 411; Charlotte Lennox, *Henrietta*, 2nd edition (London: A. Millar, 1761), vol. 2, p. 46 (chapter heading). Austen's beloved William Cowper refers to a 'Sagacious reader' in book 3 of *The Task* (1785): *The Poems of William Cowper*, 3 vols., ed. John D. Baird and Charles Ryskamp (Oxford: Clarendon Press, 1979–95), vol. 2, p. 169. On Fielding's addresses to the 'sagacious reader', see Henry Power, 'Henry Fielding, Richard Bentley, and the "Sagacious Reader" of *Tom Jones*', *Review of English Studies*, n. s. 61 (2010), 749–72. Compare Austen's letter to Cassandra of 11–12 October 1813, anticipating the 'sagacious' reference in 'Sanditon' and the name of its heroine: 'I admire the Sagacity & Taste of Charlotte Williams. Those large dark eyes always judge well.—I will compliment her, by naming a Heroine after her' (*Letters*, p. 244).

39. See for example the full title of *Shamela*, which in itself amounts to a critical review of Richardson's *Pamela; or, Virtue Rewarded* (1740): *An Apology for the Life of Mrs. Shamela Andrews. In which, the many notorious FALSHOODS and MISREPRESENTATIONS of a Book called PAMELA, are exposed and refuted; and all the matchless ARTS of that young Politician, set in a true and just Light. Together with a full Account of all that passed between her and Parson Arthur Williams; whose Character is represented in a manner something different from that which he bears in PAMELA. The whole being exact Copies of authentick Papers delivered to the Editor. Necessary to be had in all FAMILIES* (London: A. Dodd, 1741).

'Event' in fiction which is 'mainly anti-prosperous' to the hero (*JAFM*, vol. 5, p. 179).[40] As a run of other 'anti-' words in 'Sanditon' suggests, this language is likely to be related to advertising. Perhaps Austen saw some form of text promoting a sea resort and, taken with its bold claims to combat a wide range of disorders, lifted her terminology from there (if so, it would be in line with her composition of the poem on Winchester Races, most likely stimulated by a newspaper):[41]

> The Sea Air & Sea Bathing together were [. . .] anti-spasmodic, anti-pulmonary, anti-sceptic, anti-bilious & anti-rheumatic. (ch. 2, *JAFM*, vol. 5, p. 57)

'Anti-bilious', as the manuscript shows, is a late addition, suggesting a treatment for one of the complaints afflicting both Diana Parker and her author while increasing the number—and hence the absurdity—of the claims being made of 'The Sea Air & Sea Bathing together'. Austen is gathering and compacting into her sentences the very latest material available to her.

'Sanditon' arises from the collusion of loss and gain. It stages and serves as a reflection upon both past and present, as upon the relationship of the adult to the child, the new to the old, the everyday to the extraordinary. What it suggests is that, rather than discern or impose ascending or descending authorial powers upon a series of compositions, we might begin to consider each of Austen's works as a combination of advance and retreat. Even if chronology is linear, artistic development does not necessarily possess this form or shape itself to such a line. If Sir Edward Denham is anti-puerile, puerility must be an index of success. In this, her last novel, Austen endorses her beginnings.

40. On Sir Edward's language, see Jane Austen, *Sanditon*, ed. Kathryn Sutherland (Oxford: Oxford University Press, 2019), p. 79 n.

41. See Ingrid Tieken-Boon van Ostade, *In Search of Jane Austen: The Language of the Letters* (Oxford: Oxford University Press, 2014), p. 143 and n. The author notes that, with the sole exception of 'antidote' in *Emma*, all of Austen's 'anti-' words are in 'Sanditon'.

5

Histories

TO KNOW NOTHING OF HISTORY, according to Cicero, is to remain a child.[1] If so, Jane Austen's childhood ended early. The last date in 'The History of England from the reign of Henry the 4th to the death of Charles the Ist'—a self-possessed rampage through the lives of thirteen monarchs across four centuries, which cautions at the outset that it will contain 'very few Dates'—is 'Saturday Nov. 26th. 1791' (*TW*, pp. 120, 133). The author was a few weeks shy of her sixteenth birthday, but bold enough to have styled her work not '*An* History' but '*The* History of England'. This spoof has no truck with indefinite articles. Prone to some blatant internal inconsistences, it will admit only one person's version of events—that of a 'partial, prejudiced, & ignorant Historian' (*TW*, p. 120). Her reference to a 'Historian' is the sole example of teenage Austen conferring on herself a specific professional status throughout the often elaborate paratextual apparatus of the early works. Elsewhere, even when introducing texts that she calls 'novels', she never refers to herself as a novelist or writer of fiction, only as an 'Author' (*TW*, pp. 3, 10, 27, 33, 34, 37, 41, 44, 49, 52, 63, 66, 68, 96, 120, 134, 151, 160, 169). This feature alone suggests that her 'History' is conceived not as an alternative or a supplement to narratives of the past, but as a coup de force, usurping the thrones hitherto occupied by those giants of eighteenth-century historiography David Hume, William

---

1. 'Nescire autem quid ante quam natus sis acciderit, id est semper esse puerum' ('To be ignorant of what occurred before you were born is to remain always a child'). Cicero, *Brutus, Orator*, trans. G. L. Hendrickson, Loeb Classical Library, rev. edition (Cambridge, MA: Harvard University Press, 2014), ch. 34, §120, p. 395. On Austen and history, see Devoney Looser, *British Women Writers and the Writing of History, 1670–1820* (Baltimore, MD: Johns Hopkins University Press, 2000), pp. 178–203, and Christopher Kent, 'Learning History with, and from, Jane Austen', in *Jane Austen's Beginnings*, pp. 59–72.

Robertson, and Oliver Goldsmith (there is no evidence that Austen had read Edward Gibbon). It is further confirmed by the fact that the earliest monarch to appear in her work is himself a usurper, 'being the first Lancastrian to take the throne, and not the primogenitary heir'.[2] This early work is animated by a special kind of confidence, moving between intimacy and assurance, communicating knowledge that is 'confidently reported' or 'confidently asserted': at once secret, private, and confidential and self-reliant, fearless, and positively dogmatic (*TW*, pp. 100, 124).[3]

Austen's 'History' has recently been hailed as 'a multivalent, multimodal text that encompasses parody and historiography' alongside 'the traditions of martyrology and vindication, or defense'.[4] The young author, Mary Spongberg argues, responds with indignation as well as satirical intent to a Burkean apprehension of England's past, playing serio-comically with the subjects of ancestry, succession, inheritance, and 'the dispossession of women, a theme that she would return to in her novels'.[5] The 'History' has been persuasively read as a document of teenage female rebellion, a work that embraces authorial absolutism in order to dodge the two fates conventionally in store for a well-to-do girl lacking in wealth and property: marriage, or the life of a governess.[6] Austen was writing primarily in reply to Goldsmith's *The History of England from the Earliest Times to the Death of George II*, a four-volume schoolroom text of 1771 which seems to have been in regular use by the whole family. The energetic marginal comments or '*defensive* prewriting' which she entered into a copy of the 1771 *History*, perhaps just before the time that she composed her own, relate chiefly to the Stuarts, 'A Family, who were always illused, Betrayed or neglected—Whose Virtue's are seldom allowed while their Errors are never forgotten' (*Juvenilia*, p. 337: quotation corrected).[7] They are

2. Mary Spongberg, 'Jane Austen and the *History of England*', *Journal of Women's History*, 23 (2011), 56–80 (p. 73).

3. See *OED* 'confident, *adj.* and *n.*': the word is sometimes synonymous with 'confidential' and 'confidant(e)', as well as with a feeling of assurance or boldness.

4. Misty Krueger, 'From Marginalia to Juvenilia: Jane Austen's Vindication of the Stuarts', *The Eighteenth Century*, 56 (2015), 243–59 (p. 244).

5. Spongberg, 'Jane Austen and the *History of England*', p. 73.

6. See Brigid Brophy, 'Jane Austen and the Stuarts' in B. C. Southam, ed., *Critical Essays on Jane Austen* (London: Routledge & Kegan Paul, 1968), pp. 21–30.

7. Krueger, 'From Marginalia to Juvenilia', p. 246. Mary Augusta Austen-Leigh thinks Austen may have been as young as 12 or 13 when she annotated Goldsmith (*Personal Aspects*, p. 26). For further commentary on and transcriptions of Austen's marginalia, see appendix.

endorsed with the same ardent sympathy throughout her own historical narrative, where they make an appearance long before they take over the kingdom (*TW*, p. 125), and the author's special favourite, Mary, Queen of Scots, occupies most of the chapter notionally devoted to her enemy, Queen Elizabeth I.

In writing a 'History of England', Austen might be said to have been training herself as a novelist in enemy territory. The two genres had been competing with one another for decades. By the time she began to compose her teenage works, eighteenth-century writers of fiction had co-opted many of the authenticating devices of history—exact dates and real places; pseudo-editorial prefaces; the use of documentary evidence; and scholarly trappings such as footnotes—to their own ends. By mid-century, the novel could plausibly lay superior claim to possession of the innermost recesses of mind and heart, the hidden springs of human behaviour.[8] Contemporary fictional 'histories'—as novels such as *Tom Jones*, *Clarissa*, and *Sir Charles Grandison* styled themselves in their full titles—embodied, in modern and domestic contexts, many of the benefits that writers on female education had previously argued were the sole prerogative of narrative accounts of the past.[9] Samuel Richardson, a key influence on the young Austen, had sought to advance through fiction the causes of morality and virtue, and in so doing often considered the rival claims of the historian.[10] Writers of history adopted in their turn some of the novel's techniques, beginning to experiment with

8. See Neil Hargreaves, 'Revelation of Character in Eighteenth-Century Historiography and William Robertson's *History of the Reign of Charles V*', *Eighteenth-Century Life*, 23 (2003), 23–48; Looser, *British Women*, pp. 16–21, 178–203.

9. See Everett Zimmermann, *The Boundaries of Fiction: History and the Eighteenth-Century British Novel* (Ithaca, NY, and London: Cornell University Press, 1996).

10. Richardson consistently referred to *Clarissa* as a 'History', not only in the title but also in the prefatory materials; he also styled himself the editor rather than the author of his novels, defending himself in so doing with reference to the 'Historical Faith which Fiction itself is generally read with, tho' we know it to be Fiction'. See *Clarissa. Or, the History of a Young Lady: Comprehending the Most Important Concerns of Private Life. And particularly shewing, The Distresses that may attend the Misconduct Both of Parents and Children, In Relation to Marriage. Published by the Editor of Pamela*, 7 vols. (London: S. Richardson, 1748), 'Preface', vol. 1, pp. iii–viii; *Selected Letters of Samuel Richardson*, ed. John Carroll (Oxford: Clarendon Press, 1964), p. 85. Like other voluminous histories, *Clarissa* was also available in abridged form. See for example *The Paths of Virtue Delineated; or, The history in miniature of the celebrated Pamela, Clarissa Harlowe, and Sir Charles Grandison: familiarised and adapted to the capacities of youth* (London: R. Baldwin, etc., 1756).

generic boundaries in order to take in aspects of private and common life which traditionally lay outside the remit of history proper.[11]

Austen's responses, in the form of marginal notes, to Goldsmith's *History* therefore call upon fiction as readily as they do upon other sources. In a brisk analysis of the events of 1688, the character of Charlotte Smith's Frederic Delamere merges with or replaces that of Goldsmith's Lord Delamere, early champion of William of Orange. The trigger for his doing so is a perceived distinction that is perennially appealing to Austen: between a rash, hasty character and its steady, cautious opposite number. Goldsmith writes that 'Lord Delamere took arms in Cheshire'; Austen notes 'I should have expected *Delamere* to have done so, for it was an action unsuited to *Godolphin*' (*Juvenilia*, p. 334). History is made to endorse what Austen has learned of and from Smith's fictional characters: Godolphin, the slower and more reliable of the two men, wins Emmeline the heroine (who makes her own appearance, alongside Frederic Delamere, in Austen's 'History of England').[12] This habit of discovering evidence from history or the world around her that shores up, supports, or confirms 'the most thorough knowledge of human nature'—namely, that of novels—remained with Austen throughout her life (*NA*, vol. 1, ch. 5, p. 31). As Claudia L. Johnson has observed, one of her earliest proclamations as a novelist was 'the dignity of her genre as well as the authority of her command over it—both at a time when such gestures were rare'.[13] For Austen, history is the servant of fiction. Visiting the Society of Painters' Exhibition in May 1813, she found a portrait of Jane Bennet ('excessively like her') and confirmed a suspicion 'that green was a favourite colour with her'; a year later, writing to Cassandra in August 1814 about an overfull hackney coach bound for London and carrying (as it turned out) some acquaintances, Austen reports being 'put in mind of my own Coach between Edinburgh & Stirling' (*Letters*, p. 282). This Scottish stagecoach appears at a climactic moment in the epistolary spoof 'Love and Friendship', when Laura, having entered the vehicle in the dark, finds herself at daybreak 'surrounded by my nearest Relations and

11. See Peter Knox-Shaw, *Jane Austen and the Enlightenment* (Cambridge: Cambridge University Press, 2004), p. 115; Karen O'Brien, 'Historical Writing', in David Womersley, ed., *A Companion to Literature from Milton to Blake* (Oxford: Blackwell, 2000), pp. 522–35.

12. 'This unfortunate young man [Lord Essex] was not unlike in Character to that equally unfortunate one *Frederic Delamere*. The simile may be carried still farther, & Elizabeth the torment of Essex may be compared to Emmeline of Delamere' (*TW*, pp. 130–31). See Charlotte Smith, *Emmeline, the Orphan of the Castle*, 4 vols. (London: T. Cadell, 1788).

13. Johnson, *Jane Austen: Women, Politics and the Novel*, p. 28.

Connections'. The impression she describes—'Imagine my Surprize at finding myself thus seated amongst my old Acquaintance'—is redoubled in Austen's letter to Cassandra (*TW*, pp. 90–91). Twenty-four years after she wrote 'Love and Friendship', the story of rediscovering old acquaintance has itself become, to its author, an old acquaintance rediscovered (if, indeed, it ever truly left her mind: she does not feel the need to explain her reference to her sister). Such direct, simple, unworried challenges to the dividing line between fiction and reality—'green *was* a favourite'—confidently bypass the primacy of fact. They assert the right of the creative imagination to find endorsement of its suppositions and judgements not only in rival artistic forms, but in the realm of everyday life.

The first volume to be published of Hume's *History of England from the Invasion of Julius Caesar to the Revolution of 1688* (1754–62) ends with the reign of Charles I, but this does not appear to have been the prompt for Austen to conclude her own historical narrative at the same point.[14] She probably chose to break off the text here because it allows her to represent the whole of English history as the rise, fall, and romance of one dynasty—largely charted in terms of its own, and its historian's, emotions and thereby anticipating, albeit in hysterical technicolour, how she would go on to treat the '3 or 4 Families' which she described as 'the very thing to work on' in fiction (9–18 Sept. 1814, *Letters*, p. 287). Earlier reigns are invoked in fairly short order, a move which in itself enacts a parodic version of Whig history whereby the early cedes inevitably to the late, and suggesting (quite rightly) that the prime function of the introductory chapters is to lay the ground for the Stuarts. This structure seems to dictate that the 'History' will be a tragic one, even though in this same work Austen dismisses tragedy as 'not worth reading' (*TW*, p. 125). In fact, she dodges 'any particular account' of Charles's trial and execution, despite having given such detail in her commentary on Mary (*TW*, pp. 133, 130), perhaps to avoid an unduly melancholy conclusion. This historian's task is, primarily, vindication of her favourites and abuse of her enemies. Abruptly coercing her reader into agreement or submission, she plays the authorial equivalent of Charles I, insisting on the divine right of historians to rule their audiences—to supply or deny information as she sees fit; to pre-empt and pre-judge their responses. Her final rebuke to the Scottish is therefore that they should ever have 'dared to think differently from their Sovereign' (*TW*,

---

14. David Hume, *The History of England from the Invasion of Julius Caesar to the Revolution in 1688*, 6 vols. (London: A. Millar, 1754–62).

p. 133). She may not have it 'in my power', as she puts it, 'to inform the Reader who was [Henry IV's] wife' (*TW*, p. 121), but this is no concession to the reader's rival powers—merely a transparent euphemism for the ignorant historian's refusal to lift a finger.

Austen's unabashed partisanship is a riotous departure from the aspirations to dignity, objectivity, and neutrality of expressions which had, in theory, governed British historiography from the mid-eighteenth century onwards. It is also at odds with that slippery, unobtrusive, free indirect style for which her later novels are celebrated. Her loyalty to the Stuart cause sprang in large part from the fact that her maternal ancestors, the Leighs, had sheltered Charles I at their home, Stoneleigh Abbey.[15] With the weight of family history and loyalty on one side, it is not surprising that, in her closing sentence, Austen expresses the conviction that 'every sensible & well disposed person whose opinions have been properly guided by a good Education' will be satisfied by her laughably inadequate 'Argument' that all Stuarts are blameless (p. 133). After all, this was a piece of writing designed primarily to amuse (and, in a sense, to celebrate) her own relatives. It is also informed, like the novels, by the awareness that Austen and her family, however well educated, were not nearly as grand or as wealthy as their aristocratic ancestors had been; as V. S. Pritchett remarked, and as Sir Walter Elliott proves, 'no family is more tenacious of the past, more prone to fixation than the declining family'.[16]

The marginalia in Goldsmith's *History of England* make it abundantly clear whose political side the historian is on: 'Nobly said! Spoken like a Tory!' (*Juvenilia*, p. 339). 'Yes', Austen writes, 'This is always the Liberty of Whigs & Republicans', in response to the following passage in Goldsmith: 'The Whigs governed the senate and the court; whom they would, they oppressed; bound the lower orders of people with severe laws, and kept them at a distance by vile distinctions; and then taught them to call this—Liberty' (Goldsmith, *History of England*, vol. 4, p. 197; *Juvenilia*, p. 338). Commenting on Sir Robert Walpole having lessened the national debt, she writes: 'It is a pity that a *Whig* should have been of such use to his Country' (*Juvenilia*, p. 342). Such remarks, it need hardly be said, highlight the 'partial' and 'prejudiced' aspects of the young Austen's character as an historian. She also shows a novelist's instinct to appeal to secrets, domestic life, and hitherto untold stories of female suffering—as

15. See Brophy, 'Jane Austen and the Stuarts'; Austen-Leigh, *Personal Aspects of Jane Austen*, pp. 13–17.

16. V. S. Pritchett, *The Living Novel* (London: Chatto & Windus, 1946), p. 112.

opposed to the historian's endeavour to appear impartial and disinterested, and to build a case on the evidence and language of previous, public, male authorities. In the 'History of England', as in other teenage works, Austen resists through satirizing it a Whiggish model of development whereby the vantage point of the present results in a distorted view of the past. This 'mental trick' is what Herbert Butterfield would later see assuming the shape of 'something like a line of causation' in the Whig interpretation of history.[17]

In 1773, Hester Chapone had argued that 'Party so strongly influences both historians and their readers, that it is a difficult and invidious task to point out the *best* amongst the number of English histories that offer themselves'. After some hesitation, she recommended Hume's six-volume *History of England,* published between 1754 and 1762, as the 'most entertaining', albeit not the most impartial, of the lot (her next recommendation is 'my darling *Shakespear*'). And this despite the fact that Hume had staked his credibility on moderation: Voltaire praised him for being 'neither parliamentarian, nor royalist, nor Anglican, nor Presbyterian', but 'simply judicial'.[18] Hume's *History,* a set of which Austen owned in later life, sought to eschew Jacobite apologetics and Tory bias. Shunning providential explanations of past events, Hume also rejected, for the most part, the now infamous pitfalls of Whig interpretation: the Protestant affirmation of England's destiny as the birthplace of freedom, and the crude heroes-and-villains conception of historical development.[19]

Goldsmith claimed for himself a greater disinterestedness than that which purportedly characterized his predecessor: 'it is hoped', he said, in the passive voice of the seemingly neutral annalist, in the preface to his 1771 *History,* that 'the reader will admit my impartiality' (Goldsmith, *History,* vol. 1, p. viii). Young Austen, for one, did not, scribbling 'Oh! Dr. Goldsmith Thou art as partial an Historian as myself!' next to his comment that 'all the sensible part of the kingdom' forsook the cause of the Old Pretender (*Juvenilia,* p. 337)—phrasing she

17. Herbert Butterfield, *The Whig Interpretation of History* [1931] (Harmondsworth: Penguin, 1973), p. 18.

18. Hester Chapone, 'On the Manner and Course of Reading History', in *Letters on the Improvement of the Mind,* 2 vols. (London: J. Walter, 1773), vol. 2, pp. 212–3. Voltaire, cited in David Hume, *The History of England from the Invasion of Julius Caesar to the Revolution in 1688,* 6 vols. [1778 edition], intro. William B. Todd (Indianapolis, IN: Liberty Fund, 1983–5), vol. 1, p. xviii.

19. Hume judged the Whig hegemony to have been 'destructive to the truth of history' (*History of England,* vol. 6, p. 533). One of the bad things about the predominance of the Whigs for almost seventy years, according to Hume, was the alleged superiority of modern to ancient compositions.

co-opts to express the opposite view of what is 'sensible' in the closing sentence of her own 'History': 'with one argument I am certain of satisfying every sensible & well-informed person whose opinions have been properly guided by a good Education—& this Argument is that he was a **Stuart**' (*TW*, p. 133).

It was unfortunate for Goldsmith that he had chosen, in his *History of England in a Series of Letters from a Nobleman to his Son* (1764), to warn his youthful audience 'Above all things [...] to consult the original historians in every relation', and that 'Abridgers, compilers, commentators, and critics, are in general only fit to fill the mind with unnecessary anecdotes, or lead its researches astray'.[20] For Goldsmith's 1771 *History* was itself a compilation and abridgement of earlier histories, chiefly of Hume's—and it was written with the express 'aim', as he wryly and perhaps wearily acknowledged, 'not to add to our present stock of history, but to contract it'.[21] Austen's text is therefore, among other things, an extreme contraction of a miscellaneous reduction. She went on to object to historical abridgements in *Northanger Abbey*, a work in which novelists are themselves presented as 'an injured body'. In decrying 'the abilities of the nine-hundredth abridger of the History of England' by comparison with those of the novelist (*NA*, vol. 1, ch. 5, p. 31), she chimes with Hannah More in *Strictures on the Modern System of Female Education*, which condemns the 'swarms of *Abridgments, Beauties*, and *Compendiums*, which form too considerable a part of a young lady's library [...] an infallible receipt for making a superficial mind', and with William Godwin's assertion that 'the most important rule that can be laid down respecting the study of history' is 'the wisdom of studying the detail, and not in abridgement. To read historical abridgements [...] is a wanton prodigality of time worthy only of folly or of madness. [...] I believe I should be better employed in studying one man, than in perusing the abridgement of Universal History in sixty volumes'.[22]

Austen's parodic 'History' could be said to realize, in the act of ridiculing, Goldsmith's professed ambition in 1771 to 'contract' the stock of English

20. [Oliver Goldsmith,] *An History of England in a Series of Letters from a Nobleman to his Son* (London: J. Newbery, 1764), letter 1, p. 4. Unsurprisingly, given the epistolary format and the reference to 'a Nobleman' as the author, Lord Chesterfield's authorship was suspected.

21. Goldsmith, *The History of England* (1771), 'Preface', vol. 1, p. vi.

22. More, *Strictures on the Modern System of Female Education*, vol. 1, p. 160; William Godwin, 'Of History and Romance' (1797), unpublished in the author's lifetime, reproduced in *Things as They Are or The Adventures of Caleb Williams*, ed. Maurice Hindle (Harmondsworth: Penguin, 1987), pp. 363, 364.

history. Styling himself in the 'Preface' to the four-volume *History of England* a 'compiler' of successful 'abridgements', in 1774 he went on to abridge that already curtailed *History* into a single volume.[23] As in the Austen family's abridgement of Samuel Richardson's gargantuan last novel, *Sir Charles Grandison*, one flagrantly comic aspect of Jane Austen's 'History of England' is that it reduces the scope and accelerates the pace of a multi-volume work. Just as Laura, heroine of 'Love and Friendship' (written in the previous year, 1790), finds her carriage moving too fast for passers-by to have time to answer her 'repeated Enquiries' (*TW*, p. 79), so this history moves at such speed that there is no time for queries or protest (not that they would, in any event, be countenanced by the imperious historian).

The chapters of Austen's 'History' also mimic, in terms of length, the excerpts from historical narratives and speeches reprinted in popular educational anthologies such as Vicesimus Knox's *Elegant Extracts: or Useful and Entertaining Passages in Prose selected for the Improvement of Scholars* (1783). Knox's mass-produced works were designed, like this 'History', to be read aloud in family circles (Austen owned and annotated a copy of *Elegant Extracts* [. . .] *in Prose*, which she passed on to her niece Anna).[24] Another of her sources is Shakespeare—specifically, the history plays from *Richard II* to *Henry VIII*. Austen swiftly points her reader in Shakespeare's direction, as if to a work of factual reference, for a speech made by Henry IV (*TW*, p. 121). The gesture may indicate, on the one hand, her knowledge of Shakespeare's dependence on chronicles; on the other, her awareness that Hume and Robertson, following the practice of classical historians, had pasted fictional speeches into their surveys of England and Scotland. But her appeal to the history plays in this context may simply mean that, like Hester Chapone, Austen considered Shakespeare as reliable a guide to the past as any, and more delightful than most. Even gullible Catherine Morland knows that much of history is made up (she is all the more puzzled that she finds it so boring). Her friend Eleanor Tilney, however, is unfazed by what she calls the 'little embellishments' which liven up historical narratives, concluding that she is more likely to enjoy a speech concocted by Hume or Robertson than 'the genuine words' of an ancient speaker (*NA*, vol. 1, ch. 14, pp. 109–10). In this too she echoes Chapone,

---

23. Oliver Goldsmith, *An Abridgment of the History of England. From the Invasion of Julius Cæsar, to the Death of George II* (London: B. Law, G. Robinson, G. Kearsly, T. Davies, T. Becket, T. Cadell, and T. Evans, 1774).

24. See appendix.

who rated the entertainment value of history more highly than its claims to truth or neutrality.[25] The voice of young Austen the historian continues to be heard in Catherine's complaint that 'history, real solemn history' tells her 'nothing that does not either vex or weary me. The quarrels of popes and kinds, with wars or pestilences, in every page; the men all so good for nothing, and hardly any women at all—it is very tiresome' (NA, pp. 109–10). That voice is still there in the climactic scene in Persuasion, when Anne Elliot, insisting upon female constancy in a charged debate with Captain Harville, is that told 'all histories are against you, all stories, prose and verse. [...] But perhaps you will say, these were all written by men' (vol. 2, ch. 11, p. 254).[26] Decades earlier, 'A History of England' had lamented the want of 'amiable Men' in the Civil War, speculated about turning men into women, and found a way to redress the gender imbalance of previous histories by including female characters in every one of its royal portraits (TW, pp. 133, 124).[27]

From a very early age, Austen knew that history involved a large helping of imaginative licence as well as the introduction, covert or explicit, of personal feelings and affiliations. Her challenge to the line of authorial succession is so much to the fore of her own 'History' that it is this new Pretender, 'my no less amiable Self' (TW, p. 130), rather than the personalities and events she describes, that constitutes the real centre of interest. That self's unabashed partiality, prejudice, and ignorance are tested against other possible attitudes to characters in history and in the present; attitudes such as pity (staved off on two occasions, since partiality for the opposing side forbids it, TW, pp. 123, 131), disinterestedness, or indifference, that close neighbour of disinterest and the enemy of Austen's passionately interested narration. She forestalls the reader's boredom by saying that she will not repeat such events as we have not heard before—an aim which, happily, coincides with the historian's self-confessed inability to remember them, and with her dislike of reciting anything she has not herself invented (TW, pp. 126, 133). At such points in the narrative, this novelist-in-the-making sets her own talent for mimicking

25. See Chapone, Letters on the Improvement of the Mind, pp. 187–90, 199, 212.

26. See D. R. Woolf, 'A Feminine Past? Gender, Genre, and Historical Knowledge in England, 1500–1800', American Historical Review, 102 (1997), 645–79 (pp. 669–70).

27. On gender and feminism in 'The History of England', see Antoinette Burton, '"Invention Is What Delights Me": Jane Austen's Remaking of "English" History', in Jane Austen and Discourses of Feminism, ed. Devoney Looser (Basingstoke: MacMillan, 1995), pp. 35–50.

historians against her budding ability to produce fictions which are truer to life and human nature, as well as funnier, than theirs.

Like Fanny Price and the Bertram children, the young Jane Austen would have been required to read a 'daily portion of History', and 'to repeat the chronological order of the kings of England, with the dates of their accession, and most of the principal events of their reigns!' (*MP*, vol. 1, ch. 2, pp. 24, 21); in volume 1 of the family copy of Goldsmith's *History of England* there are 'some dates marked in the margins [. . .] suggesting that so many pages were read as a daily or weekly task'.[28] Beneath the signature of James Austen, there is also a chronology in Austen's hand of the chief events contained in the first volume (*Juvenilia*, p. 318). Having to compile such a timeline must have produced the joke that Austen's own 'History' would contain 'very few Dates' (five in total); behind this may also lie the knowledge that, in Goldsmith's first *History of England* (1764), there were no dates at all (*TW*, pp. 120 and 298 n.). Learning about the past in this way, and by rote, certainly proved no inhibition to Austen's own 'loose, disultary, unconnected strain' of re-making and sharing it, both in the teenage 'History of England' and in her later novels (to Martha Lloyd, 12–13 Nov. 1800, *Letters*, p. 61).

Austen's phrasing to Martha suggests she may have had at the back of her mind Chapone's caution in *Letters on the Improvement of the Mind* that mixing ancient with modern, general with particular, history, in a 'desultory manner of reading', would be likely to make girls 'distract and confound their memories, and retain nothing to any purpose from such a confused mass of materials'.[29] Chapone proceeds to recommend it as 'a useful exercise of your memory and judgment, to recount [. . .] interesting passages [of history] to a friend [. . .] not in the words of the author, but in your own natural stile—by memory and not by book—and to add whatever remarks may occur to you'.[30] Austen duly threatened Martha Lloyd with a repetition 'in any manner you may prefer' of Robert Henry's substantial *History of Great Britain*—published in six quarto volumes between 1771 and 1793—possibly

> dividing my recital as the Historian divides it himself, into seven parts, The Civil & Military—Religion—Constitution—Learning & Learned Men—Arts & Sciences—Commerce Coins & Shipping—& Manners;—So that

28. *Family Record*, p. 58.
29. *Letters on the Improvement of the Mind*, vol. 2, p. 183.
30. *Letters on the Improvement of the Mind*, vol. 2, p. 184.

for every evening of the week there will be a different subject; The Friday's lot, Commerce, Coin & Shipping, You will find the least entertaining; but the next Eveng:'s portion will make amends. (*Letters*, pp. 61–2)

The history of manners is held out as the real treat; and it is in such territory that fiction might be said to have the edge over other kinds of history-writing. In either case, the experience could and should be shared. There is a nod to Chapone's title when Austen refers in *Mansfield Park* to Edmund's 'attentions' to his cousin as being 'of the highest importance in assisting the improvement of her mind'. When Fanny learns history with Miss Lee, it is a duty, but Edmund 'made reading useful by talking to her of what she read' (*MP*, vol. 1, ch. 2, p. 25). Chapone says that, when attempting to remember history, 'the most natural and pleasing expedient is that of conversation with a friend, who is acquainted with the history you are reading.—By such conversations, you will learn to select those characters and facts which are best worth preserving'.[31] This collaborative, sometimes argumentative, experience of history—with siblings, parents, and friends—is crucial to Austen in defining a true education. It involves testing the memory, identifying what is important and rejecting what is not, forming judgements, and taking sides; in *Mansfield Park*, as in 'Kitty, or the Bower', it fosters affectionate, combative intimacies.

In view of Austen's 'History', if of nothing else, it is odd that Karen O'Brien detects no tension before the early nineteenth century between what she describes as 'the narrative form of history and its empirical or philosophical content'.[32] For 'The History of England' is determined to explode and lay bare just that division between the way that history is told and its raw materials, partly by exposing the historian as a particularly compromised and fallible variety of writer:

It is to be supposed [. . .] it is not in my power to inform [. . .] I forget what for [. . .] I cannot say much [. . .] I shall not be very diffuse in this, meaning only to vent my Spleen *against, & shew my Hatred* to *all* those people whose parties or principles do not suit with mine, & not to give information [. . .] I do not perfectly recollect [. . .] I cannot help liking him [. . .] I am myself partial [. . .] I am rather fearful of having fallen short (*TW*, pp. 121–31)

31. *Letters on the Improvement of the Mind*, vol. 2, p. 185.
32. O'Brien, 'Historical Writing', p. 522.

Moments such as these show Austen preparing for her novelistic investigations of private motivations and concealed sympathies. Austen-Leigh wrote of his aunt that

> In history she followed the old guides—Goldsmith, Hume, and Robertson. Critical enquiry into the usually received statements of the old historians was scarcely begun. [. . .] Historic characters lay before the reader's eyes in broad light or shade, not much broken up by details. The virtues of King Henry VIII. were yet undiscovered, nor had much light been thrown on the inconsistencies of Queen Elizabeth; the one was held to be an unmitigated tyrant, and an embodied Blue Beard; the other a perfect model of wisdom and policy. (*Memoir*, p. 71)

But as Austen-Leigh himself well knew, there is no reverence involved in the way Austen's 'History' treats these 'old guides' to the past, or indeed in her attitude to the male historian whom she impersonates. She roundly abuses Elizabeth as 'that disgrace to humanity, that pest of society', 'the destroyer of all comfort, the deceitful Betrayer of trust reposed in her, & the Murderess of her Cousin', a 'wicked' woman who was 'encouraged [. . .] in her Crimes' by a collection of 'vile & abandoned' male ministers (*TW*, p. 129). She frequently disdains to supply evidence to back up her claims, so that what she calls an argument is generally no more than an outrageous opinion (*TW*, p. 133). Where Austen does supply what she identifies as 'sufficient proofs' (*TW*, pp. 123, 126), they can be laughably out of kilter with the claim they are meant to be endorsing.

Take Cassandra's portrait of Edward IV, which is offered as evidence of that 'Beauty' for which the king was apparently renowned—a theory which it instantly contradicts, since it depicts a badly dressed, squat, and dumpy-looking man—while Edward's 'Courage', the only other characteristic that posterity is said to attribute to him, is exemplified by the story of his 'marrying one Woman while he was engaged to another' (*TW*, p. 123). This feature of Edward IV's conduct appears to be recalled in that of Edward Ferrars of *Sense and Sensibility*, who gains Elinor's affections while secretly engaged to Lucy Steele. When Elinor exonerates Edward to Marianne by saying that 'Nothing has proved him unworthy' (*S&S* vol. 3, ch. 1, p. 299)—note her strange external emphasis on evidence, where we might have expected Elinor to show a more intuitive, personal sense of her husband-to-be's worthiness—the effect is quieter than in young Austen's 'History', with its screaming contrast between Edward IV's supposedly 'undaunted Behaviour' (*TW*, p. 123)

FIGURE 7. Cassandra Austen, medallion portrait of Edward IV, in
Jane Austen, 'The History of England' (1791), 'Volume the Second'.
Add. MS. 59874, British Library, London.

and actual betrayal. But we should still notice the odd glitch between what
Elinor says and what Edward Ferrars has in fact done; perhaps all the more
so because Elinor has throughout the novel acted like an eighteenth-century
historian, 'by endeavouring', as she says, 'to appear indifferent where I have
been most deeply interested' (*S&S*, vol. 3, ch. 1, p. 299). Michael Prince observes that, while 'Elinor tries to teach Marianne the difficult art of probabi-
listic inference (gathering evidence through observation, testing the data in
light of fluctuating circumstances, forming tentative conclusions through
reasoned conjecture), she sometimes exempts herself from its practice'—
especially with reference to Edward's conduct and motivations.[33] In this,
again, Elinor might be said to behave as if she were an eighteenth-century
historian—one whose theory ill accords with his or her interested, partial
practice. As is suggested by its closing sentence, 'The History of England'
could be viewed as a companion piece to *Sense and Sensibility* in terms of what

33. Michael Prince, *Philosophical Dialogue in the British Enlightenment: Theology, Aesthetics
and the Novel* (Cambridge: Cambridge University Press, 1996), p. 242.

it means to be 'sensible' and how to define a good and bad 'Education' (*TW*, p. 133). On this view of things, Marianne Dashwood is, like Austen, 'Marian'—Cassandra's portrait of Queen Mary having been described as likely to be that of Austen herself—in other words, a devotee or warm adherent of Mary, Queen of Scots.[34] Marianne also represents a modern version of the doomed and martyred Mary's 'Imprudencies into which she was betrayed by the openness of her Heart, her Youth, & her Education' (*TW*, p. 130).

The treatment of Edward IV in Austen's 'History of England' hints both at the author's contempt for reputation as a guide to her characters (Edward is famous for beauty and courage, but in reality he was ugly and treacherous) and at a parodic version of the eighteenth-century historian's much-vaunted impartiality: Edward is beautiful in the text, but ugly in the illustration, just as Richard III is announced to be at once innocent and guilty of his nephews' murder (*TW*, p. 124). Character analysis and judgement are thus suspended between two fierce extremes, while our historian gallops off to her next case study. The Austen family marginalia in Goldsmith's *History of England* bring out the often equiponderant possibilities of praise and blame, good and evil, in writing about the past—even in writing of the most partial kind. Austen is herself compelled on more than one occasion in her avowedly prejudiced 'History' to express something very close to pity for the enemy, before sternly repudiating the sentiment ('Margaret of Anjou, a Woman whose distresses & Misfortunes were so great as almost to make me who hate her, pity her'; 'Elizabeth [...] died *so* miserable that were it not an injury to the memory of Mary I should pity her', *TW*, pp. 123, 131). In volume 2 of Goldsmith's *History of England*, in a passage concerning the princes in the Tower, we read that the assassins

> found the young princes in bed, and fallen into a sound sleep: after suffocating them with the bolster and pillows, they shewed their naked bodies to Tyrrel, who ordered them to be buried at the stair-foot, deep in the ground, under an heap of stones. (Goldsmith, *History of England*, vol. 2, p. 264)

In the Austen family text, this passage has a single word written next to it, 'wretches'. Sabor glosses the word as applicable only to 'the young princes murdered in the Tower' (*Juvenilia*, p. 317). But does that epithet in fact refer to the boys, or to their killers? Or even, perhaps, to both parties? 'Wretches'

---

34. On the portrait of Mary as a likeness of Jane Austen, see *Jane Austen's 'The History of England' & Cassandra's Portraits*, pp. xix–xxxvii.

might be expressive of pity or of blame (it is clearly intended to be the latter in 'Horrid wretches', *Juvenilia*, p. 350), or of both; it is at once a sentimental and a satirical term. The feelings involved here, like the various hands engaged in annotating the text, are both vehement and difficult to pin down. There is another example of such fierce unspecificity in the next volume of Goldsmith, in a note that re-writes a passage concerning the so-called Popish Plot against Charles II:

> But the parliament testified greater credulity than even the vulgar. The cry of plot was immediately echoed from one house to the other; the country party would not let slip such an opportunity of managing the passions of the people; the courtiers were afraid of being thought disloyal, if they should doubt the innocence of the pretended assassins of their king. (Goldsmith, *History of England*, vol. 3, p. 416; *Juvenilia*, p. 327)

Someone, possibly Austen (although the hand is hard to identify) has crossed out 'innocence' and replaced it with 'Guilt'. Such a diametric opposition, by way of intervention, would certainly be in line with the teenage Austen's protestations in her own 'History' that (for instance)

> It is however but Justice, & my Duty to declare that this amiable Woman [Anne Boleyn] was entirely innocent of the Crimes with which she was accused, of which her Beauty, her Elegance, & her Sprightliness were sufficient proofs, not to mention her solemn protestations of Innocence, the weakness of the Charges against her, & the king's Character (*TW*, p. 126)

Sabor writes that the alteration to the Popish Plot section of Goldsmith's text is really 'a correction, rather than a comment; the logic of Goldsmith's sentence requires the word "guilt", not "innocence"' (*Juvenilia*, p. 327). But the logic of the sentence hinges on what the verb 'doubt' means, and in this period (as indeed until the late nineteenth century) it retained both positive and negative senses. 'To doubt' could either express the suspicion that something *is* the case (as in Hamlet's 'I doubt some foul play') or the possibility that it *is not* (as in Hamlet's 'Doubt thou the stars are fire; / Doubt that the sun doth move').[35] So to 'doubt the innocence of the pretended assassins' could mean thinking that that they were innocent, as well as that they were not (just as

---

35. See *OED* 'doubt, *v.*' senses I. 2. a.; 6. b, c; *Hamlet* 1. 2. 255, 2.2.115–16. *The Riverside Shakespeare*, ed. G. Blakemore Evans, with the assistance of J.J.M. Tobin, 2nd edition (Boston: Houghton Mifflin, 1997).

'pretended' could describe someone who legitimately claims to be something, as well as someone who deceptively assumes an identity that is not his own). Goldsmith's text therefore stands in no need of correction, but the atmosphere of suspicion that is being described makes it appropriate that the reader should perform a double-take, both at 'doubt' and at 'pretended', because each word faces in two directions. Changing 'innocence' to 'Guilt', however powerful an intervention, cannot remove the central ambiguity of Goldsmith's *History*, which may even be compassing two entirely different responses to the events he is describing. To get to grips with the passage requires alertness to the historical (and double) meanings of words, while bearing in mind that Austen's 'History' grows out of a suspicion about the traditional grounds of historical enquiry and about how accounts of the past are put together. We might also remember that the young Austen's assertions typically cut both ways, so that the language of 'sufficient proofs'—used to vindicate Anne Boleyn, and to demonstrate her innocence—is also applied to Edward IV, where it performs in quite the opposite fashion (*TW*, p. 123). As in the case of her appraisal of Richard III, she is perfectly capable of embracing two mutually exclusive possibilities, guilt and innocence, at the same time. The distinctive thing about her manner is that she combines a keen sense of the doubtful status of historical truth with a bold, imperious, judgemental voice. The recognition of uncertainty—even of her own inadequacy—is not permitted to call her own authority into question. Like Eleanor Tilney in *Northanger Abbey*, Austen takes 'the false with the true' (vol. 1, ch. 14, p. 110), while asserting and adjudicating on the capacity to discriminate one from the other. The double sense of 'doubt' plays into her double character.

Throughout her 'History', Austen brings out the incongruous relationship between the brutality of what she is describing and the modern schoolroom or polite drawing-room context into which such events are necessarily being translated. Besides including anecdotes which signally fail to advance the narrative, and which might therefore invite us to mistrust the historian's discrimination, she introduces absurd touches of gentility. As elsewhere in the early works, she attaches the epithet 'amiable' to a variety of people. Sometimes she appears to mean the word seriously, as in her assessment of the 'amiable' and 'innocent' Anne Boleyn (*TW*, p. 126); at other times, it suggests its opposite: 'This Prince [Henry V] after he succeeded to the throne grew quite reformed & Amiable, forsaking all his dissipated Companions, & never thrashing Sir William again. During his reign, Lord Cobham was burned alive, but I forget what for' (*TW*, p. 122). Just as ignorance in relation to history resurfaces in

Austen's later fiction, so enquiry into the value and implications of the 'amiable' continues from this early work into *Emma*, where Knightley, 'a sensible man', defines it as a truly English epithet, involving proper awareness of the feelings of others (*Emma*, vol. 1, ch. 1, p. 8; ch. 18, pp. 160–61). The 'amiable' defines true sensibility, as opposed to the bankrupt manifestations of feeling and delicacy that are on display throughout the teenage writings. In such local repetitions lies evidence of Austen's habit of quarrying her own past, revisiting and recycling the same linguistic and moral terrain. That habit of repurposing early materials constitutes the most fruitful sense, perhaps, in which she might be thought of as a historian.

Consider, in this light, the opening words of the first regal sketch in 'History of England': 'Henry the 4th ascended the throne of England much to his own satisfaction in the year 1399' (*TW*, p. 121). The king's abrupt yet effortlessly smooth rise to power anticipates the smug provincial supremacy of a later heroine, who, in her own opening sentence appears thus: 'Emma Woodhouse, handsome, clever, and rich, with a comfortable home and happy disposition, seemed unite some of the best blessings of existence'. Like a monarch, Emma suffers, so the narrator tells us, from 'the power of having rather too much her own way, and a disposition to think a little too well of herself' (*Emma*, vol. 1, ch. 1, p. 3). Writers and readers of history may, like Emma, be led to think a little too well of themselves, in that they may be driven to understand the past as an inevitable, teleological progression towards the present. In the first chapter of the novel, Emma flatters herself that she foresaw Mr and Mrs Weston's marriage, and that her management of several 'little matters' has served to bring about the union (she does not acknowledge that these two readings of events might be incompatible). 'I made the match myself', she boasts; 'I made the match, you know, four years ago; and to have it take place, and be proved in the right, when so many people said Mr. Weston would never marry again, may comfort me for any thing.' Mr Woodhouse wholly endorses Emma's view of events, in which people and their feelings are entirely subject to his daughter's predictions: 'I wish you would not make matches and fortel things, for whatever you say always comes to pass' (*Emma*, vol. 1, ch. 1, p. 10). Knightley, however, will have none of it, and chides Emma for her partial, prejudiced, and ignorant way of referring past to present and other people to herself:

'Success supposes endeavour. Your time has been properly and delicately spent, if you have been endeavouring for the last four years to bring about this marriage. A worthy employment for a young lady's mind! But if, which

I rather imagine, your making the match, as you call it, means only your planning it, your saying to yourself one idle day, "I think it would be a very good thing for Miss Taylor if Mr. Weston were to marry her," and saying it again to yourself every now and then afterwards,—why do you talk of success? where is your merit?—what are you proud of?—you made a lucky guess; and *that* is all that can be said.' (*Emma*, vol. 1, ch. 1, p. 11)

Emma's persistent misreading of the past in terms of what she wants it to signify for the present or future—encouraged by her apparent success in the case of Miss Taylor—will shortly cause grave embarrassment and distress, when she misconstrues Elton's infatuation with her as a symptom of his passion for Harriet Smith (*Emma*, vol. 1, ch. 1, pp. 10–11; ch. 10, pp. 94–7; ch. 15, pp. 140–3). As a historian whose understanding of the past is fatally compromised by her own wish to be at once the most discerning interpreter of its ineluctable progress towards the present and its efficient cause—or something between those two positions, which Emma summarizes as 'the do-nothing and the do-all' (*Emma*, vol. 1, ch. 1, p. 11)—the heroine is a serious and threatening rival to her author.

In her 'History of England', young Austen elbowed such Whiggish tendencies as the equally confident Emma Woodhouse later displays into the realms of absurdity, while also pressing them into the service of Tory historiography. Thus Margaret Tudor, daughter of Henry VII, is said to have had 'the happiness of being grandmother to one of the first Characters in the World'—Mary, Queen of Scots—not that she knew this, unlike Austen, who also knows that she will 'have occasion to speak more at large' of Mary 'in future' (*TW*, p. 125). Historical narrative permits such magical foresight; with one of her many glances at a small domestic community of readers, Austen also 'cannot help foreseeing' that her sailor brother will equal the maritime exploits of Sir Francis Drake (*TW*, p. 130). In this prediction, she wasn't far off the mark. In view of subsequent events in her own life and afterlife, and of the illustrious careers of her sailor brothers, there is a touching as well as funny relationship throughout the 'History' between the Austen family's present genteel obscurity and the glorious renown she discerns for them. She repeatedly contrasts her own, superhuman, historian's ability to predict the future with the natural shortcomings of her paltry, all too human cast. She cannot 'pity the Kingdom for the misfortunes they experienced' during Mary Tudor's reign, she says, 'since they fully deserved them, for having allowed her to succeed her Brother—which was a double peice of folly, since they might have foreseen that as she died without Children, she would be succeeded by that disgrace to humanity, that pest of society, Elizabeth' (*TW*, p. 128). The Duke of Somerset was 'beheaded', Austen reports,

> of which he might with reason have been proud, had he known that such was the death of Mary Queen of Scotland; but as it was impossible that he should be conscious of what had never happened, it does not appear that he felt particularly delighted with the manner of it. (*TW*, pp. 127–8)

These remarks serve to collapse past and present into one mutually unillumi-nating state of co-existence. Rather than depict the past as helping to educate and inform the present and the future, Austen upbraids historical characters for not having benefitted from the knowledge of events that had yet to occur (and which, had they known about them, would not in any case have helped their own cause). These figures from the past should have seen themselves as causes of future effects, or (in the way that Milton sees Eve in *Paradise Lost*, 'fairest of her daughters') as analogues to their own posterity; instead of which they were selfish enough to live within the realm of what was merely possi-ble.[36] The point of these jokes seems to be that characters as they are conven-tionally represented in history-writing are either made to possess an inhuman ability to treat themselves and their relatives as if they were already no more than occasions for their descendants to reflect upon, or are found wanting for not quite possessing such an ability. They are expected, in life (as narrated in retrospect), to foresee their future use 'To point a Moral, or adorn a Tale', as Johnson put it in *The Vanity of Human Wishes* (1749).[37]

Her comically brisk response to and re-writing of history must have been enduring family traits, going by Austen's great-niece Fanny Lefroy's later ac-count of her ancestors on the maternal side:

> Sir John's mother was Mary daughter of Maurice Lord Berkeley, who mar-ried Sir Thomas Perrot of Hardolston, Milford and Langharne [?], etc, etc, etc, She was a great beauty, and his father was said to be that excellent man Henry VIII whom we are told he closely resembled. In plurality of wives he certainly seems to have done so, but not being able to cut off their heads,

36. John Milton, *Paradise Lost*, ed. Alastair Fowler (London and New York: Longman, 1990), book 4, l. 324: 'fairest of her daughters Eve'.

37. Samuel Johnson, *The Vanity of Human Wishes*, l. 222, in *The Complete English Poems*, ed. J. D. Fleeman (Harmondsworth: Penguin, 1971; repr. 1982).

as was his royal Sire, he unfortunately had more than one at the same time.[38]

Lefroy's joke about beheading, and her 'unfortunately', are entirely in her aunt's historical line and style—compare Austen's comment on James I: 'fortunately for him his eldest son Prince Henry died before his father or he might have experienced the evils which befell his unfortunate brother' (*TW*, p. 131). Beyond Austen's obvious joke in the passage on the Duke of Somerset's execution—that nobody is likely to be proud of or delighted by the distinction of being beheaded—there is, again, a broader historiographical comedy in play. Surveying the past, Whig historians (and other kinds of author, too) tend to assume that everything back then has been leading up to now, in a succession of characters, events, and ideas that was and is progressing towards perfection (Austen's ideal being embodied, in this case, as Mary, Queen of Scots). If only those in the past had already been conscious of future events, or realized that in their own fates lay those of greater figures, yet unborn. Quentin Skinner characterizes such techniques as belonging to the 'mythology of prolepsis': one in which 'the historian is more interested in the retrospective significance of a given historical work or action than in its meaning for the agent himself'.[39] This sense of the historian's diversion of importance from past to present is one of the many ways in which partiality, prejudice, and ignorance are shown forth in young Austen, as in the later novels such flaws are revealed in characters who are themselves bad historians of their own lives and experience, and of those around them.

A related effect—involving causality and chronology—is achieved when the seemingly accidental event is revealed to have been planned or determined well in advance. This is brought about through the supercharged use of 'happen'; in the opening sentence of the 'History of England', it describes an event which, it is heavily implied, is far from happenstance:

> Henry the 4th ascended the throne of England much to his own satisfaction in the year 1399, after having prevailed on his cousin and predecessor Richard the 2[d], to resign it to him, and to retire for the rest of his life to Pomfret Castle, where he happened to be murdered. (*TW*, p. 121)

---

38. MS Family History by Fanny Caroline Lefroy, Hampshire Record Office 23M93/85/2 [n. p.].

39. Quentin Skinner, 'Meaning and Understanding in the History of Ideas', *History and Theory*, 8 (1969), 3–53 (p. 22).

The same manipulation of 'happen' occurs in 'Love and Friendship', where Laura's reference to a 'little Accident' introduces examples of 'happening' and 'happen'—the first word indicating a chance discovery, the second acting as a euphemism for carefully planned and successfully executed theft on more than one occasion:

> Sophia happening one Day to open a private Drawer in Macdonald's Library with one of her own keys, discovered that it was the Place where he kept his Papers of consequence & amongst them some bank-notes of considerable amount. This discovery she imparted to me, and having agreed together than it would be a proper treatment of so vile a Wretch as Macdonald to deprive him of Money, perhaps dishonestly gained, it was determined that the next time we should either of us happen to go that way, we would take one or more of the Bank notes form the drawer. This well-meant Plan we had often successfully put into Execution (*TW*, pp. 84–5)

The passive construction 'it was determined' is engineered so as to skate in queenly fashion over the matter of individual criminal responsibility, straight after the masterly diversion of 'perhaps dishonestly gained'; the excision of agency is also typical of eighteenth-century historical narrative, with its bid for impartiality. Austen may have learnt her comic manipulation of happiness, happening, and happenstance from a historian who was, in other contexts, much preoccupied with cause and effect. David Hume, in a passage which perhaps illustrates how—in spite of his much-vaunted impartiality—his own sympathies inflect the account he gives of Charles I and the Star Chamber, remarks of Sir John Eliot that in 1632 he 'happened to die while in custody'.[40] Then again, a novelistic equivalent for this phrasing had also been deployed in Burney's *Cecilia, or Memoirs of an Heiress* (1782), an even more probable source for Austen. Miss Larolles complains to the heroine that what she, Miss Larolles, has undertaken 'on purpose' is thwarted by what happens, fatally, to have happened next:

> Only conceive what happened to me three weeks ago! you must know I was invited to Miss Clinton's wedding, and so I made up a new dress on purpose, in a very particular sort of shape, quite of my own invention, and it had the sweetest effect you can conceive; well, and when the time came, do you know her mother *happened to die*! Never any thing was so excessive

40. Hume, *History of England*, vol. 5, p. 216.

unlucky, for now she won't be married this half year, and my dress will be quite old and yellow.[41]

The egomaniacally poor taste of describing someone else's death as 'excessive unlucky'—as far as other people and their clothing are concerned—finds a mirror image in 'Love and Friendship' when Laura and Sophia chance upon their dead and dying spouses thanks to what Laura describes as 'a most fortunate Accident':

> From this Dilemma I was most fortunately relieved by an accident truly apropos; it was the lucky overturning of a Gentleman's Phaeton, on the road which ran murmuring behind us. It was a most fortunate Accident as it diverted the Attention of Sophia from the melancholy reflections which she had been before indulging.
>
> We instantly quitted our seats & ran to the rescue of those who but a few moments before had been in so elevated a situation as a fashionably high Phaeton, but who were now laid low and sprawling in the Dust—. 'What an ample subject for reflection on the uncertain Enjoyments of this World, would not that Phaeton & the Life of Cardinal Wolsey afford a thinking Mind!' said I to Sophia as we were hastening to the field of Action.
>
> She had not time to answer me, for every thought was now engaged by the horrid Spectacle before us. Two Gentlemen most elegantly attired but weltering in blood was what first struck our Eyes—we approached—they were Edward & Augustus—Yes dearest Marianne they were our Husbands. (*TW*, p. 87)

Here, the language of acute sensibility is plastered onto a helter-skelter narration which stubbornly, brilliantly, resists the natural feelings of humanity. Sophia's 'melancholy reflections' on her absent husband are rudely interrupted by the appearance of his corpse, thrown alongside Laura's expiring Edward before her very eyes—and the elegant clothes are more immediately striking than is the blood. (Perhaps Austen had *Tom Jones* on her mind. In her first surviving letter she wrote to Cassandra about Tom Lefroy, alluding to book 7, ch. 14, of Fielding's novel: 'He is a very great admirer of Tom Jones, and therefore wears the same coloured clothes, I imagine, which <u>he</u> did when he was wounded'; the passage in question reads: 'As soon as the sergeant was

---

41. [Fanny Burney], *Cecilia, or Memoirs of an Heiress. By the Author of Evelina*, 5 vols. (London: T. Payne and T. Cadell, 1783), vol. 3, pp. 16–17 (my emphasis).

departed, Jones rose from his bed, and dressed himself entirely, putting on even his coat, which, as its colour was white, showed very visibly the streams of blood which had flowed down it'. *Letters*, 9–10 Jan. 1796, p. 2 and n. 16.) The disconcerting indifference of Laura, the narrator, is paraded as exquisite feeling, but exposed as its opposite by the word order, and by the sequence of her observations.

Chronology (as well as partiality, prejudice, and assumed ignorance) lies at the heart of the joke. Laura knows from the start of her letter, as we on a first reading cannot, that the 'fortunate' overturning of a carriage in fact heralds the death of her beloved, although (mimicking Richardsonian convention in writing 'to the moment')[42] she reports events as if she knows no more than we do, as if she has re-inhabited her past self at the precise moment she describes. This staged ignorance of the future contrasts strangely with her reflection on hastening 'to the rescue of those who but a few moments before had been in so elevated a situation as a fashionably high Phaeton, but who were now laid low and sprawling in the Dust'. We might excuse this remark as the conventionally pious effusion of a mature narrator on a past event, writing to a much younger correspondent, even if she has not revealed the identity of those within the carriage. But her next line, quoted from the 'field of Action', tips us into full-blown absurdity: 'What an ample subject for reflection on the uncertain Enjoyments of this World, would not that Phaeton & the Life of Cardinal Wolsey afford a thinking Mind!'.

Laura senses that she ought to make use of the scene before her, to put it to some educational or improving purpose. She is remembering something from the schoolroom about falls from elevation, about applying figures from history to the purposes of everyday life. But she tries to do so before she has allowed her past self to recognize the scene for what it is in that historical present, and for her alone, without which recognition it can have no meaning. As in 'The History of England', the collapse into one another of two timeframes, past and present (here mediated through the epistolary form), produces a narrative which can only be said to afford a moral quite contrary to the one the narrator is seeking to inculcate. Laura is falling prey to the mythology of prolepsis. As hers is not, in fact, 'a thinking Mind', she is quite right to see only the potential for making something of the lesson of an overturned coach (also the opening scene of 'Sanditon'). The 'horrid Spectacle' that she and Sophia encounter

42. The phrase is originally Lovelace's: 'I love to write to the moment'. Samuel Richardson, *Clarissa*, letter 49, vol. 4, p. 288.

might well cause a more skilful moralist, given a decent lapse of time, to think of the historical figure of Cardinal Wolsey. His spectacular fall from Henry VIII's favour was often invoked to exemplify the dangers of pride and the transience of power—as, for instance, in Shakespeare and Fletcher's *Henry VIII* and in Samuel Johnson's *The Vanity of Human Wishes* (ll. 99–128). Like Austen's Lady Jane Grey and *Pride and Prejudice*'s Mary Bennet, however, Laura is far too indifferent to anyone else's suffering to make us believe in her own; otherwise, she would not be so funny ('Tho indeed my own misfortunes do not make less impression on me than they ever did', she writes her third letter to Marianne, 'yet now I never feel for those of an other', *TW*, p. 70).

'Elegantly attired but weltering in [...] blood' might stand as a description of Austen's 'History of England'. As if to demonstrate how violent episodes may be ushered into genteel company, she comments of the Civil War (which here becomes 'civil', or rather uncivil, in a different sense of that word) that: 'Never certainly were there before so many detestable Characters at one time in England as in this period of its History; Never were amiable Men so Scarce' (*TW*, p. 133). And on the Gunpowder Plot: 'Truth being I think very excusable in an Historian, I am necessitated to say that in this reign the roman Catholics of England did not behave like Gentlemen to the protestants. Their Behaviour indeed to the Royal Family & both Houses of Parliament might justly be considered by them as very uncivil' (*TW*, p. 131). The language of indulgence towards a historian who favours the truth is funny because it suggests that the historian's territory, whatever else he or she might claim, tends to be that of untruth. But even if history *were* somehow to achieve the status of naked truth, Austen suggests that it might yet call for an apology, since to make a claim which is merely factually accurate is not necessarily to make a claim that is worth hearing: 'It is [...] not a sufficient vindication of a character, that it is drawn as it appears, for many characters ought never to be drawn; nor of a narrative, that the train of events is agreeable to observation and experience.'[43]

In another of Austen's early works, 'Kitty, or the Bower', dated August 1792 (nine months after 'The History of England' was completed), the history-loving heroine endures vacuous lectures from a fierce aunt who wishes to see revived 'the Manners of the People in Queen Elizabeth's reign'. Kitty hopes she does not wish 'to restore Queen Eliz.th herself'. Her aunt, 'who never hazarded

---

43. Samuel Johnson, *Rambler* no. 4 (1750), in *The Yale Edition of the Works of Samuel Johnson*, vols. 3–5: *The Rambler*, ed. W. J. Bate and Albrecht B. Strauss (New Haven, CT, and London: Yale University Press, 1969), vol. 3, p. 22.

a remark on History that was not well founded', replies that Elizabeth 'lived to a good old Age, and was a very Clever Woman'. Kitty acknowledges that this is indeed 'True', but objects quite reasonably that its truth is beside the point:

> 'I do not consider either of those Circumstances as meritorious in herself, and they are very far from making me wish her return, for if she were to come again with the same Abilities and the same good Constitution She might do as much Mischeif and last as long as she did before' (*TW*, p. 175)

Kitty's warm, partisan love of history leads her to engage in heated discussions on the subject whenever possible. She is disappointed when her stupid new friend Camilla Stanley fails to respond to the argument about Elizabeth, and she flirts with Camilla's brother Edward by talking to him of past kings. Describing one of these encounters, Austen questions once again whether impartiality is any more desirable a trait in a historian than it is in a friend. The distinction she worries at here, as in 'The History of England', is between disinterestedness and a lack of interest or commitment—one which has implications for the development of her own discreet, mobile, perpetually engaged narrative voice. Kitty, we are told, is 'induced [. . .] to take every opportunity of turning the Conversation on History'. Soon, she and Edward Stanley are

> engaged in an historical dispute, for which no one was more calculated than Stanley who was so far from being really of any party, that he had scarcely a fixed opinion on the Subject. He could therefore always take either side, & always argue with temper. In his indifference on all such topics he was very unlike his Companion, whose judgement being guided by her feelings which were eager & warm, was easily decided, and though it was not always infallible, she defended it with a Spirit & Enthousiasm which marked her own reliance on it. They had continued therefore for sometime conversing in this manner on the character of Richard the 3^{d}, which he was warmly defending when he suddenly seized hold of her hand, and exclaiming with great emotion, 'Upon my honour you are entirely mistaken,' pressed it passionately to his lips, & ran out of the arbour. (*TW*, p. 198)

Both participants in this debate are manifestly imperfect historians. The unfixed Edward Stanley seems, initially, to fulfil the eighteenth-century brief of disinterestedness in that he has no particular cause or character to defend or attack. But the fact that he is, in Austen's cautionary wording, at once without fixity and 'calculated' for 'historical dispute' turns out not to speak in his favour. For Austen as a historian and as a novelist, it seems that cool indifference is worse than partisanship. It suggests inconstancy and flightiness of other kinds; that Stanley's passion for Kitty may well endure no longer than his whimsical support for Richard III.

So indeed it proves, when his 'ease & Indifference' suddenly strike Kitty as 'incompatible with that partiality which she had at one time been almost convinced of his feeling for her' (*TW*, p. 201). Stanley's failure is to be a less partial historian than she. His rhetorical fluency—his ability to 'argue with temper' both sides of a question—contrasts with Kitty's warm, enthusiastic feelings, which invariably govern her 'judgement'. The word is here used in the loose sense of her opinions, which she defends with gusto, but it also implies a larger concern about the nature of her historical thinking, akin to that which is examined more fully in *Emma*. Like Kitty's, and like Marianne Dashwood's, Emma's mind is too quickly made up, and she relies too securely on the acuity of her own perceptions—faults which lead her to misrepresent past, present, and future, both to herself and to other people. Nevertheless, when faced with the alternatives of detachment and partisanship, Austen will usually identify the latter as preferable. Partiality of this kind is the mark of a truly amiable character, such as that of the ardent, quasi-novelistic heroine of her 'History of England': Mary, Queen of Scots.

Alertness to the provinces of history and fiction—whether they are considered to be mutually antagonistic, or co-dependent, or indistinguishable from one another—makes its presence felt throughout Austen's work. In her resistance to the idea that open-hearted, unbounded knowledge of another person may be attained in an instant, or indeed ever, Austen is partly resisting the clichés of sentimental fiction. But she is also returning to historical debates about character, such as those surrounding Mary, Queen of Scots, and to the nature of the evidence that might be produced for and against it. Throughout her novels, Austen's heroines are engaged (more or less skilfully) in the interpretation of conflicting pieces of intelligence. Near the end of *Pride and Prejudice*, Elizabeth discusses with Darcy an important document in their shared history: his letter to her, in which he finally unmasked Wickham's treachery and suggested some painful truths about her family. Such epistolary evidence will become even more crucial in *Persuasion*, when Mrs Smith produces both documentary proof and an equally important appeal to Anne's personal observation, in order to condemn the villainous Mr Elliot (vol. 2, ch. 9, pp. 208–29).

Still, Austen makes it clear that the novel need not call upon and is not susceptible to the same kinds of proof that must, or should, govern history-writing. In her discussion with Captain Harville, and in response to his claim that—had he the memory—he could 'bring you fifty quotations in a moment on my side the argument'—Anne Elliot pleads for 'no reference to examples in books'. When Harville then objects 'how shall we prove any thing?' Anne calmly replies 'We never shall' (*Pers*, vol. 2, ch. 11, pp. 254–5). Here, in an exchange of opinions between a man and a woman that sounds very like one of the discussions between Johnson's Rasselas and his sister Nekayah, the male speaker's complaint about failing to resolve a problem or answer a question is met by a female acknowledgement of human partiality and fallibility. In their debate concerning the relative merits of marriage and celibacy, Rasselas says to Nekayah, exasperatedly, 'Both conditions may be bad, but they cannot both be worst.' His sister responds:

> 'I did not expect [. . .] to hear that imputed to falsehood which is the consequence only of frailty. To the mind, as to the eye, it is difficult to compare with exactness objects vast in their extent and various in their parts. When we see or conceive the whole at once, we readily note the discriminations and decide the preference, but of two systems, of which neither can be surveyed by any human being in its full compass of magnitude and multiplicity of complication, where is the wonder that, judging of the whole by parts, I am alternately affected by one and the other as either presses on my memory or fancy? We differ from ourselves just as we differ from each other when we see only part of the question, as in the multifarious relations of politics and morality, but when we perceive the whole at once, as in numerical computations, all agree in one judgment, and none ever varies in his opinion.'[44]

Anne echoes this view of human frailty and limitation, but she also continues to emphasize the difference between what is admissible evidence to support a female as opposed to a male point of view:

> 'We never can expect to prove any thing upon such a point. It is a difference of opinion which does not admit of proof. We each begin probably with a little bias towards our own sex, and upon that bias build every

---

44. *The Yale Edition of the Works of Samuel Johnson*, vol. 16: *Rasselas and Other Tales*, ed. Gwin J. Kolb (New Haven, CT, and London: Yale University Press, 1990), pp. 104–5. Austen's copy of volume 2 of *The Prince of Abissinia. A tale* (1759), as *Rasselas* was initially styled, survives (see *Bibliography* K15, p. 443).

circumstance in favour of it which has occurred within our own circle; many of which circumstances (perhaps those very cases which strike us the most) may be precisely such as cannot be brought forward without betraying a confidence, or in some respect saying what should not be said.' (vol. 2, ch. 11, p. 255)

The language has ceased to be that of proof gathered from books and has become that of 'cases' experienced first-hand, many of which can never be told. Where Harville would like to shore up his argument with fifty quotations that he cannot remember, Anne appeals to circumstances that cannot be openly discussed. It is the delicate business of Austen's fiction to examine the latter. Each of the two approaches—quoting numerous written authorities to prove a point; tacitly appealing to secrets—has its manifest limitations. The distinction between the two underpins Austen's insistence that she could never create a character 'occasionally abundant in quotations & allusions' (to James Stanier Clarke, *Letters*, 11 Dec. 1815, p. 319) and her professed dislike of 'enormous great stupid thick Quarto Volumes' whose readers 'must be acquainted with everything in the World' (to Cassandra, *Letters*, 9 Feb. 1813, p. 215; Catherine Morland says she dislikes history because it is narrated in 'great volumes, which [...] nobody would willingly ever look into', *NA*, vol. 1, ch. 14, p. 110). There is only one direct citation—in the strict sense of words placed within quotation marks—in the 'History of England'. Having promised 'a slight sketch of the principal Events' of the reign of Henry VIII, Austen puts at the top of her list 'Cardinal Wolsey's telling the father Abbott of Leicester Abbey that "he was come to lay his bones among them"' (*TW*, pp. 126, 303 n.). Deriving from Goldsmith and Hume, this snippet of reported speech is made even more bathetic than it might have been thanks to its billing as a 'principal Event'. Parroting 'examples from the Lives of great Men' such as Wolsey was not the kind of learning or form of writing in which Austen professed herself interested ('The female philosopher', *TW*, p. 152). Better to be partial, prejudiced, and ignorant than to 'talk from books', as Johnson disparagingly put it, meaning 'to retail the sentiments of others [...] ; in short, to converse without any originality of thinking':[45]

You distress me cruelly by your request about Books; I cannot think of any to bring with me, nor have I any idea of our wanting them. I come to you to be talked to, not to read or hear reading. I can do <u>that</u> at home; & indeed

---

45. *Boswell's Life of Johnson*, vol. 5, p. 378.

I am now laying in a stock of intelligence to pour out on you as <u>my</u> share of Conversation.—I am reading Henry's History of England. (Jane Austen to Martha Lloyd, *Letters*, pp. 61–2)

There are discussions of history as a subject in Austen's published fiction—especially in *Northanger Abbey*'s defence of the novel by way of contrast with textbook versions of 'the History of England', and in Eleanor and Henry Tilney's conversation with the heroine at Beechen Cliff. It is easy to miss the fact that, early in this exchange of views, Catherine and Eleanor jointly formulate a sophisticated criticism of historians, who are said to 'display imagination without raising interest'. Although Eleanor swiftly moves on to explain her own enjoyment of history, the point she makes in response to Catherine is a serious one. When historians depart from the truth—in other words, when they try to behave like novelists—they often fail (*NA*, vol. 1, ch. 5, p. 31; ch. 14, pp. 109–10). While 'the foes' of the novel, readers and writers who are motivated by 'pride, ignorance, or fashion' to eulogize historians (pride and ignorance also belonging to the teenage Austen in *her* character as historian), we are urged to remember that the character and judgement of such a writer may well be inferior to those of the novelist. Such overt, polemical handling of history in general and of historians as a body of authors is unusual in Austen's fiction. There, the word 'history' has, primarily, an individual or local application. It can work as a faintly comic or mock-epic device, whereby the possible range, grandeur, and breadth of history are suddenly narrowed down to a private or domestic matter. In *Sense and Sensibility*, we learn of Mrs Jennings that

> She had already repeated her own history to Elinor three or four times; and had Elinor's memory been equal to her means of improvement, she might have known very early in their acquaintance, all the particulars of Mr. Jennings's last illness, and what he said to his wife a few minutes before he died. (vol. 1, ch. 11, p. 64–5)

Here, the vestigial idea of studying history as a 'means of improvement', derived from Chapone and others, is comically applied to the circumstantial tale of a dead man's last illness—particulars hardly fit to be narrated to a new friend (Austen may have known a letter from Johnson to Hester Thrale in which he announced 'This, Madam, is the history of one of my toes').[46] Mr Wickham,

---

46. *Letters to and from the late Samuel Johnson, LL.D. To which are added some poems never before printed. Published from the original Mss. in her possession, by Hester Lynch Piozzi*, 2 vols.

who seems 'amiable', insinuates himself into Elizabeth's favour by retailing 'the history of his acquaintance with Mr. Darcy', glossed by a credulous Elizabeth as 'a history of himself [...] names, facts, everything mentioned without ceremony [...] there was truth in his looks' (*P&P*, vol. 1, chs. 16–17, pp. 86, 95, 96). In *Mansfield Park*, 'history' is again an index of character: '[William's] recitals were amusing in themselves to Sir Thomas, but the chief object in seeking them, was to understand the recitor, to know the young man by his histories' (vol. 2, ch. 6, p. 275); 'She gave the history of her recent visit' (vol. 2, ch. 9, p. 305); 'he had Fanny's history' (vol. 3, ch. 3, p. 387). When the course of Edmund Bertram's and Mary Crawford's long walk around Sotherton, a place with Stuart associations, is dutifully repeated for Fanny's benefit, the narrator sums up: 'This was their history' (vol. 1, ch. 10, p. 120).[47]

As befits a novel about attachments to the past, *Persuasion* contains the richest and most varied sense of history to be found in Austen's fiction. She began to write her last completed work on 8 August 1815, 'the day it was generally known that Napoleon had gone into permanent exile and shortly after the return of Louis XVIII to Paris on 18 July' (*Pers*, 'Introduction', p. xxx). Austen's decision to set the action of the story in the recent past—the period running up to Waterloo (18 June 1815)—gives a sad historical irony to the final sentence even as it celebrates Anne's happiness on the one hand, and the navy at home and abroad on the other: 'She gloried in being a sailor's wife, but must pay the tax of quick alarm for belonging to that profession which is, if possible, more distinguished in its domestic virtues than in its national importance' (vol. 2, ch. 12, p. 275).[48]

Persuasion opens by presenting another character opening a historical work that, like the Austen family copy of Goldsmith's *History of England*, combines

---

(London: A. Strahan and T. Cadell, 1788), vol. 2, p. 62. Writing to Cassandra (8–9 Feb. 1807), Austen cites a remark from one of Johnson's letters to Boswell: 'like my dear Dᵣ Johnson I beleive I have dealt more in Notions than Facts' (*Letters*, p. 126).

47. 'Sotherton resembles in many respects the real Stoneleigh Abbey in Warwickshire, which the Austens visited with its new owner, their cousin Rev. Leigh, in 1806. Sotherton's past likewise looks to have been shaped by its owners' loyalty to the Stuart monarchy during the seventeenth-century Civil War. Stoneleigh had sheltered Charles I in 1742'. Jane Austen, *Mansfield Park: An Annotated Edition*, ed. Deirdre Shauna Lynch (Cambridge, MA, and London: Belknap Press of Harvard University Press, 2016), p. 124, n. 4.

48. 'One might have expected [Napoleon's] defeat to usher in a long period of peace but in fact small-scale conflicts continued' (*Pers*, p. 392 n.). The editors cite the loss of 818 British sailors in Algiers in August 1816, the month in which Austen completed *Persuasion*.

print with manuscript alterations and corrections. In a hardened, aged version of young Austen's 'partial, prejudiced & ignorant Historian', Sir Walter consults the Baronetage in order to read 'his own history with an interest which never failed'; his vanity and folly on the historical front are matched by his vain and foolish endeavour to remain physically youthful (*Pers*, vol. 1, ch. 1, p. 3). Devoted to his own past, he cannot summon up the energy or interest to preserve his own estate. In the final chapter of the novel, its opening scene is revisited when Anne's sister Mary strenuously hopes 'they could but keep Captain Wentworth from being made a baronet' (vol. 2, ch. 12, p. 272).

Elsewhere in *Persuasion*, we learn that 'Mrs. Musgrove was giving Mrs. Croft the history of her eldest daughter's engagement' (vol. 2, ch. 11, p. 250). We know that Mrs Musgrove is a faulty and inherently comic narrator of her family history from the way in which Austen handles the death of Dick Musgrove, the cause of his mother's 'large fat sighings' on the sofa 'over the destiny of a son, whom alive nobody had cared for' (vol. 1, ch. 8, p. 73). Behaving like the savagely abridging teenage historian, a mature Austen treats 'this pathetic piece of family history' with brutal indifference, a refusal to extend pity, and a couple of jokes involving—like 'The History of England'—'ill fortune', 'good fortune', and 'abbreviation':

> The real circumstances of this pathetic piece of family history were, that the Musgroves had had the ill fortune of a very troublesome, hopeless son; and the good fortune to lose him before he reached his twentieth year; that he had been sent to sea because he was stupid and unmanageable on shore; that he had been very little cared for at any time by his family, though quite as much as he deserved; seldom heard of, and scarcely at all regretted, when the intelligence of his death abroad had worked its way to Uppercross, two years before.
>
> He had, in fact, though his sisters were now doing all they could for him, by calling him 'poor Richard,' been nothing better than a thick-headed, unfeeling, unprofitable Dick Musgrove, who had never done anything to entitle himself to more than the abbreviation of his name, living or dead. (vol. 1, ch. 6, p. 54)

He deserved to be called 'Dick'; that is, 'a generic name for a man or boy, esp. one considered ordinary or unexceptional'.[49] For all its justly celebrated

---

49. *OED*, 'dick' sense 1a. 'Dick' as a slang word for 'penis' seems to be a late nineteenth-century coinage (*OED*, 'dick', sense 4a).

autumnal, muted tints, *Persuasion* includes moments of sudden ferocity. Like 'The History of England', it is the work of a satirist who looks back in anger as well as with laughter; the work of a dying woman whose 'early impressions were incurable' (*Pers*, vol. 2, ch. 5, p. 175). Any reader is likely to be startled by the vitriolic pronouncement on young Musgrove, and to question its motivations. The vehemence of the judgement seems out of all proportion to the status of a very minor character who is, after all, already dead. It is hard to see what work this passage might be doing in the novel, other than perhaps to anticipate the near-fatal accident involving Louisa Musgrove, Dick's sister, at Lyme Regis. In both cases, Anne's feelings and actions are favourably contrasted with those of others, but the admirable nature of those feelings and actions in no sense relies on Dick Musgrove.

As in the opening sentence of *Northanger Abbey*, so here there seems to be something inherently suspicious about the name 'Richard'. And as in 'Love and Friendship', but in even more explicit form, the death of a young man is glossed as 'good fortune' ('an accident truly apropos [...] the lucky overturning of a Gentleman's Phaeton', *TW*, p. 87). Like the figure of Richard III in the 'History of England', Dick Musgrove generates two mutually exclusive responses—grief and ridicule—each of which is allowed to stand unmodified by the other. But the narrator's prejudice against him is made as abundantly clear as are his fond and foolish mother's feelings. In the 'History of England', we are told that Richard III, like Dick Musgrove, is 'very severely treated by Historians'; in notionally opposing such treatment, the young Austen says only that Richard was 'a very respectable man' (just as Richard Morland is 'a very respectable man, though his name was Richard'; *NA*, vol. 1, ch. 1, p. 5). Having announced in her two-sentence sketch of Edward V that the prince 'was murdered by his Uncle's Contrivance, whose name was Richard the 3ᵈ', when she next comes to the character of Richard III himself Austen then inclines to the belief 'that he did *not* kill his two Nephews'. The result of having raised both possibilities is that neither can be concluded, nor indeed be worth dwelling upon: 'Whether innocent or guilty, he did not reign long in peace...' (*TW*, p. 124).

Had Austen lived longer, the narrator's rough handling of the dead Musgrove boy might conceivably have been softened before *Persuasion* went to the press. But neither Cassandra nor Henry Austen, having overseen that process, can have judged the comments too harsh for inclusion. Dick Musgrove, reportedly an 'unfeeling' character in life, seems to merit no feeling response from *anyone* to his death: there is a strong sense throughout the narratorial commentary upon him of someone now being given exactly what he deserves. We might think that Austen is accusing Mrs Musgrove of affecting a pain that she does not truly feel, but in fact we are told that the appearance of Wentworth awakes in the mother 'greater grief than she had known on first hearing of [her son's] death' (vol. 1, ch. 6, p. 55); later in the novel, Mrs Musgrove is praised for her 'real affection' and 'sincerity' (vol. 2, ch. 10, p. 239). For her, as for the heroine of *Persuasion*, the Captain's return opens old wounds and rubs salt into them. But even if Mrs Musgrove is a more sincere figure than at first appears, it may well be this mother—or mothers in general—who is the real target of the narrator's brute indifference to Dick Musgrove. Anne's proud, hypochondriac, and carping sister Mary Musgrove comes in for comparable treatment. Working the same line as her mother-in-law, Mary complains of her husband, Charles, as 'very unfeeling [. . .] so unfeeling' towards her and his 'poor little boy', addressing Anne as 'You, who have not a mother's feelings' (vol. 1, ch. 7, pp. 60–61). These maternal figures are less developed, satirically, than Mrs Bennet or Lady Bertram, but they are equally remarkable for their helpless, unlamented stupidity.[50]

Towards the end of *Pride and Prejudice*, Elizabeth Bennet, who says that Darcy's letter marked the beginning of a process which saw 'all her former prejudices [. . .] removed', counsels her remorseful lover to adopt 'some of my philosophy. Think only of the past as its remembrance gives you pleasure.' Darcy immediately disagrees with her, arguing that 'I cannot give you credit for any philosophy of the kind. Your retrospections must be so totally void of reproach, that the contentment arising from them, is not of philosophy, but what is much better, of ignorance' (vol. 3, ch. 16, pp. 408–9). All the early editions of *Pride and Prejudice* have that sentence, at once complimentary and rebarbative, ending on a more conventional term of praise: 'innocence'. Fittingly, it was Cassandra Austen who suggested in the margin of her copy the emendation—reproduced in all modern texts of the novel—to 'ignorance'. After all, as dedicatee and illustrator of 'The History of England', and as the sister of an avowedly 'prejudiced & ignorant Historian', she would have known

---

50. Mothers are typically bad or dead in Jane Austen. Mrs Price, indifferent to Fanny when she returns home, is 'a partial, ill-judging parent, a dawdle, a slattern, whose house was the scene of mismanagement and discomfort from beginning to end, and who had no talent, no conversation, no affection towards herself; no curiosity to know her better, no desire of her friendship, and no inclination for her company that could lessen her sense of such feelings' (*MP*, vol. 3, ch. 8, pp. 451–2).

that Elizabeth's 'prejudices' are wholly compatible with her 'ignorance' in relation to the past (*P&P*, p. 537 n. 3). To be ignorant generally suggests an unfortunate want of knowledge. The fact that it is construed by Darcy as a serious
advantage in his clever wife-to-be might give pause for thought. It is a good
thing that Elizabeth is not acquainted with the past, as Darcy generously understands it at this climactic point in the book: that is, as a record, largely, of
his own offensive and awkward behaviour. Since Elizabeth, in his eyes, has
nothing with which to upbraid herself, she cannot know anything of that history at first hand. It is therefore also true to say that (as Darcy sees things) she
is innocent, as he cannot be. And yet, earlier in the novel, we have also seen
how Elizabeth's prejudices, born of pride, ignorance, and partiality, have led
her to misrepresent Darcy to herself and to others. It is only a partial and en-
amoured historian who can see her past as void of blame. Such conflicting and
overlapping perspectives on history and morality, as they are translated from
the public into the domestic spheres of conduct and emotion, lie at the heart
of Austen's fiction.

The young writer may, then, have been making a loud joke at her own and
at Goldsmith's expense when she posed as a historian who is partial, prejudiced, and ignorant. But lurking in this joke is a pervasive interest in the way
that history at large and at small affects our ethical make-up and actions in the
present. It might be a virtue to learn from the past, but it might also be a virtue
to have nothing to learn from it—or indeed to avoid knowledge of it completely. 'The History of England' pokes fun at the teachers of history and
morality—and at the whole idea of deriving and applying lessons from the
past—while also showing us that its author has already learnt a great deal from
historians. Austen's parody would not be successful unless it revealed affectionate intimacy with the works it is trouncing. In later life, she occasionally
described herself in her correspondence as deeply engaged in some unlikely
historical works. In 1813, for instance, while editing and correcting *Mansfield
Park*, she was also reading Captain Pasley's *Essay on the Military Policy and
Institutions of the British Empire* (1810), a book which she 'protested against at
first' but which proved to be 'delightfully written & highly entertaining. I am
as much in love with the Author as I ever was with Clarkson or Buchanan, or
even the two Mr Smiths of the city' (24 Jan. 1813, *Letters*, p. 207).

As has been recognized, the partial overlap in Austen's life of *Mansfield Park*
with Pasley's *Essay* is a richly suggestive one, given the emphasis of the latter
on imperial expansion and the iniquities of slavery. Brian Southam characterized Pasley's 'imperialist polemic' as 'stylish' and 'ruthless', and identified his

admirer, Austen, as an 'expansionist patriot'.[51] Vivien Jones, who observes that discussion of Austen's letter of 24 January 2013 has tended to focus on Thomas Clarkson's *History of the Rise, Progress, and Accomplishment of the Abolition of the African Slave Trade by the British Parliament* (1808), suggests that her appreciation of Pasley's *Essay* accords with her authorial 'program of conservative progress', rather than with any 'reformist, even liberal, sympathies' that might be associated with Clarkson's text.[52] Such abolitionist sympathies were in any event, by this stage, widespread and rather conventional than shocking. As Tomalin points out, the inclusion of an 'African Story' in the printed matter within Fanny Austen's 1809 diary 'shows that concern for slaves, and horror at the trade in them, was by then so general that the publishers of ladies' diaries could confidently assume that such a story [. . .] would be entirely welcome'.[53] Kathryn Davis has argued that the most important connection between Austen and Pasley is the value of 'Liberal education [. . .] on both private and political grounds'.[54] The contrasting dangers of a narrow, illiberal education lie at the heart of *Mansfield Park*; they shape at least one eighteenth-century historian's judgement of Charles I, a man who 'would probably have been a worthy prince had it not been for the principles imbibed in his education'.[55]

A great deal of critical energy has been expended over the past three decades upon Sir Thomas Bertram's Antiguan estates and the possible derivation of the family fortunes from slave labour in the West Indies. As has been noted by many commentators, certain names in the novel—'Norris' and 'Mansfield'—are pregnant with significance in the early nineteenth-century debate about abolition. As a result of such possible allusions, Austen has been construed by turns as a radical, liberal, conservative, abolitionist, imperialist, and critic of empire.[56] The episode which has provoked most discussion in

51. B. C. Southam, *Jane Austen and the Navy*, p. 171.

52. Vivien Jones, 'Reading for England: Austen, Taste, and Female Patriotism', *European Romantic Review*, 16 (2005), 221–30 (pp. 228, 223).

53. Tomalin, *Jane Austen*, p. 292.

54. Kathryn Davis, '"The First Soldier [She] Ever Sighed for": Charles Pasley's *Essay* and the "Governing Winds" of *Mansfield Park*', *Persuasions On-Line*, 35 (2014), [n. p.], http://www.jasna.org/persuasions/on-line/vol35no1/davis.html.

55. *A New History of England from the Invasion of Julius Caesar to the End of George II's Reign* (London: John Newbery, [1789]), p. 192.

56. For interpretations of the author's political sympathies and attitudes to slavery in *Mansfield Park*, see for example Edward W. Said, *Culture and Imperialism* (New York: Vintage, 1994), pp. 105–22; Susan Fraiman, 'Jane Austen and Edward Said: Gender, Culture, and Imperialism',

Mansfield Park concerns the heroine and Sir Thomas. Fanny and Edmund are talking about the resumption of the family's evening routine after the head of the family has returned from his estates:

'I suppose I am graver than other people,' said Fanny. 'The evenings do not appear long to me. I love to hear my uncle talk of the West Indies. I could listen to him for an hour together. It entertains *me* more than many other things have done—but then I am unlike other people, I dare say.' [...]

'Your uncle is disposed to be pleased with you in every respect; and I only wish you would talk to him more.—You are one of those who are too silent in the evening circle.'

'But I do talk to him more than I used. I am sure I do. Did not you hear me ask him about the slave-trade last night?'

'I did—and was in hopes the question would be followed up by others. It would have pleased your uncle to be inquired of farther.'

'And I longed to do it—but there was such a dead silence! And while my cousins were sitting by without speaking a word, or seeming at all interested in the subject, I did not like—I thought it would appear as if I wanted to set myself off at their expense, by shewing a curiosity and pleasure in his information which he must wish his own daughters to feel.'

'Miss Crawford was very right in what she said of you the other day: that you seemed almost as fearful of notice and praise as other women were of neglect.' (*MP*, vol. 2, ch. 3, pp. 230–2)

As has been pointed out by many critics, the 'dead silence' that follows the inquiry about 'the slave-trade' is not an index of the Bertram family's shame or embarrassment, but rather indicates the boredom and indifference of Fanny's cousins (*MP*, pp. lxxiv–lxxvii, 693 n.). The subject of Antigua is, as far as Fanny and Edmund are concerned, an entertaining and pleasing one that they would like to hear more about, and which Sir Thomas would be equally delighted to address. This constitutes a major obstacle to interpreting the scene as a criticism of imperialist tendencies. That said, and as has also been noted many times, *Mansfield Park* exhibits a painful, pervasive

---

Critical Inquiry, 21 (1995), 805–21; George E. Boulukos, 'The Politics of Silence: *Mansfield Park* and the Amelioration of Slavery', *NOVEL: A Forum on Fiction*, 39 (2006), 361–83; Gabrielle D. V. White, *Jane Austen in the Context of Abolition: 'A Fling at the Slave Trade'* (New York: Palgrave Macmillan, 2006); Jocelyn Harris, *Satire, Celebrity, and Politics in Jane Austen* (Lewisburg, PA: Bucknell University Press, 2017), pp. 265–98.

awareness of inequality and dependence. There is some justification for seeing Fanny Price herself as a human and sexual commodity to be traded and
exchanged: her name says as much. Austen's early works are as keenly alert as
her later fiction to the interconnected forms of cruelty and oppression that
are slavery, marriage, and the governess trade. Young women including Austen's aunt Philadelphia Hancock were routinely despatched to the East Indies
to find husbands, a fate that is contemplated with horror in 'Kitty, or the
Bower', in which the heroine's orphaned friend Miss Wynne is sent to make
a match in Bengal, 'the only possibility that was offered to her, of a Mainte-
nance'. To Miss Wynne, such a marriage is 'so opposite to all her idea of Propriety, so contrary to her Wishes, so repugnant to her feelings, that she would
almost have preferred Servitude to it, had Choice been allowed her' (*TW*,
p. 170 and p. 324 n.). But no such choice is allowed; she is to be disposed of
according to other people's wishes.

Edward Said famously proposed that *Mansfield Park* was the text in which
Austen 'more clearly than anywhere else [. . .] synchronizes domestic with
international authority, making it plain that the values associated with such
higher things as ordination, law, and property must be grounded firmly in
actual rule over and possession of territory'.[57] But in order to build on this
assertion and establish the novel's relationship to and use of 'a rich and complex history [. . .] that the Bertrams, the Prices, and Austen herself would not
recognize', he needs to subject the novel to a form of Whiggish misreading,
according to which Austen's discretion is only laying the ground for something
much worse to come:

> We must first take stock of *Mansfield Park*'s prefigurations of a later English
> history as registered in fiction. The Bertrams' usable colony in *Mansfield
> Park* can be read as pointing forward to Charles Gould's San Tomé mine in
> *Nostromo*, or to the Wilcoxes' Anglo-Imperial Rubber Company in Forster's
> *Howards End*, or to any of these distant but convenient treasure spots in
> *Great Expectations*, Jean Rhys's *Wide Sargasso Sea*, *Heart of Darkness*—
> resources to be visited, talked about, described, or appreciated for domestic
> reasons, for local metropolitan benefit. If we think ahead to these other
> novels, Sir Thomas's Antigua readily acquires a slightly greater density than
> the discreet, reticent appearances it makes in the pages of *Mansfield Park*.
> And already our reading of the novel begins to open up at those points

---

57. Said, *Culture and Imperialism*, p. 109.

where ironically Austen was most economical and her critics most (dare one say it?) negligent.[58]

The critical and political manoeuvres involved in this writing are more evasive and less defensible than the teenage Austen's bold, overt moves in favour of the Stuarts. In what sense is it imperative, before considering one work in its historical context, to cast it in terms of 'a later English history' of which Austen and her characters can have known nothing? Who is doing the 'pointing forward'? It cannot be the author. Among the most persuasive, balanced readings of the political and historical contexts of *Mansfield Park* is that of John Wiltshire, who edited the text for Cambridge University Press and who writes in his introduction to that volume that the novel

> evokes imperialism and war only to disavow them as narrative material. The tales of danger and horror with which William enthrals the Bertram family are left unspecified, whilst the narrative line [. . .] focuses the reader on the comic behaviour, at once interfering and parsimonious, of Mrs Norris' search for a second-hand shirt button. Likewise, 'the slave-trade', emerging only in Fanny's question to her uncle, recedes again into obscurity. The preparations for William's sailing in the war against Napoleon are treated as comic bustle, and his actual departure, perhaps for years, is noticed only as a loss to Fanny; the narrative attends, instead, to an incident more germane to its interests, the disturbing, distressful squabble over Susan's silver knife. (*MP*, p. lxxxiii)

In other words, the focus of attention is repeatedly diverted from subjects apparently fit for history and into local, immediate, domestic pressures; release from such pressures arrives in the form of objects: buttons, knives, jewellery, and luxury food products.

Fanny Price comes from Portsmouth, a port that, like Southampton, Jane Austen knew well. Two of her brothers were sailors. With her sister Cassandra, Austen briefly attended school in Southampton in 1783 and lived there again from 1806–9 with her mother, sister, and brother Francis and his wife, Mary (Francis had joined the Royal Naval Academy at Portsmouth in 1786, as did his younger brother Charles in 1791).[59] These small ports naturally had a lesser role to play in the slave trade than did major centres such as London,

58. Said, *Culture and Imperialism*, p. 118.
59. *Family Record*, pp. 48–9, 65, 72, 158–72; Southam, *Jane Austen and the Navy*.

Bristol, and Liverpool—although eight slave ships left Portsmouth between 1699 and 1711. But the southern English ports retained vital links with Britain's colonies in the West Indies and North America. Here, the slave trade remained legal; profits could therefore be derived from it and goods sent back home (Francis Austen wrote condemning the slave trade when he visited Antigua in 1806). Long after the British slave trade was legally abolished in 1807, Austen therefore had good cause to know that its effects persisted on home turf as well as in the plantations of Sir Thomas Bertram.[60]

Reviewing Thomas Love Peacock's novel *Melincourt* in 1817, the *Literary Gazette* complained that its 'Antisaccharine' argument had 'become obsolete' due to 'the abolition of the Slave-Trade'.[61] But, as *Melincourt* itself makes clear, ending the British slave trade did not end slavery, and Peacock introduces the products of the West Indies as a means of attending to the covert endurance of slavery itself. As Mr Forester puts it: 'every real enemy to slavery' is 'bound by the strictest moral duty to practical abstinence from the luxuries which slavery acquires'. Sugar, he argues, is 'morally atrocious, from being the primary cause of the most complicated corporeal suffering and the most abject mental degradation that ever outraged the form, and polluted the spirit of man'.[62]

Austen does not write in such explicitly political terms in any of her published works of fiction. But she is preoccupied, as Deirdre Coleman notes, with 'the metaphor of slavery' that connects domesticity and female subjection with colonialism.[63] Another example of the Regency novel's interest in the continued exploitation of slave labour, as manifested in high-end food products, is evident in the arrow-root 'of very superior quality' that Emma Woodhouse sends to cold, beautiful, dependent, and desperate Jane Fairfax (*Emma*, vol. 3, ch. 2, pp. 425–6). This is a present that cannot disguise the sender's dislike for the person to whom she affects to be generous, to whom she really believes she is being nothing *but* generous. Genuine arrow-root—a minor export from the West Indies by comparison with sugar—was a sought-after, very expensive medicinal powdered starch (or flour), a luxury thickening

60. On the Austen family and abolition, see for example Warren Roberts, *Jane Austen and the French Revolution* [1979] (London and Atlantic Highlands, NJ: Athlone, 1995), pp. 97–8.

61. *Literary Gazette* (25 Jan. 1817), p. 15.

62. *Melincourt*, vol. 2, pp. 44, 189.

63. Deirdre Coleman, 'Imagining Sameness and Difference: Domestic and Colonial Sisters in *Mansfield Park*', in *A Companion to Jane Austen*, pp. 293–303.

agent. Since Jane is ill and arrow-root is nourishing, the gift seems wholly appropriate and entirely defensible. Emma has, however, good reason to keep defending it to herself. The 'very superior quality' of her present is also at some level calculated to widen the gap between sender and recipient, not to bridge it (as true friendship might). Such behaviour really does make people ill; in *Pride and Prejudice*, Lady Catherine de Bourgh's 'sickly' daughter has her life sapped from her by the 'very superior quality' of her parent.[64] Emma's healing yet ostentatiously pricey foodstuff is a reminder of the heroine's wealth and freedom that Jane is expected to swallow. Not on this occasion, however. We are told quite clearly and firmly that 'Jane was resolved to receive no kindness from [Emma]' (vol. 3, ch. 9, p. 426).

The aloof behaviour that irks and confuses Miss Woodhouse, so determined to think well of herself and for most of the novel highly accomplished on that score, is the result not only of Jane Fairfax having to keep secret what Frank Churchill, the man who is supposed to love her, treats as a game. It lies also in the refusal to be grateful, in Jane's resistance to a fate that Mrs Elton— who comes from Bristol, and is possibly the daughter of a slave-trader—is especially keen to press upon her.[65] Jane Fairfax's privacy may be violated and toyed with. But she will not voluntarily consume a product that she knows is rare and costly; perhaps she also realizes that it is the fruit of West Indian slave labour (it was sometimes given to slaves themselves when they were ill).[66] Jane Austen, like Jonathan Swift, knew all about the relationship of solicitous, tender expressions to the appetite for 'human flesh', language to which Jane Fairfax feelingly reverts when she describes the prospect of being employed

64. 'Lady Catherine herself says that, in point of true beauty, Miss De Bourgh is far superior to the handsomest of her sex; because there is that in her features which marks the young woman of distinguished birth. She is unfortunately of a sickly constitution' (*P&P*, vol. 1, ch. 14, p. 75).

65. See Catherine Ingrassia, '*Emma*, Slavery, and Cultures of Captivity', *Persuasions*, 38 (2016), 95–106.

66. See [Dr Collins], *Practical Rules for the Management and Medical Treatment of Negro Slaves, in the Sugar Colonies. By a Professional Planter* (London: Vernor and Hood, 1803), pp. 281–2. See also J. S. Handler, 'The History of Arrowroot and the Origin of Peasantries in the British West Indies', *Journal of Caribbean History*, 2 (1971), 46–93. Gabrielle D. V. White does not mention the possible connection between arrow-root and the slave trade, although she does discuss Jane Fairfax's rejection of Emma's gift as part of an attempt 'to retain her autonomy' (*Jane Austen and the Slave Trade*, p. 158). Once she knows how things stand with Frank Churchill, Emma herself refers Jane's action to 'jealousy': 'In Jane's eyes she had been a rival' (*Emma*, vol. 3, ch. 11, p. 439).

as a governess. Mrs Elton professes herself quite shocked ('if you mean a fling at the slave-trade', she says, referring to her brother-in-law, 'I assure you Mr. Suckling was always rather a friend to the abolition', *Emma*, vol. 2, ch. 17, p. 325).[67] It is the directness that shocks her; the terms of the comparison were, in this period, familiar.[68]

Jane, seeing straight through Emma's breezy act of giving—it costs her nothing at all, since she has ordered the housekeeper to fetch it—immediately returns the gift. Miss Bates reports: 'dear Jane would not be satisfied without its being sent back; it was a thing she could not take—and, moreover, she insisted on her saying, that she was not at all in want of any thing' (*Emma*, vol. 3, ch. 9, p. 426). Miss Bates chooses to thank Emma for the arrow-root. Jane, however, does not. 'It was a thing she could not take'. She would not accept the gift because she could not endure it—she has already had to endure the painfully exposing luxury gift of a piano from Frank. Just before the truth of her feelings about Knightley darts through Emma 'with the speed of an arrow', the truth about her gift to Jane becomes apparent, too: 'arrow-root from the Hartfield store-room must have been poison. She understood it all' (*Emma*, vol. 3, ch. 11, pp. 439, 444). One of the things that Emma or her author seems to understand is that arrow-root is a powerful antidote to 'poison' (its name appears to derive from its use to cure the wounds caused by poisoned arrows). Earlier in the novel, when she reluctantly resumes her acquaintance with Jane Fairfax after a break of two years, Emma, taking in 'her history', imagines Jane having fallen in love with Mr Dixon. The metaphor she chooses when entertaining this thought already suggests the gift that she will offer Jane in the next volume: '[Jane] might have been unconsciously sucking in the sad poison' (*Emma*, vol. 2, ch. 2, p. 179). The West Indian origins of Emma's present should direct us to the realization that the way Jane Fairfax is treated, and the threat of her future life as a governess, are bound up with other forms of iniquitous servitude and confinement, some kinds of marriage included (a point that is also made clear in 'Kitty, or the Bower'). One does not take precedence over the other, in the way that 'very superior quality' might seem to imply. All of them are evil.

67. Richard Cronin and Dorothy McMillan do not interpret Jane's remark as a reference to the slave trade, but to prostitution, pp. 579–80, and think that Mrs Elton misunderstands what has been said, revealing her 'sensitivity to her Bristol origins' (*Emma*, pp. 579–80 n.).

68. See Deirdre Coleman, 'Imagining Sameness and Difference', pp. 296–302.

6

The Village and the Universe

EVERYBODY KNOWS:

> It is a truth universally acknowledged, that a single man in possession of a good fortune, must be in want of a wife. (*P&P*, vol. 1, ch. 1, p. 3)

That Austen's 'truth universally acknowledged' soon acquired some renown is affirmed by the tribute that Susan Ferrier paid it in the first line of her own second novel: 'It is a truth universally acknowledged, that there is no passion so deeply rooted in human nature as that of pride.'[1] Working this celebrated line, Ian Watt observed that 'It seems to be a universal principle in literary criticism that the more interpretation a passage has the more it shall be given.'[2] But the beginning of *Pride and Prejudice*—its first sentence also constitutes its first paragraph—is far more often quoted and adapted than it is interpreted.[3] The narrator's joke hinges on 'universally'. Replace it with, say, 'generally', as in 'It is generally evident', and the effect is lost, the voice ceasing to flaunt 'an excess of *Cockylorum*'—Austen's term, as a teenager, for an impudent sort of female confidence.[4] The sparkling command of her opening sentence is indebted to satires of her parents' generation (and therefore,

---

1. Susan Ferrier, *The Inheritance*, 3 vols., 2nd edition (Edinburgh: William Blackwood; London: T. Cadell, 1825), vol. 1, ch. 1, p. 1.

2. Ian Watt, *Conrad in the Nineteenth Century* (Berkeley: University of California Press, 1979), p. 325.

3. This is the shortest opening paragraph of any of Austen's novels; the first paragraph of *Emma* also consists of a single sentence.

4. 'Cockalorum' (*OED*): Austen is given as the earliest recorded example of the word in the sense of 'Self-important behaviour; conceitedness, vanity'. She applied the word to Lady Jane Grey in the 'History of England', then crossed it out and replaced it with 'vanity' (*TW*, pp. 128, 305 n.).

presumably, the generation of Mr and Mrs Bennet): to works such as Henry Fielding's 'Modern Glossary' (1752), a list of short, sharp definitions of words as deployed by the type of vacuous wealthy people with whom a social aspirant might long to be seen. In such chat, meaning and its application have been radically curtailed. The 'WORLD', in this context, signifies nothing more global than 'Your own Acquaintance' (as if to say, in a tone that harbours a certain aggression and exclusivity, 'But darling, *everybody* was there'). Its flipside is 'NO BODY. All the People in Great Britain, except about 1200'.[5] (Emma Woodhouse reflects that, by comparison with her own family, 'the Eltons were nobody' (vol. 1, ch. 16, p. 147); Sir Walter Elliot refers to Captain Wentworth as 'nobody'—that is, someone 'quite unconnected; nothing to do with the Strafford family' (*Pers*, vol. 1, ch. 3, p. 26).) Such abuses of language and the blind spots that they perpetuate occupied Fielding throughout the *Covent-Garden Journal*; as for the consequences, opposing himself to 'the World' in its socially restricted form, he remarked that 'whilst the Author and the World receive different Ideas from the same Words, it will be pretty difficult for them to comprehend each other's Meaning'.[6]

That Austen inherited the atmosphere and idiom of Fielding's 'Modern Glossary', perhaps as a sort of family shorthand, and perhaps via such imitators of his style as Burney, is evident from her play with the senses of 'every Body' in an early letter to Cassandra:

> Miss Fletcher says [. . .] that as every Body whom Lucy knew when she was in Canterbury, has now left it, she has nothing at all to write to her about. By Everybody, I suppose Miss Fletcher means that a new set of Officers have arrived there—. But this is a note of my own.—(15–16 Sept. 1796, *Letters*, p. 10)

As the underlining of the second term and the 'note of my own' seem designed to emphasize, 'every Body' and 'Everybody' are being put to two distinct uses as well as indicating two different groups of people: first, those who have 'left'; second, those who 'have arrived'. Those uses map onto the difference between 'Lucy' Lefroy (referred to informally, by her first name, as a family friend of the Austens) and 'Miss Fletcher' (referred to formally, as a

---

5. *The Wesleyan Edition of the Works of Henry Fielding, The Covent-Garden Journal and A Plan of the Universal Register-Office*, ed. Bertrand A. Goldgar (Oxford: Clarendon Press, 1988), *The Covent-Garden Journal* no. 4 [1752], pp. 37, 38.

6. *Covent-Garden Journal* no. 4, p. 34.

friend of Lucy's, someone whom Jane Austen has just met and Cassandra does not know). 'Every Body' describes a group of people known to another person or 'Body', in this case Lucy.[7] 'Everybody' means 'a new set', hitherto not fully individuated and appealing to Miss Fletcher because of their uniformity—indeed, because of their uniforms (Mrs Bennet wistfully recalls 'the time when I liked a red-coat myself very well', vol. 1, ch. 7, p. 33). 'Everybody' has not yet become 'every Body' because these people are not yet individuated or familiar, but the strong hope is that they soon will be, a hope that is spelt out in single days of long female sighs in *Pride and Prejudice*: 'Every day added something to their knowledge of the officers' names and connections. Their lodgings were not long a secret, and at length they began to know the officers themselves' (vol. 1, ch. 7, p. 32).

The compound words 'Everybody', 'everyone', and 'everything' do not appear in Samuel Johnson's *Dictionary*; 'EVERY' is 'Each one of all'. But his practice of separating 'every' from 'body', 'one', and 'thing' was, by the late eighteenth century, in the process of changing, and Austen's manuscripts duly hover between 'every body', (more rarely) 'every Body'—where the capitalized 'Body' perhaps also signals an awareness of physical presence—and 'everybody'.[8] Alternation between the separated and compound forms suggests an intuitive or working distinction in her mind between a crowd as a collection of individuals and that crowd considered from a greater distance—a 'set', like that of the officers in *Pride and Prejudice*—the latter usage being the more recent. 'Every Body' stresses single members of a group, and therefore that any collective is made up of many particular bodies potentially at variance with one another, eluding or striving for attention; 'everybody' treats that group itself as an indivisible single entity.

The ways in which those two senses might be tussling for prominence, and the preferences or exclusions implied in identifying yourself with one side or

---

7. Austen occasionally capitalizes 'Body' in this way in other letters, whether indicating a single person or collective entity: 'If the warmth of her Language could affect the Body, it might be worth reading in this weather'; 'that Pious, Learned & disinterested Body'; 'a weak Body must excuse weak Nerves' (*Letters*, 17–18 Jan. 1809, 6 April 1817, 27 May 1817, pp. 174, 354, 357).

8. For 'every body', see for example 'Collection of Letters' and 'Kitty, or the Bower' (*TW*, pp. 145, 178) and *Letters*, pp. 10, 31, 134, 163, 218, 276, 290, 340; for 'every Body', see for example *Letters*, pp. 5, 10; for 'everybody', see for example 'Lady Susan (*JAFM*, vol. 3, p. 349) and *Letters*, pp. 5, 28, 43, 45, 73–4, 84, 117, 128, 132, 166, 190, 312, 328, 343. Compare *OED* definitions of 'Everybody', 'Every one' (under 'Every', sense 10c.), 'Everything'.

the other, might also be one means of understanding how Austen's variety of free indirect style—with its alertness to competing points of view, communal and individual—comes into being. Emma Woodhouse, a committed 'imaginist', frequently insinuates her faulty and lightly scornful appraisals of other, less fortunate characters, into the narrative (vol. 3, ch, 3, p. 362). But when we come to the first sustained third-person account of what Miss Bates really thinks and feels, Emma's judgement is not permitted to intrude:

> Miss Bates stood in the very worst predicament in the world for having much of the public favour; and she had no intellectual superiority to make atonement to herself, or frighten those who might hate her, into outward respect. She had never boasted either beauty or cleverness. Her youth had passed without distinction, and her middle of life was devoted to the care of a failing mother, and the endeavour to make a small income go as far as possible. And yet she was a happy woman, and a woman whom no one named without good-will. It was her own universal good-will and contented temper which worked such wonders. She loved every body, was interested in every body's happiness, quick-sighted to every body's merits; thought herself a most fortunate creature, and surrounded with blessings in such an excellent mother and so many good neighbours and friends, and a home that wanted for nothing. The simplicity and cheerfulness of her nature, her contented and grateful spirit, were a recommendation to every body, and a mine of felicity to herself. (*Emma*, vol. 1, ch. 3, p. 20)

Miss Bates is, like every other human being, in some sense 'in the world' and in 'public'; she is possessed of 'universal' feelings and stands in a human relation 'to every body' she knows—in her case, that relation is decidedly local, individual, and particular. 'Universal' here means not only that she feels good will towards every single body around her, but also that she does not resent her own place in the universe. One lesson of *Emma* is that any human perspective on reality—in particular, the heroine's—should not assume the status of a universal truth. But another lesson is that the universal may sometimes be quite properly synonymous with the local. *Emma* inhabits a realm in which the 'small' may not only be made to 'go as far as possible', but should be understood as possessing an importance beyond the claims it would ever think to make for itself. This is the home truth that Emma is brought to learn after her humiliation of Miss Bates at Box Hill. It is also the moral of *Middlemarch* (1871–2), the conclusion of which presents Dorothea as a Miss Bates of sorts:

But the effect of her being on those around her was incalculably diffusive: for the growing good of the world is partly dependent on unhistoric acts; and that things are not so ill with you and me as they might have been, is half owing to the number who lived faithfully a hidden life, and rest in unvisited tombs.[9]

'Kitty, or the Bower' includes some earnest scrutiny of 'every body'. Its apparent breadth of application is shown to mean something cruelly narrow:

> [Kitty:] 'But as to the Wynnes; do you really think them very fortunate?'
>
> [Camilla:] 'Do I? Why, does not every body? Miss Halifax & Caroline & Maria all say that they are the luckiest Creatures in the World. So does Sir George Fitzgibbon and so do Every body.'
>
> [Kitty:] 'That is, Every body who have themselves conferred an obligation on them. But do you call it lucky, for a Girl of Genius & Feeling to be sent in quest of a Husband to Bengal, to be married there to a Man of whose Disposition she has no opportunity of judging till her Judgement is of no use to her, who may be a Tyrant, or a Fool or both for what she knows to the Contrary. Do you call *that* fortunate?' (*TW*, p. 178)

Kitty's side of this exchange possesses the same bridling sense of injustice as that which animates Fielding's definitions of 'WORLD' and 'NO BODY'. 'Every body' means, as Kitty vainly endeavours to show her dull companion, only very rich patrons—in other words, hardly anyone at all. To understand 'Every body' in any other way means ignoring the sufferings of a poor girl compelled to marry in order to survive. Something of this story's indignation persists in the third of Austen's 'Collection of Letters', perhaps (going by the dedication) written soon after 'Kitty, or the Bower', in autumn 1792 (*TW*, xxxvii). The author of this third letter, 'A young Lady in distress'd Circumstances to her freind' has to endure continual social humiliations, snubs, and displays of 'insulting importance' (*TW*, p. 140) from the insufferable Lady Greville. Her condescension, and the young lady's responses to it ('I saw that she wanted to mortify me, and was resolved if I possibly could to prevent her seeing that her scheme succeeded'; 'I could hardly help laughing'; 'leaving me in a great passion with her', *TW*, pp. 140–2), find their counterparts in Elizabeth Bennet's

---

9. *The Clarendon Edition of the Novels of George Eliot: Middlemarch: A Study of Provincial Life*, ed. David Carroll (Oxford: Clarendon Press, 1986; rep. 1992), p. 825 [book 8, finale].

exchanges with Lady Catherine de Bourgh, and (in a less amused way) in Jane Fairfax's conversations with Mrs Elton.

'Kitty, or the Bower' shows how impassioned a vein of social and satirical complaint could be Austen's, how quick and bristling was her sense of the contrast between individuals and the world to which they do and do not belong (one note in Goldsmith's *History*, responding to an anecdote about a desperate couple who murdered their child before hanging themselves, says: 'How much are the Poor to be pitied, & the Rich to be blamed!', *Juvenilia*, p. 344). When Mrs Percival complains, having discovered her niece alone in the bower with Edward Stanley, that Kitty has offered 'a bad example to the World, and the World is but too well disposed to receive such', Kitty is instantly riled by the exaggeration: 'I *can* have given an Example only to *you*, for you alone have seen the offence' (*TW*, p. 199).[10] Austen's early letters abound, too, in Fielding's style of comedy, playing narrowness of scope against the seeming breadth of a surface claim implied by words such as 'Every body'.[11] These jokes, pitching large against small and regulating one by the other, gesture towards the origins of *Pride and Prejudice*'s celebrated 'universal' opening, as well as (more obviously) towards the perspective of small-minded characters such as Lydia and Kitty Bennet, who 'could talk of nothing but officers' (*P&P*, vol. 1, ch. 7, p. 32).

Isobel Grundy understandably discerns a resemblance between the opening line of *Pride and Prejudice* and Samuel Johnson's *Rambler* essays (1750–52). Johnson was undoubtedly fond, as Grundy says, of sending up 'the aphoristic manner with unreliable matter'; however, Austen's 'truth universally acknowledged' has only an indirect connection with her 'favourite' prose moralist.[12] There are many more plausible sources for her best-known words. Jonathan Swift's *Tale of a Tub* (1704), for one, alights on the 'universal' as the satirical pivot of the subtitle ('Written for the Universal Improvement of Mankind'),

10. Camilla refers to 'Every Body', two words again freighted with stupidity, later in 'Kitty, or the Bower': 'Gold Net. It will be a most angelic thing—Every Body will be longing for the pattern—'; Camilla's brother, Kitty's suitor, says: 'this will be a most agreable surprize to every body to see you enter the room with such a smart young Fellow as I am' and 'Every body gives Balls now I think; I beleive I must give one myself soon—' (*TW*, pp. 180, 189).

11. Samuel Beckett saw a kinship between Austen's 'manner' and that of Henry Fielding. *The Letters of Samuel Beckett*, ed. George Craig, Martha Dow Fehsenfeld, Dan Gunn, and Lois More Overbeck, 4 vols. (Cambridge: Cambridge University Press, 2009), vol. 1, pp. 252–3.

12. Isobel Grundy, 'Jane Austen and Literary Traditions', p. 203; Henry Austen, 'Biographical Notice of the Author', in *Memoir*, p. 141.

and Swift's truths continually present themselves, in the mouths of absurdly compromised speakers—speakers who anticipate Austen's 'partial, prejudiced, & ignorant Historian'—as 'bold', 'momentous', or 'universal' (*TW*, p. 120).[13] Like Austen, Swift enjoys setting up large truth claims that are quickly riddled with suspicion. One way in which each of them does so is to contaminate or insinuate doubt into what presents itself as truth by emphasizing its origins as some form of 'account' or 'report' (reported speech, collective gossip, or a private delusional fantasy). Towards the end of *Pride and Prejudice*, Lady Catherine demands 'a report universally contradicted', as if by way of reply or rebuke to 'a truth universally acknowledged'. Her peremptory request is met with a blank refusal from Elizabeth Bennet, who by now sees how things are (*P&P*, vol. 3, ch. 14, p. 392).

How you take a 'universal truth' will necessarily depend on the limits of your definition of the universe; on where your own world starts and ends. For some characters, the universe very quickly fades into nothing when it extends beyond the immediate gratification of their own wants and needs; this is Mrs Bennet's case, and Mary Elliot's in *Persuasion*. It is also true of Marianne Dashwood for the bulk of *Sense and Sensibility*. Just before she is struck down by fever, Marianne is said to feel 'herself universally ill' (vol. 3, ch. 7, p. 348). In other words, she doesn't feel right at all, in any part of her mind or body— but *universally*? This appears to be an elephantine overstatement of some sort, when applied to how one individual might be feeling. But that, it seems, is the whole point of the word: the relationship Marianne has constructed between 'herself' and the world is a form of sickness. She has embraced a code of conduct and form of living that allow her to be entirely engulfed in her own concerns—so that she is, as it were, her own universe. This reading of 'universally' is supported by the fact that she fails to notice that most of the inhabitants of the house where she is staying have been forcibly evacuated due to the gravity of her potentially infectious condition. She is not told that this has happened; but nor does she enquire. 'It gave her no surprise that she saw nothing of Mrs. Palmer; and as it gave her likewise no concern, she never mentioned her name' (*S&S*, vol. 3, ch. 7, p. 349). Such a condition as Marianne's

---

13. *The Cambridge Edition of the Works of Jonathan Swift*, vol. 1: *A Tale of a Tub and Other Works*, ed. Marcus Walsh (Cambridge: Cambridge University Press, 2010), p. 3. For 'bold' affirmations, 'momentous Truths', and 'universal Benefit', see for example the final paragraph of section 9 of *A Tale*, 'A Digression concerning the Original, the Use and Improvement of *Madness* in a Commonwealth', p. 116.

sometime universal selfhood comes close to being the antithesis of Miss Bates's 'universal good-will'.

There is a dense cluster of 'truths' being 'universally acknowledged' in publications of the 1780s and 90s, the years of Austen's literary apprenticeship.[14] Going by the deployment in print of such phrasing, 'It is a truth universally acknowledged' might be the opening of a sermon about human fallibility, or of a satirical tract in the Swiftian vein, or of a sweeping historical survey or schoolroom textbook, even of a political argument about (say) the rights and wrongs of democracy, or a speech concerning the legitimacy of an administration. Edmund Burke, more strikingly and more comprehensively than any other writer, joins these disparate elements together, and his conclusions—in their wish to unite and to counterbalance the claims of community with those of individuals—come closest to Austen's. In *Reflections on the Revolution in France* (1790), he asked

> Is it then a truth so universally acknowledged, that a pure democracy is the only tolerable form into which human society can be thrown, that a man is not permitted to hesitate about its merits, without the suspicion of being a friend to tyranny, that is, of being a foe to mankind?[15]

In 1791, Charles de Calonne presented some universal truths with which Burke would have been far more willing to agree: 'That this is the present

14. See for example Jacob Duché, *Discourses on Various Subjects*, 2 vols. (London: T. Cadell, 1779), vol. 2, p. 270; Anon., *God Justified, Man Condemned, and Grace Magnified. A Sermon on Ecclesiastes vii. 29* (Canterbury and London: J. Marsom and D. Taylor, 1795?), p. 23; *The Methodist Magazine* (1799), vol. 2, p. 34; Joseph Priestley, *A Free Address to Protestant Dissenters, as such*, 3rd edition, enlarged (Birmingham and London: J. Johnson, 1788), p. 3; Philip Pyle, *One Hundred and Twenty Popular Sermons*, 4 vols. (Norwich: for the author, 1789), vol. 1, 121; John Skinner, *A Course of Lectures; delivered on the six Sundays in Lent, to a congregation of the Episcopal Church of Scotland* (Aberdeen: J. Chalmers & Co., 1786), p. 98; Robert Woodward, *A System of Christian Theology* (Northampton: T. Dicey & Co., 1791), p. 15; William Jackson, *The Four Ages; together with essays on various subjects* (London: Cadell and Davies, 1798), p. 87; Charles Rollin, *The Ancient History of the Egyptians, Carthaginians, Assyrians, Babylonians, Medes and Persians, Macedonians, and Grecians*, 8th edition, 10 vols. (London: J. Rivington and Sons; G. G., J., and J. Robinson, etc., 1788), vol. 8, p. 96; Robert Lowth, *Lectures on the Sacred Poetry of the Hebrews*; translated from the Latin, 2 vols. (London: J. Johnson, 1787), vol. 2, pp. 237–8.

15. Edmund Burke, *Reflections on the Revolution in France and on the Proceedings in Certain Societies in London relative to that Event* [1790], in *The Writings and Speeches of Edmund Burke*, vol. 8: *The French Revolution, 1790–1794*, ed. L. G. Mitchell and William B. Todd (Oxford: Oxford University Press, 2014), pp. 173–4.

disastrous situation of France, is universally acknowledged'; 'That, in every truly monarchical state, the right of declaring war and concluding treaties resides in the Monarch, is a truth so universally acknowledged'.[16] Like Burke, Austen endorsed both the communal view of things and the moral reality of exceptions to that view. Her near-contemporary John Grose was generally convinced of the power of the local: 'The great force of example', he wrote, 'is a truth universally acknowledged'.[17] He would probably have agreed with Austen that the only proper answer to a universal truth claim is that 'Seldom, very seldom, does complete truth belong to any human disclosure; seldom can it happen that something is not a little disguised, or a little mistaken' (*Emma*, vol. 3, ch. 13, p. 470). Not 'never'—that would let everybody off the hook—but 'seldom'.

Austen began from a very young age to think about the motives and scope of universal truths. What purchase, if any, does the universal continue to possess, when exemplified in a number of different situations and individual people? The starting point of *Pride and Prejudice* is that a universal truth means no more than local twittering about a single man (albeit of the general type). A similar reflex appears in a letter to Cassandra of 1808: 'I am to be in Bombazeen & Crape, according to what we are told is universal here; & which agrees with Martha's previous observation' (*Letters*, p. 148). The playing off in that instance of the universal against the local—'here', as well as the endorsement of the truth by Martha Lloyd—is even more extreme than in the opening sentence of the novel.

Another way of thinking about how the 'universal' relates to 'here' would be to ask what happens when 'Everybody' is understood as 'every Body', or when 'the whole World' turns out to be no greater than (say) a neighbourhood. Austen wrote with creative irritation on this latter score to Cassandra in January 1801:

> Mr Peter Debary has declined Dean Curacy; he wishes to be settled nearer London. A foolish reason—! as if Deane were not near London in comparison of Exeter or York.—Take the whole World through, & he will find

16. Charles de Calonne, *Considerations on the Present and Future State of France [...] Translated from the French* (London: J. Evans, 1791), pp. 8, 215. See also pp. 78–9, 290.

17. *Ethics, Rational and Theological, with cursory reflections on the general principles of deism* (London: for the author, 1782), p. 437.

many more places at a greater distance from London than Deane, than he will at a less.—What does he think of Glencoe or Lake Katherine?—I feel rather indignant that any possible objection should be raised against so valuable a peice of preferment, so delightful a situation!—that Deane should not be universally allowed to be as near the Metropolis as any other Country Village.—(*Letters*, p. 70)

Austen's objections to the foolish Mr Debary start in reasonable vein; Deane, a village and civil parish in Hampshire, is indeed much closer to London than is Exeter or York. It follows that there are many other places farther from London than Deane is, and among those places are the picturesque locations of Glencoe and Lake Katherine (both in Scotland). But when we reach what 'should' be 'universally allowed'—the same province of truth as that with which *Pride and Prejudice* opens—we have also reached an absurdity to parallel Mr Debary's. This time it works in the opposite direction, panning out rather than narrowing down: Deane is 'as near the Metropolis as *any other* Country Village'. Austen cannot resist flipping the perfectly sensible argument against Debary's provincialism into a form of universality that in its own, knowingly absurd overreaching offers a satirical counterweight to his excessively bounded views.

The early works repeatedly pitch themselves in this way: as flagrantly above or below an unspoken borderline of respectability or normality, offering us far too much or far too little. There is a relic of that technique in the ways in which the 'universal' is set against the 'single' in the first sentence of *Pride and Prejudice*, as in how we might understand the workings of 'everybody' versus 'every Body' in Austen's fictional and epistolary prose. These satirical techniques are especially flagrant at the beginning of a novel first called 'First Impressions', the work that may also have been intended as the first of Jane Austen's novels to appear in print: its attention to opening gambits is even more charged than it might otherwise be. Its status as the first of Jane Austen's novels to be finished—albeit perhaps not the first to have been started—has already been mentioned, and could supply one reason for Austen's description of *Pride and Prejudice* as 'rather too light & bright & sparkling' (*Letters*, 4 Feb. 1813, p. 212). As Margaret Anne Doody has suggested, by the time it finally appeared in print the novel may have struck its author as having too much of the eighteenth century about it. 'Sparkle' is the name of a character in Richard Brinsley Sheridan's *The Rivals* (1775); more generally, it stands for 'that old Augustan style, that taste for paradox and wit, for snip-snap antithesis—all things Jane Austen inherited'.[18] It is the kind of word and stylistic quality that the older Austen might well have thought in need of updating. Maybe the opening sentence of *Pride and Prejudice*, with its flavour of Henry Fielding, has a sort of fusty, tarnished grandeur about it—like that of the amateur or provincial theatricals beloved of the Austen clan and often featuring seventeenth- and eighteenth-century comedies as part of the repertoire.

The same atmosphere of slightly hackneyed brightness shapes many of Austen's teenage spoofs. Part of what she is joking about is how tired and trite the idioms of fiction, history, and conduct books have become. One of only two authorial notes appended to her early works occurs in the course of the unfinished epistolary novel 'Lesley-Castle'. Margaret Lesley is writing about her brother to a friend, Charlotte Lutterell:

> Never was there a better young Man! Ah! how little did he deserve the misfortunes he has experienced in the Marriage state. So good a Husband to so bad a Wife!; for you know my dear Charlotte that the worthless Louisa left him, her Child & reputation a few weeks ago in company with Danvers & +dishonour. Never was there a sweeter face, a finer form, or a less amiable Heart than Louisa owned!
> +Rakehelly Dishonor Esqre. (*TW*, pp. 96–7)

Louisa is abandoning a set of real and abstract things ('him, her Child & reputation'), in exchange for another seeming combination of the human and the non-human, the briskly alliterative pairing of 'Danvers & dishonour'. Austen might have had in mind Imlac's advice to the astronomer in Johnson's *Rasselas*—'fly to business or to Pekuah', as the sage advises—or at least the basic structure of that formula, an abstraction (business or dishonour) combined with a person (Pekuah or Danvers).[19] But thanks to the authorial footnote, that structure is itself retrospectively exploded, or realized on earth, and Danvers now becomes one of *two* people with whom the doubly worthless Louisa has thrown in her lot. She has, to repeat Austen, 'left [...] with Danvers & dishonour', or rather 'Rakehelly Dishonor Esqre'. The remote abstraction has become one of two single male realities, albeit one whose name is so absurdly implausible as

---

18. Margaret Anne Doody, 'The early short fiction', in *The Cambridge Companion to Jane Austen*, pp. 72–86 (p. 76). See also *OED* 'sparkle' (sense 6b): 'Brightness or liveliness of spirit; smartness; wittiness'.

19. *Rasselas and Other Tales*, p. 163.

to remove him again into the realm of semi-allegorical types. Imagine, for a moment, an eighteenth-century assisted suicide corporation called 'Dying with Dignity': one reason it might not have succeeded or proved a confusing sort of euphemism is because the temptation to read 'Dignity' as a female allegorical figure, encouraged by the habitual eighteenth-century capitalization of abstract nouns as if they are names of individual agents, would be too strong. This kind of joke is still more or less current. In a 1980s spoof of *Dracula*, Stephen Fry's character talks about leaving 'Prudence' behind, at the gates of Count's castle, but what initially seems to be the abstract virtue turns out to be a girl with the same name. Immediately thereafter, he tell us 'Of all the hideous spectacles I ever beheld, those perched on the end of this man's nose remain forever pasted into the album of my memory'.[20] This is the coming-down-to-earth strain of humour that shapes *Northanger Abbey*: Gothic is sapped of its capacity to intimidate or frighten, being rendered human, local, and domestic; the personification is reduced to a person, the terrifying and incomprehensible spectacle to an instrument that helps you see things more clearly.

The passage from 'Lesley-Castle' seems to reveal a combination of theatrical and textual modes: if Austen were reading this letter aloud, her audience would be unable to tell whether 'dishonour' was capitalized or not, allowing for greater comic ambiguity in regard to the distinction between abstract qualities and realized agents; yet the footnote which decisively completes the joke cannot be experienced in the same way if it is heard rather than read. This doesn't so much suggest the priority of the real over the fictional as the ceaseless reference of one to the other. The movement between abstractions and persons is quick and constant in Austen's adolescent tales, which at the level of action sometimes feature human beings in the guise of abstract qualities, and (at the other end of the scale) inanimate accessories standing in for people themselves. 'Female Masks' in 'Jack & Alice' are, metonymically, the masqueraders who wear them. Popular characters to impersonate at such masquerades included Virtue, Hope, Temperance, and Liberty, so that the process of translating a disembodied abstraction or truth universally acknowledged into a real, single person might be tantamount to a genuine human experience, a movement from glancing at something unknown and not yet individuated to recognition of a friend or relative. Lady Williams, also in 'Jack & Alice', appears in the 'character of Virtue' at a ball, for instance, as well as impersonating a virtuous character in the rest of

20. Stephen Fry, 'The Letter', *Cambridge University Footlights Review* (televised version, 1982). 'Prudence had demanded that I leave her behind, so I was alone'.

the story. Repeated glimpses of her bitchiness and inconsistency do a lot to compromise this vision, as does the entirely banal and deliberately unconvincing way in which her virtue is stylistically represented (*TW*, pp. 10–11). But you couldn't say that Austen wants to uncover a *real* Lady Williams behind all this, or even that Lady Williams amounts to a 'person' or 'character' in any meaningful sense of those words. This is what makes another female masquerader's studied lament, 'Oh Cecilia, I wish I was really what I pretend to be', all the better as a joke (*TW*, p. 11: the speaker is Caroline Simpson, disguised as a Sultana). Rather, Lady Williams' personification of virtue permits Austen to adopt the mask of an author for whom perfect men and women are by turns the goal of her spoof conduct-book writing, and the enemy.

One way of construing the relationship of general to particular truth, of types to individuals, is in terms of how Austen gathers her people into large parties and then separates them again. Characters repeatedly join and part company in all her fiction (even if it amounts to no more than a page); indeed, her plots might be said to consist of little else.[21] The gathering up, pairing off, and dispersal of groups, families, couples, body parts, and words constitute one of the mechanisms that she is testing out in her early tales. She commented in later life to her niece Anna, who was working on her own novel: 'You are now collecting your People delightfully, getting them exactly into such a spot as is the delight of my life' (*Letters*, 9–18 Sept. 1814, p. 287). In the early tales, clusters of words (as of people) are often collected, with gusto, by creakily overdone devices such as alliteration. One dedication (to Jane Austen's cousin, Jane Cooper) runs in its entirety:

> To Miss Cooper—
>
> Cousin
>   Conscious of the Charming Character which in every
> Country, & every Clime in Christendom is Cried, Concerning
> you, with Caution & Care I Commend to your Charitable
> Criticism this Clever Collection of Curious Comments, which
> have been Carefully Culled, Collected & Classed by your
> Comical Cousin
>
> > The Author.
> > ('Collection of Letters',
> > *TW*, p. 134)

---

21. On this aspect of Austen's writing, see also Yoon Sun Lee, 'Austen's Swarms and Plots'.

Alliteration—always something of a cheap trick—is both a matter of chance and the result of contrivance. Does anything bind this run of c-words together, the author seems to be asking, beyond the fact that they start with the same letter? But the dedication happens accurately to be reproducing the titles of other collections of 'curious', 'compendious', and 'copious' letters and, in view of her lasting solicitude for her own early works, Austen's emphasis on the pains of art ('Carefully Culled, Collected & Classed') is more than a joke. The figure of 'The Author' in this composition is permitted to stand both within and outside its own tightly woven confines. Jane Austen may be 'your Comical Cousin', sharing a first name with Miss Cooper and allowing that cousin's surname as well as the relationship of cousinhood to determine the first letter of most words in her dedication. But Austen is something and someone else, too: namely, 'The Author', a character whose name does not begin with 'c' and who has a vantage point on the imposition of alliterative uniformity as well as being implicated in it. She is both subject to a rule and (having formulated that rule) an exception to it. In playing the author, we might also say that she is at once impersonating a type and becoming an individual. 'The Author' will be how she is later primarily identified on the title pages of her published novels, where she never appears in her own name.[22]

'There's a divinity that shapes our ends', says Hamlet, and in the teenage writings, that divinity is unmistakeably and tyrannically authorial.[23] Overly determined syntactical structures enclose unpredictable endings. What seems to be a foregone conclusion turns out to be a punchline that shirks respectability and decorum, as well as the generic requirements either of a marriage plot or a conduct book. It may be true of many child writers that they are trammelled in routines contrived by other people, routines from which their fictions are an exercise in evasion; in other words, that their imaginative licence arises from an inability to make their own choices or govern their own lives. J. M. Barrie observed of the nine-year-old Daisy Ashford that her writing possessed 'an air of careless power'—an air directly related to the fact that the

---

22. *Pride and Prejudice* is 'By the author of "Sense and Sensibility"', *Mansfield Park* 'By the Author of "Sense and Sensibility" and "Pride and Prejudice"', *Emma* 'By the Author of "Pride and Prejudice"'. Even the posthumously published *Northanger Abbey* and *Persuasion* are announced as 'By the Author of "Pride and Prejudice", "Mansfield Park", etc.', supplemented with a 'Biographical Notice of the Author'.

23. *Hamlet*, act 5, scene 2, line 10.

author herself 'was hauled off to bed every evening at six.'[24] But resisting the schematic tendencies of other novels, valuing the exception to a rule, cherishing the possibility of things having turned out differently—or carrying beyond the formal close of her own fiction a consciousness of things having indeed worked out other than the way it seemed they had—all these things mattered very much to Austen as a grown-up writer, too.

John Bayley pointed out more than fifty years ago that Austen's freedom in her writing sprang precisely from a lack of it in her life. The fiction, he argued, was located in a 'reality' that 'depends on its inescapability'; '"constraint" for Jane Austen is the condition of life.'[25] Bayley's suggestion is borne out by comments such as that recorded of a Mrs Pole, about *Mansfield Park*: 'the situations & incidents are told in a manner which clearly evinces the Writer to <u>belong</u> to the Society whose Manners she so ably delineates' ('Opinions of Mansfield Park and Opinions of Emma', *JAFM*, vol. 4, p. 327). Writing from inside that society, belonging to it whether she liked it or not, Austen does not seem to have drafted her novels with an unchanging sense of how they would end. One reason why she continues to provoke so many sequels or re-writings is that— like Shakespeare—she exhibits a strong consciousness that human lives, including those within her fictions, are at once confined by and something other than exemplary of the general truths they embody, or of the genres in which they appear. Stephen Wall wrote of Anthony Trollope's characters that 'it is clear that they are not there just to demonstrate something that he wants proved.'[26] The same is true of Austen's people, whose lives extended in their author's mind beyond the novels in which they come into being and who contain the potential to behave differently from the ways in which they are shown to behave in print.[27]

In one sense, what Austen achieves in the opening line of *Pride and Prejudice* is a sudden, comic narrowing of horizons. Yet her first sentence keeps up the appearance of perfect equipoise thanks to the even-handed syntax and the

24. Daisy Ashford, *The Young Visiters or Mr Salteena's Plan* [1919], intro. J. M. Barrie (London: Chatto & Windus, 2008), 'Preface', p. 7.

25. John Bayley, 'The "Irresponsibility" of Jane Austen', in *Critical Essays on Jane Austen*, ed. B. C. Southam (1968), pp. 1–20 (pp. 9, 13).

26. Stephen Wall, *Trollope and Character* (London: Faber, 1988), p. 13.

27. 'According to a less well-known tradition, the delicate Jane Fairfax lived only another nine or ten years after her marriage to Frank Churchill. It seems that Jane was not prepared to discuss her characters' lives until after they had finally appeared in print'. *Family Record*, p. 241. See also *Memoir*, p. 119.

balance of supply ('possession') and demand ('want') that it deals out to us with a poker face. This must be part of what Austen meant when she referred in 1813 to 'the playfulness & Epigrammatism of the general stile' of *Pride and Prejudice* (*Letters*, p. 203). And it is right to feel that we are here reading a truth that does generally hold in some way, as an epigram does, albeit not a truth of the stature heralded by 'universally': could any human truth live up to such a billing? Carey McIntosh writes that

> The words 'truth universally acknowledged' are the semantic counterparts of the syntax that delays closure past the verb of the *that*-clause to its object, since by their abstractness and hyperbole they promise that the single man will be in want of something exalted like 'prudence' or 'a guardian angel' or 'a worthy purpose in life,' not merely (such is the attitude comically / ironically implied by the presence of all that universally acknowledged truth) a 'wife.'[28]

But, as suggested at the beginning of this chapter, the ironic emphasis of the sentence appears to fall rather on 'universally' than on 'wife'. Once we realize what sort of 'neighbourhood' we are in, 'universally' is made to seem as if it means 'locally': albeit that the truth in question perhaps applies to any village across the globe, so this might be described as universal insofar as it applies to each and every small (and possibly small-minded) place. The province of truth we had thought belonged to the universe is native to a mere village. Perhaps, then, it is not so much that we expect a bigger and better goal than 'wife', as McIntosh claims, as that we expect the sentence's adjudication to emanate from a larger realm than that of the provincial. A universal truth cannot, it seems, derive from a mere village.

William Empson's gloss on Fielding's double irony suggests how Austen's truth about men and women might be read as both universal and not universal, and at the same time:

> the style of Fielding is a habitual double irony. [. . .] Single irony presumes a censor; the ironist (A) is fooling a tyrant (B) while appealing to the judgement of a person addressed (C). For double irony A shows both B and C that he understands both their positions; B can no longer forbid direct utterance, but I think can always be picked out as holding the more official

---

28. *The Evolution of English Prose, 1700–1800: Style, Politeness, and Print Culture* (Cambridge: Cambridge University Press, 1998), pp. 87–8.

or straight-faced belief. [. . .] Presumably A hopes that each of B and C will think 'He is secretly on my side and only pretends to sympathize with the other'; but A may hold some wise balanced position between them, or contrariwise may be feeling 'a plague on both your houses.'[29]

The tyrannical perspective in Austen is that which declares a truth universally acknowledged; that superhuman perspective itself becomes the butt of irony when it is yoked to an imperative about nothing more significant than a rich man's marital prospects in the neighbourhood. (It matters, additionally, that this process involves the translation of an epigram into a novel; the expansion of the pithy general truth into its dispersed, multiple, and particularized applications.) The supremely even-handed narrator understands both positions, the 'universal' and the 'single', and the compromises—in other words, omissions from a full picture of reality—that each involves when one is taken in isolation from the other. She therefore not only permits but requires the articulation of both within the first sentence. There is a joke in the opening line of *Pride and Prejudice*, then, about mere locality, and at the same time a feeling that it is indeed quite true that '3 or 4 Families in a Country Village is the very thing to work on' (*Letters*, 9–18 Sept. 1814, p. 287). Such material is not 'everything' or 'every thing'. It is, rather, 'the very thing', both general and particular.

To begin with, Austen's works were praised more for their moral content— the conduct that they were understood to recommend—than for their stylistic merits. But many reviewers, as well as Austen's immediate circle, were also quickly alerted to the sheer *interest* of her works, the ways in which they draw us in. Austen's was a fiction with a broader, more familial scope than was typically the case in novels of the early 1800s, as the *Critical Review* immediately realized in the opening sentence of its appreciative comments on *Pride and Prejudice*:

> Instead of the whole interest of the tale hanging upon one or two characters, as is generally the case in novels, the fair author of the present introduces us, at once, to a whole family, every individual of which excites the interest, and very agreeably divides the attention of the reader.[30]

29. William Empson, '*Tom Jones*', *Kenyon Review*, 20 [1958], 217–49 (p. 219).

30. *Critical Review*, 4th ser., 3 (March 1813), 318–24 (pp. 318–9). On the romantic and aristocratic implications of 'interesting' fiction in this period, see *Jane Austen: The Critical Heritage*, vol. 1, p. 9.

Before we even get to that family, the appeal of Austen's beginning is that it immediately commits itself to at least two perspectives on reality; to more than one way of weighing up the importance of things. This is itself a truth about Austen's style in general, and perhaps remains its chief draw for readers. Our attention is at once excited and divided: the narrator's perspective never reposes securely in a single consciousness—even if the heroine occupies most of our interest—but takes note at some level of 'every individual' in her cast.

In the preface to the revised edition (1907) of his novel *Roderick Hudson*, Henry James came up with his own version of Austen's universal truth claim in order to contrast the achievements of literature with the interconnections and ramifications of real lives: 'Really, universally, relations stop nowhere, and the exquisite problem of the artist is eternally but to draw, by a geometry of his own, the circle within which they shall happily *appear* to do so'.[31] It is hard to understand how anyone might possess 'a geometry of his own'; for, if any laws are universal, wouldn't they be the laws of geometry? But perhaps what James is getting at is that perfect circularity in literature is not desirable, or that a fictional circle must be not quite finished (even if it initially appears to be so) in order to satisfy its readers. The opening line of *Emma* could thus be read as the impersonation of completeness, an impersonation whose lacunae we are invited to recognize:

> Emma Woodhouse, handsome, clever, and rich, with a comfortable home and happy disposition, seemed to unite some of the best blessings of existence; and had lived nearly twenty-one years in the world with very little to distress or vex her. (*Emma*, vol. 1, ch. 1, p. 3)[32]

The imperfections of this geometry are 'seemed', 'some', and 'nearly'; they leave the surface claim that is 'unite' open to question and investigation. *Emma* concerns the misguided arrogance of youth and its collisions with illegitimacy and poverty. It is therefore fitting that it begins not only with a title and a first word of the first sentence that are obediently identical to the name of its highly superior heroine—no other Austen novel, at least in its published form, is either named after the heroine or begun with her name—but also with a dedication

---

31. Henry James, 'Preface to the New York Edition' [1907], *Roderick Hudson*, ed. Geoffrey Moore and Patricia Crick (Harmondsworth: Penguin, 1986), pp. 35–48 (p. 37).

32. The 'best blessings of existence' are invoked again (vol. 3, ch. 12, p. 12, p. 460), with reference to what it would mean to be Knightley's wife.

to the Prince Regent, a spoilt, undisciplined, and headstrong man, the epitome of a character who gets his own way.

Frank Kermode argued that the novel answers a paradigmatic demand for form, 'an irreducible minimum of geometry—of humanly needed shape or structure'. There is, he said, a connection between fictions, time, and apocalyptic modes of thought, the last of which Kermode suggests provides a useful analogy with the process of reading and writing fiction. In imagining an end for the world, apocalyptic thinkers are imposing a pattern on history, making possible 'a satisfying consonance with the origins and with the middle'.[33] Since any human prediction of the end is continually being falsified, we are compelled to adjust our response to such patterns in the light and interests of reality. Austen famously remarked to a niece in 1817 that 'pictures of perfection' made her 'sick & wicked' (*Letters*, 23–25 March 1817, p. 350). Samuel Beckett appears to have felt something similar when he complained in 1931 that two novels of T. F. Powys (*Mark Only* (1924) and *Mr Tasker's Gods* (1925)) exhibited a 'painfully organised unified tragic completeness'. He thought that 'the divine Jane', by contrast, had 'much to teach me'—even if being taught by her that 'completeness' was not desirable also (later) entailed recognizing that her endings could be 'a mess'.[34] In this recognition he was at one with an early reader of *Sense and Sensibility*, Lady Bessborough, who praised it as 'a clever novel [. . .] tho' it ends stupidly' (*A Family Record*, p. 188).

Beckett's pain sprang from apprehending a work of art that struck him as too finished, too closed. The universal, if not held in check by consciousness of the possible exception to its rule—and such consciousness need not be tantamount to thinking 'the Doom of Man revers'd for thee'—will become a form too 'unified' to reflect life and will therefore not console but discomfort its reader.[35] Because Austen writes not as one of the elect but as one of her own community, her narratorial perspective is subject to error, change, and obscurity. Her fictions are not 'universally shut up' as stories perhaps in theory ought to be, at least according to the rules of decorum.[36] Instead, they remain

33. Frank Kermode, *The Sense of an Ending: Studies in the Theory of Fiction with a new epilogue* (Oxford and New York: Oxford University Press, 2000), pp. 132, 17.

34. Beckett, *Letters*, vol. 1, pp. 94, 250. 'Poor Jane has got herself into a mess at the end of S. & S., the big scene between Elinor & Willoughby could hardly be worse' (Beckett, *Letters*, vol. 3, p. 525).

35. Samuel Johnson, *The Vanity of Human Wishes*, l. 156, in *The Complete English Poems*.

36. Laurence Sterne, *The Life and Opinions of Tristram Shandy, Gentleman* [1759–67], ed. Howard Anderson (New York and London, 1980), vol. 4, ch. 27, p. 224.

knowingly within the circumstances in which a universal claim is made: by a single, fallible human voice. *Persuasion* has its own mature and considered view on the limits of universal characteristics; one expression of that view occurs just after Louisa has fallen from the steps on the Cobb:

> Anne wondered whether it ever occurred to [Wentworth] now, to question the justness of his own previous opinion as to the universal felicity and advantage of firmness of character; and whether it might not strike him, that, like all other qualities of the mind, it should have its proportions and limits. She thought it could scarcely escape him to feel, that a persuadable temper might sometimes be as much in favour of happiness, as a very resolute character. (*Pers*, vol. 1, ch. 12, p. 126)

Limits need to be set even to the advantageous quality of firmness or resolution—because no such quality is *universally* advantageous. *Persuasion* spells out the cost, to individuals, of thinking otherwise. The limits of types are balanced against the proportions of individuals (and vice versa) from the title pages of Austen's novels onwards. The qualities of pride and prejudice, for example, might be applied to either or both of the central characters whose separate ruling passions the respective abstractions seem intended to capture. The adjective 'sensible' encompasses both Elinor and Marianne Dashwood, each of whom possesses a greater or lesser degree of sense and of sensibility; the fact that there is a third sister in the picture, Margaret, seems designedly to unsettle the schematic relationship of titular abstractions to family members.

The 'gift of reticence' that was Jane Austen's, early and late, may be an index of tact; it can also be a satirical thrust. Emma Woodhouse, the only heroine whose fiction is named after her when it appears in print, is rewarded for that distinction by having recognition of herself as a type thrust upon her. At the moment at which she accepts Knightley's proposal, when he expressly asks to hear her voice, she is silenced by her author. She says 'Just what she ought, of course. A lady always does' (*Emma*, vol. 3, ch. 13, p. 470). Having set out to become the exception to a rule, Emma is made to conform to the generic requirements of a marriage plot that is itself the work of a lady: Jane Austen. Richard Simpson observed that '*Pride and Prejudice*, *Emma*, and *Persuasion* all end with the heroes and heroines making comparisons of the intellectual and moral improvement which they have imparted to each other'.[37] He was right

---

37. *The Critical Heritage*, vol. 1, p. 244.

to say so, but the conclusions he invoked do something other than enlighten the central characters in regard to one another. Those three novels also reach a conclusion partly by attending to matters that are absent or withheld: Elizabeth is celebrated for her ignorance of the past (vol. 3, ch. 16, pp. 408–9); Emma resolves to say nothing to her future husband about Harriet's infatuation with him (vol. 3, ch. 13, pp. 469–70); Anne Elliot chooses not to betray to Wentworth her knowledge of his 'blunder' (vol. 2, ch. 11, p. 264). Such rituals of closure are both open and shut. They show Austen's characters thinking and feeling their way into a new life, one in which silence or suppression of one truth indicates the reception or recognition of another. These people and their stories do not end. They grow.

A Note on Marginalia

A HANDFUL of Austen's annotations to Oliver Goldsmith's *The History of England, from the Earliest Times to the Death of George II*, 4 vols. (1771), were first transcribed, inaccurately, in 1920, in Mary Augusta Austen-Leigh's *Personal Aspects of Jane Austen* (pp. 26–9). They next appeared, in much fuller form, in appendix B of Peter Sabor's edition of the *Juvenilia* (2006) for Cambridge University Press. Their availability has contributed to a welcome appraisal in recent years of Austen's early responses to and re-writing of history.[1] However, a fresh examination of the physical evidence suggests that not all the marginalia identified in the *Juvenilia* as Jane Austen's may in fact be hers, while others omitted from the *Juvenilia* could feasibly be ascribed to her. This is perhaps only to be expected, given the resemblance of one family member's hand to another and the fact that the book has remained in private ownership; opportunities to study and analyse its many comments and markings have been very limited. In my discussion in chapter 5 of Austen's 'History of England', unless indicated otherwise, I have cited only the marginalia that may confidently be attributed to her. This note considers some of the problems involved in securely identifying authorship of the rest.

Sabor explains that 'The various comments, corrections and markings' on the pages of Goldsmith's *History* 'in hands other than Austen's are not reproduced here, with the exception of two (pp. 328, 335) that respond to Austen's own marginalia' (*Juvenilia*, p. 318). It is hard to know how to interpret this. If a reader turns, as directed, to page 328 of the *Juvenilia*, there is a transcription of 'a pencilled comment', interpreted by the editor as Austen's, but 'inked over

---

1. See for example Misty Krueger, 'From Marginalia to Juvenilia: Jane Austen's Vindication of the Stuarts'; *Jane Austen's 'The History of England' and Cassandra's Portraits*; Juliet McMaster, *Jane Austen, Young Author*; Mary Spongberg, 'Jane Austen and the *History of England*'.

by another hand'. Are we therefore to understand that this is the first of the two responses to Austen's marginalia by other hands, as described on page 318? If so, is it the act of inking over a pencilled original which is understood by the editor to constitute a response to Austen's marginalia by someone else? If that is indeed the case, why are other pencilled comments written over in ink by another hand (transcribed on pp. 321, 322, 325), not also listed as responses by another person or people to Austen's original comments, rather than (presumably) being interpreted as Austen's property alone? On page 335 of the *Juvenilia*, there is no editorial indication as to which (if any) of the transcribed notes is presumed to derive from someone other than Austen; but a comment identified as by James Edward Austen (later Austen-Leigh), explicitly replying to his aunt's, is transcribed on page 337. Earlier in appendix B, mention is made of another response to one of Jane Austen's marginalia, in the form of the word 'Detesbaly', 'written (and thus misspelled) in another, childish hand; the same hand has apparently inked over her pencilled remark' (*Juvenilia*, p. 323). This word, 'Detesbaly', is (unlike James Edward's response on p. 337) not formally listed as one of the marginalia, so it is not 'reproduced' in the same form that other notes are. What status does this comment then possess, in relation to James Edward's—and his aunt's?

Issues of identification and attribution—to one person, and if so which one, and to more than one person—such as are raised by the marginalia in Goldsmith's *History of England* are very difficult to resolve. This is not only because it can be tricky to differentiate Jane Austen's writing from that of some other family members. As H. J. Jackson points out, marginalia demonstrate (among other things) that reading 'always involves an element of contest or struggle, and an oscillation between surrender and resistance, identification and detachment'.[2] Austen's confident, defiant marginalia often sound very like those of William Blake (both of them write 'A lie' in response to claims by another author which they hotly dispute); like Blake, she wrote such comments in the expectation that they would be circulated within and provoke a response from a known audience.[3] The various Austen marginalia are embedded in the semi-private contexts of education, communication, imitation, and

---

2. H. J. Jackson, *Marginalia: Readers Writing in Books* (New Haven, CT, and London: Yale University Press, 2001), pp. 85–6.

3. On Austen's use of this phrase, see her annotations to Goldsmith, *Juvenilia*, appendix B, p. 337 ('a lie'; 'another'), and to Vicesimus Knox, *Juvenilia*, appendix C, pp. 353 ('A lie'), 354

collaborative writing within one family across generations, with marks of identification and detachment being recorded between and among the different annotators as well as between the printed author and his marginal commentators.[4]

Prime candidates (other than Austen herself) for annotating the text must be her niece Anna Austen (later Lefroy) and Anna's half-brother James Edward; the latter has already been identified as a contributor to the Goldsmith notes (see chapter 5 of this volume and *Juvenilia*, p. 337). If Anna, too, were commenting in this way, it would be entirely consistent with the continuations that she and James Edward appended to Austen's 'Evelyn' and 'Kitty, or the Bower' in 'Volume the Third', most likely during Austen's lifetime and with her knowledge (*TW*, pp. xxi–xxiii, 205–9). James Edward's hand was long confused with Austen's in this last volume of the teenage writings, such that his ending of 'Kitty, or the Bower' was for decades attributed to Austen herself. In her edition of the text, Juliet McMaster concluded that changes in hand evident in the story might be attributed to 'a natural transition between Austen's youthful and her mature penmanship'.[5] Peter Sabor rejected this view as implausible, convincingly matching the conclusion of 'Catharine, or the Bower' (as 'Kitty, or the Bower' is re-styled in its revised form) to other examples of James Edward's writing. Sabor makes a strong case for a date of 1815–6, when James Edward was seventeen to eighteen, for his conclusion to 'Evelyn' and a first attempt to finish 'Catharine' (*Juvenilia*, pp. 363–5).[6] Kathryn Sutherland has subsequently and persuasively argued that James Edward made far more

('another lie'), 355 ('a lie'; 'A Lie—an entire lie from beginning to end'). On Blake's use of 'A lie' in annotations, see Jackson, *Romantic Readers*, p. 160.

4. On Blake's marginalia as a means of formulating and defending his own opinions, frequently in vitriolic, hostile, or sarcastic terms, see Jackson, *Romantic Readers*, pp. 153–63. On the circulation of his annotated books, see p. 157: 'The essence of Blake's practice of annotation [. . .] was that he indicated approval or disapproval of parts of the text with a view to exhibiting the results to other people'.

5. See Kathryn Sutherland, 'From Kitty to Catharine', 124–43. See also *TW*, p. xxiii, 236–43; *Catharine, or, The Bower*, ed. Juliet McMaster and others (Edmonton, Alberta: Juvenilia Press 1996), p. xv.

6. See also Peter Sabor, 'James Edward Austen, Anna Lefroy, and the Interpolations to Jane Austen's "Volume the Third"', *Notes and Queries*, 245 (2000), 304–6. On the basis of differences in hand, and following Doody and Murray, Sabor argues that James Edward's continuation of 'Catharine' is divided into two periods, the first c. 1815–6 and the second post-1845, a view disputed in Sutherland, 'From Kitty to Catharine', p. 131.

substantial interventions in 'Kitty, or the Bower' than has previously been recognized—including the change in title to 'Catharine, or the Bower', and amounting to overwhelming 'evidence for reattribution'.[7] This argument is developed in *Jane Austen's Fiction Manuscripts*, which concludes that

> Though impossible to identify or to date in all cases, the hands other than Austen's at work on *Volume the Third* offer sufficient clues to suggest that both Anna and James Edward contributed to the revision of its contents (probably under Austen's guidance) and that their interpolations are closely linked to their own experiments in fiction (between 1814 and 1817). (*JAFM*, vol. 3, p. 6)

In the case of the annotations to Goldsmith's *History of England*, it looks as if more than four separate hands have been contributing, over a long period, responses of various kinds in the margins (and sometimes within the body of the text itself). If a younger relative chose to write in ink on top of one of Austen's pencilled notes, does that act signal endorsement of her opinion, or simply a wish to preserve it (especially once Austen had gained some renown as a novelist)? Can we be sure that other comments made in ink on Goldsmith's *History* are not also preserving pencilled remarks originally made by Jane Austen that have subsequently been rubbed off, so that these notes too might be reporting her views? Certain words—for instance, 'worthy', 'wretches', 'charming', 'creature'—are characteristic not only of Austen's sentimental-satirical idiom but also of language used by other family members, suggesting a shared vocabulary of rebellious, vituperative responses to history.

A representative selection of the surviving marginalia in Goldsmith's *History* is shown here, in order to demonstrate something of the range of hands at work and in play, and the difficulties of identifying those hands (images of many other notes could not be included, as the pencil has become too faint to be legible). For comparison purposes, readers may wish to consult images of Anna Lefroy's handwriting in *Jane Austen's Fiction Manuscripts*, volume 3 (pp. 272–86), and of James Edward Austen's in 'From Kitty to Catharine: James Edward Austen's Hand in *Volume the Third*', *Review of English Studies*, 66 (2015), 124–43, and in *Jane Austen's Fiction Manuscripts*, volume 3 (pp. 56–68, 262–8).

---

7. Sutherland, 'From Kitty to Catharine', p. 137.

FIGURE 8. The Austen family's annotated copy of Oliver Goldsmith, *The History of England, from the Earliest Times to the Death of George II*, 4 vols. (1771), vol. 3, p. 281: 'Horrible wretches'. This marginal comment is not transcribed in appendix B of the *Cambridge Edition* of the *Juvenilia*, where Sabor writes that 'Horrible wretches' is 'not in Austen's hand' (p. 317). It is, however, in the same hand as that which is elsewhere identified as having written over comments made in pencil by Austen (see for example the note to Goldsmith, *History*, vol. 3, p. 314; *Juvenilia*, p. 322), which might have disappeared beneath the ink here. Another annotation, 'wretches' (Goldsmith, *History*, vol. 2, p. 264), is accepted as Austen's, as is a note to Goldsmith, *History*, vol. 4, p. 320: 'Horrid wretches' (*Juvenilia*, pp. 319, 350). Writing over 'Horrible wretches' in ink might have resulted in 'wretches' being squashed into a semi-vertical position on the page, whereas the pencilled original could perhaps have fitted horizontally into the margin.

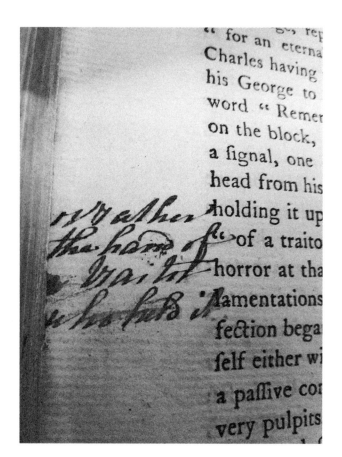

FIGURE 9. Goldsmith, *History*, vol. 3, p. 314: 'or rather the hand of a traitor who held it'. Included in the *Juvenilia* as Austen's 'pencilled comment [. . .] written over in ink by another hand' (p. 322).

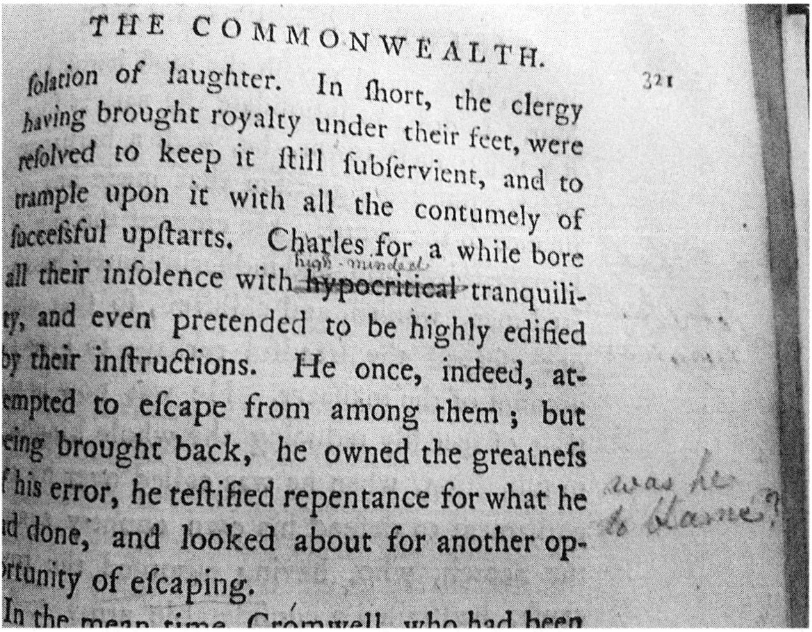

folation of laughter. In fhort, the clergy having brought royalty under their feet, were refolved to keep it ftill fubfervient, and to trample upon it with all the contumely of fuccefsful upftarts. Charles for a while bore all their infolence with high-minded hypocritical tranquili-ty, and even pretended to be highly edified by their inftructions. He once, indeed, at-tempted to efcape from among them ; but being brought back, he owned the greatnefs of his error, he teftified repentance for what he had done, and looked about for another op-portunity of efcaping.

In the mean time, Cromwell, who had been

was he to blame?

FIGURE 10. Goldsmith, *History*, vol. 3, p. 321: 'was he to blame?' (in the margin). This pencilled comment appears to be in a different hand from Austen's; it is included as hers in the *Juvenilia* (p. 323). (For a brief comment on this annotation as part of Austen's 'genuine, sympathetic image of Charles I', see Krueger, 'From Marginalia to Juvenilia', p. 247.)

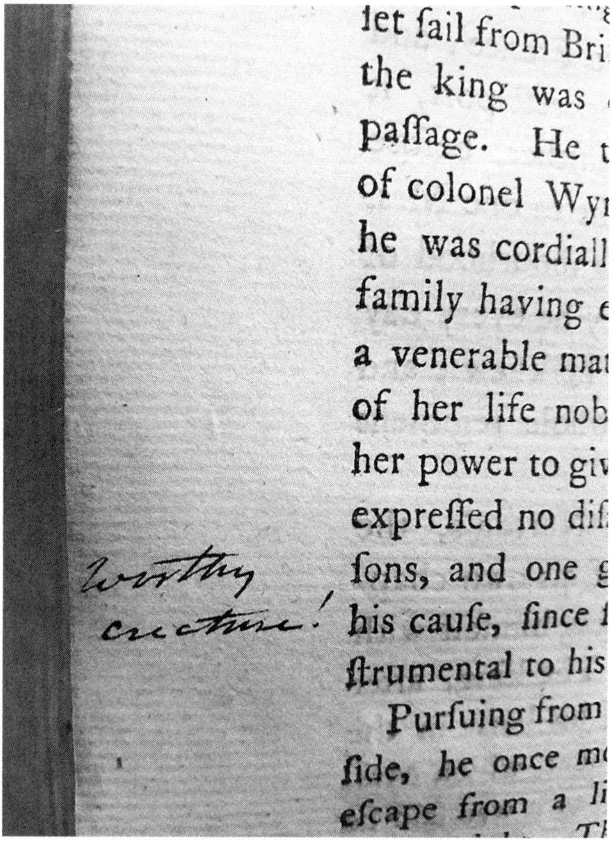

let fail from Bri

the king was

paſſage. He

of colonel Wy

he was cordiall

family having

a venerable ma

of her life nob

her power to gi

expreſſed no di

worthy creature! ſons, and one

his cauſe, ſince

ſtrumental to his

Purſuing from

ſide, he once m

eſcape from a li

Th

FIGURE 11. Goldsmith, *History*, vol. 3, p. 328: 'worthy creature!' (compare later marginalia: 'elegant creature what charming eloquence!' and 'Charming Creatures!', *Juvenilia*, pp. 328, 336). Not Austen's hand; not included in *Juvenilia*.

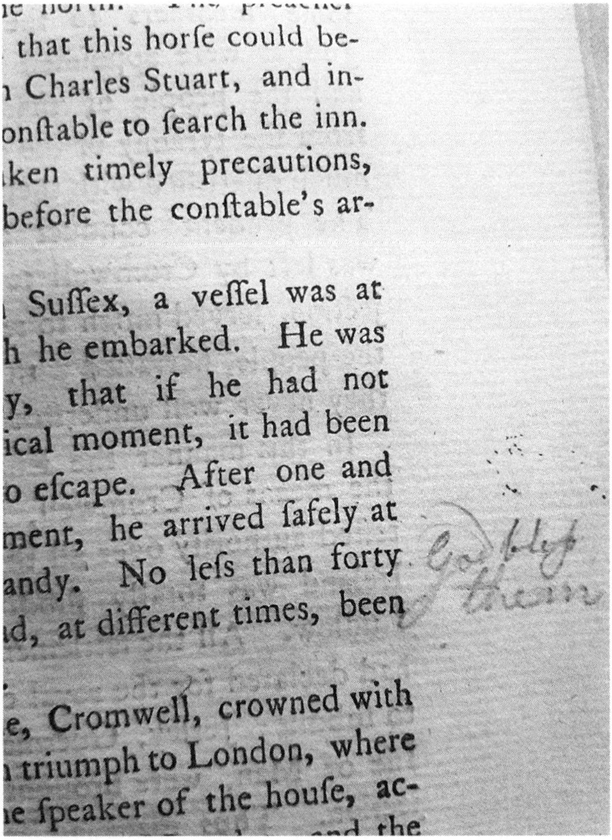

that this horſe could be-
Charles Stuart, and in-
onſtable to ſearch the inn.
ken timely precautions,
before the conſtable's ar-

Suſſex, a veſſel was at
h he embarked. He was
y, that if he had not
ical moment, it had been
o eſcape. After one and
ment, he arrived ſafely at
andy. No leſs than forty
d, at different times, been

e, Cromwell, crowned with
triumph to London, where
e ſpeaker of the houſe, ac-

FIGURE 12. Goldsmith, *History*, vol. 3, p. 329: 'God bless them'. Probably Austen's hand; included as hers in *Juvenilia* (p. 324).

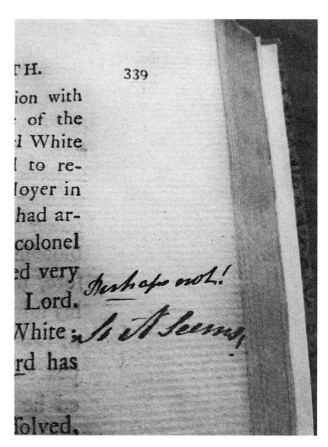

FIGURE 13. Two different hands in Goldsmith, *History*, vol. 3, p. 339: 'Perhaps not!'; 'So it seems!'. Neither comment is in *Juvenilia*.

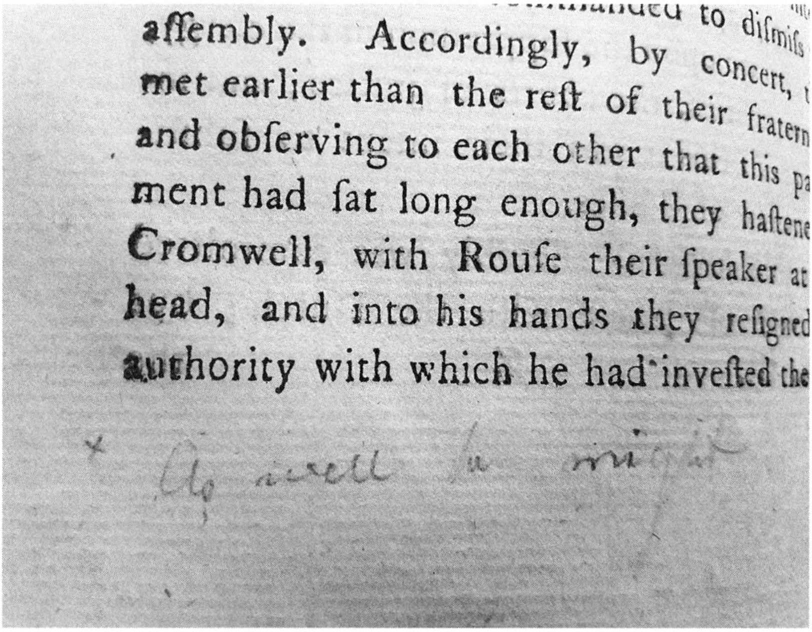

affembly. Accordingly, by concert, t
met earlier than the reft of their fratern
and obferving to each other that this pa
ment had fat long enough, they haftene
Cromwell, with Roufe their fpeaker at
head, and into his hands they refigned
authority with which he had invefted the

As well he might

FIGURE 14. Goldsmith, *History*, vol. 3, p. 338: 'As well he might' (included as Austen's in *Juvenilia*, p. 326). This does not look like Austen's hand; it does resemble that of the comment on vol. 3, p. 321 of the *History*.

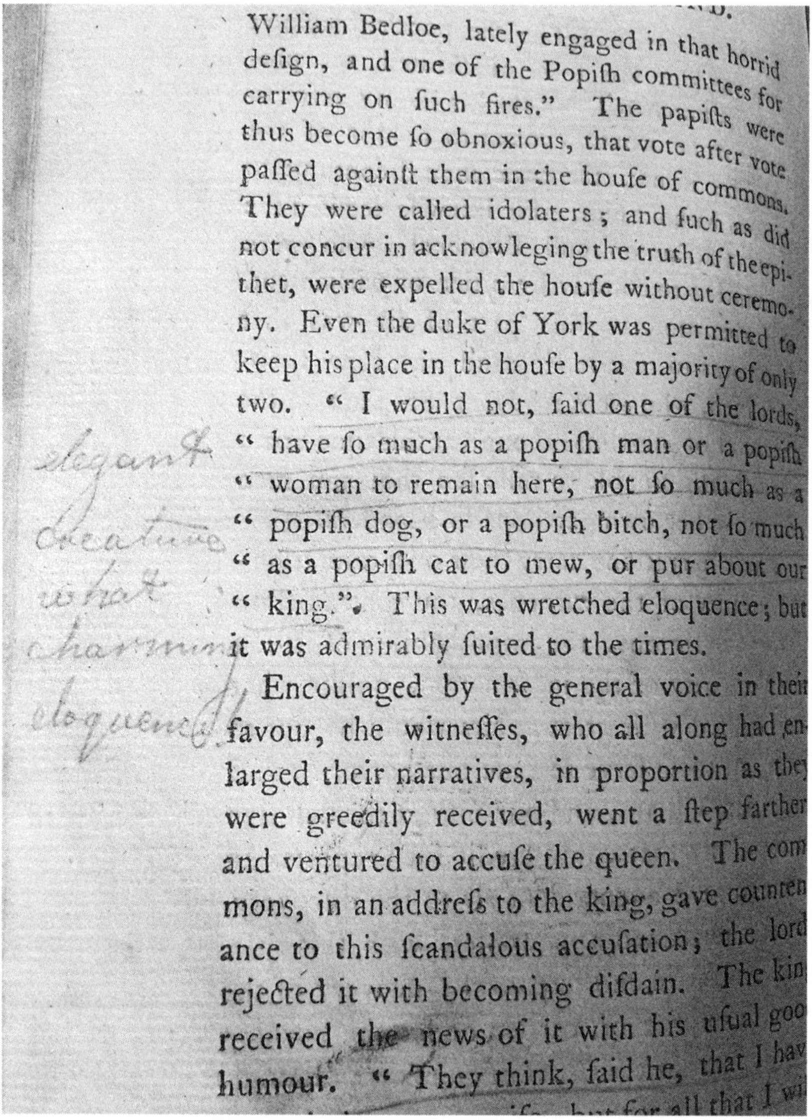

William Bedloe, lately engaged in that horrid
defign, and one of the Popifh committees for
carrying on fuch fires." The papifts were
thus become fo obnoxious, that vote after vote
paffed againft them in the houfe of commons.
They were called idolaters; and fuch as did
not concur in acknowleging the truth of the epithet, were expelled the houfe without ceremony. Even the duke of York was permitted to
keep his place in the houfe by a majority of only
two. " I would not, faid one of the lords,
" have fo much as a popifh man or a popifh
" woman to remain here, not fo much as a
" popifh dog, or a popifh bitch, not fo much
" as a popifh cat to mew, or pur about our
" king." This was wretched eloquence; but
it was admirably fuited to the times.

Encouraged by the general voice in their
favour, the witneffes, who all along had enlarged their narratives, in proportion as they
were greedily received, went a ftep farther
and ventured to accufe the queen. The commons, in an addrefs to the king, gave countren
ance to this fcandalous accufation; the lord
rejected it with becoming difdain. The kin
received the news of it with his ufual goo
humour. " They think, faid he, that I hav

[marginal handwritten notes:] elegant creature what charming eloquence

FIGURE 15. Goldsmith, *History*, vol. 3, p. 420: 'elegant creature what charming eloquence!' (included as Austen's in *Juvenilia*, p. 328). This does not resemble Austen's hand.

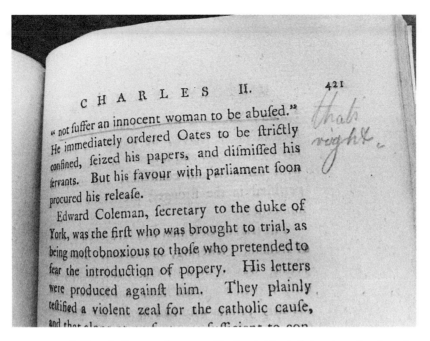

FIGURE 16. Goldsmith, *History*, vol. 3, p. 421: 'that's right.' (included as Austen's in *Juvenilia*, p. 328). Not a plausible match for Austen's hand, but possibly the same as that of vol. 3, p. 420.

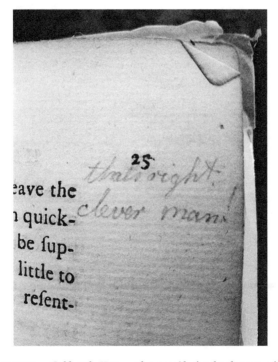

FIGURE 17. Goldsmith, *History*, vol. 4, p. 25: 'that's right, clever man!':
presumably the same hand as that of vol. 3, p. 421, perhaps also
as that of vol. 3, p. 420 (included as Austen's in *Juvenilia*, p. 331).

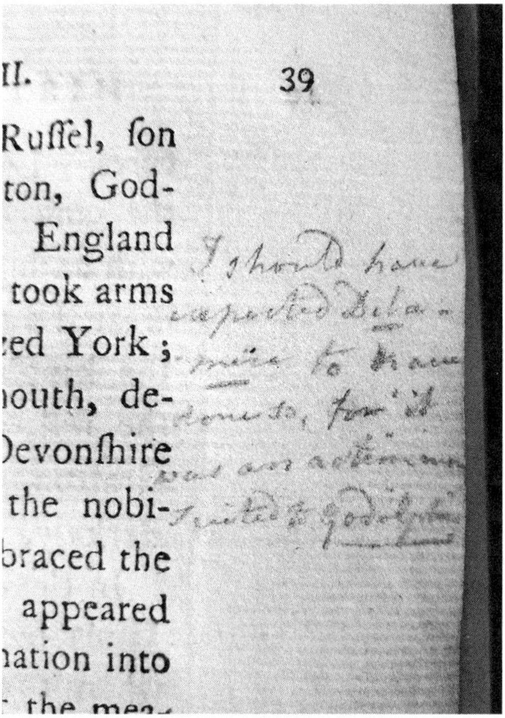

FIGURE 18. Goldsmith, *History*, vol. 4, p. 39: 'I should have expected <u>Delamere</u> to have done so, for it was an action unsuited to <u>Godolphin</u>'. Austen's hand (*Juvenilia*, p. 334).

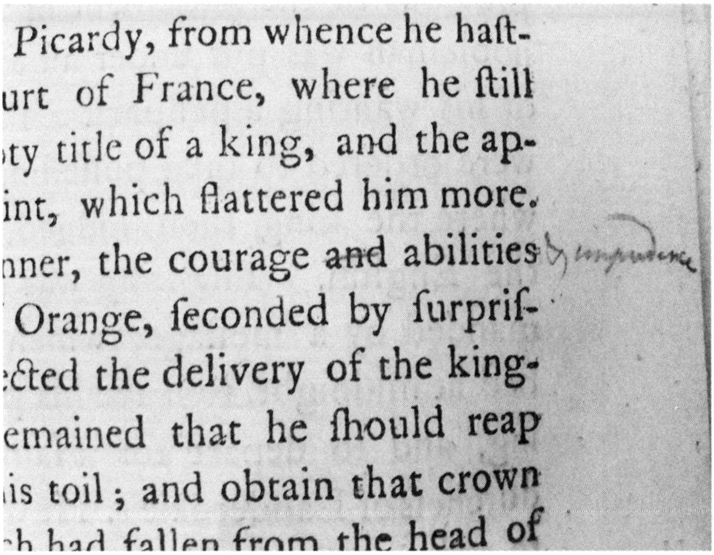

Picardy, from whence he haſt-
urt of France, where he ſtill
ty title of a king, and the ap-
int, which flattered him more.
nner, the courage ~~and~~ abilities _& impudence_
Orange, feconded by furprif-
:écted the delivery of the king-
emained that he fhould reap
.is toil ; and obtain that crown
.h had fallen from the head of

FIGURE 19. Goldsmith, *History*, vol. 4, p. 46: Goldsmith's description of the 'courage and abilities' of William of Orange has been revised to read 'courage abilities &
impudence'. Austen's hand. Mistranscribed as 'courage, abilities, & *insolence*' in
Juvenilia, p. 335 (punctuation and italics added by the editor).

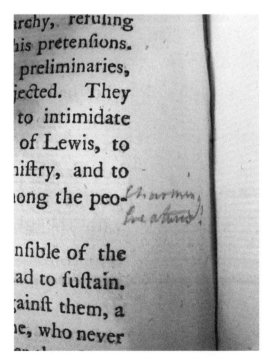

irchy, refuling
.his pretenſions.
preliminaries,
jected.   They
to intimidate
of Lewis, to
.iſtry, and to
iong the peo- _Charming_
creatures!

nfible of the
.ad to fuſtain.
:ainſt them, a
.e, who never

FIGURE 20. Goldsmith, *History*, vol. 4, p. 174: 'Charming
Creatures!' Probably Austen's hand (*Juvenilia*, p. 336).

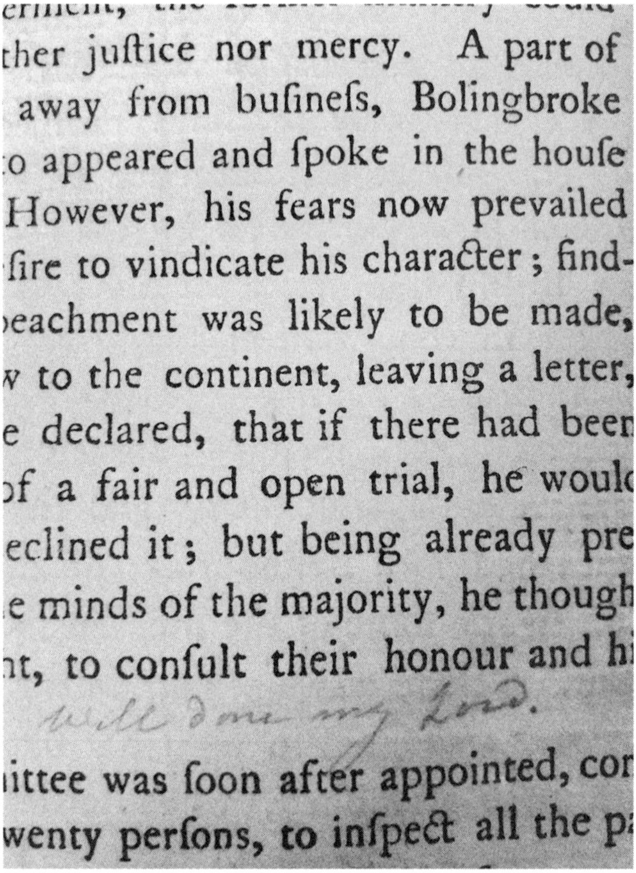

ther juſtice nor mercy. A part of
away from buſineſs, Bolingbroke
o appeared and ſpoke in the houſe
However, his fears now prevailed
fire to vindicate his character ; find-
eachment was likely to be made,
v to the continent, leaving a letter,
e declared, that if there had been
of a fair and open trial, he would
eclined it ; but being already pre
e minds of the majority, he though
nt, to conſult their honour and hi

well done my Lord.

iittee was ſoon after appointed, cor
wenty perſons, to inſpect all the pa

FIGURE 21. Goldsmith, *History,* vol. 4, p. 203: 'Well done my Lord.' Austen's
hand (*Juvenilia,* p. 339).

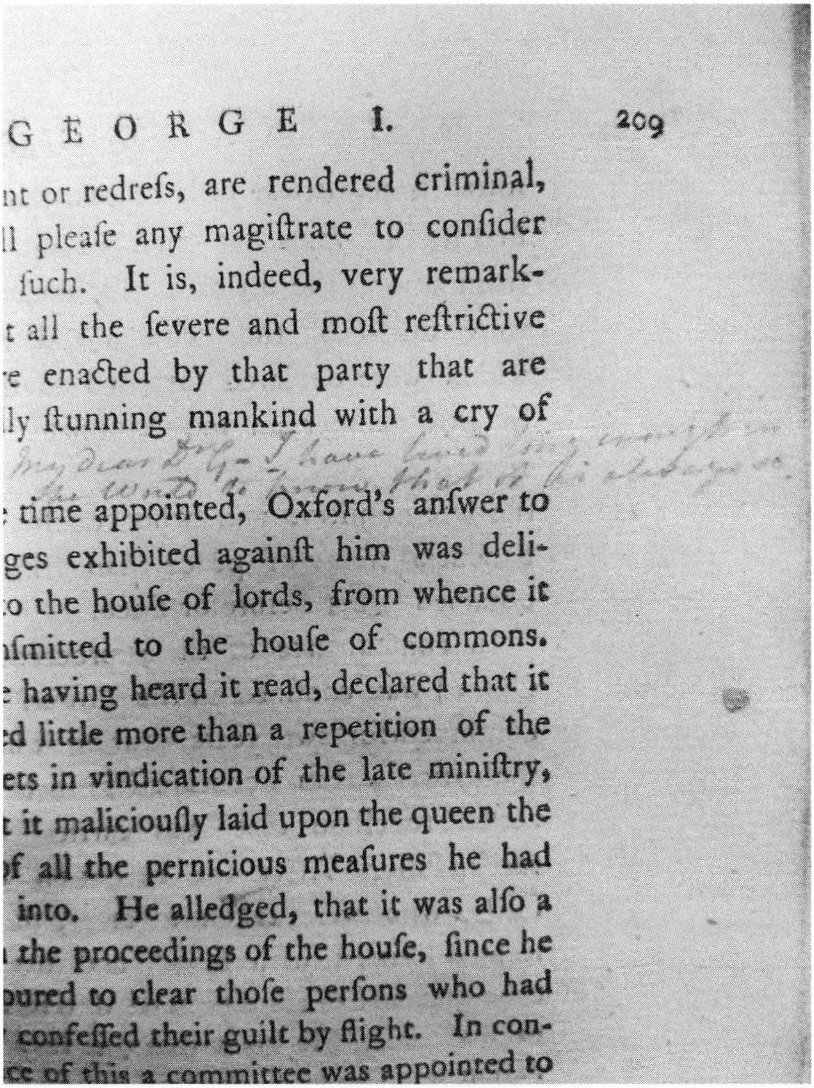

nt or redrefs, are rendered criminal,
ll pleafe any magiftrate to confider
fuch.   It is, indeed, very remark-
t all the fevere and moft reftrictive
e enacted by that party that are
ly ftunning mankind with a cry of
: time appointed, Oxford's anfwer to
ges exhibited againft him was deli-
o the houfe of lords, from whence it
fmitted to the houfe of commons.
having heard it read, declared that it
d little more than a repetition of the
ets in vindication of the late miniftry,
t it malicioufly laid upon the queen the
f all the pernicious meafures he had
into.   He alledged, that it was alfo a
the proceedings of the houfe, fince he
ured to clear thofe perfons who had
confeffed their guilt by flight.   In con-
ce of this a committee was appointed to

FIGURE 22. Goldsmith, *History*, vol. 4, p. 209: 'My dear Dʳ G—I have lived long enough in the World to know that it is always so.' Austen's hand (*Juvenilia*, p. 340 (with an exclamation mark in place of a full stop)). The author may have been no more than fifteen years old when she wrote this; she later ascribed such teenage world-weariness to Fanny Price, who at eighteen 'began to feel that she had not yet gone through all the changes of opinion and sentiment, which the progress of time and variation of circumstances occasion in this world of changes. The vicissitudes of the human mind had not yet been exhausted by her' (*MP*, vol. 3, ch. 6, p. 431).

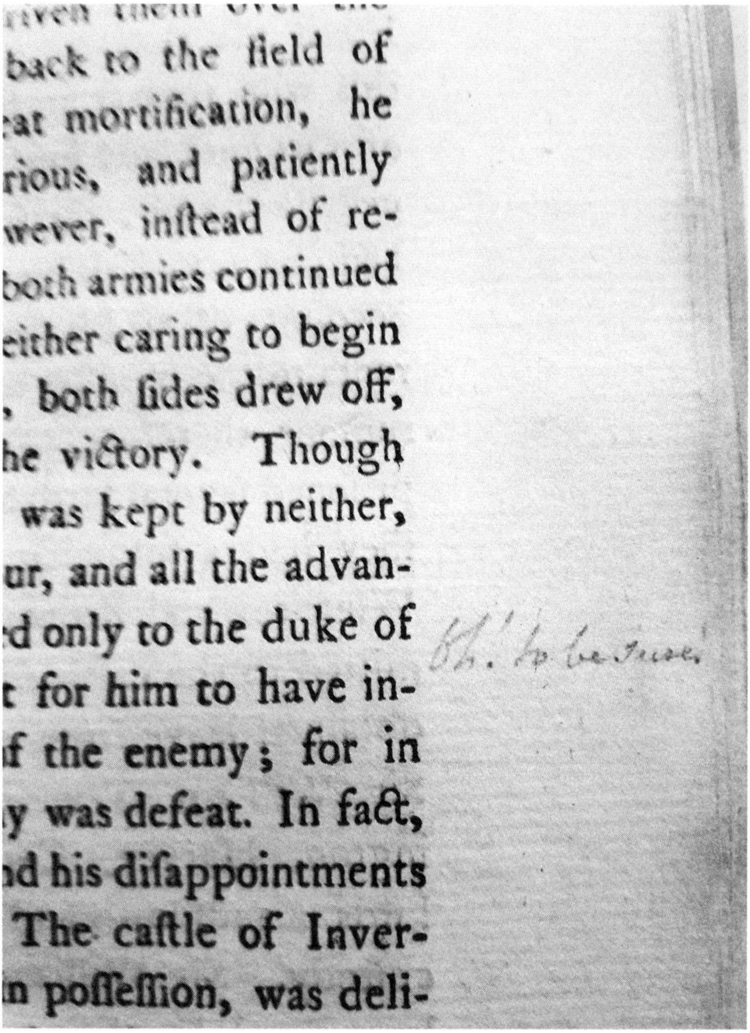

back to the field of
at mortification, he
rious, and patiently
wever, inftead of re-
both armies continued
either caring to begin
, both fides drew off,
he victory. Though
was kept by neither,
ur, and all the advan-
d only to the duke of
t for him to have in-
f the enemy; for in
y was defeat. In fact,
d his difappointments
The caftle of Inver-
n poffeffion, was deli-

Oh! to be sure!

FIGURE 23. Goldsmith, *History*, vol. 4, p. 217: 'Oh! to be sure!' Austen's hand (*Juvenilia*, p. 341).

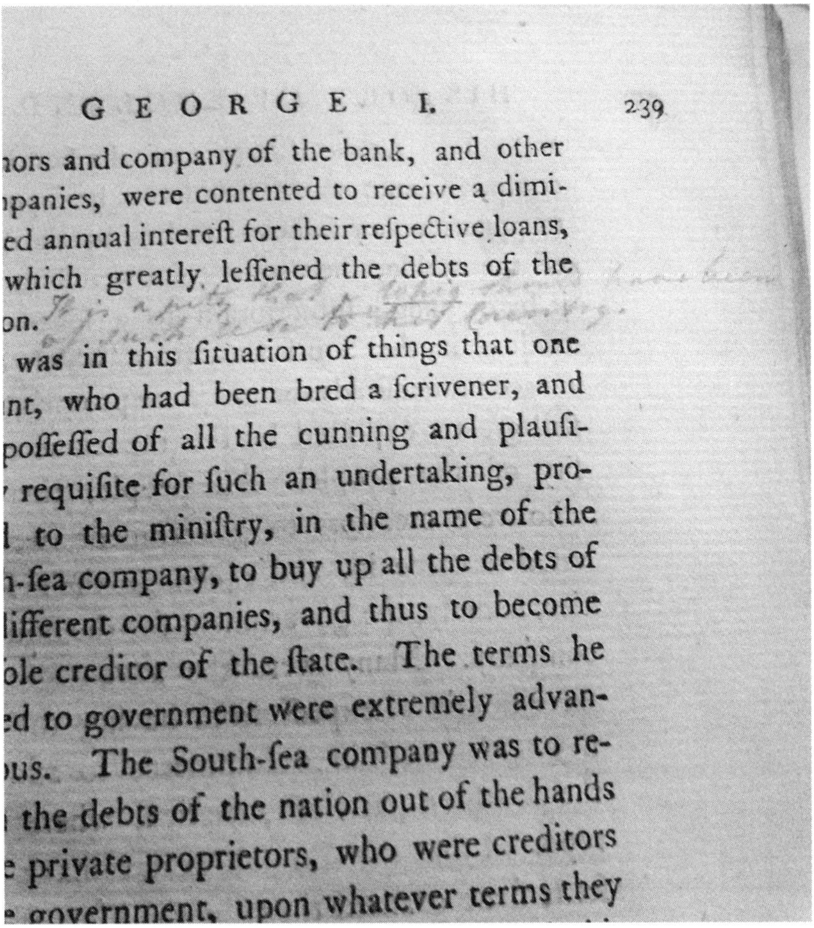

ıors and company of the bank, and other
ıpanies, were contented to receive a dimi-
ed annual intereſt for their reſpective loans,
which greatly leſſened the debts of the
on.
was in this ſituation of things that one
ınt, who had been bred a ſcrivener, and
poſſeſſed of all the cunning and plauſi-
requiſite for ſuch an undertaking, pro-
l to the miniſtry, in the name of the
ı-ſea company, to buy up all the debts of
lifferent companies, and thus to become
ole creditor of the ſtate. The terms he
ed to government were extremely advan-
us. The South-ſea company was to re-
the debts of the nation out of the hands
e private proprietors, who were creditors
e government, upon whatever terms they

FIGURE 24. Goldsmith, *History*, vol. 4, p. 239: 'It is a pity that a <u>Whig</u> should have been of such use to his Country.' Austen's hand (*Juvenilia*, p. 342).

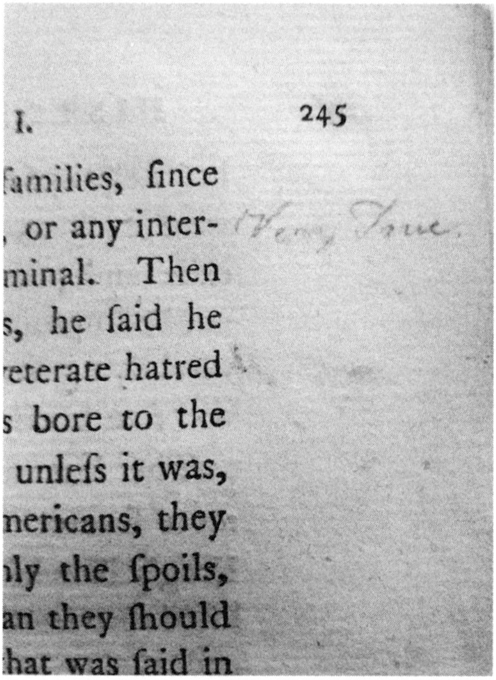

I. 245

families, ſince
, or any inter- (Very True.
minal. Then
s, he ſaid he
eterate hatred
s bore to the
unleſs it was,
nericans, they
ly the ſpoils,
an they ſhould
hat was ſaid in

FIGURE 25. Goldsmith, *History*, vol. 4, p. 245: 'Very True.' Austen's hand (*Juvenilia*, p. 342).

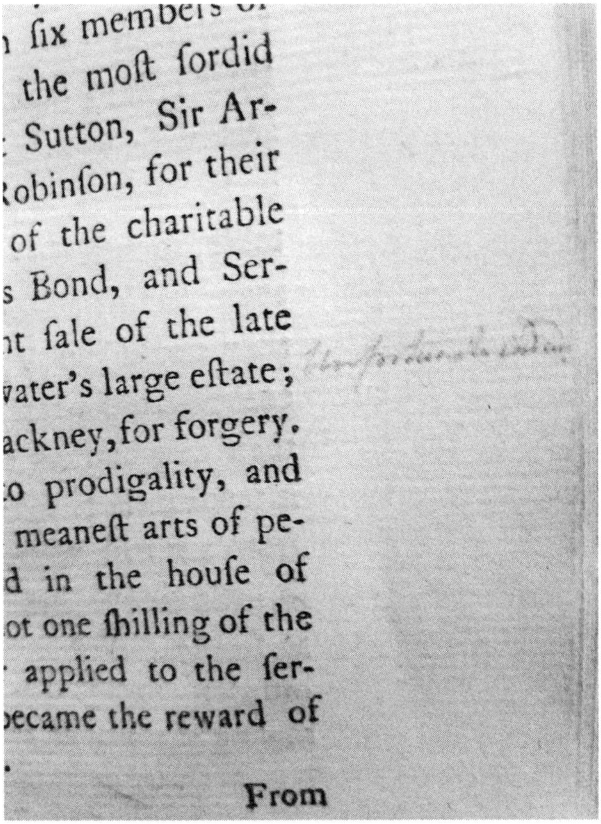

ſix members of
the moſt ſordid
Sutton, Sir Ar-
obinſon, for their
of the charitable
s Bond, and Ser-
t ſale of the late
ater's large eſtate;
ackney, for forgery.
o prodigality, and
meaneſt arts of pe-
d in the houſe of
ot one ſhilling of the
applied to the ſer-
ecame the reward of

From

FIGURE 26. Goldsmith, *History*, vol. 4, p. 263: 'Unfortunate indeed'. Austen's hand (*Juvenilia*, p. 344).

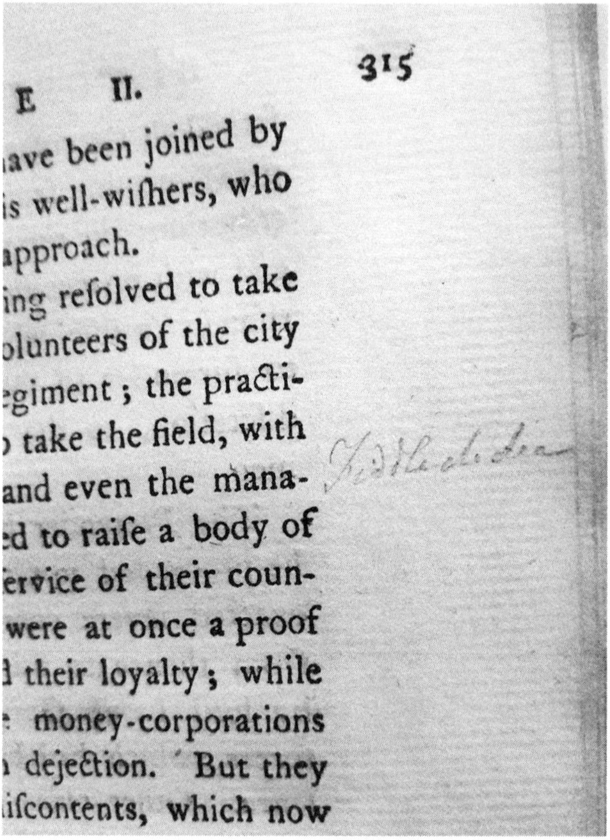

ave been joined by
is well-wifhers, who
approach.
ing refolved to take
olunteers of the city
egiment ; the practi-
) take the field, with
and even the mana-
ed to raife a body of
ervice of their coun-
were at once a proof
l their loyalty ; while
e money-corporations
n dejection.   But they
ifcontents, which now

Fiddlededia

FIGURE 27. Goldsmith, *History*, vol. 4, p. 315: 'Fiddlededia'. Austen's hand (*Juvenilia*, p. 348). 'Fiddlededia', also 'fiddlededee', means 'Nonsense!'; the *Oxford English Dictionary* traces it back to Samuel Johnson, as quoted in James Boswell's *Life of Johnson*, a work published in the same year (1791) in which Austen finished her 'History of England'.

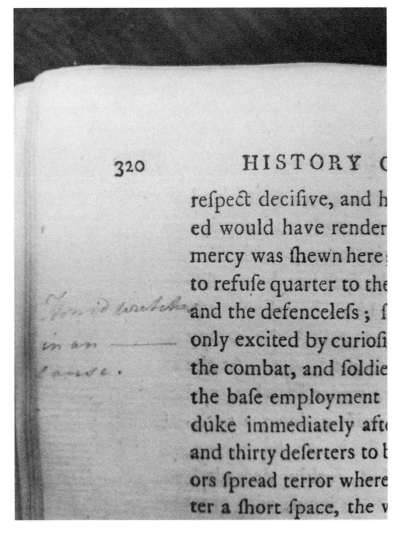

FIGURE 28. Goldsmith, *History*, vol. 4, p. 320: 'Horrid wretches in an ——— cause.'
Austen's hand (*Juvenilia*, p. 350). Compare 'Horrible Wretches', another annotation to
Goldsmith, *History*, vol. 3, p. 281; 'horrid Wretches' and 'Horrid Wretch' also appear in
'Kitty, or the Bower' (*TW*, pp. 177–8).

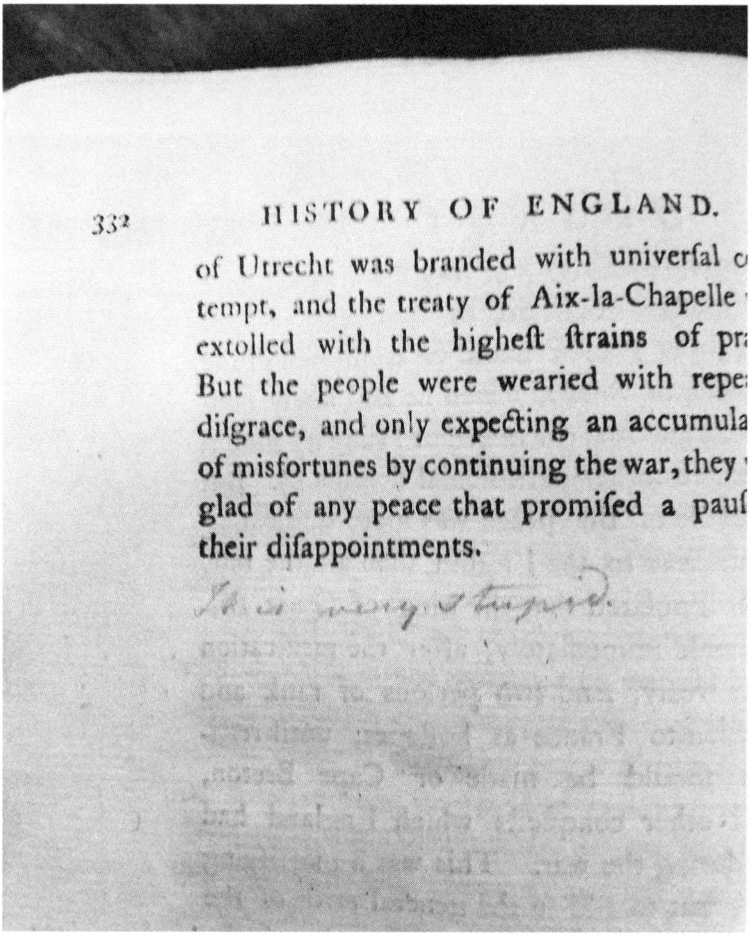
332 HISTORY OF ENGLAND.

of Utrecht was branded with univerſal c
tempt, and the treaty of Aix-la-Chapelle
extolled with the higheſt ſtrains of pr
But the people were wearied with repe
diſgrace, and only expecting an accumula
of misfortunes by continuing the war, they
glad of any peace that promiſed a pauſ
their diſappointments.

It is very stupid.

FIGURE 29. Goldsmith, *History*, vol. 4, p. 332: 'It is very stupid.' Austen's hand (*Juvenilia*, p. 351).

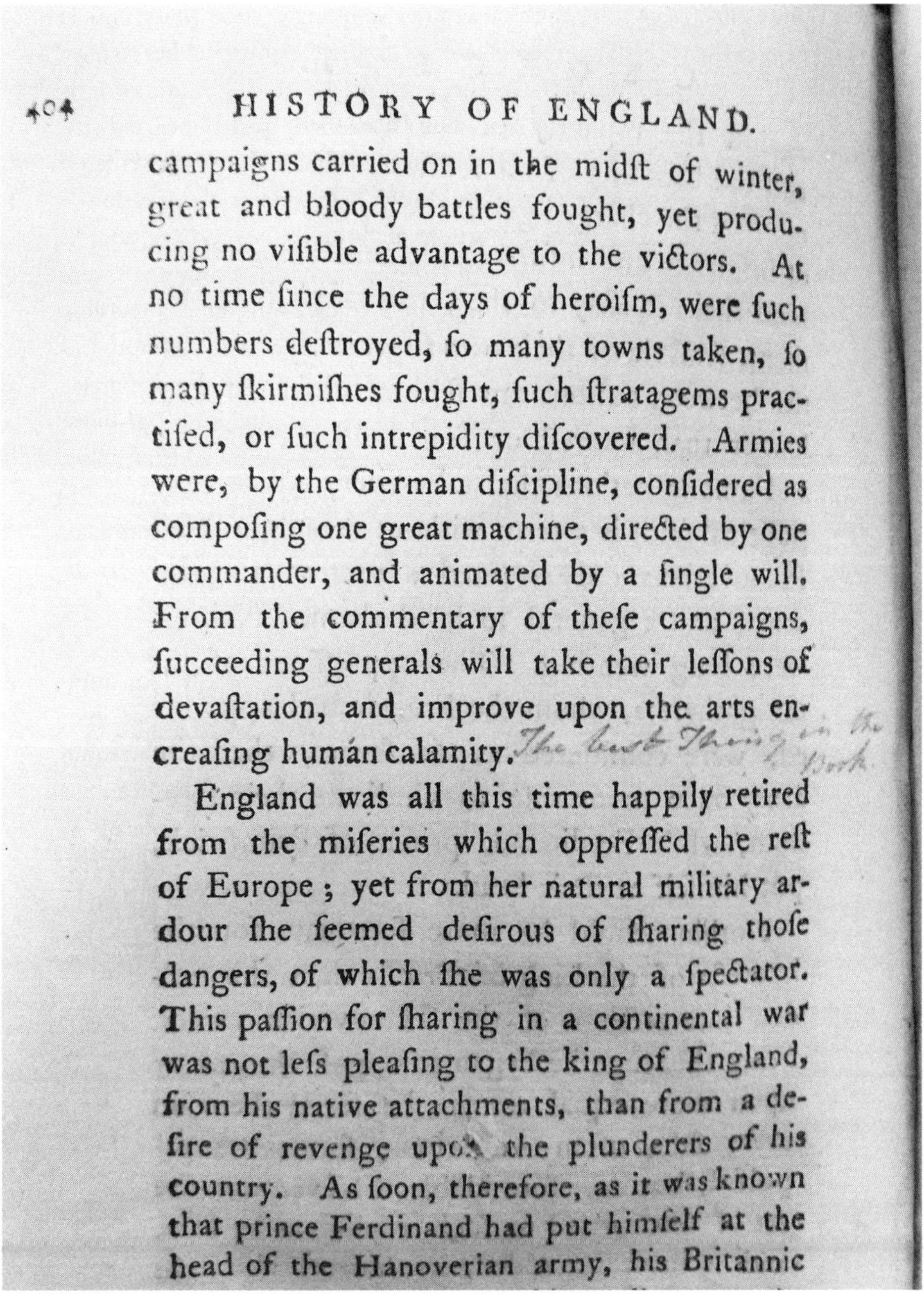

campaigns carried on in the midft of winter, great and bloody battles fought, yet producing no vifible advantage to the victors. At no time fince the days of heroifm, were fuch numbers deftroyed, fo many towns taken, fo many fkirmifhes fought, fuch ftratagems practifed, or fuch intrepidity difcovered. Armies were, by the German difcipline, confidered as compofing one great machine, directed by one commander, and animated by a fingle will. From the commentary of thefe campaigns, fucceeding generals will take their leffons of devaftation, and improve upon the arts encreafing human calamity. *The best Thing in the Book.*

England was all this time happily retired from the miferies which oppreffed the reft of Europe ; yet from her natural military ardour fhe feemed defirous of fharing thofe dangers, of which fhe was only a fpectator. This paffion for fharing in a continental war was not lefs pleafing to the king of England, from his native attachments, than from a defire of revenge upon the plunderers of his country. As foon, therefore, as it was known that prince Ferdinand had put himfelf at the head of the Hanoverian army, his Britannic

FIGURE 30. Goldsmith, *History*, vol. 4, p. 404: 'The best Thing in the Book.' Austen's hand. Her unusually admiring comment on the *History* is prompted by a Johnsonian passage about the misery of war, with its 'lessons of devastation' and 'arts encreasing human calamity'.

Where attribution is doubtful, it is often tempting to think that a note is Austen's on the basis of comments that we might like or expect her to have made (such as in response to the 'popish bitch' passage in Goldsmith, *History*, vol. 3, p. 420, reproduced on page 232), rather than on the basis of the handwriting. A further complicating factor is that Austen could in theory have entered remarks into the margins and text of Goldsmith's *History* over a long period—first, as a schoolroom reader of set portions of the book, then as a rival adolescent historian, later still as a novelist and beloved aunt whose comments were evidently viewed by her family as prompts for their own agreement or revision. Just as the teenage Austen was herself engaged in buttressing or (more frequently) disagreeing with Goldsmith's text, and went on to read and appraise the novelistic writing of her niece Anna and nephew James Edward, so those younger relatives and others themselves read and disputed Goldsmith's account, at the same time responding and adding to notes made by Austen. Although it is not always possible to disentangle individual commentators from one another, there is one marginal note that we can certainly identify as a direct reply to and endorsement of Aunt Jane's because it announces to everyone that that is exactly what it is (see figure 31).

If, as has been suggested, the early writings became a 'workshop or storehouse of ideas', not only for their author but also for the next generation of novelistic Austens when their aunt moved to Chawton, might the schoolroom texts that were read and annotated across the generations not have been put to similar use?[8] Jane Austen passed on such books to those younger relatives, Goldsmith's *History of England* going to James Edward; Vicesimus Knox's *Elegant Extracts: or Useful and Entertaining Passages in Prose* (first published in 1783 and frequently revised and reprinted) and Ann Murry's *Mentoria: or, the Young Ladies Instructor* (first published in 1778 and frequently reprinted) to Anna Austen. All three texts are 'annotated in Austen's opinionated way, as preliminary to conversation or practice for it';[9] *Elegant Extracts* includes some typically fervid endorsements of Mary, Queen of Scots, and equally typical condemnations of Elizabeth I (see *Juvenilia*, pp. 352–5).[10] That Austen's

8. Sutherland, *Jane Austen's Textual Lives*, p. 204, and 'From Kitty to Catharine', p. 129; see also Jane Austen, *Catharine and Other Writings*, p. xx.

9. H. J. Jackson, *Romantic Readers*, p. 136.

10. See also Deirdre le Faye, 'New Marginalia in Jane Austen's Books', *Book Collector*, 49 (2000), 222–6. As Sabor notes, there are problems with attribution here, too. Le Faye suggests that the pencilled comments in *Elegant Extracts* are in Austen's hand, but references to Henry

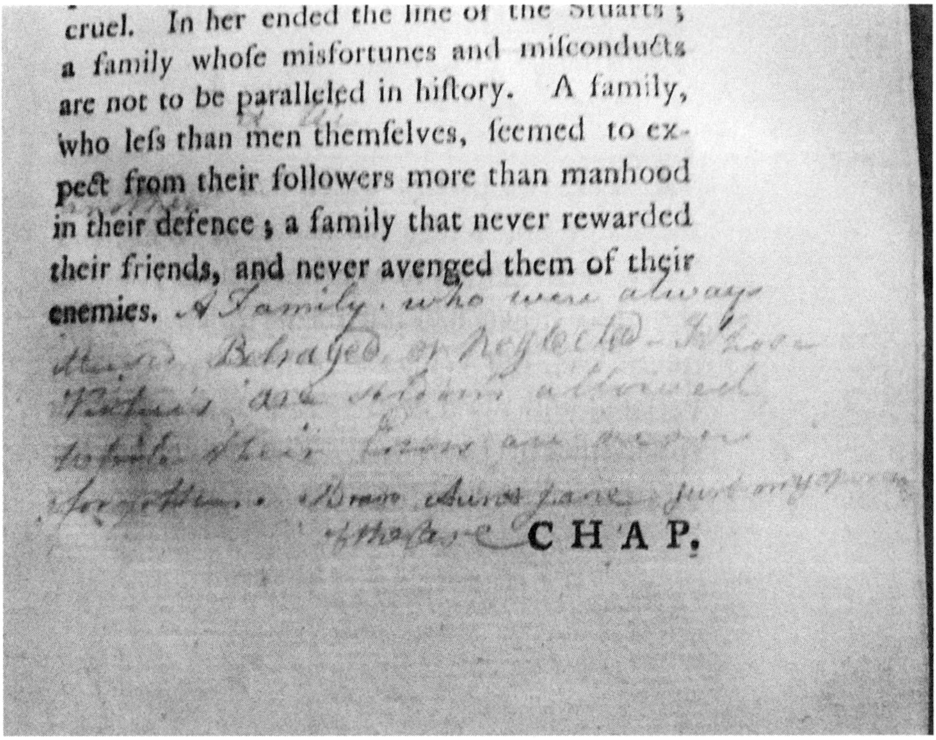
cruel. In her ended the line of the Stuarts; a family whoſe misfortunes and miſconducts are not to be paralleled in hiſtory. A family, who leſs than men themſelves, ſeemed to expect from their followers more than manhood in their defence; a family that never rewarded their friends, and never avenged them of their enemies.

CHAP.

FIGURE 31. Goldsmith, *History*, vol. 4, p. 191: The last sentence of this chapter, 'A family, who less than men themselves, seemed to expect from their followers more than manhood in their defence; a family that never rewarded their friends, and never avenged them of their enemies', has been re-written as 'A Family, who were always illused, Betrayed, or neglected—Whose Virtue's are seldom allowed while their Errors are never forgotten.' Austen's hand, although it looks as if another hand has retraced some of her words in pencil, either for additional emphasis or to ensure their preservation. Directly following this comment (and on the same line) is James Edward's response, also in pencil: 'Bravo Aunt Jane just my opinion of the Case.' (*Juvenilia*, p. 337).

'History of England' appears to be her most overtly participatory, collaborative work—with signed portraits contributed by Cassandra, direct addresses to the audience, and several internal references to relatives and friends—suggests that partisanship was always a family business.[11]

John Todd's edition of Johnson's *Dictionary*, first published in 1818 (that is, after Austen's death), rule this out.

11. See for example references to 'you, Reader' and to 'Mrs Lefroy, Mrs Knight & myself', as well as to Francis Austen (*TW*, p. 130).

BIBLIOGRAPHY

Primary Works: Manuscripts

Austen, George, Letter to Thomas Cadell (1 Nov. 1797), MS 279—Letter 1, St John's College, Oxford

Austen, Jane, Lines on Winchester Races, MS 209715B (No. 410–12), The Henry W. and Albert A. Berg Collection of English and American Literature, The New York Public Library, Astor, Lenox, and Tilden Foundations

——, 'Volume the First', MS. Don. E. 7, Bodleian Library, Oxford

——, 'Volume the Second', Add. MS. 59874, British Library

——, 'Volume the Third', Add. MS. 65381, British Library

Lefroy, Fanny Catherine, Family History, 23M93/85/2, Hampshire Record Office

Wingfield, Mrs 'Character, given by Mrs Wingfield when holding a letter written by Jane Austen', 23M93/64/4/1/2, Hampshire Record Office

Primary Works: Books, Chapters, and Articles

Aikin, John, *Evenings at Home; or, the Juvenile Budget Opened. Consisting of a variety of miscellaneous pieces, for the amusement and instruction of young persons*, 6 vols. (London: J. Johnson, 1792–6)

Anderson, James, *The Constitutions of the Antient and Honourable Fraternity of Free and Accepted Masons* (London: Brother J. Scott, 1756)

Anon., 'ART. XIII. *Camilla: or, A Picture of Youth*', *The British Critic, A New Review*, VII–VIII (1796), 527–36

——, 'Art. 14. *The Effusions of Friendship and Fancy*', *The Monthly Review or Literary Journal Enlarged*, vol. 34 (1766), 313–4

——, *The Blossoms of Early Genius and Virtue; containing a great variety of juvenile memoirs and anecdotes* (Burslem: J. Tregortha, 1800)

——, *Elizabeth Percy; A Novel, Founded on Facts*, 2 vols. (London: A. Hamilton, 1792)

——, *God Justified, Man Condemned, and Grace Magnified. A Sermon on Ecclesiastes vii. 29* (Canterbury and London: J. Marsom and D. Taylor, 1795?)

——, *The History of Little Goody Two-Shoes* (London: J. Newbery, 1765)

——, *A History of the Ridiculous Extravagancies of Monsieur Oufle* (London: J. Morphew, 1711)

Anon., *The Paths of Virtue Delineated; or, The history in miniature of the celebrated Pamela, Clarissa Harlowe, and Sir Charles Grandison: familiarised and adapted to the capacities of youth* (London: R. Baldwin, etc., 1756)

——, *The Posthumous Daughter: A Novel*, 2 vols. (London: G. Cawthorn, 1797)

——, *Royal Magnificence; or the Effusions of Ten Days: A Descriptive and Satirical Poem, in three cantos. On the subject of His Majesty's late visit to Worcester, on the sixth of August, 1788* (London: for the author, 1788)

——, *The Sentimental Connoisseur: or, Pleasing and Entertaining Novelist. Being an elegant and new assemblage of lively effusions of fancy, polite tales, diverting essays, droll adventures, pleasing stories, entertaining novels, comic characters, facetious histories, affecting examples, striking remarks, pointed satires, &c. &c. Entirely calculated to form in the Mind the most Virtuous Sentiments: and Adapted to promote a Love of Virtue and Abhorrence of Vice* (London: R. Newton, etc., 1778)

——, 'To Mrs Charlotte Lennox, upon seeing her Poems, and Proposals for printing them', *Gentleman's Magazine*, 19 (June 1749), p. 278

——, 'WINCHESTER RACES', *The Hampshire Chronicle and Courier* (Monday, 14 July 1817), p. 1, col. 2

Ashford, Daisy, *The Young Visiters or Mr Salteena's Plan*, intro. J. M. Barrie (London: Chatto & Windus, 2008)

Austen, James, *The Complete Poems of James Austen, Jane Austen's Eldest Brother*, ed. David Selwyn (Chawton: Jane Austen Society, 2003)

——, *The Loiterer: A Periodical Work in Two Volumes Published at Oxford in the Years 1789 and 1790 by the Austen Family*, ed. Robert L. Mack (Lewiston, NY; Queenstown, Ontario; and Lampeter: Edwin Mellen Press, 2006)

——, and Henry Austen, et al., *The Loiterer, A Periodical Work*, 2 vols. ([Oxford]: for the author, [1789–90])

Austen, Jane, *The Beautifull Cassandra: A Novel in Twelve Chapters*, ed. Claudia L. Johnson (Princeton, NJ: Princeton University Press, 2018)

——, *The Cambridge Edition of the Works of Jane Austen*, gen. ed. Janet Todd (Cambridge: Cambridge University Press, 2005–8):

   Emma, ed. Richard Cronin and Dorothy McMillan (2005)

   Juvenilia, ed. Peter Sabor (2006)

   Later Manuscripts, ed. Janet Todd and Linda Bree (2008)

   Mansfield Park, ed. John Wiltshire (2005)

   Northanger Abbey, ed. Barbara M. Benedict and Deirdre le Faye (2006)

   Persuasion, ed. Janet Todd and Antje Blank (2006)

   Pride and Prejudice, ed. Pat Rogers (2006)

   Sense and Sensibility, ed. Edward Copeland (2006)

——, *Catharine and Other Writings*, ed. Margaret Anne Doody and Douglas Murray (Oxford: Oxford University Press, 1993)

——, *Jane Austen's Fiction Manuscripts*, 5 vols., ed. Kathryn Sutherland (Oxford: Oxford University Press, 2018)

——, *Jane Austen's Lady Susan: A Facsimile of the Manuscript in the Pierpont Morgan Library and the 1925 Printed Edition*, intro. A. Walton Litz (New York and London: Garland Publishing, 1989)

———, *Jane Austen's Letters*, ed. Deirdre le Faye, 4th edition (Oxford: Oxford University Press, 2014)

———, *Jane Austen's 'The History of England' and Cassandra's Portraits*, ed. Annette Upfal and Christine Alexander (Sydney: Juvenilia Press, 2009)

———, *Love and Freindship and Other Early Works Now First Printed from the Original MS.* (London: Chatto & Windus, 1922)

———, *Love and Freindship and Other Youthful Writings*, ed. Christine Alexander (London: Penguin, 2014)

———, *Mansfield Park: An Annotated Edition*, ed. Deirdre Shauna Lynch (Cambridge, MA, and London: Belknap Press of Harvard University Press, 2016)

———, *Plan of a Novel, according to hints from various quarters by Jane Austen; with opinions on Mansfield Park and Emma, collected and transcribed by her, and other documents, printed from the originals*, [ed. R. W. Chapman] (Oxford: Clarendon Press, 1926)

———, *Sanditon*, ed. Kathryn Sutherland (Oxford: Oxford University Press, 2019)

———, *Sanditon: An Unfinished Novel: reproduced in facsimile from the manuscript in the possession of King's College, Cambridge*, ed. Brian Southam (Oxford: Clarendon Press, 1975)

———, *Sense and Sensibility: A Novel*, 3 vols. (London: T. Egerton, for the author, 1811)

———, *Teenage Writings*, ed. Kathryn Sutherland and Freya Johnston (Oxford: Oxford University Press, 2017)

———, *The Works of Jane Austen*, ed. R. W. Chapman, 6 vols. (Oxford and New York: Oxford University Press, 1923–54)

———, and Charlotte Brontë, *The Juvenilia of Jane Austen and Charlotte Brontë*, ed. Frances Beer (Harmondsworth: Penguin, 1986)

———, et al., *Charades &c. Written a Hundred Years Ago by J. Austen and her Family* (London: Spottiswoode & Co., 1895)

———, et al., *Collected Poems and Verse of the Austen Family*, ed. David Selwyn (Manchester: Carcanet, 1996)

Austen-Leigh, J. E., *A Memoir of Jane Austen* (London: Richard Bentley, [1869])

———, *A Memoir of Jane Austen and Other Family Recollections*, ed. Kathryn Sutherland (Oxford: Oxford University Press, 2002)

Austen-Leigh, R. A., ed., *Austen Papers, 1704–1856* (London: Spottiswoode, Ballantyne, 1942)

Austen-Leigh, William, and Richard Arthur, *Jane Austen: Her Life and Letters* (London: Smith Elder, 1913)

Bage, Robert, *Hermsprong; or Man as he is not*, 3 vols. (London: William Lane, 1796)

Bancks, John, *The History of the House of Austria, and the German Empire: containing the Germanick constitution, and an account of all their emperors* (London: [n. p.], 1743)

Barker, Mary, *A Welsh Story*, 3 vols. (London: Hookham and Carpenter, 1798)

Beckett, Samuel, *Disjecta: Miscellaneous Writings and A Dramatic Fragment* (London: John Calder, 1983)

———, *The Letters of Samuel Beckett*, ed. George Craig, Martha Dow Fehsenfeld, Dan Gunn, and Lois More Overbeck, 4 vols. (Cambridge: Cambridge University Press, 2009)

Bennett, Alan, Peter Cook, Jonathan Miller, and Dudley Moore, *The Complete Beyond the Fringe*, ed. Roger Wilmut (London: Methuen, 1987)

Bennett, Mrs., *Juvenile Indiscretions. A novel*, 5 vols. (London: W. Lane, 1786)

Bennett, Mrs., *Les imprudences de la jeunesse, par l'auteur de Cécilia; traduit de l'anglois, par Madame la Baronne de Vasse*, 4 vols. (London [Paris?]: Buisson, 1788)

Boswell, James, *Boswell's Life of Johnson: together with Boswell's journal of a tour to the Hebrides and Johnson's diary of a journey into North Wales*, ed. G. B. Hill, rev. and enlarged L. F. Powell, 6 vols., 2nd edition (Oxford: Oxford University Press, 1934–64)

Brontë, Charlotte, et al., *The Clarendon Edition of the Novels of the Brontës*: [Charlotte Brontë], *The Professor*, ed. Margaret Smith and Herbert Rosengarten (Oxford: Oxford University Press, 1987)

Burke, Edmund, *The Writings and Speeches of Edmund Burke*:

    Vol. 4: *Party, Parliament, and the Dividing of the Whigs: 1780–1794* (Oxford: Oxford University Press, 2015)

    Vol. 8: *The French Revolution, 1790–1794*, ed. L. G. Mitchell and William B. Todd (Oxford: Oxford University Press, 2014)

[Burney, Frances], *Camilla: or, A Picture of Youth*, 5 vols. (London: T. Payne, T. Cadell Jr., and W. Davies, 1796), Bodleian Library Arch. A. e. 108 / 1

——, *Cecilia, or Memoirs of an Heiress. By the Author of Evelina*, 5 vols. (London: T. Payne and T. Cadell, 1783)

——, *The Witlings and the Woman-Hater*, ed. Peter Sabor and Geoffrey Sill (Peterborough, Ontario: Broadview Press, 2002)

Byron, Lord George Gordon, *Hours of Idleness, A Series of Poems, original and translated, by George Gordon, Lord Byron, a Minor* (Newark: S. and J. Ridge; London: B. Crosby and Co.; Longman, Hurst, Roes, and Orme; F. and C. Rivington; and J. Mawman, 1807)

——, *Lord Byron: The Complete Poetical Works*, ed. Jerome J. McGann, 7 vols. (Oxford: Clarendon Press, 1980–93)

Calonne, Charles de, *Considerations on the Present and Future State of France. By M. de Calonne, Minister of State. Translated from the French* (London: J. Evans, 1791)

Chapone, Mrs. [Hester], *Letters on the Improvement of the Mind: Addressed to a Young Lady*, 2 vols., 2nd edition (London: J. Walter, 1773)

Chesterfield, Lord Philip Dormer Stanhope, *Letters written by the Late Right Honourable Philip Dormer Stanhope, Earl of Chesterfield, to his son, Philip Stanhope, Esq.*, 4 vols., 6th edition (London: J. Dodsley, 1775)

Cicero, Marcus Tullius, *Brutus, Orator*, trans. G. L. Hendrickson, Locb Classical Library, rev. edition (Cambridge, MA: Harvard University Press, 2014)

Clark, Hugh, *A Concise History of Knighthood*, 2 vols. (London: W. Strahan, J. F. and C. Rivington, T. Payne, etc., 1784)

Coleridge, S. T., *The Collected Works of Samuel Taylor Coleridge*, vol. 14: *Table Talk*, part 2, ed. Carl Woodring (Princeton, NJ: Princeton University Press, 1990)

——, *Poems on Various Subjects* (London: G. and G. Robinson; Bristol: J. Cottle, 1796)

[Collins, Dr.], *Practical Rules for the Management and Medical Treatment of Negro Slaves, in the Sugar Colonies. By a Professional Planter* (London: Vernor and Hood, 1803)

Courtenay, John, *Juvenile Poems, by the late John Courtenay, jun. With an elegy on his death* (London: J. Jones, 1795)

Cowper, William, *The Poems of William Cowper*, 3 vols., ed. John D. Baird and Charles Ryskamp (Oxford: Clarendon Press, 1979–95)

Donoghue, J., *Juvenile Essays in Poetry* (Barnstaple: L. B. Seeley; London: J. Owen, 1797)

Duché, Jacob, *Discourses on Various Subjects*, 2 vols., 3ʳᵈ edition (London: T. Cadell, 1779)

Edgeworth, Maria, *Letters for Literary Ladies to which is added An Essay on the Noble Science of Self-Justification*, ed. Claire Connolly (London: Everyman, 1993)

Eliot, George, *The Clarendon Edition of the Novels of George Eliot: Middlemarch: A Study of Provincial Life*, ed. David Carroll (Oxford: Clarendon Press, 1986; rep. 1992)

Eliot, T. S., *The Poems of T. S. Eliot*, ed. Christopher Ricks and Jim McCue, 2 vols. (London: Faber & Faber, 2015)

E.N., 'To Mrs. Charlotte Lennox. On reading her Poems, printing by Subscription, in one Vol. 8vo, price 5s.', *Gentleman's Magazine*, 20 (Nov. 1750), p. 518

Evans, John, *Juvenile Pieces: Designed for the Youth of Both Sexes* (London: B. Crosby, [1797])

Fanshawe, Catherine, *The Literary Remains of Catherine Maria Fanshawe, with notes by the late Rev. William Harness* (London: Basil Montagu Pickering, 1876)

Ferrier, Susan, *The Inheritance*, 3 vols., 2ⁿᵈ edition (Edinburgh: William Blackwood; London: T. Cadell, 1825)

Fielding, Henry, *An Apology for the Life of Mrs. Shamela Andrews. In which, the many notorious FALSHOODS and MISREPRESENTATIONS of a Book called PAMELA, are exposed and refuted; and all the matchless ARTS of that young Politician, set in a true and just Light. Together with a full Account of all that passed between her and Parson Arthur Williams; whose Character is represented in a manner something different from that which he bears in PAMELA. The whole being exact Copies of authentick Papers delivered to the Editor. Necessary to be had in all FAMILIES* (London: A. Dodd, 1741)

———, *The Wesleyan Edition of the Works of Henry Fielding* (Oxford: Clarendon Press, 1967–):
The Covent-Garden Journal and A Plan of the Universal Register-Office, ed. Bertrand A. Goldgar (1988)
The History of Tom Jones, A Foundling, ed. Fredson Bowers and Martin C. Battestin, 2 vols. (1974)
Joseph Andrews, ed. Martin C. Battestin (1967)
The Journal of a Voyage to Lisbon, Shamela, and Occasional Writings, ed. Martin C. Battestin (2008)

Fielding, Sarah, *The Governess or, Little Female Academy* (London: Oxford University Press, 1968)

Forster, E. M., *Howards End* (London: E. Arnold, 1910)

Gilbert, Sandra M., and Susan Gubar, eds., *The Norton Anthology of Literature by Women* (New York: Norton, 1985)

Godwin, William, *Things as They Are or The Adventures of Caleb Williams*, ed. Maurice Willians (Harmondsworth: Penguin, 1987)

Goldsmith, Oliver, *The History of England, from the Earliest Times to the Death of George II*, 4 vols. (London: T. Davies; Becket and De Hondt; and T. Cadell, 1771)

———, *An History of England in a Series of Letters from a Nobleman to his Son* (London: J. Newbery, 1764)

[Gray, Thomas], *Elegy Wrote in a Country Churchyard* (London: R. Dodsley, 1751)

Griffiths, Miss J., *A Collection of Juvenile Poems, on Various Subjects* (Warwick: for the author, [1784])

Grose, John, *Ethics, Rational and Theological, with cursory reflections on the general principles of deism* (London: for the author, 1782)

Hardy, Thomas, *Jude the Obscure* (London and New York: Penguin, 1998)

——, *The Works of Thomas Hardy in Prose and Verse, with Prefaces and Notes*, 23 vols. (London: Macmillan, 1912–20)

Hogarth, William, *The Analysis of Beauty. Written with a view of fixing the fluctuating ideas of taste* (London: for the author, 1753)

Hume, David, *The History of England from the Invasion of Julius Caesar to the Revolution in 1688*, intro. William B. Todd, 6 vols. (Indianapolis, IN: Liberty Fund, 1983–5)

Jackson, William, *The Four Ages; together with essays on various subjects* (London: Cadell and Davies, 1798)

Jackson, William, *The New and Complete Newgate Calendar; or, Villany* [sic] *Displayed in All its Branches*, 6 vols. (London: Alex. Hogg, [1795])

James, Henry, *Roderick Hudson*, ed. Geoffrey Moore and Patricia Crick (Harmondsworth: Penguin, 1986)

Johnson, Samuel, *The Complete English Poems*, ed. J. D. Fleeman (Harmondsworth: Penguin, 1971; repr. 1982)

——, *A Dictionary of the English Language*, 2 vols. (London: for J. and P. Knapton, T. and T. Longman, C. Hitch and L. Hawes, A. Millar, R. and J. Dodsley, 1755)

——, *The Yale Edition of the Works of Samuel Johnson*, 20 vols. (New Haven, CT, and London: Yale University Press, 1958–2019):

Vol. 2: *The Idler and the Adventurer*, eds. W. J. Bate, John M. Bullitt, and L. F. Powell (1963)

Vols. 3–5: *The Rambler*, ed. W. J. Bate and Albrecht B. Strauss (1969)

Vol. 16: *Rasselas and Other Tales*, ed. Gwin J. Kolb (1990)

——, and Hester Lynch Piozzi, *Letters to and from the late Samuel Johnson, LL.D. To which are added some poems never before printed. Published from the original Mss. in her possession, by Hester Lynch Piozzi*, 2 vols. (London: A. Strahan and T. Cadell, 1788)

Joyce, James, *Ulysses*, ed. Jeri Johnson (Oxford: Oxford University Press, 2008)

Keats, John, *The Poems of John Keats; Arranged in Chronological Order with a Preface by Sidney Colvin*, 2 vols. (London: Chatto & Windus, 1909)

——, *21ˢᵗ-Century Oxford Authors: John Keats*, ed. John Barnard (Oxford: Oxford University Press, 2017)

Knight, Frances, *Fanny Knight's Diaries: Jane Austen through Her Niece's Eyes*, ed. Deirdre le Faye ([Winchester]: The Jane Austen Society, 2000)

[Knight, Mrs?], *Flights of Fancy, or Poetical Effusions, by a Lady, Late of Mitcham, in the County of Surry* (London: J. Long, 1791)

[Langhorne, John], *The Effusions of Friendship and Fancy. In Several Letters to and from Select Friends. The Second Edition, with Large Additions and Improvements*, 2 vols. (London: T. Becket and P. A. De Hondt, 1766)

[Lennox, Charlotte], *Henrietta*, 2ⁿᵈ edition (London: A. Millar, 1761)

——, 'Of the Studies Proper for Women. Translated from the French', in *The Lady's Museum. By the author of The Female Quixote*, 2 vols. (London: J. Newbery and J. Coote, 1760–61) vol. 1, no. 1, p. 13

Litchfield, R. B., *Tom Wedgwood, the First Photographer: An Account of His Life, His Discovery and His Friendship with Samuel Taylor Coleridge, Including the Letters of Coleridge to the Wedgwoods and an Examination of Accounts of Alleged Earlier Photographic Discoveries* (London: Duckworth & Co., 1903)

Lowth, Robert, *Lectures on the Sacred Poetry of the Hebrews; translated from the Latin*, 2 vols. (London: J. Johnson, 1787)

Milner, John, *The History Civil and Ecclesiastical, & Survey of the Antiquities, of Winchester*, 2 vols. (Winchester: Jas. Robbins; London: Cadell and Davies, etc., 1798–1801)

Milton, John, *Paradise Lost*, ed. Alastair Fowler (London and New York: Longman, 1990)

Mitford, Mary Russell, *The Life of Mary Russell Mitford, Authoress of 'Our Village', etc., Related in a Selection from her Letters to her Friends*, ed. Rev. G. A. L'Estrange, 3 vols. (London: Richard Bentley, 1870)

——, *Our Village: Sketches of Rural Character and Scenery*, 5 vols. (London: Geo. B. Whitaker, 1824–32)

——, *Recollections of a Literary Life; or, Books, Places, and People*, new edition, 2 vols. (London: Richard Bentley, 1857)

Momus, Marmaduke, *The Jolly Jester; or The Wit's Complete Library* (London: W. and J. Stratford, 1794)

[Moore, John], *Mordaunt. Sketches of Life, Characters, and Manners, in Various Countries*, 3 vols. (Dublin: W. Watson and Son, 1800)

More, Hannah, *Strictures on the Modern System of Female Education*, 2 vols. (London: T. Cadell Jun. and W. Davies, 1799)

Morris, Edward, *False Colours, A Comedy* (Dublin: P. Byrne, W. Jones, J. Jones, and J. Rice, 1793)

Motley, John Lothrop, *The Correspondence of John Lothrop Motley*, ed. George William Curtis, 2 vols. (London: John Murray, 1889)

[Owen, Harriet May], ed., *The Works of Mrs Hemans; with a Memoir of her Life*, 7 vols. (Edinburgh: William Blackwood and Sons; London: Thomas Cadell, 1839)

Parsons, Eliza, *Women as They Are. A novel*, 4 vols. (London: William Lane, 1796)

Peacock, Thomas Love, *Headlong Hall* (London: T. Hookham, Jun., and Co., 1816)

——, *Melincourt*, 3 vols. (London: T. Hookham, Jun., and Co.; Baldwin, Cradock, and Joy, 1817)

——, *The Works of Thomas Love Peacock*, ed. H.F.B. Brett-Smith and C. E. Jones, 10 vols. (London: Constable & Co.; New York: Gabriel Wells, 1924–34)

Piozzi, Hester Lynch, *British Synonymy; or, an attempt at regulating the choice of words in familiar conversation*, 2 vols. (London: G. and G. Robinson, 1794)

——, *The Cambridge Edition of the Novels of Thomas Love Peacock*, gen. ed. Freya Johnston (Cambridge: Cambridge University Press, 2016–): *Crotchet Castle*, ed. Freya Johnston and Matthew Bevis (2016)

Pope, Alexander, *The Twickenham Edition of the Poems of Alexander Pope*, 11 vols., gen. ed. John Butt (London: Methuen & Co.; New Haven, CT: Yale University Press, 1939–69):

Vol. 1: *Pastoral Poetry, and, An Essay on Criticism*, ed. E. Audra and Aubrey Williams (1961)

Vol. 2: *The Rape of the Lock and Other Poems*, ed. Geoffrey Tillotson (1940; repr. 1966)

Porter, Anna Maria, *Artless Tales, by Anna Maria Porter, ornamented with a frontispiece, designed by her brother, R. K. Porter* (London: L. Wayland, 1793)

———, *Artless Tales; or, Romantic Effusions of the Heart* (London: for the author, 1795)

Priestley, Joseph, *A Free Address to Protestant Dissenters, as such*, 3rd edition, enlarged (Birmingham and London: J. Johnson, 1788)

Pyle, Philip, *One Hundred and Twenty Popular Sermons*, 4 vols (Norwich: for the author, 1789)

[Ramsay, Charlotte], *Poems on Several Occasions. Written by a Young Lady* (London: S. Paterson, 1747)

[Richardson, Samuel], *Clarissa. Or, the History of a Young Lady: Comprehending the Most Important Concerns of Private Life. And particularly shewing, The Distresses that may attend the Misconduct Both of Parents and Children, In Relation to Marriage. Published by the Editor of Pamela*, 7 vols. (London: S. Richardson, 1748)

———, *The History of Sir Charles Grandison*, 6 vols. (Oxford: B. Blackwell, 1931)

———, *Selected Letters of Samuel Richardson*, ed. John Carroll (Oxford: Clarendon Press, 1964)

Robinson, Henry Crabb, et al., *Correspondence of Henry Crabb Robinson with the Wordsworth Circle*, ed. Edith Morley, 2 vols. (Oxford: Clarendon Press, 1927)

Rollin, Charles, *The Ancient History of the Egyptians, Carthaginians, Assyrians, Babylonians, Medes and Persians, Macedonians, and Grecians*, 8th edition, 10 vols. (London: J. Rivington and Sons; G. G., J., and J. Robinson, etc., 1788)

Romilly, S. H., *Letters to 'Ivy' from the First Earl of Dudley* (London: Longman, 1905)

Scott, Walter, *Waverley Novels*, 48 vols. (Edinburgh: Robert Cadell; London: Simpkin and Marshall, 1829–33)

Shakespeare, William. *The Riverside Shakespeare*, ed. G. Blakemore Evans, with the assistance of J.J.M. Tobin, 2nd edition (Boston: Houghton Mifflin, 1997)

Skinner, John, *A Course of Lectures; delivered on the six Sundays in Lent, to a congregation of the Episcopal Church of Scotland* (Aberdeen: J. Chalmers & Co., 1786)

Smith, Adam, *The Theory of Moral Sentiments*, ed. Knud Haakonssen, Cambridge Texts in the History of Philosophy (Cambridge: Cambridge University Press, 2004)

Smith, Charlotte, *Emmeline, the Orphan of the Castle*, 4 vols. (London: T. Cadell, 1788)

Spark, Muriel, *Memento Mori* (Harmondsworth: Penguin, 1961; repr. 1996)

Sterne, Laurence, *The Life and Opinions of Tristram Shandy, Gentleman*, ed. Howard Anderson (New York and London: Norton, 1980)

Swift, Jonathan, *The Cambridge Edition of the Works of Jonathan Swift*, gen. eds. Claude Rawson, Ian Gadd, Ian Higgins, James McLaverty, Valerie Rumbold, Abigail Williams, and Linda Bree (Cambridge: Cambridge University Press, 2010–):
Vol. 1: *A Tale of a Tub and Other Works*, ed. Marcus Walsh (2010)
Vol. 15: *Gulliver's Travels*, ed. David Womersley (2012)

Taylor, Isaac, *Advice to the Teens; or, Practical Helps towards the Formation of one's own Character* (London: Rest Fenner, 1818)

Thomson, Charles, trans., *The Holy Bible, containing the Old and New Covenant, commonly called the Old and New Testament* (Philadelphia: Jane Aitken, 1808)

Trusler, John, *The Distinction between words esteemed synonymous in the English language, pointed out, and the proper choice of them determined. Useful to all who would either write or speak with Propriety and Elegance*, 2nd edition (London: for the author, 1783)

Vasari, Giorgio, *Lives of the Artists*, trans. George Bull, 2 vols. (Harmondsworth: Penguin, 1987)

Walpole, Horace, and William Cole, *Horace Walpole's Correspondence with the Rev. William Cole*, ed. W. S. Lewis and A. Dayle Wallace, 2 vols. (London: Oxford University Press; New Haven, CT: Yale University Press, 1937)

Warton, Joseph, *An Essay on the Writings and Genius of Pope*, 2 vols. (London: M. Cooper, 1756–82)

White, Gilbert, *The Natural History and Antiquities of Selbourne, in the County of Southampton* (London: B. White and Son, 1789)

Wollstonecraft, Mary, *Mary, A Fiction* (London: J. Johnson, 1788)

———, *A Short Residence in Sweden, Norway, and Denmark*, and William Godwin, *Memoirs of the Author of A Vindication of the Rights of Woman*, ed. Richard Holmes (Harmondsworth: Penguin, 1987)

———, *The Works of Mary Wollstonecraft*, 7 vols., ed. Janet Todd and Marilyn Butler (London: Pickering & Chatto, 1989)

Woodward, Robert, *A System of Christian Theology* (Northampton: T. Dicey & Co., 1791)

Wordsworth, William, *Poems by William Wordsworth: including Lyrical Ballads, and the Miscellaneous Pieces of the Author. With additional poems, a new preface, and a supplementary essay*, 2 vols. (London: Longman, Hurst, Rees, Orme, and Brown, 1815)

———, *Poems, Chiefly of Early and Late Years; including The Borderers, A Tragedy* (London: Edward Moxon, 1842)

———, *The Poetical Works of William Wordsworth*, ed. E. de Selincourt and Helen Darbishire, 5 vols., 2nd edition (Oxford: Clarendon Press, 1954)

———, and Dorothy Wordsworth, *The Letters of William and Dorothy Wordsworth*, ed. E. De Selincourt, rev. Alan G. Hill, 4 vols. (Oxford: Clarendon Press, 1978–88)

Young, Edward, *Conjectures on Original Composition. In a Letter to the Author of Sir Charles Grandison* (London: for A. Millar, and R. and J. Dodsley, 1759)

Secondary Works

Alexander, Christine, and Juliet McMaster, ed., *The Child Writer from Austen to Woolf* (Cambridge: Cambridge University Press, 2005)

Austen-Leigh, Mary Augusta, *Personal Aspects of Jane Austen* (London: John Murray, 1920)

Barchas, Janine, *Matters of Fact in Jane Austen: History, Location, and Celebrity* (Baltimore, MD: Johns Hopkins University Press, 2012)

Barnard, John, 'The Harvard Manuscript of Keats's "On First Looking into Chapman's Homer", Joseph Severn, Leigh Hunt, and Its Transmission into Print', *Romanticism*, 25 (2019), 157 68

Bellow, Saul, 'The Civilized Barbarian Reader', *New York Times* (8 March 1987), section 7, p. 1

Bishop, Elizabeth, *Poems, Prose, and Letters*, ed. Robert Giroux and Lloyd Schwartz (New York: Library of America, 2008)

Boulukos, George E., 'The Politics of Silence: *Mansfield Park* and the Amelioration of Slavery', *NOVEL: A Forum on Fiction*, 39 (2006), 361–83

Brownstein, Rachel M., *Why Jane Austen?* (New York: Columbia University Press, 2013)

Butler, Marilyn, *Jane Austen and the War of Ideas* (Oxford: Clarendon Press, 1975)

Butterfield, Herbert, *The Whig Interpretation of History* (Harmondsworth: Penguin, 1973)

Byrne, Paula, *Jane Austen and the Theatre* (London: Hambledon and London, 2002)

Chandler, James, *England in 1819: The Politics of Literary Culture and the Case of Romantic Historicism* (Chicago and London: University of Chicago Press, 1998)

Chapman, R. W., *Jane Austen: Facts and Problems* (Oxford: Clarendon Press, 1948)

——, 'Jane Austen's Text: Authoritative Manuscript Corrections', *Times Literary Supplement* (13 Feb. 1937), p. 116

Chwe, Michael Suk-Young, *Jane Austen, Game Theorist* (Princeton, NJ: Princeton University Press, 2013)

Clark, Lorna J., 'Teaching "The Young Idea How to Shoot": The Juvenilia of the Burney Family', *Journal of Juvenilia Studies*, 1 (2018), 20–36

Copeland, Edward, and Juliet McMaster, ed., *The Cambridge Companion to Jane Austen*, 2nd edition (Cambridge: Cambridge University Press, 2011)

Craik, W. A., *Jane Austen: The Six Novels* (London: Methuen, 1965)

Davis, Kathryn, '"The First Soldier [She] Ever Sighed For": Charles Pasley's *Essay* and the "Governing Winds" of *Mansfield Park*', *Persuasions On-Line*, 35 (2014), [n. p.], http://www.jasna.org/persuasions/on-line/vol35no1/davis.html

Doody, Margaret Anne, *Jane Austen's Names: Riddles, Persons, Places* (Chicago: University of Chicago Press, 2015)

Dow, Gillian, and Katie Halsey, 'Jane Austen's Reading: The Chawton Years', *Persuasions On-Line*, vol. 30 (2010), [n. p.], http://www.jasna.org/persuasions/on-line/vol30no2/dow-halsey.html

Duckworth, Alistair M., *The Improvement of the Estate: A Study of Jane Austen's Novels* (Baltimore, MD, and London: Johns Hopkins, 1971)

Empson, William, 'Donne the Space Man', *Kenyon Review*, 19 (1957), 337–99

——, 'Tom Jones', *Kenyon Review*, 20 [1958], 217–49

Everett, Barbara, *Poets in Their Time* (London: Faber and Faber, 1986)

——, *Young Hamlet: Essays on Shakespeare's Tragedies* (Oxford: Clarendon Press, 1989)

Ferry, Anne, *The Title to the Poem* (Stanford, CA: Stanford University Press, 1996)

Forster, E. M., 'Miss Austen and Jane Austen', *Times Literary Supplement* (10 Nov. 1932), pp. 821–2

Fraiman, Susan, 'Jane Austen and Edward Said: Gender, Culture, and Imperialism', *Critical Inquiry*, 21 (1995), 805–21

Garrod, H. W., 'Jane Austen: A Depreciation', in *Essays by Divers Hands: Transactions of the Royal Society of Literature*, 8 (1928), 21–40

Gay, Penny, *Jane Austen and the Theatre* (Cambridge: Cambridge University Press, 2002)

Gill, Stephen, *William Wordsworth: A Life*, 2nd edition (Oxford: Oxford University Press, 2020)

Gilson, David, *A Bibliography of Jane Austen*, rev. edition (Winchester: St Paul's Bibliographies; New Castle, DE: Oak Knoll Press, 1997)

Grandison, Julia, 'Jane Austen and the Almanac', *Review of English Studies*, 70 (2019), 911–29

Grey, J. David, *Jane Austen's Beginnings: The Juvenilia and* Lady Susan, intro. Margaret Drabble (Ann Arbor, MI, and London: UMI Research Press, 1989)

———, ed., *The Jane Austen Handbook* (London: Athlone, 1986)

Handler, J. S., 'The History of Arrowroot and the Origin of Peasantries in the British West Indies', *Journal of Caribbean History*, 2 (1971), 46–93

Harding, D. W., 'Regulated Hatred: An Aspect of Jane Austen', *Scrutiny*, 8 (March 1940), 346–62

———, 'Two Aspects of Jane Austen's Development', *Theoria: A Journal of Social and Political Theory*, 35 (1970), 1–16

Hardy, John, *Jane Austen's Heroines* (London: Routledge, 2011)

Hargreaves, Neil, 'Revelation of Character in Eighteenth-Century Historiography and William Robertson's *History of the Reign of Charles V*', *Eighteenth-Century Life*, 23 (2003), 23–48

Harris, Jocelyn, *Satire, Celebrity, and Politics in Jane Austen* (Lewisburg, PA: Bucknell University Press, 2017)

Heath, William W., ed., *Discussions of Jane Austen* (Boston: Heath and Company, 1961)

Hutcheon, Linda, and Michael Hutcheon, 'Late Style(s): The Ageism of the Singular', *Occasion: Interdisciplinary Studies in the Humanities*, 4 (2012), https://arcade.stanford.edu/occasion/late-styles-ageism-singular

Ingrassia, Catherine, '*Emma*, Slavery, and Cultures of Captivity', *Persuasions*, 38 (2016), 95–106

Irvine, Robert P., *Jane Austen* (London and New York: Routledge, 2005)

Jackson, H. J., *Marginalia: Readers Writing in Books* (New Haven, CT, and London: Yale University Press, 2001)

———, *Romantic Readers: The Evidence of Marginalia* (New Haven, CT, and London: Yale University Press, 2005)

Johnson, Claudia L., *Jane Austen: Women, Politics and the Novel* (Chicago and London: Chicago University Press, 1988)

———, *Jane Austen's Cults and Cultures* (Chicago: University of Chicago Press, 2012)

———, and Clara Tuite, eds., *A Companion to Jane Austen* (Malden, MA, and Oxford: Wiley-Blackwell, 2009)

Jones, Mark, 'Parody and Its Containments: The Case of Wordsworth', *Representations*, 54 (1996), 57–79

Jones, Vivien, 'Reading for England: Austen, Taste, and Female Patriotism', *European Romantic Review*, 16 (2005), 221–30

Kermode, Frank, *The Sense of an Ending: Studies in the Theory of Fiction with a New Epilogue* (Oxford and New York: Oxford University Press, 2000)

Kettredge, Katharine, 'Early Blossoms of Genius: Child Poets at the End of the Long Eighteenth Century', *Looking Glass: New Perspectives on Children's Literature*, 15 (2011), http://www.the-looking-glass.net/index.php/tlg/article/view/274/271

Kinkead-Weekes, Mark, *Samuel Richardson: Dramatic Novelist* (London: Methuen, 1973)

Kirkham, Margaret, *Jane Austen, Feminism and Fiction* [1983] (London and Atlantic Highlands, NJ: Athlone, 1997)

Kneale, J. Douglas, *Romantic Aversions: Aftermaths of Classicism in Coleridge and Wordsworth* (Montreal; Kingston; London; and Ithaca, NY: McGill-Queen's University Press, 1999)

Knox-Shaw, Peter, *Jane Austen and the Enlightenment* (Cambridge: Cambridge University Press, 2004)

Krueger, Misty, 'From Marginalia to Juvenilia: Jane Austen's Vindication of the Stuarts', *The Eighteenth Century*, 56 (2015), 243–59

Lane, Maggie, *Growing Older with Jane Austen* (London: Robert Hale, 2014)

Langbauer, Laurie, *The Juvenile Tradition: Young Writers and Prolepsis, 1750–1835* (Oxford: Oxford University Press, 2016)

———, 'Leigh Hunt and Juvenilia', *Keats-Shelley Journal*, 60 (2011), 112–33

Lascelles, Mary, *Jane Austen and Her Art* (Oxford: Clarendon Press, 1939)

Leader, Zachary, 'Daisy Packs Her Bags', *London Review of Books*, 22 (2000), 13–5

———, *Revision and Romantic Authorship* (Oxford: Clarendon Press, 1996)

Leavis, F. R., ed., *A Selection from Scrutiny*, 2 vols. (Cambridge: Cambridge University Press, 1968)

Leavis, Q. D., 'A Critical Theory of Jane Austen's Writings', *Scrutiny*, 10 (1941–2), 61–87, 114–42, 272–94; and 12 (1944–5), 104–19

Lee, Yoon Sun, 'Austen's Swarms and Plots', *European Romantic Review*, 30 (2019), 307–14

Le Faye, Deirdre, *A Chronology of Jane Austen and Her Family* (Cambridge: Cambridge University Press, 2006)

———, *Jane Austen: A Family Record*, 2nd edition (Cambridge: Cambridge University Press, 2004)

———, 'Jane Austen's Verses and Lord Stanhope's Disappointment', *Book Collector*, 37 (1988), 86–91

———, 'New Marginalia in Jane Austen's Books', *Book Collector*, 49 (2000), 222–6

Levy, Michelle, 'Austen's Manuscripts and the Publicity of Print', *ELH*, 77 (2010), 1015–40

Litz, A. Walton, 'Chronology of Mansfield Park', *Notes and Queries*, 8 (June 1961), 220–21

———, *Jane Austen: A Study of Her Artistic Development* (New York: Oxford University Press, 1965)

Looser, Devoney, 'Age and Aging Studies, from Cradle to Grave', *Age Culture Humanities*, 1 (2014), https://ageculturehumanities.org/WP/age-and-aging-studies-from-cradle-to -grave/

———, *British Women Writers and the Writing of History, 1670–1820* (Baltimore, MD: Johns Hopkins University Press, 2000)

———, *Women Writers and Old Age in Great Britain, 1750–1850* (Baltimore, MD: Johns Hopkins University Press, 2008)

———, ed., *Jane Austen and Discourses of Feminism* (Basingstoke: MacMillan, 1995)

McGann, Jerome, *Don Juan in Context* (Chicago: University of Chicago Press, 1976)

McIntosh, Carey, *The Evolution of English Prose, 1700–1800: Style, Politeness, and Print Culture* (Cambridge: Cambridge University Press, 1998)

McMaster, Juliet, *Jane Austen, Young Author* (Farnham: Ashgate, 2016)

Michals, Teresa, *Books for Adults, Books for Children: Age and the Novel from Defoe to James* (Cambridge: Cambridge University Press, 2014)

Miller, D. A., *Jane Austen, or The Secret of Style* (Princeton, NJ: Princeton University Press, 2003)

Moody, Ellen, 'A Jane Austen Event Calendar' (10 Jan. 2001), https://janeausten.co.uk/blogs /jane-austen-life/jane-austen-event

Mudrick, Marvin, *Jane Austen: Irony as Defense and Discovery* (Princeton, NJ: Princeton University Press, 1952)

Murphy, Olivia, *Jane Austen the Reader: The Artist as Critic* (Basingstoke: Palgrave Macmillan, 2013)

O'Gorman, Francis, 'Matthew Arnold and Rereading', *The Cambridge Quarterly*, 41 (2012), 245–61

Owen, David, 'The Failed Text That Wasn't: Jane Austen's *Lady Susan*', in *The Failed Text: Literature and Failure*, ed. José Luis Martínez-Duenãs Espejo and Rocío G. Sumerilla (Newcastle upon Tyne: Cambridge Scholars Publishing, 2013), pp. 81–96

Parrish, Stephen M., 'The Whig Interpretation of Literature', *Text*, 4 (1988), 343–50

Paulson, Ronald, *Breaking and Remaking: Aesthetic Practice in England, 1700–1820* (London: Rutgers, 1989)

Piper, David, *Shades: An Essay on English Portrait Silhouettes* (New York: Chilmark Press; Cambridge: Rampant Lions Press, 1970)

Power, Henry, 'Henry Fielding, Richard Bentley, and the "Sagacious Reader" of *Tom Jones*', *Review of English Studies*, n. s. 61 (2010), 749–72

Prince, Michael, *Philosophical Dialogue in the British Enlightenment: Theology, Aesthetics and the Novel* (Cambridge: Cambridge University Press, 1996)

Pritchett, V. S., *Books in General* (London: Chatto & Windus, 1953)

——, *The Living Novel* (London: Chatto & Windus, 1946)

Quayle, Eric, 'Porter, Anna Maria', *Oxford Dictionary of National Biography*,https://doi.org/10 .1093/ref:odnb/22559

Rawson, Claude, *Satire and Sentiment, 1660–1830: Stress Points in the Augustan Tradition* (Cambridge: Cambridge University Press, 1994)

Reiman, Donald H., *The Study of Modern Manuscripts: Public, Confidential, and Private* (Baltimore, MD, and London: Johns Hopkins University Press, 1993)

Richards, Bernard, 'George Eliot's GSOH', *Essays in Criticism*, 69 (2019), 399–421

Ricks, Christopher, *Dylan's Visions of Sin* (London: Viking, 2003)

——, 'Neurotic Editing', *Essays in Criticism*, 62 (2012), 474–82

Roberts, Warren, *Jane Austen and the French Revolution* [1979] (London and Atlantic Highlands, NJ: Athlone, 1995)

Robson, W. W., *Critical Essays* (London: Routledge & Kegan Paul, 1966)

Rutherford, Andrew, ed., *Lord Byron: The Critical Heritage* (London: Routledge, 2010)

Sabor, Peter, 'James Edward Austen, Anna Lefroy, and the Interpolations to Jane Austen's "Volume the Third"', *Notes and Queries*, 245 (2000), 304–6

Said, Edward W., *Culture and Imperialism* (London: Vintage, 1994)

——, *On Late Style* (London: Bloomsbury, 2006)

Saintsbury, George, *The English Novel* (London: J. M. Dent & Sons Ltd; New York: E. P. Dutton & Co., 1913)

Sitter, Zak, 'On Early Style. The Emergence of Realism in Charlotte Brontë's Juvenilia', in *Charlotte Brontë from the Beginnings: New Essays from the Juvenilia to the Major Works*, ed. Judith E. Pike and Lucy Morrison (London and New York: Routledge, 2017), pp. 30–43

Skinner, Quentin, 'Meaning and Understanding in the History of Ideas', *History and Theory*, 8 (1969), 3–53

Snart, Jason, 'Recentering Blake's Marginalia', *Huntington Library Quarterly*, 66 (2003), 134–53

Southam, Brian, *Jane Austen: A Students' Guide to the Later Manuscript Works* (London: Concord Books, 2007)

———, *Jane Austen and the Navy* (London and New York: Hambledon and London, 2000)

———, *Jane Austen's Literary Manuscripts: A Study of the Novelist's Development Through the Surviving Papers*, new edition (London and New York: Athlone Press, 2001)

———, 'Mrs. Leavis and Miss Austen: The "Critical Theory" Reconsidered', *Nineteenth-Century Fiction*, 17 (1962), 21–32

———, ed., *Critical Essays on Jane Austen* (London: Routledge & Kegan Paul, 1968)

———, ed., *Jane Austen: The Critical Heritage*, 2 vols. (London: Routledge & Kegan Paul; New York: Barnes & Noble, 1968–87)

Spongberg, Mary, 'Jane Austen and the *History of England*', *Journal of Women's History*, 23 (2011), 56–80

Stephen, Leslie, *Studies of a Biographer* [1898–1902], 4 vols. (Cambridge: Cambridge University Press, 2012)

Stillinger, Jack, 'The Multiple Versions of Coleridge's Poems: How Many "Mariners" Did Coleridge Write?', *Studies in Romanticism*, 31 (1992), 127–46

Sutherland, James, *English Satire* (Cambridge: Cambridge University Press, 1962)

Sutherland, Kathryn, 'From Kitty to Catharine, James Edward Austen's Hand in *Volume the Third*', *Review of English Studies*, 66 (2015), 124–43

———, *Jane Austen's Textual Lives: From Aeschylus to Bollywood* (Oxford: Oxford University Press, 2005)

Tandon, Bharat, *Jane Austen and the Morality of Conversation* (London: Anthem, 2003)

Tanner, Tony, *Jane Austen* (Basingstoke: Macmillan, 1986)

———, 'Jane Austen: "By a Lady"', *New York Times* (6 May 1979), p. 266

Todd, Janet, 'Ivory Miniatures and the Art of Jane Austen', in *British Women's Writing in the Long Eighteenth Century: Authorship, Politics, and History*, ed. Jennie Batchelor and Cora Kaplan (Basingstoke: Palgrave Macmillan, 2005), pp. 76–87

Tomalin, Claire, *Jane Austen: A Life*, rev. edition (London: Penguin, 2012)

Tucker, George Holbert, *A Goodly Heritage: A History of Jane Austen's Family* (Manchester: Carcanet, in association with Mid Northumberland Arts Group, 1983)

Tuite, Clara, *Romantic Austen: Sexual Politics and the Literary Canon*, Cambridge Studies in Romanticism, no. 49 (Cambridge: Cambridge University Press, 2002)

Tytler, Sarah [Henrietta Keddie], *Jane Austen and Her Works* (London: Cassell, Petter, Galpin, [1880])

Upfal, Annette, 'Jane Austen's Lifelong Health Problems and Final Illness: New Evidence Points to a Fatal Hodgkin's Disease and Excludes the Widely Accepted Addison's', *Medical Humanities*, 31 (2005), 3–11

Van Ostade, Ingrid Tieken-Boon, *In Search of Jane Austen: The Language of the Letters* (Oxford: Oxford University Press, 2014)

Wall, Stephen, *Trollope and Character* (London: Faber, 1988)

Watt, Ian, *Conrad in the Nineteenth Century* (Berkeley: University of California Press, 1979)

———, *The Rise of the Novel: Studies in Defoe, Richardson and Fielding* (London: Chatto & Windus, 1957)

Wenner, Barbara Britton, *Prospect and Refuge in the Landscape of Jane Austen* (Aldershot: Ashgate, 2006)

White, Gabrielle D. V., *Jane Austen in the Context of Abolition: 'A Fling at the Slave Trade'* (New York: Palgrave Macmillan, 2006)

Woloch, Alex, *The One vs. the Many: Minor Characters and the Space of the Protagonist in the Novel* (Princeton, NJ: Princeton University Press, 2003)

Woolf, D. R., 'A Feminine Past? Gender, Genre, and Historical Knowledge in England, 1500–1800', *American Historical Review*, 102 (1997), 645–79

Womersley, David, ed., *A Companion to Literature from Milton to Blake* (Oxford: Blackwell, 2000)

Wright, A. R., *British Calendar Customs*, ed. T. E. Jones, 3 vols. (London: William Glaisher Ltd; Glasgow: John Wylie & Co. for the Folk-Lore Society, 1936–40)

Zimmermann, Everett, *The Boundaries of Fiction: History and the Eighteenth-Century British Novel* (Ithaca, NY, and London: Cornell University Press, 1996)

INDEX

abolition, 192–9. *See also* Austen, Jane: slavery and slave trade, references to

abridgements, 62, 160 n10, 165–6

age and ageing studies, 17

Alexander, Christine, 16

Anjou, Margaret of, 172

Antigua, 74, 193–7

Anne, Queen of Great Britain, 120

arrow-root, 197–9

Ashford, Daisy, 213–4

Austen, Anna (JA's niece). *See* Lefroy, Jane Anna Elizabeth

Austen, Caroline Mary Craven (JA's niece), 1, 6, 8, 19, 26, 55, 101, 132–3, 149, 150

Austen, Cassandra (JA's mother), 31, 59–60, 105n12, 114, 122, 196

Austen, Cassandra Elizabeth (JA's sister), 20–5, 27–8, 30–1, 46n33, 51–5, 58–60, 61, 62, 63, 65, 78, 91, 96nn42 and 43, 99–100, 102, 105, 106, 107–8, 113, 114, 115n36, 116, 121–2, 123, 124–5, 128, 133nn6 and 8, 134, 135, 138, 139, 140, 142–3, 144–6, 147, 149–50, 151, 152, 152–3n32, 156n38, 161–2, 170–1, 172, 180, 186, 187–8n46, 190, 191, 196, 201–2, 208, 247

Austen, Catherine Anne (JA's niece). *See* Hubback, Catherine Anne

Austen, Charles John (JA's brother), 59–60, 196

Austen, Francis William (JA's brother), 59–60, 176, 196, 197, 247n11

Austen, George (JA's father), 3, 22n56, 31, 79, 46–7n33, 78–9, 85, 104–5, 125, 153

Austen, Henry Thomas (JA's brother), 19, 22, 52n45, 61n63, 61–2n64, 69, 86, 102, 111n26, 112, 113, 132–3, 140, 149, 152–3n32, 190, 205

Austen, James (JA's brother), 53, 89n34, 102, 132–3, 135, 168

Austen, Jane: alliteration, use of, 212–3; allusion and quotation, habits of, 90, 118–21, 185–6; attribution of her works, 222–4, 246–7; beheading, depictions of, 122–3, 178; childhood, 31–2, 54, 70–1, 102, 118–9, 124–9; chronology of works, 2, 17, 28, 33, 48, 51–63, 92; collaborations with family, 6n16, 8, 14, 142, 169, 170–2, 222–3, 247; complete and incomplete works, 1, 3–5, 7–10, 12, 13, 15, 43–4, 45n26, 48–9, 52–5, 57–9, 61, 80, 91, 148, 150–1, 152–4, 209, 210; compositional methods, 1–2, 5, 8, 9–10, 12, 42, 44, 45–8, 50, 51, 55–6, 59, 61, 70–1, 89–91, 107–9, 113, 117–22, 132–5, 138–44, 147–9, 150–7, 208–9, 212–13; critico-poetical character, 131–2; death, 2, 10, 48, 51, 52n45, 53, 58, 60–1, 85–6, 86–7, 101, 127, 132, 139–45, 149–51, 190; dress, 8, 147; education, 64–5, 89, 117, 159, 163, 164–5, 166, 169, 171–2, 177, 181–2, 193, 222–3, 246; face, 18–25; food, representations of, 146–7, 155, 196–9; funeral, 140, 145–6; handwriting, 2, 5–6, 14n37, 19, 27n66, 52 n45, 78, 135, 155, 168, 173, 221–47; ignorance, 64–5, 69, 101, 132, 167, 174–6, 178, 181, 186, 187, 191–2, 220; illness, 21–2, 86–7, 124, 142–4, 150–1, 155, 157, 187–8, 206–7; mothers, portrayals of, 9n22, 30–1, 32, 60, 73, 93–4, 96, 99, 100,

A NOTE ON THE TYPE

This book has been composed in Arno, an Old-style serif typeface in the classic Venetian tradition, designed by Robert Slimbach at Adobe.